After
the Galleons

Probst 1748 Map

After the Galleons

Foreign Trade, Economic Change & Entrepreneurship in the Nineteenth-Century Philippines

Benito J. Legarda, Jr.

Published in cooperation with
Ateneo de Manila University Press

CENTER FOR SOUTHEAST ASIAN STUDIES
UNIVERSITY OF WISCONSIN-MADISON

MONOGRAPH NUMBER 18

Library of Congress Catalog Card Number
98-061609   ·

ISBN Cloth: 1-881261-29-8
ISBN Paper: 1-881261-28-x

Published by the
CENTER FOR SOUTHEAST ASIAN STUDIES
University of Wisconsin-Madison
Madison, Wisconsin 53706 U.S.A.
Tel: (608)263-1755 / FAX: (608)263-3735

Edited by Janet Opdyke
Design of cover and dividers by J. B. de la Peña
Book design by Joel and Bernardita Lozare
Printed in the Philippines
Cover print: "Das Zollhaus in Manila" by Ernest Heyn et al. (Wilhelm
Sievers, *Asien* [Berlin, 1893]).

Distributed in the Philippines exclusively by the Ateneo de Manila
University Press; in Asia by both the Ateneo and the Center for Southeast Asian Studies, University of Wisconsin-Madison; and in the rest of
the world by the Center for Southeast Asian Studies, University of
Wisconsin-Madison.

To My Father and My Mother
Without Whom This Work Could Not Have Been
Started, and

To Lita and Isabel
Without Whom It Could Not Have Been
Completed.

After the Galleons

CONTENTS

TABLES

ABBREVIATIONS

AdM .... Aduana de Manila Papers, PNA
AHC .... Augustine Heard Collection, BL-HBS
BL-HBS .... Baker Library, Harvard Business School
BR .... Blair and Robertson, *The Philippine Islands*
DAP .... Dexter-Appleton Papers, BL-HBS
DIU .... *Documentos Inéditos de Ultramar*
ECP-RIHS ..... Edward Carrington Papers, Rhode Island Historical Society
HBS .... Harvard Business School
               (Graduate School of Business Administration),
               Harvard University
MHS .... Massachusetts Historical Society
NWGPC .... *New Weekly General Price Currentt*
PCCP .... Plymouth Cordage Co. Papers, BL-HBS
PCM .... *Precios Corrientes de Manila*
PEM .... Peabody Essex Museum, Salem, Massachusetts
PFP-SUL .... Peirce Family Papers, Stanford University Libraries
PHC .... Peele, Hubbell & Co.
PNA .... Philippine National Archives, Manila
RIHS .... Rhode Island Historical Society
SSPP-PEM .... Stone, Silsbee & Pickman Papers, Peabody Essex Museum
SUL .... Stanford University Libraries

PREFACE

The present work is published in part as a response to suggestions and even requests from scholars in the Philippines, the United States, and England who have had occasion to read it, and in some cases work through it, in its original form as a doctoral dissertation submitted to Harvard University in 1955. In that form, it was the object of some quite generous commentary, for which I am grateful.

Among the comments are some that describe the work as a pioneering study, which is perhaps an overstatement, as the seminal idea was contained in Dr. T. H. Pardo de Tavera's 1912 lecture on Philippine economic development (cited in the notes and bibliography). What I did was give quantitative measurement and geographical dimension to that idea, elaborate on the mechanisms through which the observed results came about, identify the principal players, and start weighing the economic and social costs.

The present version was projected to be little more than a sprucing up of the original, but as I undertook the task of revision it proved impossible to avoid both later research on the topic and the exploration of archival material that came to light after my retirement from government service. There is, therefore, considerably more detail in this revision than in the original.

For the revision project, thanks are due in the first place to Henry Rosovsky, who encouraged me to proceed with it despite my own hesitation, and to Jeffrey G. Williamson, who amid his multifarious academic duties read the draft patiently and critically as it reached him in installments.

For the final steps toward publication, credit should go to Alfred W. McCoy, Daniel Doeppers, and Paul Hutchcroft of the Center for Southeast Asian Studies at the University of Wisconsin.

For the original thesis, acknowledgment is due to those who helped me as I groped my way into the subject. Alexander Gerschenkron, my first thesis adviser, turned my sights to concepts of economic dependence and entrepreneurship. John King Fairbank, who took over as adviser after Gerschenkron went on sabbatical, imparted a broad historical perspective to the work and first raised the possibility of publication. (One of his other students, the eminent Filipino historian Horacio de la Costa, S.J., published the first excerpt in *Philippine Studies*.) Josef Solterer, my mentor at Georgetown, helped me to keep my focus on the larger picture and avoid bogging down in minor issues and directed my steps to Schumpeterian paths.

Personal thanks are also due to my Filipino contemporaries (many of whom have since made their mark on our national life), who cheered me on in my work, and other fellow students who helped out with such mundane matters as translations. Fernando Zóbel y Montojo, with his profound insights into Philippine life and history, raised far above the ordinary level by his artistic vision, was a constant source of fresh ideas. Particular thanks are due to Mrs. Elizabeth Menzel Davis for help with typing at crucial stages of the work.

Two fellow scholars in particular provided invaluable help. Edgar Wickberg assisted in the early stages with material from the Philippine National Archives and with scholarly ideas and input. To Onofre D. Corpuz I entrusted the unenviable chore of retrieving my final text from the typist, giving it at least a cursory inspection, and taking it to the bindery in time to be passed on within the academic year at a time when I was called away on official business. Despite such interruptions, I am thankful to my employers at the time, the Central Bank of the Philippines, for assistance during part of my graduate studies.

Also helpful were the years of dialogue I carried on with friends like Amado A. Castro, Thomas and Mary McHale, Alain Miailhe, and Richard Wheeler. Of special help was the information that surfaced and the many ideas exchanged on numerous drives between Cambridge and Salem, Massachusetts, with H. A. Crosby Forbes.

Acknowledgment is also made of the help received from libraries, archives, and museums at both stages of the work; they are listed in the notes and bibliography.

Special mention should be made of private collections like the George R. Russell papers (then in the care of Dr. Charles P. Lyman of Cambridge, Mass.) and the George Sturgis papers (then in the care of Mrs. David Little of Weston, Mass.), which were located through a combination of detective work, persistence, and luck and to which as a young foreign graduate student I was given unhesitating and generous access. I must also thank the custodians of other private collections, like the Burke-Miailhe papers and the Felipe Liao collection in the Philippines. Not least deserving of recognition is my typist, Mrs. Carolina P. Dimalanta, who patiently typed the text, the statistical tables, and the bibliography.

Finally, I must thank my parents for seeing me through my student days and my wife and daughter for putting up with a lengthy rewriting process. It is not given to many to review and revise work done forty years previously. The modifications are minor in substance, somewhat more in nuance, and greatest in richer detail. It is my hope that publication of this study will finally give it the accessibility that so many scholars on the Philippines have been seeking.

Part 1

The Age of Transshipment:
Philippine Foreign Trade
to the Early Nineteenth Century

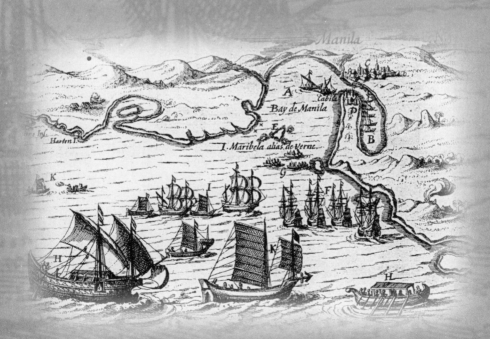

As the entrepot between Asia and the West,

Manila became the no. 1 city in the Orient in galleon days. . . .

Philippine agriculture, commerce and industry

were enriched and advanced by the Manila Galleon. . . .

Epochal enough was the transfer of

Western flora and fauna to the Philippines.

Even more epochal was the transfer here

of Western technology, with the galleons serving, literally,

as vessels and media. . . .

It was on the Manila Galleon that we began

to become the Philippines.

—NICK JOAQUIN (1990)

Print overleaf: "Spilbergen Map" (*Speculum Orientalis Occidentalisque Indiae Navigationum* [1620] by Joris van Spilbergen and Jacques Le Maire).

PROLOGUE

Philippine exports appeared in substantial amounts in international markets for the first time in the nineteenth century. At the same time, domestic needs came to be met more and more often through imports rather than domestic output. Starting with a collection of minimally interdependent communities forming a subsistence economy, the Philippines developed over the century into an agricultural export economy, with greater specialization and greater dependence on external trade.

The country was land rich and a food exporter, but it was also short of labor and capital poor. In the late eighteenth century, it had been an arsenal for Mexico's Pacific defenses, and in the following century it provided rice to China, Cuba, and California. But tightening linkages with the world trading economy had effects that went beyond the purely commercial to more profound structural economic changes, with demographic and social ramifications.

Four questions suggest themselves. First, when did the Philippines definitely become an agricultural export economy? Around 1820, there was still a substantial transshipment trade and among exports of domestic origin a wide variety of commodities (including textiles and rice), if at low aggregate levels. By the latter part of the century, trade levels had multiplied fifteen- to twentyfold, but between two-thirds to four-fifths of total exports were accounted for by only two commodities, sugar and abaca, and most of the minor exports had become marginalized. Textiles, formerly a minor export, became the country's major import, while rice, formerly a major export, became an import. Evidence points to the half century ending in the early 1870s as the period of transformation.

Second, what forces brought about this change? Those identified in other tropical dependencies (the impact of estates and pressures on the peasantry) were largely absent in the Philippines for much of the nineteenth century. It was a country of predominantly small cultivators and did not have the large and tightly managed commercial plantations of other colonies. Estates followed rather than preceded the rise of exports. Likewise, the administering authorities had neither the means nor an overriding interest in pressuring the population to produce specifically for export. Other priorities were ranked higher: the fairly successful policy over time of assuring adequate rice supplies and keeping rice prices moderate, and rather ineffectual efforts to protect domestic industry and encourage (somewhat fitfully) preferential trade with the metropole. In fact, the Philippines was never economically complementary to Spain and in this specific sense was not a colonial economy. Trade flows moved from China, India, and Mexico early in the century to Great Britain, the United States, and China later on, with Spain ranking only fourth. What was actually achieved resulted from the activities of private, largely Anglo-American, commercial firms, few in number, dealing through domestic and Chinese intermediaries in their local operations.

Third, what was the modus operandi of these forces? Quite simply, they worked through a system of flexible prices and exchange rates. Tendencies toward monopsony or concerted buying were effectively countered by the workings of competition. The Americans were most active in export promotion. They induced growers to shift to export crops by noncoercive means such as favorable prices and cash advances. The last they did initially with capital imports and then with intermediated funds, making them in effect merchant-financiers. They also introduced innovations such as the development of new products (abaca), the use of bills of exchange, and the application of steam power in manufacturing. The English initially concentrated on imports; undercut the textile industry with factory-made goods and plunged it into decline; and late in the century, with operations in both exports and imports, rode out the economic turmoil that bankrupted the export-oriented Americans.

Fourth, what were some of the major consequences of these developments? The outcomes were fully consonant with the Smithian dictum that division of labor depends on the extent of the market. In this case, the

4

market had grown from local and regional early in the century to global by the third quarter of the century, and from the reordering of factors of production emerged a pattern of concentration and specialization. The larger market meant an increase in domestic incomes, rises in standards of living and educational attainment, and a growing assertiveness and national consciousness that contributed to impulses toward revolution. There is also evidence of growing activity by domestic entrepreneurs. But the linkage to the world market, while it opened up prospects of great gains, also meant exposure to great hazards: short- and long-term shifts in demand, an increase in competing products, and the prevalence of cyclical movements. These meant that the great increases in income would be unevenly spread, resulting in a widening distance between income extremes, and that the balance in rural production relations would be disrupted. These crosscurrents interacted, in the quarter of a century or so before the Revolution, in a world environment shadowed by crises and depressions in the country's major markets and depreciation in its main currency medium, silver.

The examination of these four questions will be the main theme of this work. But the nineteenth-century Philippine economy did not start from scratch. The preceding Age of Transshipment dated back to pre-Hispanic times, and, during the centuries when it was in effect, a process of administrative unification and geographic consolidation took place that laid the groundwork for the rise of national consciousness. By the middle of the eighteenth century, economic policy began to focus on reducing commercial dependence on transshipment, promoting the geographic diversification of trade, and stimulating the production of domestic goods so as to increase the domestic content of foreign trade. Before taking up the nineteenth century, then, it is appropriate that we should look at its historical antecedents.

CHAPTER I

Philippine Foreign Trade
to the Spanish Contact

*The Filipino race, before its union with Spain, had its own
civilization . . . and its agriculture and industry nourished
its commercial traffic. . . . The history of the Philippines in
its three centuries of union with Spain is a sequence of heroic
loyalty toward its metropole . . .*

—*Marcelo H. del Pilar (1890)*

Pre-Hispanic Trade

The pre-Hispanic Filipinos lived by and large in small, independent, coastal and riverine communities of fifty to two hundred
people, with two main residential patterns: nucleated, or composite;
and lineal, or dispersed. The latter, with dwellings built close to each
other in single file along the seacoast and riverbanks, was the more
common one, a function of the predominant system of shifting cultivation (although there was some wet rice cultivation on Luzon) as well
as dependence on seas and rivers as avenues of communication and
sources of protein. This led to residential mobility and impermanence
of settlements, and there was no megalithic building as elsewhere in
Southeast Asia. From about the middle of the fifteenth century, under

7

the influence of Chinese and Muslim traders, people from the hinter-lands were drawn by trade to the coastal areas and there was an in-crease in nucleated settlements characterized by the clustering of houses at the center of a village, sedentary agriculture, and crafts. Plows were not in use; nor were wheeled vehicles. Cattle were kept as sources of milk and meat rather than as draft animals.

Class structures varied, ranging from classless societies through warrior societies and petty plutocracies to principalities with relatively centralized political organizations. Even within similar kinds of societies there were marked differences; for example, most of the classless societies did not make war and had no weaponry or warrior traditions, while oth-ers were notorious head takers.

The most common form of organization was the *barangay* (named after the boat in which groups of settlers came), a bilaterally extended kin-ship unit. Where there were recognized rulers, dominion was personal rather than geographic; the concept was one of dependency or authority over people rather than one of territory (although there were reported ex-ceptions to this). In some villages, there were several *barangays*, each one an independent social, political, and economic unit. A weakness was that a disgruntled member could simply move to another village where he had relatives.[1]

These demographically and politically fragmented units carried on trade among themselves, with the rest of Southeast Asia, and with China. Of the foreign traders, the Arabs (and Persians) and the Chi-nese were the most active. Apparently their activity dates at least to the ninth century A.D. during the later years of the T'ang dynasty (618–906), although there were earlier cultural contacts. Trade activity rose markedly in the Sung dynasty (960–1279), when Chinese accounts de-scribe Philippine contacts and porcelain ware attained a quality supe-rior to that imported in the subsequent Yuan and Ming dynasties. The first recorded mention by the Chinese of what is now the Philippines is a brief reference in the year 982 A.D. More detailed accounts of trading practices came in the thirteenth century.

There were also Indian commercial contacts, which are blurred in the mists of general cultural contacts; they may have represented activity by the so-called Hinduized or Indianized states of Southeast Asia. Again, the ninth century seems to be some sort of watershed period. Siamese and Vietnamese porcelain and the large earthenware jars that until recently were called *martabanas* (from Martaban in Burma) attest to trade with con-tinental Southeast Asia, especially from the fourteenth century on. Much of this may have been carried on by Chinese junks, but Magellan's expedition did find that a Siamese junk had just left Cebu with a cargo of gold and slaves.

Filipinos themselves made trading voyages to what was later known as Indochina, and a Chinese source refers to Filipino traders in Canton in the tenth century. A Portuguese apothecary in Malacca on the eve of the Spanish contact testified to a community of "Lucoes," as the Filipinos were called then (derived from the island of Luzon), with the observation that they had two or three junks at most. At the time of the Spanish contact, it was observed that all the traders were Muslims. Japanese trading contacts are believed to date from the fifteenth century.

They had different kinds of seacraft. The *barangays*, or *binidays*, were medium-sized vessels used in wars or raids. Larger *vireyes* could carry between fifty and a hundred men and were equipped with long oars, with three tiers of rowers and outriggers. Still larger craft were *birocos*, probably sailing vessels for long voyages.

Trading practices varied in different places and at different times, with characteristics of both confidence and mistrust. In some localities, Chinese traders left their goods with local people and waited a few months, confident of collecting barter items later; in effect, they were selling on credit. Elsewhere the Chinese would keep two local residents as hostages on board their junks until they were ready to depart, usually in three or four days.

On the other side, some communities removed the rudders and sails from the Chinese junks to make sure they disposed of all their goods. Where there was a more centralized authority, as in Muslim principalities such as Sulu, Chinese traders were given legal safeguards; they were under the protection of the sultan and were exempt from slavery. But it was here also that, when Chinese vessels departed for their homeland, some of their men were detained as hostages to make sure the vessels would call again. In certain minor emporiums such as Cebu, both local and foreign vessels registered, paid harbor dues, and loaded transshipped merchandise. Some Philippine political units sent tribute to the Chinese emperors, especially during the Ming dynasty. Sulu seems by far to have been the most important tributary among these units.

When disagreements arose, the consequences could sometimes be deadly. When members of the Legazpi expedition were reconnoitering Luzon, they came upon a horrible sight in the town of Taal. Apparently there had been an altercation between Chinese traders and townspeople in which a native chief had been killed. The Chinese had tried to flee, but their ships ran aground and they were captured and condemned to the lingering death of having their faces skinned alive and exposed to the sun. Only two were saved by the coming of the Spaniards.

Exports from what is now the Philippines in pre-Hispanic times and at the time of Spanish contact included beeswax, tortoiseshell, edible birds' nests, honey, medicinal betel nuts, *laka* wood, pearls, coral, gold, mats, cotton (kapok in one translation), native textiles, foodstuffs, and slaves. Imports consisted of porcelain, iron censers, lead, tin, colored glass beads, silks, iron needles, bronze gongs, small bells, and trade gold.

Although regionally extensive, Philippine pre-Hispanic trade was limited by the structure of the native societies. As clan communities, they were largely self-contained economic units producing little more than a sufficiency for their own needs in a delicate balance between nature and people, and there was probably little taxable surplus.

Against this, there is the existence in grave sites of large quantities of pre-Hispanic porcelain numbering in the tens of thousands of pieces. Their value then was of course far different from modern-day values, and we do not know the terms of exchange for Philippine products, some of which, like Sulu pearls, were described as highly priced. Beeswax was also important for candle making.

As to how their importation was paid for, certain possible explanations come to mind. One is that even societies practicing swidden farming could, with integrated agricultural techniques, produce a sufficient surplus to accumulate such heirloom items as porcelain and brass gongs. Another is that gold exports underwrote these imports. Still another clue may lie in the transshipment trade; the pre-Hispanic Filipinos traded not only their own products but goods they had acquired from neighboring countries. These could have been paid for with slaves or the imported goods traded for porcelain. Perhaps no single explanation will suffice but a combination of all of them.

Or perhaps the relevant concept for the trade of these early societies was not a taxable surplus but a food surplus. Even if such a surplus was small, it would not preclude the exchange of valuable items like gold and slaves. Pigafetta, the chronicler of Magellan's voyage in 1521, describes a village in Mindanao in which he saw many gold articles but little food.[2] The meagerness of the food surplus would become evident with the arrival of the Legazpi expedition in 1565.

The Coming of Spain

The Legazpi expedition was the high point of Spanish expansion in the sixteenth century. But that expansion, to put it in context, was only a part of the general expansion of certain Mediterranean nations based on a Greco-Hebraic cultural synthesis and having both Islamic and Christian branches. The Muslims, the first to develop the sciences of geography and navigation and to awaken Western interest in Asian trade, expanded in an eastward direction through Persia, India, and finally Southeast Asia. The Portuguese, in the Christian van, sought the most direct route to China by carefully and methodically following the African coastal route to its logical destination in the Indian Ocean and beyond.

The situation was complicated when Columbus, under Spanish auspices, sailed west to reach the East and thought that the land he came upon was part of Asia. Unlike the careful and scientific Portuguese effort, this was a mere stroke of fortune, but it launched Spain's overseas expansion. To defuse the prospect of conflict between the only Christian nations that until then had shown any interest in world exploration, the famous Papal Bull of 1493 delineated the respective spheres of action for the two nations. This was followed by the Treaty of Tordesillas in 1494. The route around the Cape of Good Hope was reserved for the Portuguese, a stipulation that would greatly affect the future commerce and governance of the Philippines. The bull and the treaty accomplished their objectives of eliminating the chance of war, and in the hundred years that followed there were only two violations of the agreement—the return of the sole surviving ship of Magellan's expedition via the Portuguese sea route and the Spanish conquest of the Philippines.

Magellan's expedition of 1519–21 can be viewed as an extension of Columbus's voyages, for it was soon realized that what had been reached on the Atlantic was not Asia but a new world. Balboa's sighting of the Pacific Ocean from Panama showed that there was another ocean to cross in order to reach the Spice Islands and the fabled treasures of China. But the search for a passage to that ocean, including the much talked about Northwest Passage, invariably ended in failure, although other European nations now joined the effort. The New World seemed to present an impassable barrier.

For nearly thirty years after Columbus's first voyage, efforts at both settlement and exploration more often than not were unsuccessful. And despite the well-intentioned and explicit decrees of Queen Isabella the cost in human lives (mostly indigenous but also European) and money was appalling, giving rise to denunciations by priests (most prominently Bartolomé de las Casas) against the injustices taking place in the West Indies.

In the meantime, the Portuguese had established trading centers in India, taken Malacca, and reached the Moluccas or Spice Islands. Wealth poured into Lisbon. In Spain, Ferdinand of Aragon, ruling as regent after Isabella's death and facing the prospect of the total failure of the kingdom's American venture, listened in near desperation to a scheme propounded by a Portuguese sailor who had already served in Southeast Asia, Ferdinand Magellan. The latter claimed to know of a map showing a passage to the Pacific and that he could prove the Spice Islands were on the Spanish side of the papal demarcation line. The king commanded Magellan to find the passage and, regardless of whether he found it or not, to proceed by the shortest route to the Spice Islands and establish Spanish trade there. Thus, Magellan's expedition was intended to be an undertaking not of conquest but of discovery and commerce.

After a long and epoch-making voyage, Magellan, who had sailed ten degrees too far north to hit his target in the Moluccas, made landfall at Samar on March 16, 1521, and the Philippines became the meeting point of East and West, where the eastern and western routes of Mediterranean expansion converged and closed the worldwide circle of exploration.[3] Magellan had given geography for the first time the true dimensions of the globe. He was not the first European to land on Philippine soil; that distinction belongs to his friend and countryman Francisco Serrao, who landed in Mindanao in 1512. And the honor of being first to circumnavigate the world goes to his Malay slave Enrique, variously described as being a native of Malacca and having been born in Sumatra, who understood the language of the inhabitants of northern Mindanao. And, although he was averse to needless bloodshed, Magellan's "mad mismanagement" (to use one biographer's words) of the attempt to subjugate the chief of Mactan, Lapu-lapu, led to his death and gave the future Filipino nation a powerful symbol of anticolonial resistance.

The first man to circumnavigate the globe in a single journey was the Basque sailor Juan Sebastián de Elcano, who led the sole surviving vessel of Magellan's expedition back to Spain, arriving on September 7, 1522. Of the five ships and about 265 men who had sailed in 1519, only 18 men returned on a single ship, the *Victoria* (a few stragglers who had fallen into Portuguese hands followed later). Despite the heavy losses of ships and men, the expedition was a commercial success, for a cargo of spices picked up by the *Victoria* in the Moluccas on its way home covered the cost of the expedition and provided a tidy profit besides.

Three more expeditions were sent by the Spanish authorities after Magellan's voyage and before Legazpi's. Elcano was engaged as the pilot major of an expedition headed by García Jofre de Loaisa, which was to follow Magellan's route to the Moluccas and also establish forts and trading posts in China and Japan. Of the seven ships that left Spain on July 25, 1525, only one made it across the Pacific, and both Loaisa and Elcano died during the crossing. The solitary ship picked up a survivor of Magellan's expedition in the Ladrones, proceeded to Mindanao (where it met with a hostile reception) and the Visayas, and finally broke up after reaching the Moluccas. The remaining members of the expedition carried on a desultory struggle with the Portuguese while awaiting rescue. This expedition is remembered for two things: one of its members was a young Basque sailor, Andrés de Urdaneta, who was to figure importantly in the future history of Pacific navigation; and it was the last expedition to sail from Spain to the Orient until the end of the eighteenth century.

It was clear to the Spanish authorities that the route below South America via the Strait of Magellan was long and impractical. With the conquest of Mexico, it was now more logical to launch trans-Pacific expeditions from there. This, too, was to have an important effect on Philippine history. The tender *Santiago,* which had become separated from Loaisa's fleet, had managed to reach Tehuantepec, and its chaplain, Father Areizaga, was taken to Mexico to see Hernán Cortés himself, who had already been thinking about new discoveries in the southern seas.

In 1526, Emperor Charles V wrote Cortés from Granada, ordering him to ascertain the fate of the *Trinidad,* a ship from Magellan's voyage, and investigate the outcome of other expeditions with a fleet from Mexico. This Cortés did by dispatching three vessels commanded by his kinsman, Álvaro de Saavedra, from the port of Zihuatanejo on November 1, 1527. After coming on what are thought to have been the Marshall Islands, two of the ships drifted off course and were not seen again. The remaining ship, the *Florida,* reached the Ladrones, which Saavedra renamed the Marianas, then proceeded to Mindanao, where he rescued a shipwrecked member of the Loaisa expedition. From this man he learned that eight members of Magellan's ill-fated expedition had been sold in Cebu to the Chinese in exchange for metal goods. From Mindanao, Saavedra went to Gilolo and then to the fort at Tidore. This fort had been built by the remaining survivors of the Loaisa expedition, who, after three years of terrible experiences, now heard for the first time of the existence of New Spain.

Saavedra refused to take part in fights with the Portuguese, since his mission was to explore the Spice Islands and then return to New Spain. He made two attempts to return to Mexico, first sailing east and encountering New Guinea and then reaching the Admiralties and some of the Bismarcks before being forced back by contrary winds and currents to Tidore in October 1528. Finally, he set out on a more northerly course in May 1529 and reached the Caroline Islands (named after Emperor Charles V). But he died in October, and, although his successors followed his instructions to seek winds favorable for the return trip at about the thirty-fifth parallel, they did not find them. With only eighteen men, they returned to Tidore, where they discovered that the Spaniards there had moved to Gilolo.

Later the Portuguese brought the news that the emperor in the Treaty of Zaragoza of 1529 had renounced all claim to the Moluccas for the sum of 350,000 ducats. The surviving Spaniards, now numbering only seventeen, were persuaded to surrender on the condition that they would be shipped back to Portugal. They eventually returned to Spain in 1536. Among the returnees was Urdaneta, who arrived just twenty-eight days short of eleven years after he started out on the Loaisa expedition.

With the Spice Islands legally out of bounds, Spanish attention shifted primarily to the Philippines, formerly a peripheral concern. Both Cortés and his fellow conquistador in Guatemala, Pedro de Alvarado, maintained a lively interest in overseas exploration, but the expeditions they attempted to send to the Philippines proved abortive. Alvarado's most important act was probably the bringing to the New World of Andrés de Urdaneta in 1538.

After Alvarado's death, command of the ships he had prepared was first offered to Urdaneta, who declined the offer, and then to Ruy López de Villalobos, who believed that the archipelago of San Lázaro (the name Magellan had given the Philippines) and New Guinea were on the Spanish side of the papal demarcation line. Villalobos sailed with three ships from Mexico on November 1, 1542, probably came across the Hawaiian Islands, reached Leyte two and a half months later, formally took possession of the archipelago, and renamed it Islas Filipinas in honor of then Prince Felipe of Asturias, later to become King Philip II. But the local rulers resented Spanish interference with their independence and customs, and the people, unlike the isolated indigenous cultures of the Americas, already had trading and other contacts with the great Eurasian cultures.

Villalobos realized that with his small contingent he could not carry out his orders to establish permanent settlements and defend them against the Portuguese, who were beginning to trade with China and Japan and had even called at some of the Visayan islands. But his attempted return to New Spain was dogged by the same misfortunes as the previous expeditions, and after losing two ships he was driven back to the Moluccas by contrary winds, disease, and the danger of mutiny, finally arriving at Amboina toward the end of 1544. There he died during Holy Week of 1546 in the arms of St. Francis Xavier.

With this failure, coming after the earlier ones, the emerging opinion was that no one should go because no one would return. Only one man was thought capable of finding the return route, Andrés de Urdaneta, but he had entered the Augustinian monastery in Mexico City in 1552, so his seafaring days seemed to be over.

The Legazpi Expedition

It took a letter from Philip II himself to draw Urdaneta out of the cloister. Having determined to undertake an expedition to the "western islands" from Mexico, the king wrote the viceroy, Luis de Velasco, ordering him to make the necessary preparations. Enclosed was a letter to Urdaneta. In it, the king entreated and charged him ("Yo vos ruego y encargo") to accompany the expedition, as he had been on the Loaisa voyage, had great knowledge of that part of the world, was familiar with the sailing routes, and was a good cosmographer. In his instructions to the viceroy of the same date (September 24, 1559), the king says that the expedition should not tarry in trading and bartering but return immediately to New Spain, as the principal reason for the voyage was to ascertain the return route.

Urdaneta, of course, obeyed the royal order, however politely it might have been worded, but appended to his letter of acceptance was an opinion to the effect that the Philippines lay on the Portuguese side of the demarcation line and the projected expedition should remain on the Spanish side. In Urdaneta's view, the only legitimate reason for going to the Philippines would be to ransom any Spanish captives from previous expeditions who might be held there. If there was to be a settlement, it should not be in the Philippines but in New Guinea. In this, he was supported by the viceroy. In a later communication, he stated that he would refuse to embark if the fleet was to head for the Philippines. But a contrary view was held by Admiral Juan Pablo de Carrión, a survivor of the Villalobos expedition, with consequences that will be apparent later.

Since Urdaneta was a clergyman, command of the expedition could not given to him. Velasco, upon his recommendation, selected the chief clerk of the Mexico city council, Miguel López de Legazpi, a man enjoying his senior years surrounded by his children and grandchildren. He was not only a fellow Basque but more specifically a fellow Guipuzcoan and a kinsman of Urdaneta. Legazpi supervised the outfitting of the expedition, from the construction of ships to their provisioning and manning, using up much of his personal fortune in the process (for this he was later to receive several honors and titles but little in the way of actual recompense).

Five years would pass between the king's command to go to the western islands and the actual departure of the fleet from Puerto de la Navidad, Mexico, on November 21, 1564. Velasco died in July of that year, and in the absence of a viceroy the Audiencia (supreme court) of Mexico assumed executive power. Influenced by Carrión's views, the Audiencia's detailed instructions to Legazpi diverged from Urdaneta's recommendations; he was ordered to sail directly to the Philippines. Since it was known that Urdaneta, indispensable to the enterprise, would not sail on a voyage contrary to his conscience, the Audiencia's stratagem was to hand Legazpi sealed orders that would only be opened when he was a hundred leagues out to sea. At that point, as a royal official, he would have no recourse but to comply, and Urdaneta and his four fellow Augustinians would have to swallow their umbrage at the deception and accept their destination as an accomplished fact. Following the breaking of the news, the fleet, which had been sailing southwest in accordance with the late viceroy's instructions, headed west-southwest until it reached nine degrees north latitude. Then it turned due west. Later, on Urdaneta's advice, it would climb to thirteen degrees and thus come upon the Ladrones.

The vessels composing it were the five hundred ton *capitana,* or flagship, *San Pedro,* which either carried a small frigate or brigantine on her poop deck or towed it astern. The *almiranta,* or second in command, was the three to four hundred ton *San Pablo.* Escorting them were two small, fast tenders meant for navigating in shallow waters, the eighty ton *San Juan* and the forty ton *San Lucas.* Aboard were 380 men.

On the twenty-ninth, the numbers were reduced by the disappearance of the *San Lucas* under circumstances that indicated desertion. Its rascally but able leaders apparently sailed ahead to the Philippines and then back to Mexico in a feat of navigation that was remarkable even if shadowed by disloyalty. (Later it would be discovered that the desertion conspiracy was much bigger and would have involved the *almiranta* had not the master of camp insisted on following the flagship.)

The bulk of the fleet made a trans-Pacific crossing in which Urdaneta's calculations of distance were invariably more accurate than those of the pilots. After stopping in Guam, the ships made landfall at Samar on February 13, 1565.

Legazpi's enterprise cannot be looked on as simply the fifth of various expeditions that reached the Philippines. It was of transcendental importance in the country's development. The larger framework is beyond the scope of this study and can only be referred to briefly here. Spanish historical writing has been, as expected, uniformly laudatory of Legazpi's work. American historians of the early twentieth century, from the perspective of a different culture, seem to have been in substantial agreement. The editors of the largest compilation of Philippine historical material, Emma Helen Blair and James Alexander Robertson, opined that with his expedition "begins the real history of the Philippine Islands." Writing the historical introduction to the this collection of documents, Edward Gaylord Bourne said: "The work of Legaspi during the next seven years entitles him to a place among the greatest of colonial pioneers. In fact he has no rival."

Two generations later, less Eurocentric historians from the former colonies, the Philippines and Mexico, have weighed in with their own evaluations, which reinforce the high regard in which Legazpi has been held. The Filipino editors of a collection of source documents compiled on the occasion of the quadricentennial of the Christianization of the Philippines wrote: "There is one incontrovertible fact on which all historians agree—that the expedition, more than any other events, served as the turning point that changed the course of our history. That great enterprise . . . laid down the foundation of our present-day political and social organizations . . ." In the introduction to this work, the Mexican diplomat, writer, and scholar Rafael Bernal wrote:

> It was an extraordinary moment in the history of the Philippines because, in those first ten years of the Hispanic settlement here, the die was cast. . . . In those years the actual boundaries of the nation came into being. In those few years of history, the Philippines were molded into a cast that has solidified in time, never to be destroyed or thrown away. . . . The documents in this volume . . . reveal the actions and thoughts, and the hopes of the men that made possible that conquest, with so little bloodshed, in comparison with the conquests done by other western nations.

More recently, a Filipino historian has put it succinctly: "Before Legazpi there were no Philippines and no Filipinos." Some anthropologists have discerned a latent unity, based on shared cultural characteristics, among the numerous political units of the pre-Hispanic Philippines, but it was the positive act of Legazpi's expedition that gathered most of them together within a short span of time.

Legazpi had behind him the accumulated experience of two generations of exploration and settlement, starting with the demographic disasters of the Caribbean and continuing through the struggles on the American mainland. Some hard lessons had been learned, most importantly that the native population had to be conserved, both because it was the Christian thing to do and because it was economically sound; without native labor, the land was useless. As Bernal points out, the Spanish pattern of settlement was different from that of the Portuguese, who, for lack of sufficient men, only established factories or trading posts in which they remained foreigners in the new land. It also differed from the British and Russian patterns of occupying land, displacing natives, and transplanting their cultures and ways of life. The Spanish policy of conserving the native population meant keeping a great part of its culture and mixing it with Spanish and Christian elements. The Spanish themselves were partly indigenized, and this occurred in varying degrees and in various ways in the Americas and later in the Philippines.

Legazpi proceeded with tact and caution, preferring diplomacy to force; in fact, the Audiencia's detailed instructions left open the possibility that he might have to return with his whole fleet if settlement was not possible due to lack of men or opposition among the inhabitants. Whenever he could, his senior officers entered into blood compacts of friendship with the chieftains (*principales*) whom they encountered, some anonymous but others identified by name—Caobos, Calayon, Urrao, Tandaya (which was also a name given to Samar Island), Balaniga, Maletec, and Camutuan. When armed bands in some localities showed hostility and pelted their boats with stones, Legazpi ordered his men not to retaliate.

Legazpi himself entered into the most famous blood compact in Philippine history with a chieftain of Bohol, Si Katuna (Katurnao in some modern renderings), immortalized in a painting by the great Filipino painter Juan Luna, which hangs in Malacañang Palace. This compact has given rise to the Order of Sikatuna, conferred by the Republic of the Philippines on foreign nationals who have rendered some notable service to the country. In effect, Si Katuna has become a symbol of diplomacy.

The historical irony is that he was not the most important chieftain on Bohol. There was also Si Gala, described as being a greater chieftain of higher rank ("mas principal y de mas calidad") than Si Katuna, with whom he also entered into a blood compact. From both chieftains, Legazpi obtained confirmation of a story, previously told by a Bornean, that they had initially been reluctant to make contact because two years previously Moluccans aided by "Castilians" had killed or carried off into slavery more than eight hundred of their people. Legazpi told them that those were the Portuguese, who were different from Castilians, but the Boholanos said since their gestures, arms, and dress were similar they did not perceive them to be different. Legazpi assured them that he represented a different kingdom and a different sovereign and proceeded to win them over with gifts.

Up to this point, the native leaders are referred to in the documentation as chieftains (*principales*), but in exploring for trade reference is made to the ruler of Butuan as a king and the ruler of Cebu, Tupas, as a king and lord. If there was any basis for this upgrading in designation, it may have been because both places were trading ports.

Legazpi had to exercise firm leadership in controlling his own forces. His policy of paying for all goods taken, of returning captured goods and vessels to their owners, and of restraint in the face of provocation did not sit well with the soldiers, who found such diplomacy a source of irritation. On the other hand, when the decision was made in a general meeting of officials to establish a settlement in the country, the religious, who had strongly favored the policy of restitution, refused to accede to the decision (doubtless reflecting Urdaneta's reservations about their legal right to be there at all).

Cebu was selected for settlement as the most populous locality and best provided with food. Here Legazpi could play another card: if the indigenous people were not friendly, he could remind them of their treachery to Magellan's party after the Mactan disaster, despite their having sworn fealty to the Spanish crown, which in his view meant that he could justly wage war upon them.

The expedition arrived in Cebu on April 27, forty-four years to the day after Magellan's death. Several days were spent in inconclusive negotiations. The inhabitants were seen evacuating the town, probably fearing that this was the reprisal for the attack on Magellan's party, and when sufficient warriors with reinforcements from neighboring towns had assembled on the seashore and offshore in canoes and praus with warlike yells and gestures, the issue was joined. Fire from the Spanish naval artillery scattered them and paved the way for an unopposed landing.

Legazpi set about tracing the outlines of the new Spanish garrison. Feelers from the local inhabitants for peace were subsequently received with a great coming and going of chieftains and messengers, but it was some days before Tupas appeared, accompanied by a chieftain named

Tamuñon. Both of them entered into a blood compact with Legazpi. The Spaniard noted the unhappy antecedents of the survivors of Magellan's company but offered a royal pardon in exchange for renewed vows of fealty. He also asked that the other chieftains of the island make peace (apparently Tupas's writ as king and lord did not extend very far). This was agreed to by the rulers, although they mentioned the obvious fact that they had been children when it all happened; again, this led to some delays.

Finally Tupas arrived with several chieftains—Pisuncan, Si Catepan, Si Batumay, Si Maquio, Si Cabun, Si Giguin, Si Carlic, Si Cagumo, Si Batala, and Si Linti—all of whom signified their acceptance of Legazpi's terms in their names and those of the other chieftains and inhabitants of the islands. (The last two may not have been the names of anyone but rather the oaths "By God" and "By the lightning," mistaken by Spanish chroniclers for personal names). In the days following, more chieftains came to submit, of whom five are named: Si Carasi, Si Ra, Si Cao, Si Dala, and Nique.

While this was going on, the main objective of the expedition was being set in motion, the *tornaviaje* or return trip to Mexico. The flagship, the *San Pedro*, under the command of Legazpi's grandson Felipe de Salcedo, departed from Cebu on June 1, 1565, with two hundred people aboard, including Urdaneta, Fr. Andrés de Aguirre, and ten soldiers, thus drastically reducing the strength of the Cebu garrison. The *San Pedro* sailed northeast and by August 3 had reached 39° N. It descended to just below 31° N on August 11 before again climbing to a little above 39° N on September 4. On the eighteenth, an island was sighted just below 34° N (off today's Los Angeles, California), and on the twentieth they were abreast of Cedros Island. On the twenty-sixth, they passed the southernmost point of California, and (again with some guidance from Urdaneta) they reached Navidad on October 1 and Acapulco on the eighth. Sixteen men had died on the voyage, including the chief pilot; many were ill, with only ten to eighteen men still fit to work.

The *tornaviaje*, which followed Urdaneta's plan of sailing northeast from the Philippines and then catching the northwesterlies off the North American coast, was now reality. Although it had been upstaged by the tender *San Lucas*, which had arrived in Navidad on August 9, that has been considered a lucky improvisation, whereas Urdaneta's plan represented a solid contribution to nautical science.

Urdaneta and his fellow friar Aguirre were feted on their return to Mexico, where they reported to the authorities and then proceeded to Spain to report further and submit their papers. There were rumors of honors, prizes, and possible bishoprics, but these never materialized. Urdaneta met with the Council of the Indies on October 8, 1566, but it is thought he never saw Philip II, and the urgent request made by Legazpi and his officers for his return to the Philippines was not granted. By Lent of 1567, he was back in the Augustinian cloister in Mexico, where he died the following year.

In the meantime, Legazpi was marking time in Cebu awaiting definitive orders concerning what to do next. He is said to have worked so hard that it was said a twenty-five-year-old youth could not do more. Even with his reduced forces, the Cebuanos were calling on him to help them in their wars against hostile villages, which he could not totally avoid doing. But the main dangers were hunger, mutiny (on land and sea), and external attack.

Food procurement was a problem because Legazpi initially refused to send his Spaniards to secure supplies for fear that they would harm and rob the inhabitants. Instead he asked the chieftains of Cebu to buy rice where they could, and he gave them money and goods for the purpose. But they gave him short measure, alleging that they were unable to buy much, although it became known that their boats came back loaded. Even more serious was an agricultural strike, in which both friend and foe refrained from planting their fields in the hope of starving the Spaniards into departing. The Spaniards were reduced to eating cats, rats, and iguanas, which abounded on the island. They overcame the emergency when Moro traders from Luzon arrived with rice cargoes and when Legazpi had two frigates built on which he could send his own senior officers, who could keep military discipline, on rice-buying trips. On one of these trips, to Leyte, they received the first gold for the king in the form of earrings of light weight.

The attempts at mutiny stemmed from the food shortages and Legazpi's policies of restraint toward the local people; the men must have thought it was not for this that they had crossed two oceans and a continent and risked their lives. A serious plot was uncovered toward the end of November 1565 involving more than forty people. After executing the ringleaders, Legazpi pardoned the rest at the urging of the religious. A smaller mutiny in the making, which was uncovered in July 1566, could have had serious consequences because so few men were left in the camp. Again the ringleaders were executed. A mutiny at sea on a frigate that had taken the master of camp on a trading voyage to Mindanao was averted in April 1567 but not before the master was killed; two soldiers and a sailor paid with their lives.

In the meantime, the galleon *San Gerónimo* had arrived from Mexico in October 1566 after a terrible crossing that witnessed the captain's death in a mutiny led by Lope Martín (the pilot of the renegade *San Lucas* of the previous year), who in turn was marooned by loyal sailors with twenty-six mutineers on what is believed to have been one of the Marshall Islands. The galleon was so unseaworthy that it had to be broken up. It brought no food, and no dispatches from the Audiencia, but the reinforcements helped to fill the ranks, which had been depleted by death and disease.

To complicate matters, the Portuguese, who had not bothered to establish themselves in the Philippines because there were no spices, began scouting the Spanish garrison in November 1566. "It may well be imagined," wrote Legazpi to the king, "that they were not pleased to see Spaniards in these parts." After some inconclusive diplomatic sparring, the Portuguese mounted a full-scale blockade with superior forces toward the end of 1568. With a combination of military readiness, bravado, and brazen prevarication, Legazpi held them off until their strength proved to be their weakness: they ran out of provisions before the Spaniards did and lifted the siege on New Year's Day of 1569. While they did no harm to the Spaniards, they attacked and destroyed some local villages—a foretaste for the Filipinos of what it would be like to be caught in the middle of great power struggles in their future history.

Nevertheless, the Portuguese blockade impelled the Spaniards to move their settlement early in 1569 to a more defensible river position in Panay, where food was also reported to be more abundant. The friars looked on all this with a critical eye. Panay was hot and unhealthy, located along the swampy shore of a river, had no port, and was much less defensible than Cebu. Military discipline was lax, and punishment for infractions was light. What were needed were settlers, not soldiers who only knew how to amass wealth quickly and return home.

Legazpi's stay on Panay can be regarded as a demarcation period between a time of doubt and a time of decision. Until then, he had put up a brave front, acting as a supreme arbiter before the indigenous population; for example, one of his earlier acts was to forbid the burial of slaves with their dead masters. But his whole enterprise hung in doubt, awaiting more explicit directives from the king. As late as July 1569, Legazpi wrote the viceroy in Mexico, imploring him to send him what he asked if there was a warrant to do so from the king: "[O]therwise, may Your Excellency favor us by sending vessels by which we might leave this land, and not perish here without any profit." From the religious side, writing to the same viceroy at the same time, Fr. Martin de Rada wrote: "I trust in our Lord that this land may . . . receive the faith . . . but, on account of our great uncertainty and because we do not know whether his Majesty will order us to abandon this land, we have not dared to baptize." In fact, the friars had proceeded very circumspectly. There were no mass conversions, and by 1570 only about a hundred persons had been baptized. For his part, Tupas had cannily declared that he would receive baptism when he saw Spanish women joining the men because until then his people would not believe in the permanence of the Spanish presence and feared that they would be shipped off in what might only be an expedition to take captives.

Panay, despite the scant attention it has been given, also seems to have marked a moral and psychological nadir in the Spanish enterprise. Fr. Diego de Herrera, writing to the viceroy in June 1570, complained of military brutality, extortion, and lack of discipline. Safe conducts given by some commanders to local travelers were not respected by others. Even the soldiers wrote to protest the excesses of their commanders, and corruption had infected the highest levels, not excluding Legazpi himself. The portrait of Legazpi as a covetous old man susceptible to bribes and unable to control his subordinates is difficult to square with the earlier one of the wise, tolerant, and just governor who attracted even those who initially fled by protecting them from his own men, themselves in need as they got neither pay nor rations from the royal treasury. Was this a departure from his earlier stance? Had he grown tired of waiting for recompense for his efforts? (The cost of preparing for the expedition had exceeded 400,000 pesos, and he had met at least a part of it by drawing upon his personal fortune.) Were the reports a form of protest in the tradition of Las Casas in the Americas—in Bernal's words, "demagogic at times, truthful at others"?

Whatever the case, this period would soon come to an end, but not until one major operation was mounted. For three years, Legazpi had been hearing of Luzon, where the Chinese and Japanese came yearly to trade, but he did not have enough men to send an expedition. From the Portuguese, it was heard that they were maintaining themselves through a lucrative trade conducted with China and Japan. This trade could be tapped from that island. On May 8, 1570, the new master of camp, Martín de Goiti, left Panay on two small ships (a fifty-ton junk and a frigate), carrying three cannons, with a hundred men aboard, and accompanied by fourteen or fifteen praus manned by about five hundred Visayan allies from Cebu and Panay, on the first voyage to Luzon.

They would meet the first Chinese they had encountered since coming to the Philippines under circumstances that seemed far from auspicious but eventually would redound to their favor. On Mindoro, they heard of two Chinese vessels in a river, and since the winds were unfavorable they sent some praus ahead to reconnoiter and request peace and friendship. But the Chinese were alarmed at what they took to be an attack and came out side by side with their foresails up, firing rockets and culverins to the accompaniment of drums and fifes. The Spaniards on the praus, without waiting for orders, attacked and captured the junks with several Chinese casualties. The captain, Legazpi's grandson Juan de Salcedo, and the master of camp, who both came up in the rear guard, were displeased at what had happened, apologized to the Chinese, and promised them their freedom and a ship in which to return to their country along with whatever was needed for the voyage. They had one of the ships sent to Panay for repairs along with four Chinese who knew something about the construction of vessels (this was one of the incidents complained of by Father Herrera). The second meeting with the Chinese has already been mentioned: the captives who were flayed in Taal after a dispute with the local inhabitants.

A few days later, the small Spanish fleet entered Manila Bay, anchored at Cavite, and sent word to the ruler Raja Soliman (Sulayman in a modern rendering), requesting peace and friendship. Soliman reciprocated the friendly greeting and gave the Spaniards permission to settle on his land. Goiti then decided to go personally to Manila to meet the king. As he sailed along, people came in praus from the villages to complain that Soliman had plundered their towns and killed many of the inhabitants. As they passed the bar of the river at Manila, Chinese from the four ships at anchor came with gifts and complained that the people of Manila had removed the helms of their ships (a prevalent custom in the islands, as the people of Cebu had related five years earlier) and taken away the best of their goods without paying for them.

Goiti refused to be drawn into the dispute and went ashore to the palisaded town, where he was met by old Raja Laya (Soliman's uncle) and by Soliman himself. They were a study in contrasts, as the older man was soft-spoken and diplomatic, while the younger one was imperious and impetuous. The three made a blood compact of friendship, with the local rulers agreeing to support the Spaniards who settled there but to pay no tribute. But there was an air of tension, with an increasing number of armed men noted, and from their native allies who had relatives ashore they heard that an attack was being planned for the first rain, when the Spaniards could not fire their arquebuses. A confusing message was received from Soliman, saying that the ruler of Tondo, Lakandula, on the other side of the river, had invited him to join an attack on the Spaniards but that he had refused and would aid the Spaniards.

A misunderstanding brought matters to a head. The Spaniards sent a prau to reconnoiter some vessels that were sailing toward them, but on seeing that they were light merchant vessels they recalled the scouting prau by firing a cannon seaward. Soliman's artillerymen (said to be Borneans and Portuguese, Soliman being himself of Bornean ancestry) may have mistaken this for a hostile act and fired three shots, one or two of which hit the Spanish junk. At that point, Soliman appeared to have the military advantage. He had twelve or thirteen cannons to the Spaniards three and large numbers of men on land, and a later report had it that he fired the first shot himself. But some Spaniards had slept ashore, and Goiti with eighty men rushed the palisades through the wide embrasures of the artillery, captured the pieces, turned them on their adversaries, and set fire to the town. He ordered the return of the sails and helms to the Chinese vessels, which proceeded to cast anchor near the Spanish ships to get out of the line of fire. A large, oared vessel with three or four hundred warriors was seen upriver, mounted with culverins and large pieces of artillery and surrounded by more than five hundred praus, but these were scattered by cannon fire from the Spanish junk.

This happened on May 24, 1570. Goiti waited a couple of days for some message from the local rulers, but none came. As the prevailing winds would soon be changing, he had to leave soon if he wanted to make it back to Panay. But first, since Manila had now been taken in combat, he had the notary in chief, Hernando Riquel, draw up an official act, dated June 6, 1570, taking possession and declaring royal ownership of Luzon. Lakandula of Tondo he left undisturbed and sailed away accompanied by four Chinese junks, with whom his men bartered some goods for local wax.

As he made his way south, news reached him in Mindoro of the arrival of three ships from Mexico with Father Herrera and two other Augustinians as passengers. He hastened to Panay, arriving in mid-June, where he joined all the other commanders, who had been summoned by Legazpi to hear the newly received royal letters and orders. In brief, these orders, after commending the "sensible policy in not waging war," provided for the settlement of the country, the conversion of its inhabitants, and the grant to Legazpi for life of the title governor and captain general "of the said islands," with full administrative, judicial, and military powers. The period of hesitation was over; both the civil officials and the religious now had definite instructions.

The viceroy ordered Legazpi to return to Cebu, now that he had reinforcements and supplies, to prevent its falling into Portuguese hands in case of a subsequent attack. This Legazpi did in November 1570, and by

January 1571 he had officially founded the City of the Most Holy Name of Jesus, with fifty married Spanish settlers. He returned to Panay at the end of the month to undertake from there the occupation of Manila.

The move to Manila must have arisen from a conscious decision to take part in the China trade because as late as July of the previous year Legazpi was writing the viceroy that he wished to know the royal desire on whether to contact the Moluccas, for which Cebu would be the appropriate location, or go north to trade on the coast of China, for which a settlement on Luzon would be better given the master of camp's recent discovery of an adequate port.

He sailed from Panay on April 20 with all his officers, 230 soldiers, and Father Herrera and other priests on twenty-six or twenty-seven vessels, large and small, including those of his Visayan allies. He tarried a fortnight on Mindoro and arrived in Manila in mid-May. Legazpi noted that the town had been rebuilt after the previous year's fire, but on seeing the Spaniards the inhabitants burned it again and fled to Tondo on the north bank of the Pasig River.

However, neither side wanted a renewal of hostilities. Lakandula came out in a boat to welcome Legazpi, soliciting peace and friendship also for the other two rajas, Soliman and Laya. This was granted, and the next day Legazpi disembarked, met the three rulers, and made peace. The Spaniards were allowed to occupy the site of the burned village, commanding the entrance to the river. In return, exemption from tribute would be granted to the rajas and their descendants.

On June 3, 1571, Legazpi formally conferred the status of city on the new settlement. He appointed the first City Council on June 24, a date that is still observed as Manila Day. On the twenty-eighth he submitted the first ordinances to the council. From Manila, the conquest of the rest of Luzon would follow quickly.

Legazpi died suddenly on August 20, 1572. The Augustinian friar Francisco de Ortega, in a letter to the viceroy, and in contrast to Father Herrera's earlier opinion, wrote that "he governed this country with great quietness and prudence, spent upon it his own property, and died poor in the service of his Majesty."[4]

Trade Aspects

From its earlier stages, the members of the Legazpi expedition actively accumulated knowledge about the archipelago's commercial conditions and prospects. They were fortunate in that, even before they reached

Cebu, they received the fullest body of information on the subject that they were to get during their entire stay. This came about when some Spanish boats hailed a Bornean vessel (referred to most frequently as a prau but some times as a junk in the same document), seeking to parley. Fearing hostile intent, the prau, which was armed with a small culverin and two arquebuses in addition to bows and arrows, chose to fight. It was captured after a fierce battle, in which the captain was killed, and taken to Legazpi's anchorage.

The prau was much larger than those used by the local inhabitants, with a mainmast, foremast, and mizzenmast and three decks (though little space between them). It was estimated to be a little smaller than the tender *San Lucas*, which would mean just under forty tons, and carried forty-five men. Its owner was a Portuguese residing in Borneo, Anton Maletis, but the cargo belonged to the king of Borneo (i.e., Brunei).

Through Urdaneta, who had learned Malay during his years in the Moluccas as a young sailor on the Loaisa expedition, Legazpi spoke with the Borneans, clarified the misunderstanding, and restored to them their freedom, their vessel, and their cargo. This gave rise to some discontent among the soldiers, who had already taken some things for themselves.

Legazpi also had a long conversation with the pilot, who had extensive knowledge of and experience in trade and navigation in Southeast Asia. The pilot gave him what may have been the first detailed commercial report on pre-Hispanic trade—or at least on Philippine trade at the time of Spanish contact. He looked at Legazpi's large ships and samples of his cargo and frankly told him that his goods were not suitable for these islands. In ten years, they would not be able to sell all their silks, linens, and textiles. They should go to Borneo, where the cargo could be disposed of in eight days, or to Siam, Patani, or Malacca, where it would also sell well.

The cargo on the Bornean prau consisted of iron and tin from Borneo; porcelain, copper bells, benzoin, and colored blankets from China; pots of brittle iron and pans from India; and lances, knives, and other baubles. These they traded for gold, slaves, shells used as money in Siam and Patani (cowries), wax (which abounded in the islands), and white blankets (which were cheap and plentiful among the people).

The cargo found aboard the Chinese junks taken by Goiti's men on the first voyage to Manila confirms and expands the list of imports supplied by the Borneans. On those junks were found, although not in large quantities considering the size of the ships, silk (woven and in skeins); gold thread; musk; gilded porcelain vases, plates, and bowls; fine porcelain jars; iron and steel; and wax that had been purchased in the country.[5]

The Bornean identified Butuan as an active trading port because there was gold there both from its own rivers and from Surigao, Caraga, and other islands. Everywhere the people had gold earrings, bracelets, and necklaces. He said there were at that time two Luzon junks in Butuan trading gold, wax, and slaves for much the same kind of cargo as that carried by the Borneans. Because they carried Chinese goods, both the Bornean and Luzon vessels were called China junks in the islands. Authentic Chinese junks did not visit the Philippines because they were too large for the island trade.[6]

Since no values are given, it is difficult to judge the relative importance of the goods traded, but a general impression can be gathered from various accounts. On the import side, there seems to have been a great desire for metal goods, as is indicated by certain incidents that will be cited later. To judge by the listing of cargoes and the finds in excavations of burial sites, porcelain ware was also important. On the export side, the triad of gold, wax, and slaves mentioned by the Bornean pilot is repeated by Legazpi's high officials in a letter to the king in 1567: "The Chinese go to their land [Luzon and Mindoro] to trade and carry away all the products of this archipelago, namely, gold, wax, and slaves." Likewise, Fr. Martin de Rada, writing two years later to the viceroy in Mexico, says: "Many merchants of Lusson, Bornei, Xolo, and other parts travel continually throughout these islands, and the object of their search is either gold or slaves."[7]

Two questions may be taken up briefly at this point. The first is whether slaving was a component of trade with China. At first glance, this would seem an absurdity because China is such a populous country. In fact, most references to the China trade do not mention it. But, aside from Father Rada's general observation, there are specific instances cited in the documentation. Members of the Loaisa expedition learned that eight survivors of Magellan's complement who had fallen into an ambuscade in Cebu following the battle of Mactan had been sold to the Chinese in exchange for metal goods (an example of the local demand for metals). Years later, when Legazpi's grandson Juan de Salcedo was in the process of completing the conquest of Luzon in 1572, he came across a Chinese junk in Bolinao loaded with slaves, including a chieftain, and he compelled the Chinese to free them, thus earning the Filipinos' gratitude.[8]

The second question is whether there was some kind of change in the pattern of the Philippine overseas trade between Magellan and Legazpi. Pigafetta, it will be recalled, mentioned that a Siamese junk had come to Cebu in 1521 to buy gold and slaves. Urdaneta, while in the Moluccas with the stragglers of the Loaisa expedition, heard that there was gold in Cebu (this is inaccurate, as the Cebu chieftains told Legazpi years later) and that Chinese junks went there annually to trade. He also heard that two junks a year went to Mindanao, where they traded for cinnamon, gold, and pearls.[9] By Legazpi's time, however, the Borneo pilot was saying that overseas junks went only to larger ports like Borneo and Manila, from whence smaller vessels carried goods in the interisland trade. During Legazpi's five years or so on Cebu, no overseas trading ships came, but a number of praus and junks from Luzon and Mindoro either put in to sell iron, tin, wax, porcelain, blankets, China cloth, fragrances, gold, and rice or were seen on trading voyages to Butuan.

What seems to have developed is that Manila had become a transshipment port, foreshadowing the coming era of the galleon trade, when it would become the entrepôt for transoceanic voyages to Acapulco and the Manila galleon would also be known as the China ship because of its cargo, much as the Luzon and Borneo vessels were known as China junks in the southern Philippine islands. There was, however, one difference. In pre-Hispanic times, transshipment was of the break-bulk kind, with the larger cargoes from Chinese junks split into smaller lots for the interisland trade. In the days of the galleons, the opposite was the case: Chinese junks sold their wares in Manila so that these could be assembled for shipment in larger cargoes to Mexico.

Following the Bornean pilot's advice, the tender *San Juan* went to Butuan to explore the coast and scout its commercial prospects, with instructions from Legazpi that the vessel should allow no harm to come to the natives and take nothing from them without pay but also should guard against harm or deception perpetrated by them. The sailors found the two junks from Luzon, gave gifts on Legazpi's behalf to the local king, and acquired gold dust, cheap jewels, and wax. They also began trading for cinnamon and in subsequent years sent several expeditions to Butuan, Dapitan, and the Zamboanga coast in search of this commodity. Cinnamon was found to be plentiful on Mindanao, provided the right goods could be found for barter, since much of what the Spaniards carried was not acceptable to the natives. On their return from one such expedition, fifteen or sixteen Spaniards died of diarrhea, the result of eating too much cinnamon.

Cinnamon formed the main local export item for the galleons that went to Acapulco from the new settlement, starting with the *San Pedro* on the first *tornaviaje* when a small quantity was carried. The quantities increased in subsequent years, with 70 quintals shipped in 1567 and four hundred in 1568 (these were lost, however, in a shipwreck). In 1573, 372 quintals were sent.[10]

In an undated report, Legazpi wrote that cinnamon was the only article from which profit could be derived since the gold supply would be small until the mines were worked. In another report, dated July 7, 1569, to the viceroy he wrote: "If his Majesty has an eye only on the Felipina islands, they ought to be considered of little importance, because at present the only article of profit we can get from this land is cinnamon; and unless order is established and a settlement is made, his Majesty will continue to waste money. . ." But in 1573 the viceroy in Mexico wrote the king: "I do not believe cinnamon will prove a success in this land, for it is very little used, because of the use here of other spices which grow in these regions."[11] Clearly something else was needed, and unknowingly they had already stumbled on it during the early days of the expedition.

When Legazpi wanted to send a scouting party to look for a frigate he had sent to Cebu, Si Katuna and Si Gala provided a large prau with thirty oarsmen, and after some bargaining it was agreed that they would be paid the equivalent of two gold taydes (eighteen and a quarter pesos or Mexican dollars). The transaction went as follows: the Borneo merchants would give the Boholanos the value of the two gold taydes in iron (another indication of the local demand for metal), and Legazpi would pay the Borneans in testoons (pieces of four, or half pesos, for which they showed a great desire) at a ratio of five of silver to one of gold.

Shortly afterward the tender that went to Butuan found the Luzon merchants there equally eager to acquire silver testoons, and they agreed to accept six of silver to one of gold by weight. The Spaniards tried to barter with the Butuan people using linens and taffeta, but they would accept nothing but testoons. This was apparently at the prompting of the Luzon merchants, who expected to acquire the coins in trade later because the Spaniards said that the islanders there "do not recognize testoons, nor trade in them, nor know what they are. . ."

Later, when Legazpi was established on Cebu and the Luzon merchants came to trade, they were offered a silver to gold ratio of five to one, but they refused, citing the transaction at Butuan as a precedent. Before they left, however, they said they would accept the five to one ratio, but this time Legazpi refused, claiming that the gold being offered was of low grade.

During Goiti's first voyage to Manila, Legazpi's chief notary, Fernando Riquel, wished to buy some gold trinkets. He was asked to provide a five to one ratio of silver to gold, but he offered only three to one. However, the transaction was interrupted by a call to return to his ship.[12]

From these transactions it was evident that the Borneo and Luzon traders, who dealt with the Chinese, were familiar with the use of silver in trade even if the local people were not and that the accepted ratio among them was 5 or 6 of silver to 1 of gold by weight. In 1560, the silver to gold ratio was 11 to 1 in Europe and at least 13 to 1 in Mexico, while in China it was only 4 to 1. This last ratio varied from time to time between 5.5 and 8 to 1 in the last two decades of the sixteenth century and the first three of the seventeenth, but then the ratio in the western world also rose until it reached 15.5 to 1 in the late eighteenth century, around which level it hovered well into the nineteenth. In Japan, the source of silver for the Portuguese in Macao before the coming of Spanish-American silver, the ratio was fixed in 1592 at 10 to 1, while in Moghul India it was around 9 to 1. If one were dealing with foreign exchange, these would represent broken cross-rates. The opportunities for arbitrage profits were staggering.

Later Spanish mercantilist complaints about home industries being undercut by Chinese textiles reflected not so much the low prices of Chinese goods as the high price placed on silver by the Chinese. Bernal points out that Mexican silver entering China immediately tripled in value, while Boxer cites opinions to the effect that China was long the suction pump that absorbed silver from the whole world. This was to be the driving force in Manila's nascent entrepôt trade with Acapulco.[13]

Legazpi sought to welcome foreign merchants, whether Muslim, pagan, or of any other nation, by providing fair dealing, security of persons and goods, and freedom from exactions by councilors or deputies in his first ordinances to the Manila City Council on June 28, 1571, reiterating that special care should be taken to give good treatment to both natives and foreigners.[14]

Legazpi also proposed a voyage of exploration to China, but this was not carried out for lack of interest by his successor, Guido de Lavezaris. However, the new governor wrote the king in 1573 that "during the two years we have spent on this island, they [the Chinese] have come in greater numbers each year . . ."

Among them were the Chinese merchants whom Legazpi had rescued from a shipwreck off Mindoro on his way to Manila and who, early in 1572, had arrived "with a great deal of rich merchandize . . . together with others of that nation, who brought damasks, satins, taffeties, silks, porcelain, and other things, with which the foundation of a lucrative commerce with Acapulco was laid."[15] Actually, it is doubtful that a single act of rescue can be credited with having sparked the Acapulco trade, as the Spaniards had had at least three prior contacts with the Chinese during Goiti's first voyage to Manila. With the unspoken factor of arbitrage profits underlying all transactions, the Manila galleon's long career was under way.

CHAPTER 2

The Galleon Trade

The Manila Galleon was . . . the first medium to reduce the world to a village.

—*Nick Joaquin (1990)*

The galleon trade lasted for two and a half centuries after Legazpi's settlement in Cebu, from 1565 to 1815, the period in the Western world falling approximately between Lepanto and Waterloo.[1] It was the longest shipping line in history. One hundred and eight galleons were used, and of this number thirty were lost by shipwreck (ten of them in the turbulent waters of the San Bernardino Straits, also known as the Embocadero) or capture (four by the British).

In the context of late-sixteenth-century East Asian commerce, the Philippines-Mexico trade was the one completely new and important creation, stimulating a greatly increased traffic between China and the Philippines even while the rest of the traditional framework of Asian trade remained largely the same.[2]

From the point of view of regional geography, the galleon trade made Manila the first primate city in Southeast Asia by the early seventeenth century, as much as two centuries ahead of other regional centers, which attained this status only in the nineteenth century. In

32

population, prosperity, and social complexity, it far outstripped the country's second- and third-ranked settlements combined.[3]

From a broad economic point of view, the Philippines through the era of the galleon trade became part of what has been called the first-world economy of modern times, namely, that based on Seville and the Atlantic. The Pacific trade moved in phase with economic activity in the Atlantic. If mercantilist strictures had been correct in claiming that the drain of silver into East Asia was the cause of economic depression in Mexico and Spain, a negative correlation would have emerged between Atlantic and Pacific activity, each one being autonomous and with its own dynamic; prosperity in one (the Pacific) would have meant depression in the other (the Atlantic). But in fact there was a positive correlation; the cycles in both areas were similar in timing. The galleon trade was more the result than the cause of the ups and downs in the economy of the Spanish Empire.[4]

General View

The Philippines, whose geographical position as an outlier of the Southeast Asian island arc had made it in pre-Hispanic times among the last to receive some of the major cultural influences of the region, now found itself in a position to gather together trade flows from many directions. A capsule summary of the galleon trade is that it attracted silks from the north, spices from the south, and cottons and ivory from the west, exchanging them for silver and friars from the New World.

This sweeping generalization, however, hides a wealth of detail to which even lengthy accounts can hardly do justice. General categories of exports to Mexico were textiles (silk and cotton), porcelain, ivory (especially carved religious images), furniture (including inlaid and lacquered items), metalwork (from grills to delicate filigrees), and various foods and plants of Philippine or other Asian provenance (rice, tea, mangoes, and orchids and other flowering plants).[5] Despite official restrictions, slaves were sometimes carried. Domestic Philippine exports were gold dust, wax, cordage, and various kinds of sheeting and textiles from Manila, Ilocos, Cebu, and Lubang; these amounted to no more than about 10 percent of the value of the shipments.

Contemporary accounts are more specific and mention (to name only some commodities) carpets from Persia, jewels from India, rich hangings and bed coverings from Bengal, cinnamon from Ceylon, pepper from Java and Sumatra, spices from the Moluccas, balsam and ivory from Cambodia, camphor from Borneo, civet from the Ryukyus, silverware and lacquer from Japan, and silks of all kinds from China. Reference is also found to trade with Macassar, Siam, and Cochin China. Mercury from China was at times carried for use in the Mexican mining industry.

Certain items for public use carried by the galleons have endured to this day as reminders of that period. The most important is the choir grille of the Mexico Cathedral, made in Macao after a Mexican design and installed in March 1730. Another item in the same cathedral is a choir-book lectern carved in Manila and sent as a present by the archbishop of that city.[6] Of much humbler dimensions is the revolving tabernacle carried on the galleon *San Carlos* in 1781 as part of a cargo of supplies for the northern California missions. After a couple of transshipments, it arrived in 1783 in San Francisco Bay and was placed in the mission of San Francisco de Asís, known to modern San Franciscans as Mission Dolores, where it can still be seen today. In the same shipment were three consecrated and eleven unconsecrated altar stones, Philippine contributions to the California missions.[7]

On the return voyage from Mexico, probably between 90 and 99 percent of the value of the cargo was made up of silver—irregular cob coins at first and then milled coins after 1732 with the introduction of the pillar dollar, considered in numismatics to be the coin that has gained acceptance in more lands and across a greater area than any coin ever minted by man. The rest was a mixture of New World products (cochineal, cacao, leather bags) and transshipped Spanish items (wine, olive oil, woolen cloth).[8] Perhaps of greater future significance, although of inconsequential invoice value, was the carrying of plants and plant products from Mexico and Central America, some of which enriched the diet of Filipinos while others became important in trade and public finance. The most important of these were maize, tobacco, indigo, maguey, cacao, papaya, pineapple, eggplant, cassava, tomatoes, potatoes, and coffee (transshipped from Africa), but there were many others, including decorative and flowering plants, shrubs, and trees.[9]

The Sampan Trade

In the early years, trading between Chinese and Manilans was unrestricted, but lack of confidence in their own bargaining ability led the

Spanish to propose in 1586 a wholesale arrangement (approved by the Crown in 1589) under which representatives of local merchants met with those of Chinese importers and negotiated prices for the cargo of each incoming junk. The arrangement, called the *pancada*, was subject to numerous evasions and proved unfeasible, gradually giving way to the *feria* or fair. The Portuguese, who resented it, and the Japanese, who preferred to barter, were not subject to the *pancada*.

In fact, the trade with Japan (until it closed its ports to foreign trade in 1639) had a different underlying dynamic because it was a silver-producing country and so did not seek Mexican silver. The Japanese brought cutlery, some silks, wheat flour, and dried meat and carried away raw Chinese silk, jars, gold, dyewoods, deerskins, honey, glass, and Spanish curiosities.[10]

But the most important cargo commercially was silk—of all kinds and in every stage of manufacture from raw silk to wearing apparel and church vestments. Mexican art historians also give prominence to porcelain.[11] Both of these types of goods came primarily from China, hence the name China ship, which was sometimes applied to the Manila galleon.

In view of their limited numbers and the dangers of external attack (the Portuguese had besieged Cebu and the corsair Limahong, or Lin Feng, had tried to take Manila three years after Legazpi had transferred his garrison there), the Spanish were not allowed to embark on trading expeditions. Even if they had been, foreigners were barred from Chinese ports until they were allowed into Canton in 1685 under highly restrictive rules, although Spain was given special port rights in Amoy. These have been little noted historically; for example, in November 1794 the packet boat *San José*, alias *El Cavallo*, returned to Manila from a trading voyage to Amoy. The Portuguese, during the union of the Portuguese and Spanish Crowns from 1580 to 1640, tried to act as intermediaries through Macao, but they could not proceed beyond that city. The concession by China to Spain of a trading post on an island called El Pinal (probably Hong Kong) in 1598 failed to improve matters owing to opposition from Macao. Thus, the bulk of the trade with China was carried out by sampans from Fujianese ports like Amoy and Chincheo (Zhangzhou). Other ports named in the Spanish records are Lanquin and Limpo. Among the sampan captains in the late eighteenth century were Christian Chinese bearing names like Juan Fantengco, Santiago Fantengco, and José Tuasiong.

These sampans ranged from one hundred to three hundred tons burden, and they arrived during the prevailing northeasterlies between November and May, taking about fifteen sailing days from Fujian to Manila. Yearly, an average of thirty to forty sampans called at Manila, and there could be as many as fifty in good times. They brought highly salable items, already mentioned, for the galleons. But they were not confined to the luxury trade. They also brought foodstuffs for local consumption such as wheat flour, fruit preserves, salted meats, live fowls, fresh fruits, and nuts. Other important items consisted of domesticated animals such as buffaloes, horses, mules, asses, and birds. Supplies for shipbuilding and military use included iron, saltpeter, gunpowder, copper, nails, and other metal items. The wide assortment of imports demonstrates the heavy dependence of the new colony on the sampan trade.

The sampans did take home Philippine products such as gold dust, raw cotton, deerskins, wax, dyewoods, and seashells. In the eighteenth century, more commodities, such as indigo, rattan, ebony, tortoiseshell, bird's nests, and lead, were added to the list. But these exports were minor in quantity and value compared to Mexican silver.

The sampan voyages affected not only trade but immigration. The Chinese, aside from being merchants, were also financiers, and they gave credit or advanced loans to needy Spanish merchants (although the main sources of financing for such people were the *obras pías* or pious foundations). There was also an influx of artisans and tradespeople—ironsmiths, carpenters, brick makers, silversmiths, stonemasons, druggists, bakers, butchers, fishermen, and truck gardeners, to name a few. The Chinese population of Manila, numbering forty at the time of the Spanish contact, soared into the tens of thousands, increasing to twenty to thirty thousand by 1603, when the country's population was estimated to be about half a million.[12]

Faced with such numbers and fearful of their own numerical inferiority, the Spanish blew hot and cold in their policy toward the Chinese, with periods of encouragement or tolerance alternating with periods of expulsion or repression. This resulted in several sanguinary uprisings beginning in 1603. But the trade connections were of mutual benefit, not only to the individuals involved but to the revenue authorities in both Fujian and Manila. The governor of Fujian annually collected eighty to one hundred thousand pesos from the sampan trade with Manila, while at Manila the sampan traders had to pay a 3 percent import duty (later raised to 6 percent for luxury items) as well as anchorage fees, freight charges, and license fees for staying in the Chinese quarter, known as the Parian. Customs collections by 1620 had risen to eighty thousand pesos a year. This was in fact the major, if indirect, impost on the galleon trade at the Manila end, since direct taxation of the trade was unpopular and only a light export duty was collected. Commerce therefore generally resumed after the suppression of each uprising.

The heyday of the sampan trade was from 1570 to 1670. Its flourishing state attracted the attention of enemies both foreign and Spanish. During the Dutch wars of the first half of the seventeenth century, Dutch fleets prowled Philippine waters and blockaded Manila in order to intercept the sampans and choke off the Philippines' lifeline. While they achieved a marked reduction in the sampan trade in some years, they were on the whole singularly unsuccessful owing to the superiority of the Basque naval officers, the loyalty of the Christian Filipinos (who made up most of the crews in the Spanish vessels), and the sturdy construction of the galleons, which were made from Philippine hardwoods.[13] There were also attacks by Chinese pirates and refugees from the mainland, including the Taiwan-based Koxinga or Cheng Ch'eng-Kung.

The Restrictive System

More ominous was the hostility generated in Spain by the lucrativeness of the trade long before the Dutch appeared on the scene. The first heady years of the trade saw exports not only to Mexico but also to Peru, where expeditions were sent in 1581 and 1582. But by then the silk industry of Andalusia, protected by laws enacted prior to the conquest of the Philippines, including a decree of Charles V dating to 1523, had become alarmed by the inroads of Asian silks into its monopoly position in Spain's New World possessions. The royal government also harbored mercantilist fears about the heavy drain of silver from its colonies.

A royal order in 1582 cut off the Peruvian trade at its very inception. This was followed by laws passed in 1591, 1592, 1593, 1595, and 1604 prohibiting trade between China and the Philippines with all of Spain's American possessions except Mexico. To ensure that no Asian silks reached Peru, a drastic measure was decreed in 1604, suppressing all trade between Mexico and Peru (the decree had to be reissued several times until 1706, indicating chronic conditions of noncompliance).

There remained the viceroyalty of New Spain, from whence the Philippines was administered. In this case, however, cutting off the galleon trade would have meant relinquishing the colony, as that trade was the major source of revenue and the major inducement for officials and soldiers to go there. As a compromise with the Andalusian interests, it was decided not to suppress the trade but to limit it, and this gave birth to the restrictive system that was to form such a large part of the history of the trade for more than two centuries and over which Manila and Andalusia struggled at court for nearly a century and a half until Manila won a victory of sorts in 1734.

In a decree of January 11, 1593, limitations were set on numbers of vessels (only two might cross yearly), on their tonnage (not more than three hundred tons each), and on the value of their cargoes (250,000 pesos outgoing and 500,000 returning). Manilans could not consign their cargoes to merchants in Mexico, who like all residents of Spanish America were forbidden to trade directly with Asia; instead, they had to send supercargoes on the galleons to Acapulco, where an annual fair was held during which the goods might be disposed of to Spanish American buyers. The galleons became state vessels, with the costs of construction and operation borne by the royal treasury.

In carrying out the restrictive system, it became necessary to measure cargo space on the galleons and allot rights to such space to shippers. A committee measured the ship's hold and divided the space into equal parts corresponding to a bale, or *fardo*, of definite and uniform size. Each bale was in turn subdivided into four packages, or *piezas*, and the right to ship on the galleon was represented by a *boleta*, or ticket corresponding to one *pieza*. Dividing four thousand *boletas* (representing *piezas*) into the return quota of 500,000 pesos gave a value of 125 pesos for each *boleta* in Manila, which provided a convenient criterion for assessing duties and making statistical returns, although in practice its value could be much higher.

The 1593 decree provided that "all the citizens of those islands, in proportion to their wealth" were eligible to be *boleta* holders, or *boleteros*, on the theory that the body of citizens and the merchant class (*ciudad y comercio*) were identical. The distribution of *boletas* was handled differently at different times. In the early days, it was the exclusive prerogative of the governor, but a 1604 decree forced him to share his powers with a *junta de repartimiento* or board of apportionment representing the principal interests of the community—the royal government, the Church, and the "city and commerce." This ex officio committee included the governor, the senior judge of the Audiencia (supreme court), the *fiscal* (attorney general), two *regidores* (members of the city council), and the archbishop of Manila (who seldom participated actively in the committee's sessions). This board was to allocate the lading space on the galleons during most of their history. There were some changes in 1734, when one of the city councilors was replaced with a district judge of the city and the other councilor had to alternate every other year with one of the eight *compromisarios* representing the *comercio* or strictly mercantile element of the colony, attesting to its growing distinction from the community at large.

It is hard to see how this committee could be expected to function harmoniously and honestly, composed as it was of persons of unequal influence whose self-interest as potential beneficiaries of the apportionment system undercut their duty to make the allocation equitably. The governor tended to dominate his fellow committee members, and some usurped and temporarily overrode the authority of the *junta*. As a rule, forty-five tons of each vessel's cargo were reserved for him, and in one instance he did not allow the citizens a single ton of space. He also had the lucrative prerogative, with occasional interference from the viceroy, of naming the officials of the galleons. At a later stage in the trade, city councilors and provincial governors were allocated eight *boletas* each; members of the *consulado*, citizens of Manila, widows of Spaniards, and others received half, or one or more *boletas*.[14]

There were charges of fraud and favoritism. Extensive trading in *boletas* arose between those who could afford to ship but lacked *boletas* and those who had *boletas* but could not afford to ship. This was not supposed to happen, and a decree of 1638 forbade the transfer of *boletas* without the *junta*'s intervention. Those who could not use all their *boletas* were required to return the unused ones to the *junta* for distribution to those who could and be compensated at the assessed value of the *boletas* for that year. Regulations in 1734 reaffirmed the principle of the 1638 decree, but allowed "the poor and widows" to sell their *boletas* outright to active merchants. The granting of boletas to widows, orphans, ecclesiastical organizations, and public officials either as outright charity or as income supplements allowed the speculative traffic to continue.

When the last major reform was made in the allocation system in 1769 by replacing the *junta* with a *consulado* of merchants composed of a *prior*, two *consuls*, and four deputies, the exceptions remained. (The *consulado* actually began functioning only in 1771.) This led Francisco Leandro de Viana, former attorney general of the Philippines, to denounce the *boleta* system as the root of all evil in the galleon trade in a report submitted on May 9, 1780, to the Council of the Indies, on which he sat as the count of Tepa. He favored assigning *boletas* only to bona fide merchants and deplored the despotism and greed of the governors; the intrusions of the clergy, the military, and the bureaucracy; and the provisions for widows and the poor among the *boleteros*. He observed sarcastically about this unique scheme of social security that "there did not remain anyone in the Philippines who did not share in the *repartimiento*." He proposed that the

churches, pious foundations, widows, orphans, soldiers, and city councilors not be deprived of the distribution quota "with which it has been cus-
tomary to help them" but that they be given in money the same amount
they would have received from the sale of their *boletas*. This aid would be
underwritten by the merchants, which could then assign all *boletas* to
qualified individuals, the aid to last until the beneficiaries could amass a
sufficient endowment but in no case to exceed ten years, after which time
the merchants could ship in their own vessels or buy *boletas* directly from
the royal government. He also struck a refreshing developmental note by
trying to link the allocation system to investment and economic growth;
boletas should be given to registered merchants with various qualifications
"and principally to those who may distinguish themselves in developing
with their capital agriculture, manufactures, and industry . . . that they
may be rewarded with *boletas* according to the greater or less capital invested in the said fields."[15]

There is no record that Viana's reforms on this point were ever
adopted, and the *boleta* system appears to have persisted to the end in
about the same state as in 1769. A lengthy discussion took place in 1804
around the nagging question of placing the trade in the hands of traders
and commuting the entitlements of nontraders to a cash payment at the
official price of one hundred pesos per *boleta* in times of peace, but the city
councilors remained exempt from this and could still receive their entitle-
ment in a permit (*en poliza*). So they could use the lading space if they
wished or sell their rights at not more than the official price, subject in case
of violation to the penalty of losing half the value of their right to the ac-
cuser (even if he was the buyer) and the other half to the royal treasury. In
any event, Viana's recommendations and other attempted modifications,
while they would have allowed a greater role for the forces of demand and
the pricing mechanism in the allocation system, failed to address its major
defect, namely, the *permiso*, or export quota, that hung over the whole
trade. This quota, whether expressed as the number of *piezas* or the value
of the cargo, and the restrictions on the tonnage of the galleons were ignored with cynical consistency throughout the history of the trade.

While the officially permissible number of *piezas* was four thousand,
some galleons carried six, twelve, or even eighteen thousand in good
years. In bad years, especially around the mid–eighteenth century, the
number of *piezas* fell below the official limit. Nor were the tonnage limitations enforced. Although the limit was set at 300 tons, some galleons were
as heavy as 1,600 tons. Although the official limit was raised to 560 tons in
1720, there were ships of 1,700 and 2,000 tons subsequent to that.

The most flagrant evasions, and those that were most infuriating to the mercantile interests of Cadiz and Seville, came in the matter of the value of the cargo. Despite being set originally at 250,000 pesos outgoing (500,000 pesos incoming), some galleons carried as many as 2 million pesos on the return voyage. Official regulations tried to accommodate increasing amounts. The *permiso* was revised to 300,000 pesos outgoing in 1702, to 500,000 in 1734, and finally (as an extraordinary increase) to 750,000 pesos in 1776 (with the incoming quota double these respective figures), but mercantile practice continued to outrun official theory and galleons carried from 1.5 million to as many as 3 million pesos in the later years.

The excess cargo was accommodated in a number of ways. There was often tonnage in excess of the legally prescribed limits. The decks were frequently piled high with chests and bales. Appraisers undervalued goods. Officers, sailors, and passengers took silks along in their personal baggage. Minimal amounts of food and water were taken aboard, with rain squalls at sea counted on to maintain the supply of drinking water. Many guns were stowed away on the eastward passage, putting the galleons at a serious disadvantage if enemies should be encountered. Additional cargo was loaded during the ships' progress through the island-studded channels south of Luzon leading to the Embocadero to such an extent that when an alternative route through more open sea north of Luzon was suggested the Manila shippers opposed it.[16]

There were also legal loopholes. Philippine goods did not fall under the *permiso*. In Acapulco, additional funds were often remitted representing proceeds from transactions left over from previous voyages and payments sent for official or religious purposes. Above all, there was the *situado*, or subsidy, through which the import duties collected at Acapulco (10 percent ad valorem much of the time, later raised to 16.6 percent) were rebated to Manila instead of going to the viceregal treasury, which had to send additional sums if the collections fell short of the amount needed in the Philippines. All of these and other factors combined to raise the value of the cargo on the return trip far above *permiso* levels.

The incentives for evasion existed not only at the personal level but also institutionally at the levels of local and viceregal government. The latter was always anxious to increase customs revenue, which could only be accomplished with higher levels of trade. The personal factor also entered, in that 10 percent of any excess above the *permiso*, it was charged in the Council of the Indies, was divided between the viceroy and among the officials at Acapulco.

Profits in the Restrictive System

With regard to the restrictive system, it is possible to identify at least conceptually some sources of private gain over and above the premium on silver and normal commercial margins. Restricted entry into a lucrative market gave an implicit monopoly to those with official access to it. Evasions were another source of gain. There was a quantifiably calculable subsidy in freight rates on what were state galleons. In 1596, a viceroy calculated that it cost about 150,000 pesos annually in excess of the freight revenue to maintain the shipping line, and later Viana stated that freight was originally paid by the shippers of merchandise but that the governor had suspended this and charged the freight to the royal treasury.[17] There were proposals to have the Manila interests take over and support the shipping line without using royal funds, but these were opposed by the governors, who were among the biggest shippers, and in any event private operators could not compete with the state-owned, subsidized galleons.

Aside from the explicit subsidy of operating costs, there was a further implicit subsidy in what might be called the capital costs of the trade, namely, the construction of the galleons. Although one galleon was made in Siam and another in Japan, and in emergencies some vessels were purchased from other countries, the great majority were built in the Philippines—at Cavite, Bagatao in Sorsogon Bay, Albay, Masbate, Mindoro, and Pangasinan. They were made of Philippine hardwoods, which were almost impervious to contemporary cannonballs, and the few that were taken surrendered because their upper works had been raked with grape shot or because sharpshooters perched on masts had picked off individual officers and sailors. Also their size and wide beam made them hard to maneuver. For cordage, abaca was used, while the sails were manufactured in Ilocos. Metal fittings were imported from China, Macao, Japan, and even India and were worked by Chinese laborers.

Hardships for the Filipinos

The hardest work, the cutting of timber in the interior and getting it to the coast as well as the rough work in the shipyards, was performed by Filipinos. They were pressed into service by the *repartimiento* or the *polo*, a kind of corvée system also in effect in Spain under which able-bodied males between certain ages had to contribute their labor for a certain number of days (usually forty) a year. Although there were provisions in the Laws of the Indies designed to prevent exploitation, there were many abuses, which in 1660 provoked a revolt among the Pampangos, who were usually the most loyal and valiant of the Spanish auxiliaries. By then, the Dutch wars were over, and with the reduction of that threat the urgency to construct galleons diminished. It was estimated at one time that a galleon had cost the king 60,000 pesos but the Filipinos 150,000 pesos.

With the interplay of the various premiums both implicit and explicit, it would be difficult to calculate a rate of net profit on the trade, although it must have been high in a trade rife with shady practices. The Manilans admitted to a ludicrously low 5 or 10 percent, their enemies alleged 500 percent, and the central government allowed an arbitrary 83 percent. Scholars estimate that net profits ran between 100 and 300 percent.

The venerable *obras pías*, pious foundations supported with money bequeathed by wealthy persons and entrusted to lay brotherhoods affiliated with religious orders or chapters, came in for their share of criticism for their role in financing the trade. Toward the end of the galleon era, the terms of the bequests usually provided that the original endowment be divided into three parts: one-third for the Acapulco trade, one-third for ventures to China and India, and one-third to be retained as a reserve fund. The funds lent for commercial purposes had the character of both bank loans and marine insurance. The premiums charged probably reflected the perceived differences in risk between the various branches of trade and economic activity in the following rate structure.

For the Acapulco trade	20 to 50 percent (27 to 45 percent in 1810)
For ventures to Madras, Calcutta, and Batavia	16 to 22 percent
For the China trade	12 to 18 percent
For mortgages	5 percent (legal limit)

Sometimes interest-free loans were made to the government in times of need, as when the *situado* failed to arrive or when foreign invasion threatened. But they were censured for being too influential, diverting funds from agriculture and industry to the Acapulco trade, and swallowing up the profits from foreign trade. Fr. Martínez de Zúñiga in the early 1800s estimated that a doubling of the procurement price would still fall short of covering costs and that regular sales would have to be made at 300 percent above the purchase price, but by then the trade was on the wane.

Borrowers from the *obras pías* also engaged in questionable practices. Often twice as much was borrowed as was needed, so that interest and premiums could be paid in case payment of the principal had to be postponed. Since the *obras pías* assumed sea risks only in cases of total loss, salvageable wrecks were in some cases left to deteriorate so that the merchants could pass the risk on to them. There were also instances of borrowers renewing their loans by paying the yearly interest until the loss of a galleon freed them from the obligation to repay the principal.

There were many such losses during the 250 years of the galleon trade, with four ships captured by the English, more than thirty wrecked or lost at sea, thousands of people lost, and property losses calculated at more than 60 million pesos. From a cold-blooded actuarial point of view, one modern commentator opines that, against the total numbers involved—about 108 ships—total losses were comparatively few and the percentages of missing and captured crewmen would have caused no great concern to modern underwriters. Comyn estimated that in the approximately 250 years from the conquest to his day, 400 million pesos entered the Philippines. Chaunu calculated the flow of silver to the Far East to be between four and five thousand tons over two centuries and roughly one-third of the American output if one includes both direct (Pacific shipments) and indirect (reexport from Europe) flows.

The income of the *obras pías* therefore reached very respectable proportions. From 1599 to 1650, the Hermandad de la Misericordia (founded in 1596) spent 540,446 pesos on works of charity (an annual average of 10,809 pesos). In good times, this confraternity disbursed up to 70,000 pesos a year. Between 1734 and 1766, it loaned 3,319,787 pesos to galleon traders, an annual average of more than 100,000 pesos.[18]

Filipinos in the Galleon Trade

Filipinos made up from 50 to 80 percent of the crews of the galleons and were paid less than Spanish sailors, who, if they were common seamen, received 100 pesos for a round trip while the Filipinos received 48 to 60 plus a rice ration. At the end of the voyage, the sailors also received a sum of money, 330 pesos in the case of the Filipinos, and enjoyed some profit from the sale of goods they were permitted to carry. In the early days, there were complaints of lack of skill, partly perhaps because the need for crewmen led to the hiring of men without seafaring experience from the interior of Luzon. But by the mid–eighteenth century the liberal Viana was paying Filipinos high tribute, saying in effect that there were no

better sailors in the world, that they could teach many of the Spanish sailors in those seas, and that they fought bravely.[19] They suffered from the
unaccustomed cold of the high latitudes; from fraud or delays in getting
their wages, which were often paid in treasury warrants discounted by
those who cashed them; and from bad treatment aboard. But they were not
lacking in advocates like Governors Vera, Corcuera, and Manrique de Lara
and the colony's agent, Hernando de los Ríos Coronel. A law of 1633
aimed to protect them from the predations of Acapulco officials.

Those who put little trust in laws had other, more informal rem-
edies. They could profit from selling the goods that they were allowed to
carry as crewmen, and they could and did jump ship in Acapulco. There
were several long-term results of this. One is that thousands of Filipinos
settled in Mexico (as did thousands of Mexicans in the Philippines) and in
the *costa chica* and *costa grande* of the state of Guerrero, especially in
Espinalillo, one can see marked Malay features in much of the population
as well as Philippine words, family names, and customs such as the manner of cooking rice.[20] Another result stems from the 1618 desertion from
the *Espíritu Santo* of seventy-four (out of seventy-five) Filipino seamen,
who had been hired by Mexican Indians to teach them how to make palm
wine, called *tuba* in the Philippines. Both the drink and the word have remained in Mexico, and one can see on the outskirts of Acapulco roadside
stands selling "*tuba fresca.*" This beverage was so appreciated by Mexicans
that imports of Spanish brandy and wine fell and the king was petitioned
to send the Filipinos back to their homeland as punishment for interfering
with Spanish trade[21]—an ironic footnote demonstrating how nameless
common people practicing a humble trade could disrupt imperial policy.
Some Mexicans also aver that their ceviche (marinated raw fish) is of Asian
origin (based on Philippine *kinilaw*). The Spanish spoken in the Philippines became sprinkled with Mexican words such as *mecate* (rope), *petate*
(mat), and *zacate* (grass).

Trade with India

While debates raged over the workings of the restrictive system, a
change was coming that involved the feeder trade for the galleons. India
was growing in importance. The East Asian trade had declined owing to
the Dutch wars, the closing of Japan to foreign commerce in 1639, the rup-
ture of relations with Portuguese Macao, and the disruption of the junk
trade following the collapse of the Ming dynasty in 1644.[22] Trade with
mainland Southeast Asia was reported to have begun with Cambodia in

1594, Cochin China in 1596, and Siam in 1599, and a ship from Malacca was reported in 1597, but this trade was never very large or regular.

The Portuguese connection during the period when the Spanish and Portuguese Crowns were united (1580–1640) was more important. In years when few Chinese junks came to Manila, either because of expulsions from Manila or the Dutch wars, Macao was an important supplier for the galleons, especially in the years after 1619. At about the same time, there were some ships from India. But with the regaining of independence by Portugal in 1640, trade with Macao and India declined.

However, new players appeared on the scene. The British East India Company, like every other European trading entity, needed silver for its operations in China. Manila was a logical source, but the Spanish government never gave the company permission to trade there. However, its servants were permitted to venture out on their own, and they and the English "free merchants" (unaffiliated with the company) accounted for the bulk of the "country trade" (as the intra-Asian trade between East Africa and China was known). Trade with Manila began in 1644 but was infrequent and sporadic for some decades. In the meantime, some Spanish traders, disregarding their own government's strictures, began making voyages to the Malabar coast. After 1674, ships from Madras and other Indian ports voyaged to Manila under Asian (including Indo-Portuguese) flags since European vessels were barred. Three or four of these ships were owned by Elihu Yale. These country ships of up to five hundred tons were larger than sampans and took ten months for a round-trip voyage.

The early phase, which continued with only brief interruptions until 1708, was dominated by company servants. Though the later phase (1708–62) was carried on mostly by the free merchants, the company's share rose gradually.

The cargoes to Manila consisted of silk, blue cloth, painted fabrics (i.e., batiks), iron anchors, and various other textiles, including calicoes. Some of these items (such as iron for the construction of galleons) were for Philippine consumption, but large quantities of calico and chintz were loaded on the galleons. In the 1740s, the annual value of Madras exports to Manila was nearly 300,000 pesos. For the return cargo, the main item was silver, of course; it is estimated that 25 to 30 percent of the annual amount of silver shipped to Madras came from the Manila trade. Philippine products consisted of sugar, *sapan* wood, brimstone, copper, tobacco, wax, deer nerves, cowries, silver and gold wares, and leather. Later, horses and pearls were added to the list.

There was some competition from French traders based in their Indian possessions, but the loudest complaints were lodged against the Armenians. European wars caused interruptions in trade, and English naval captains were not above stopping Armenian vessels to extort money. After the British occupation of Manila in 1762–64, a resident agent was appointed to act on damage claims and pave the way for the resumption of the country trade. By 1787, customs duties (*almojarifazgo*) paid on Indian goods in Manila were almost 90 percent of those paid on Chinese goods. By 1810, the value of imports from India and China was equal.[23] Fine cottons from India were held in as much esteem as Chinese silk.

The Last Years of the Trade

At the same time, in Manila, professional merchants were assuming a greater portion of the trade. In 1586, there had been 194 shippers sending cargo on the annual galleon. Two centuries later, there were only 28. By then, there were notorious inequalities of fortune among Manila's citizens. Of the original 150 members of the *consulado*, only 25 were active merchants, while 56, including eight women, traded on a commission basis through the merchants. The rest had other occupations or were idlers.

The last half-century of the galleon trade was a period in which Spain introduced new economic initiatives (as will be seen later). But Spain was also embroiled in a series of wars, and there is some haziness about trends at that time. Cyclical analysis discerns five distinct periods: expansion in 1580–1620, a severe contraction to 1670, recovery to 1720, a mild recession to 1750, and a resumption of expansion until the end of the eighteenth century. At this time, the galleons called at ports in California, which was ordered by the Council of the Indies on June 22, 1773. Although the galleon captains preferred to bypass the Californian capital at Monterey in their eagerness to sell their cargoes at Acapulco, visits were recorded in 1779, 1780, 1784, 1795 (two galleons), and 1797. In 1781, the *San Carlos* put in unexpectedly at San Diego with supplies for the California missions. It is postulated that it was only in the last phase of the trade that the peak of prosperity reached in the initial expansion was once again attained.[24]

But the data peter out about 1790, and the postulate sits uneasily beside reports of the decline of the galleon trade, although it has some support in that duties in Manila reached a record level in 1787 and the galleon of 1784 carried a return cargo to Manila of 2,791,632 pesos, one of the highest on record.[25] These however, may have been monetary illusions because the entrance of the Dutch, English, French, and other nationalities into the Chinese market raised prices there. Prices had also risen in India, and indeed throughout the world, as was stated by the Manila *consulado* in a 1772 representation aimed at securing an increase in the *permiso* to accommodate these increases.

Price comparisons between specific commodities between 1734 and 1770 have led to estimates indicating that prices for Chinese goods had risen on average 147 percent, while those for Indian goods had risen 165 percent (although rates of increase varied widely among individual commodities). The temporary increase of the *permiso* by 250,000 pesos in 1776 was granted in response to the representation. But the first galleon that carried the increased quota was lost without a trace in 1782, and it was not until 1786 that another galleon carried the increased *permiso*, only to find at Acapulco that a *feria* could not be held because the trade liberalization scheme of 1778 (which will be looked at again) had allowed other suppliers to bring in Asian goods and these had accumulated in large amounts in Mexico.[26] The last phase of expansion therefore may have reflected inflationary trends rather than a real increase in the volume of trade.

In any event, by the 1790s the galleon trade had fallen on hard times. New efforts to promote trade liberalization and economic development had been made under Charles III. Viceroy Revilla Gigedo in 1794 wrote that the decline of the trade was a natural consequence of industrial progress in Europe, increased demand for English and European cottons, and decreased esteem for Asian silks and cottons. Only Asian muslins maintained a part of their market, and even this was being eroded by European muslins, especially those from Catalonia. He also reported that in the years 1790–92 the Royal Philippine Company (established in 1785) had landed 450,000 pesos worth of East Indian goods at the gulf port of Veracruz, cutting further into the market for the Acapulco ships. As a consequence, paying customers had become scarce at the Mexican port and the last two galleons had not been able to hold fairs. A decade later, the Manila *consulado* reported that three ships had lain in Acapulco harbor without being able to dispose of their merchandise for between one and three years. English and American ships traded more frequently on the Pacific coast of Spanish America. The Mexican War of Independence broke out in 1810, and in 1813 the Mexican patriot Morelos took and held Acapulco for a few months; during this occupation, the Manila galleon was prevented from unloading and had to retire to San Blas up the coast.[27]

In the meantime, with Napoleon's invasion of Spain and the capture of King Ferdinand VII, the Spanish resistance convened the Cortes of

Cádiz in 1810 with representatives from throughout the empire, with the aim of establishing a constitutional monarchy. One of the Philippine deputies, the Manila merchant Ventura de los Reyes, assumed his seat in 1811 and early in 1813 proposed discontinuing the galleon trade, a solution that had already been visualized in 1811. In the ensuing debate, there was a strong current of opinion in favor of opening up more Spanish American ports to Philippine trade, with some, however, wishing to limit such liberalization to Philippine goods. Finally, a conservative position was taken in a decree of September 14, 1813: the galleon trade was to be discontinued, but in its place private Philippine ships could trade at Acapulco (and San Blas, with Sonsonate in today's El Salvador as an alternative port) in Chinese and other Asian goods carried on privately owned national ships but within the limits of the basic *permiso* of 500,000 pesos outgoing and 1 million pesos for the return voyage. In adopting this hybrid arrangement, the Cortes may have been trying to strike a balance between two branches of commerce approved by the Crown, namely, the Royal Philippine Company's operations and trading by ships of Philippine registry. The decree was received in Mexico on July 14, 1814, but it was not put into effect because by then Ferdinand VII had been reinstated as absolute monarch and the Cortes dissolved. However, de los Reyes persuaded the king to ratify the decree on April 23, 1815, and gave further proof of his political agility by securing a royal order on January 18, 1819, allowing him to bring up to 100,000 pesos' worth of Chinese and other Asian goods to both New Spain and Guatemala through authorized Pacific ports.[28]

A Brief Appraisal

A full evaluation of the galleon trade lies beyond the scope of the present work, but some points can be made briefly. The restrictive system would not pass muster in a court of economic inquiry, although it would have to be recognized that it was a political compromise for which there were few realistic alternatives. Contemporary and later writers, both Spanish and non-Spanish, deplored the formation of an indolent, unimaginative, monopolistic, and numerically small merchant class; the failure to realize Manila's full potential as an entrepôt; the tolerance or encouragement of widespread official corruption and evasion of the law; and the neglect of the country's agricultural and industrial development. But the social concomitant of the last point was avoidance of the horrors of a colonial plantation system and mitigation of the abuses of the early *encomenderos*. And, despite the charge of industrial neglect, the galleons to the end carried Philippine textiles, which could not be said of subsequent phases of the trade. Already noted has been the creation of a new current in East Asian trade and the beginning of large-scale Chinese immigration, which could be regarded as both a boon (for the goods and the skills that the Chinese brought) and a bane (for the difficulties created by a large-scale external demographic presence and the persistence of long-term immigration problems). Also noted have been the establishment of Manila as the first primate city in Southeast Asia and the incorporation of the Philippines into the first modern world economy based on Seville and the Atlantic.

This enabled Spain to hold the Philippines and maintain an administrative and cultural unity that would lead to the formation of a Filipino national consciousness. It meant the advent of Christianity and Roman Law and a trans-Pacific cultural interaction that saw a mixing of Filipino, Chinese, Mexican, and Spanish elements. It meant the transfer of technology from both the West and China and the transport of useful plants that over the long term enriched the diet of the common man and helped to diversify the economy. The *obras pías*, which financed and profited from the trade, undertook a multitude of good works. One such endowment resulted in Manila's first waterworks.

Schurz has written that "no ship ever played the part in a city's life which the galleon did in that of Manila"—and by extension the rest of the country. The modern Filipino author Nick Joaquin has observed: "It was on the Manila Galleon that we began to become the Philippines."[29]

The galleon trade was assaulted by the world's mightiest navies and undermined by the misdeeds of the knaves and fools who clutter its annals. But despite loss and adversity the ships sailed on year after year, for the trade was not merely a commercial or economic institution but a multifaceted historical phenomenon that surmounted its handicaps and had pervasive and enduring effects. When the last galleon, named the *Magallanes* after the explorer who first claimed the Philippines for Spain, left Mexico in 1815, it sailed west, literally into the sunset.

CHAPTER 3

Eighteenth-Century
State-Sponsored Efforts at
Trade Diversification and Economic Development

The 18th century is one of the least known areas of our history.

—*Julián Marías (1963)*

The dawn of the eighteenth century saw the end of the Habsburg dynasty in Spain and the beginning of Bourbon rule. The country had been in economic and political decline for a century, from about the death of Philip II in 1598, owing to the drain of foreign wars and domestic misgovernment. The nadir was reached with the last Habsburg, Charles II, who was not only inept but demented and could neither govern personally nor choose and maintain capable ministers.[1]

The first Spanish Bourbons found that substantial inroads had been made in their colonial trade by Dutch and Hamburg merchants, and the warfare attending their accession was disastrous for what trade remained. Although of only moderate ability, these kings benefited from brilliant advisers supplied by the French monarchy in their efforts to revive the economy. It was French influence that facilitated the entrance of the Enlightenment into Spain.

The stimulus provided by the new dynasty was felt earliest in the work of theorists. The greatest Spanish mercantilist of the new regime,

Gerónimo de Uztáriz, best known for a work published in 1724, followed Colbert's doctrines closely but not blindly, and his theories became the basis of Spanish economic thought for a century.

This current of ideas culminated in the reign of Charles III (1759–88), when many writers advocated state-directed agricultural and industrial development. The revival was marked in the Philippines by more vigorous and honest public administration, more intensive development of domestic resources, efforts to diversify and reorient trade by encouraging direct voyages to Spain, and a more liberal stance toward foreign traders.[2] It was under this monarch, the ablest of the Spanish Bourbons, that numerous proposals were made and new initiatives undertaken regarding Philippine trade and economy.

Since Spain's eighteenth-century economic revival was based on colonial trade, it was that sector that received the greatest emphasis in the new schemes and initiatives. It will be recalled that the galleon trade, with its major Asian currents from China and India feeding into the trans-Pacific route to the Americas, had made Manila the predominant port in the East Asian trade despite the restrictions imposed thereon, and it was the principal outlet for Chinese goods for more than two centuries.[3]

Despite the regional importance attained by Manila and the pervasive effects of the galleon voyages on Philippine life, one consequence of the restrictive system that provoked strong reactions among the reformist Bourbon officials was the growth of a complacent and unimaginative merchant class. That class, in the reformists' view, should have led in the development of the country's internal resources, especially for the export trade, and its failure to do so prompted active intervention by the state. The galleon trade was too important to dispense with, but efforts could be made to intensify trade relations with other Asian countries, establish direct trade with Spain, and stimulate domestic Philippine production of items that could figure in these trade initiatives. In a sense, it would require a new overlay on the existing trade pattern centered on the galleon trade and might be described as aiming for its euthanasia.

The initiatives had mixed results, in part due to the hostility of the Manila merchants, who rightly feared that they were meant to undermine the galleon trade; in part because that trade remained more profitable than many of the new ventures; in part because some prospects were unsound and others could not escape the logic of opportunity costs; and in part because of Spain's involvement in naval wars beginning in the 1790s. Yet many positive features remained, and these were carried over into the next century.

Plans and Proposals

Just before the mid–eighteenth century, several proposals were made for Philippine trade expansion and diversification and economic development. The first came in 1746 from an Irish pilot in the galleon trade, Richard Bagge. Unlike most of the other projects to come, this one was oriented exclusively toward a two-way trade with China, envisioning Philippine exports of cocoa, sea slugs, camphor, pearls, and gold in exchange for cotton goods, silk, and porcelain. The Bagge plan also advocated silkworm culture in the northern, textile-weaving provinces of Ilocos and Cagayan as well as the mining of saltpeter for the manufacture of gunpowder.

Funding would come from certain *obras pías,* which already were making loans for the Acapulco trade; from Manila residents; and from the Crown (for which a one-fifth interest was reserved). Although favorably endorsed by the *fiscal* of the Council of the Indies, the plan apparently did not advance beyond the talking stage.

The next proposal came in 1753 from the Jesuit procurator Fr. José Calvo. He envisioned the formation of a company in Spain in order to exploit the agricultural and mineral possibilities of the Philippines and trade directly with the peninsula. He attributed the country's underdeveloped state to the existing commercial system, illustrated by the fact that in the 188 years since its conquest not a single hereditary estate had been founded. A start would be made with gold and cinnamon, with additional items to be added by forcing tribute-paying natives to devote a part of their holdings to pepper, cloves, cocoa, and mulberry trees (for silkworm culture). Nutmeg was also mentioned. Silk and cotton weaving would be developed under master craftsmen brought over from China and the Malabar Coast. Aside from the trade and development aspects, the fiscal impact would reduce the need for the *situado* (subsidy) from Mexico. The route to be taken to Spain would be via Cape Horn. Again, nothing came of this proposal.

Of greater importance and effect were the ideas of Francisco Leandro de Viana, attorney general of the Audiencia (Supreme Court) of Manila from 1756, whose views on the galleon trade have already been noted. His first report, in 1760, concerning abuses in the collection of customs duties and the conduct of the galleon trade, was little heeded. His second report, submitted in 1765 after the British occupation of 1762–64, was more detailed and aimed to transform the Philippines from a financial burden to a source of wealth. He tried to link the enjoyment of municipal offices to the cultivation of rice, wheat, sugar, cotton, beeswax, and other products and advocated exempting industrious farmers from statute labor. His ideas concerning trade centered on opening direct trade with Spain via the Cape of Good Hope. Ships would leave Spain with cottons, wine, hats, silk stockings, mirrors, tableware, and other articles made of glass, paper, and various textile fibers; unload part of their cargo in Manila; take in such goods as edible birds' nests, mother of pearl, seashells, cochineal, indigo and other dyes from Pampanga, sea slugs, dried deer meat, deer sinews, leather, *sapan* wood, ebony, and other woods; and proceed to Canton to exchange these products and the remainder of the European cargo for the Chinese goods hitherto taken to Europe by foreigners. On their return voyage, they should again call at Manila to take on Philippine products salable in Spain such as woven mats, palm leaf hats, raw cotton, tortoiseshell, *sapan* wood, and various other kinds of wood. Cinnamon could also become an article of commerce if its cultivation were pursued.

To conduct this trade, an East India Company should be organized, with the king holding a portion of the shares. The company's shipyards would be located in the Philippines to take advantage of its excellent timber resources. Once organized, the company could embark on larger scale enterprises. After giving pride of place to cinnamon, pepper, and other spices, Viana mentions sugar, cocoa, coffee, rice, wheat, tobacco, indigo, the mulberry tree, and cotton. Weaving existed in Ilocos, Cagayan, Bicol, and the Visayas but was underdeveloped; master weavers could be imported to train the native operators and achieve domestic self-sufficiency, obviating the need to import textiles from the Chinese, Dutch, and English. Minerals such as iron, gold, sulfur, and rock crystal awaited exploitation.

Viana's plan was endorsed by Simón de Anda, who became governor in 1770. In view of the country's damaged condition following the British occupation, he suggested making no immediate changes in the commercial system but taking up the matter after a few years. He enumerated the country's commercial products as spices, gold, indigo, rattan, high-grade cotton, beeswax, and hardwoods. He also advocated resumption of iron mining and the development of weaving.

Some of Viana's most important ideas were put into practice later, although he was overoptimistic about the prospects for certain products.

In 1778, he submitted still another paper, this time as a member of the Council of the Indies, in which he elaborated on some of his earlier ideas. He broached the possibility of having Spanish ships round Cape Horn to supply Chile and Peru with textiles, take on silver for Manila, load Chinese goods in Manila, and return to Spain via the Cape of Good Hope.

Other minor proposals were made. One, submitted in 1764 by two Cádiz merchants, Bernardo Van Dahl and Pedro Tomás Vergara, proposed organizing a company to engage in direct trade between Cádiz and the Philippines. However, the scheme depended excessively on privileges such as exemption from tonnage duties, sales taxes, and other charges; exemption of the company's cargoes from inspection by treasury officials in the Philippines; and the authority to engage occasionally in the slave trade. A charter was therefore denied the company.

A proposal in 1779 by the learned historian Juan Bautista Muñoz called for direct trade with the Philippines via Cape Horn, with stops in the Malvinas (Falklands) and Tahiti on the outgoing voyage and in Australia on the return. There he recommended establishing a colony. He felt that encouragement should be given to the Philippines' natural products and protection extended to the cotton and silk industries.[4]

While none of the proposals had immediate concrete results, some of the main ideas were adopted later. Such was the desirability of having direct voyages to Spain, the formation of a company for this purpose, the encouragement of native Philippine products, and the development of the textile industry. Although the old dream of the spice trade lingered and items proper to the China trade (like birds' nests and sea slugs) also figured in the plans, the future was adumbrated with the inclusion of items of increasing commercial importance such as sugar, indigo, coffee, tobacco, and rice. There was also recognition of the growing importance of Canton in the China trade; the main trade currents had come and still came at the time from Fujian, but this situation, too, was undergoing change.

There were also proposals regarding trade with neighboring countries such as Borneo, Cambodia, Siam, and the then independent sultanate of Jolo. There had been a modest level of trade with these countries from the beginning of Spanish rule in the Philippines. From Jolo came beeswax, birds' nests, mother of pearl, tortoiseshell, and sea slugs. From Borneo, the main products were pepper and beeswax, although there was also a trade in copper, brass, diamonds, camphor, benzoin, and aromatic woods. Trade with Siam had never amounted to much, as its products had no market in Acapulco, but owing to lower costs the building of ships there was proposed in the early and middle eighteenth century. At the time, the king of

Siam was willing to grant trading rights, but a royal order in 1755 disapproved the founding of a company in Manila for this purpose and prohibited ships from being built outside the country, although not until after a hull had been constructed in Siam. At about the same time (in 1751), the king of Cambodia sent two ambassadors to Manila to invite ships to trade there, and this invitation was repeated two years later.

By 1785, trade with these countries appeared to be at a low level, in part due to a partial closure of the port of Manila during the British occupation of 1762–64. A prize-winning study submitted to the Economic Society of Manila by José García Armenteros recommended measures to stimulate this trade. For Jolo and southern Mindanao, Armenteros called for light vessels like sloops to call at Iloilo, discharging articles commonly sent from Manila to the Visayas, and load rice (always assured of a market in Jolo), sugar (which was even more profitable), and local textiles. This trade had a political dimension, being conceived as a way of fending off piracy without recourse to costly military operations. For Borneo, the same route through Philippine waters was recommended, with the stop at Iloilo to load the same products but in greater quantities owing to the larger size of the market. In addition, Indian textiles should prove profitable, because the Borneans went to Batavia to buy them and thus gave evidence of a ready market, but Chinese goods were to be avoided because one or two junks came annually from Amoy. The return cargo would consist of the products mentioned earlier. For trade with Siam, the Philippines could sell sugar and cowries and buy saltpeter and teak as well as lead, ivory, camphor, pepper, and rhubarb. Resumption of trade with Cambodia was also recommended.

The Armenteros plan included not only a resumption of trade with the Moluccas but the reestablishment of Spanish garrisons on Ternate and Tidore in order to sell ordinary Indian textiles, Iloilo textiles, abaca cloth, tobacco, palm wine, and rice, with a return cargo of cloves. But the reoccupation was viewed as temporary; clove plantings would be collected in places not under Dutch domination and sent to the Philippines. Once cloves were acclimated there (a delusion), the Spanish would withdraw. The Armenteros plan served as the basis for the intensification of trade with neighboring countries in the last decade of the eighteenth century.[5]

The plans so far examined either were not carried out or served only as general indications for economic policy. Three specific initiatives, however, did get under way, although they did not get very far. The first was launched under Governor Pedro Manuel de Arandía as an offshoot of his strict enforcement of a decree expelling the Chinese.

To replace the Chinese in Manila's textile trade, a joint stock company was formed, open to all Spaniards and natives of the islands, in order to take charge of textile supplies and stores. The plan had been suggested by Pedro Calderón Enríquez, a member of the Audiencia.

In addition to the apparently negative thrust, there were constructive aspects. The company was to set aside a portion of its profits to encourage the weaving of as many cotton textiles as possible, in the process modernizing the country's textile industry. To spin and weave cotton, it would build sheds outside the city walls, where instruction would be given on spinning and weaving not only to the many idlers abounding in the city's vicinity but to those who might be brought in from the provinces and on their return home could pass their knowledge on to others. To ensure the supply of cotton, the company would stimulate planting by buying, with the help of parish priests, all the cotton grown in the provinces at prevailing prices for ready cash.

In recompense for its public policy objectives—namely, to raise employment, lower prices, prevent the outflow of money for imports and commercial profit remittances, and provide a ready outlet for native products—the company was to be given a monopoly of the textile trade around Manila; enjoy tax exemption on its cotton manufactures for ten years; be permitted to trade with other countries, enjoying duty-free entry for its imports in this trade; take charge of various types of trust funds and *obras pías* in order to invest them at 5 percent in its business; and be secure from financial exactions by the governors, even in the most urgent cases, so as to maintain public confidence in its financial integrity. But the scheme was disapproved by Madrid and failed by itself after less than a year of operation.[6]

The second initiative was a project suggested by Nicolas Norton Nicols, an Englishman who became a naturalized Spaniard in 1758, for the cultivation of spices on Mindanao and the institution of direct voyages between Spain and the Philippines. The usual advantages were cited—a reduction in the outward flow of silver; employment and income for the natives, leading to higher tax collections; direct communication with Spain; diversion of spice purchases from the Dutch; lower costs of production; and others. Norton had been in the Philippines during the governorship of the marquis of Obando (1750–54) and claimed to be well traveled, knowledgeable, and experienced. His memorandum to the king, sent in 1759, is of interest not only for the main project he espoused but because he made favorable mention of Francisco Salgado (who was to figure actively in Philippine economic and other matters during the rest of the century) and provided a listing of Philippine exports to various parts of Asia. After deploring the ban on the export of sugar that had been in effect during his first Philippine visit, he went on to mention the normal exports to different Asian regions—to China, rice, sugar, cotton, indigo, rattan, sea slugs, pepper, tortoiseshell, mother of pearl, brazil wood (*sapan* wood), ebony, dried meat, cattle sinew, edible birds' nests, and lead when available; to the Coromandel Coast and Bengal, sugar, indigo, brazil wood, pepper, cowries, birds' nests, cotton, and rice; and to the Malabar Coast and Persia, sugar in large quantities, which was sold for cash.

The centerpiece of his project was the cultivation of cinnamon, which grew wild on Mindanao, for export to Spain and America. He would also look for cloves, and he was certain he would find nutmeg and pepper. He was given the right to occupy and use Crown lands for ten years, after which time the plantation would revert to government ownership, and he was to hire only natives, not aliens, as farmhands. In exchange, he requested exemption from import, export, and excise duties and other taxes. He was in Manila by 1761 and in Mindanao in December 1762. The following year, word arrived that he had found cinnamon trees of superior quality, but in July he died from a fall. Viana referred to him as

> this famous and skilful Englishman. . . . It was necessary that a foreigner should accomplish what no Spaniard had done in some two hundred years; he died on account of our misfortunes, and now there will be no one who will devote himself to the same enterprise; for these citizens have no thought of any further occupation than their everlasting laziness, nor have they the spirit to risk four reals, or any zeal for the nation.

It was probably well that he did not live to see the failure of future cinnamon schemes in the country.[7]

The third of the aborted projects was launched in 1776, when Governor Simón de Anda, desirous of initiating trade with the kingdom of the nabob Myer Alican on India's Malabar Coast, sent two representatives to the port of Mangalore. One of them died, but the survivor returned to Manila and (Anda also having died in the meantime) reported to the new governor, the development-oriented José Basco y Vargas. Basco found the nabob's proposals excellent, but there were few formal guarantees and, fearing opposition from the British East India Company and the Dutch, he felt that the project was beyond the scope of Manila's merchants and would require the backing of a powerful company.[8]

One feature that characterized most of the specific proposals was the need for government participation in commercial companies (Bagge, Viana), the concession of certain monopolies (Van Dahl–Vergara for the exclusive use of the Cádiz-Manila route; Arandía for a textile monopoly), and tax exemptions (Van Dahl–Vergara and Arandía). The Norton Nicols plan also depended on certain fiscal concessions, but these seem to have been considered compensation for the fulfillment of certain obligations. These concessions probably reflected the spirit of that age, aiming at profitability and development but with little competitive pressure for efficiency.

Direct Voyages to Spain: The Major Guilds and the Ustáriz Company

Manila's trade could be looked on as having two principal branches: the eastern or trans-Pacific branch to silver-rich Mexico and the western or Asian branch to China and India, the sources of supply for the Acapulco galleons and Philippine import needs. The new initiatives would greatly expand the western branch of the trade by extending it all the way to Spain, but modifications were also made in the eastern branch through both policy design and improvisation.

Amid the plethora of plans and proposals, the first concrete action was taken by the Crown after the British occupation of 1762–64 when it initiated annual sailings of war frigates from Cádiz to Manila. These ships carried European merchandise and had the authority to take on cargoes of Philippine and other Asian goods on account for Manila's merchants, thus in effect ending the prohibition laid on all Spanish subjects against trading with the East Indies. They followed the Cape of Good Hope route first advocated by Norton Nicols and later by Viana. This had earlier been held to be barred to Spain by papal bulls of demarcation and treaties with Portugal, Holland, and England, but by the mid–eighteenth century the reduction of Portugal to military and commercial impotence, the more secular atmosphere, and the entrance of new players like the French into the picture made the earlier strictures academic.

The maiden voyage was undertaken in 1764–65 by the sixty-four-gun frigate *Buen Consejo* (Good Counsel). It was the first direct trip from Spain to the Philippines since the Loaisa expedition of 1525. The ship's reception in Manila was chilly, the merchants there fearing, perhaps with some justification, that this augured the suppression of their cherished Acapulco trade. With a play on words, they jeeringly referred to the frigate as the *Mal Consejo* (Bad Counsel). They refused the invitation to supply the return cargo, making it necessary to load the ship on the king's account.

They even hid the wheat supplies earmarked for the provisioning of the vessel. The situation was saved by Francisco Xavier Salgado, who chartered a ship to procure wheat in China and sold it at cost for the baking of biscuits. There was also an attempt at sabotage in Cavite, where the vessel's hull was perforated, causing it to ship water on the high seas on its return voyage in 1767, spoiling its provisions, and imperiling the entire enterprise.

Fourteen voyages were made in all, the last one in March 1783, when the *Asunción* carried to Manila the glad tidings of the peace concluded at Paris that year; it returned to Cádiz in July 1784. The volume of trade represented by these sailings was not large, owing to the limited cargo space on warships, but they introduced Spain to new Philippine products and stimulated interest in the archipelago. This is illustrated by the manifest of the ship *Juno*, which in 1777 carried to Cádiz a varied cargo largely composed of what appear to be transshipped Chinese goods and Moluccan spices but including items that were almost certainly of Philippine provenance such as 450 *piculs* of *sapan* wood (1 *picul* = 63.262 kilograms), 10,737 pounds of wax, 340 *arrobas* of sugar (1 *arroba* = 11.5 kilograms), 10,680 rolls of abaca cloth, and articles made of tortoiseshell and mother of pearl.

The voyages had been an experiment, a means of clearing the way for private interests to take advantage of such navigation. And the edict of *libre comercio*—free trade—of October 12, 1778, ratifying the end of the Cádiz-Seville monopoly on trade with the Indies and opening up direct navigation between these and most ports in Spain, was an invitation to private traders to launch enterprises themselves.

A company formed by the five *gremios mayores* (major guilds) of Madrid in 1763 was encouraged to try Asian ventures, having been conceded by a royal order of June 12, 1776, loading space at moderate rates on the frigates and passage for factors or commissioners who would carry sufficient funds to engage in trade. In 1778, the guilds made their first shipment to the Philippines of goods and specie worth a little over a million reals on two ships accompanied by two commissioners. A smaller cargo of half a million reals in specie and nearly a hundred thousand reals in merchandise was sent the following year, and one of the commissioners set up shop in Canton.

Then the company strayed from its original objectives. It secured loading privileges on the Acapulco galleon on a par with the merchants of Manila's Consulado, and its commissioner sailed from Cavite to Acapulco in 1780 with Canton textiles, which were sold for 130,000 pesos. This sum was remitted for reinvestment in the following year's Canton trade to Manila, where in the meantime a third commissioner was taking up residence. The company's involvement in the galleon trade grew to the point where by 1783 it was taking up at least one-fifth of the lading space. This also signified that its operations had become global, since it sent voyages from Spain to both coasts of the Americas, possibly the first Spanish company to attain this distinction.

This diversion seemed to show that profits were still greater in the Acapulco trade than in the direct trade to Spain despite all the privileges that went with the latter, and the director of the Economic Society of Manila, Ciraco González Carbajal (also spelled Carvajal) proposed channeling the firm's efforts toward iron and copper mining, processing indigo and sugar, and promotion of the textile industry. This would make available substantial cargoes for Cádiz, and by setting up agencies in Ilocos, Camarines, and Iloilo they could sell many Spanish goods. The guilds did in fact continue to engage in direct trade between Spain and the Philippines on their own ships after the naval frigates ceased their voyages, but without much success, and their later Philippine operations became intermingled with those of the Royal Philippine Company.

Another firm that set up a factory, or agency, in Manila was Ustáriz, San Ginés, and Company of Cádiz, which in 1779 managed to secure exemption from import and export duties in Manila on the specie, products, and textiles loaded on the two vessels it was authorized to send yearly. With Spain's involvement in the American Revolution, the company's Manila factors thought of sending their frigate *Hercules* to Canton to load textiles for disposal in Lima or Acapulco, as wartime conditions had made the return route to Spain dangerous. This was tenaciously opposed by Manila's Consulado but was approved by Governor Basco, who felt that if the company could not compensate with this trip for the losses it would suffer in not being able to make a return voyage to Spain it might close down its Manila agency.[9]

It was clear that the government was in earnest in pushing these first ventures for direct commerce between Spain and the Philippines. But it was equally clear that the big profits still lay in the trans-Pacific transshipment trade to the Americas.

The San Blas–Manila Trade

The trans-Pacific trade was due to undergo changes that would overlap some of the events taken up in this section. Since these changes encroached upon certain established interests, they were made in the obscurity of historical shadows, making them difficult to trace clearly.

The impetus for new moves along the American Pacific coast was the Russian fur trade. The voyages of Bering and Chirikof to Alaska in 1741 had led to the founding of Russian colonies in North America,[10] and this had alarmed the revived Spanish monarchy, which responded by initiating the long-deferred occupation and settlement of California. The naval springboard for this effort and subsequent Spanish expeditions to what is now the Northwest of the United States was the port of San Blas, six hundred miles up the coast from Acapulco, whose establishment in 1766 would affect the commerce of the Philippines. In 1767, San Blas sent what was probably its first vessel to Manila, a thirty-ton, topsail schooner carrying the order for the expulsion of the Jesuits. The merchants of Manila were made to pay for this schooner. This was not trade—yet.

In the 1770s, merchant frigates that cannot definitely be characterized as Acapulco galleons began to make occasional voyages between Manila and San Blas in both directions. The first merchant frigate to sail from the former port to the latter was the *Buen Fin* in 1773, owned by private Manila merchants, which, directed by its English chief pilot Philip Thompson, pioneered a new route that swung out from the southern Philippines in an arc past northern New Guinea before turning northward. For bureaucratic reasons, however, it was not allowed to unload its cargo in San Blas, where it was detained for two and a half months. Eventually, it was sent to Acapulco, where it arrived almost simultaneously with the regular Manila galleon, thus frustrating its intention of making early entry into the Mexican market.[11]

The following year, permission was granted, after an almost two-century lapse, to land Philippine goods in Peru. In 1779, owing to the American Revolution, two shipments of 300,000 silver pesos were made to Manila from San Blas to strengthen Spain's Asian bastion against a possible British attack. In that same decade, Spanish expeditions to the American Pacific Northwest in 1774, 1775, and 1779 led to recognition of the possibilities of the fur trade. Thus, in addition to excluding the Russians from California by means of physical occupation, Spanish interest was awakened in the trade of Northwest furs with China, with the Philippines as a stopover.

The next decade saw a strengthening of the Manila–San Blas link. The *San Carlos*, mentioned earlier as having carried supplies from Manila for the California missions, put in unexpectedly at San Diego but was made to discharge its cargo in San Blas. In 1784, the first plan for sending furs to China in exchange for quicksilver was made by one Vicente Vasadre y Vega. This was a major departure from the silk-for-silver pattern of the regular galleon trade. On May 10, 1785, the *Hercules* arrived at San Blas from Manila and Canton. The following month the king approved Vasadre's plan, and he went to California in 1786 to collect pelts. San Blas was the Mexican terminus of this operation, and it was to remain so for other ventures of the same nature.

On June 5 of that same year, González Carvajal wrote Viceroy Gálvez that the newly formed Royal Philippine Company had sent to China the frigate *San Francisco*, which had just arrived in Manila from San Blas with what he suspected was a cargo of sea otter pelts. Also in that year the botanist Juan de Cuéllar wrote that the packet boat *San Carlos* had left Manila for San Blas a few days after his arrival at the former port; this seems to have been the same 196 ton ship that carried a cargo of California furs to San Blas the following year.

Toward the end of 1787, Vasadre made a definite proposal for a voyage from San Blas to Canton via Puget Sound and Manila. In November of that year, after a stop in Manila, he arrived in Canton and by means of lavish spending in high society was able to dispose of his California furs. Difficulties with the Manila authorities and the hostility of the Royal Philippine Company caused him to give up the business and return to Spain. But this was not the end of the Spanish fur trade. Nootka Sound was occupied in 1789. In 1790, one Don Ninante Maximi arrived in Canton with the same purpose as Vasadre in mind, and there were other plans for the fur trade following Vasadre's.[12]

The ordinary procedure was for the pelts to be sent inland to Mexico City for processing and then to Acapulco for loading on the Manila galleon. The convenience of both San Blas and Manila as way stations in this trade might have suggested to the makers of high policy that here was another way in which the Acapulco trade might be eroded. Since, however, this trade was a monopoly of the Manila merchants protected by law and long-standing custom, and since the right to import quicksilver into the Americas was reserved to the Royal Philippine Company, it would not do to have the new trade out in the open where it was certain to provoke bitter protests from the galleon traders and the Royal Philippine Company. The triangular trade between Spanish America, Nootka Sound, and East Asia, which would be conducted with signal success by Yankee sailors in the late eighteenth and early nineteenth centuries, was therefore carried on in a clandestine fashion, and the maneuverings attendant on the San Blas trade took place in a murky haze.

In the decade of the 1790s, however, the Acapulco traders appear to have awakened to the threat posed by the new trade. Efforts were made, with temporary success, to strengthen their privileged monopolistic position, but in April 1794 one Nicolas Manzanali of San Blas solicited permission to take skins from the Californias to Canton. The petition was granted in February of the following year.

Reference has already been made to the breakdown of the Acapulco monopoly in the late eighteenth and early nineteenth centuries. The Royal Philippine Company landed a large amount of goods at San Blas. At the same time, the fur trade with California and the Northwest was well under way. Perhaps the best index of the rise in importance of San Blas is that when the galleon trade was replaced with private ventures it was designated one of the few termini of the new arrangement in Spanish America.[13]

Francisco Xavier Salgado

No survey of this period in the Philippine economy would be adequate without reference to some of the personalities that played active roles in it. In the private sector, the outstanding entrepreneurial figure was Francisco Xavier Salgado, who was active in commerce, mining, industry, and agriculture. He lived long enough to straddle almost the whole period under discussion, and he experienced many ups and downs depending on who was governor and what their mutual relations were. He also performed signal services for his country during the British occupation of Manila in 1762–64, suffering financial losses as a consequence. At various times, he was a member of the Consulado, a commissioner of the Company of the Major Guilds, and a member of the Manila Council of the Royal Philippine Company.

Born in Madrid in 1713, he went to the Philippines in 1735 and never saw Spain again. During his early years in the Philippines, he was in the Civil Service, serving as principal officer of the Colonial Secretariat. He then became a permanent clerk in the accounting office of the Finance Department. In 1747, he was *maestre de plata* (supercargo for silver) on the *patache* (tender or dispatch boat) *Santo Domingo,* which voyaged to Acapulco to pick up the royal subsidy for the Philippines. Later he was sergeant major of soldiers and seamen at the Zamboanga garrison and a captain of Spanish infantry. In 1750, he was deputy to the governor and captain general of the province of Camarines. For more than twenty years, he was also the general contractor for the revenue from palm and coconut wine.

His service in Camarines must have aroused his interest in mining. Some previously worked mines at Mambulao lay in a state of abandonment, and the governor, the marquis of Obando (1750–54), sent an Augustinian Recollect, Fr. Sebastián de San Vicente, to conduct a survey. Salgado offered to finance the venture and accompanied the friar. The mine site was close to the coast, which facilitated loading the ore on boats, and had an abundance of mangrove trees, a source of charcoal for the foundries. But these local advantages were offset by the long and arduous journey to Manila (transportation costs to Manila were one and a half pesos per *picul*) and the threat of Moro attacks. Although the iron extracted by Chinese methods tested well, Salgado had difficulty in arranging a suitable development contract with the government, such as occurred with his request to ship two thousand *piculs* in ballast to Acapulco and to extend his lease of the wine monopoly for six years without bidding. Governor Obando threw his weight in Salgado's favor, but the favorable decision was nullified after he left office.

Salgado found a more suitably located mine at Santa Inés in the Lanatin Valley among the hills east of Manila, eight or nine leagues distant, behind the towns of Morong and Tanay. The valley was fertile and forested, suitable for settlement and farming, and had an abundance of building materials. The mineral was found in the surrounding mountains in the form of loose stones, and the cost of transporting it to the ironworks was low.

The lease contract with the government called for delivery of two thousand *piculs* of iron annually for nine years at one peso less than the current price in the city plus five hundred pesos a year. In the four or five years that he actually worked the mine and foundry, he invested more than fifty thousand pesos and extracted more than three thousand *piculs* of iron, manufacturing plows, artillery projectiles of various calibers, *kawas* and *carajais* (large native pots and pans), and other pieces. Despite an existing order for the expulsion of non-Christian Chinese, Salgado early in 1758, claiming that he had the tacit approval of Governor Arandía, contracted with skilled Chinese workmen to make anchors, ordnance, and other items. But when Arandía denied having given permission the Chinese were expelled. Salgado then suspended operations at the mines, alleging that the skills of the Chinese could not be found locally.

After Arandía's death, the acting governor, Archbishop Manuel Rojo, sent for Salgado, offering to authorize the reentry of Chinese workmen and to extend whatever help was needed to continue the enterprise. But Salgado had lost interest, and he turned over to the government the existing installations for free, to be used by new lessees Juan Francisco Solano, Juan de Asso y Otal, and Francisco Casañas. (The first two, both Manila merchants, would finance the voyage of the *Buen Fin* to San Blas in 1773.) The military engineer of Manila, Miguel Antonio Gómez, was appointed intendant of the mine to oversee the making of ordnance, bullets, bombs, anchors, and nails, the last two badly needed at the Cavite shipyards. In January 1762, Gómez moved to Santa Inés, and between March and the British invasion late in September of that year the facility's output was 2,500 plows, 16,000 bullets of different calibers, 4,000 grenades, 650 metric *quintals* of beaten iron balls similar to those of China, 400 *quintals* of European-type platen, 150 *quintals* of assorted ship's nails, and another 150 *quintals* used to manufacture mining equipment. A new foundry with twenty forges was also nearing completion.

The breakdown of law and order with the British invasion brought about destruction of the facilities by Aeta tribesman and some local inhabitants, who attacked the workmen and engaged in killing, looting, and arson. Among those killed were nine master founders. Santa Inés would rise again but not until the term of Governor Basco, as will be seen.

In the meantime, Salgado also had investments in industry in the form of a sailcloth factory. Data on the enterprise are scarce, but it is known that it had twenty-one looms in operation and wove more than seventy thousand *varas* (Spanish yards) of sailcloth for the royal navy and other uses. It was good enough to become an export item to Batavia. Cloth was made for the uniforms of soldiers and sailors and the clothing of the poor. But when for unspecified reasons the supply of cotton yarn dwindled, despite the efforts of Governor Obando to promote cotton growing, Salgado closed his factory. During the British invasion of 1762, the occupying forces used the looms for firewood, thus destroying the installation.

Salgado's career during that invasion was one of outstanding service under the resistance governor, Simón de Anda, a judge of the Audiencia who left Manila on the eve of its fall in order to organize opposition to the invaders. All the citizens of substance were in the occupied city except Salgado, his son-in-law Joseph Eslava, and one Andrés Blanco Bermúdez. Salgado transported out of the city at his expense royal funds amounting to 111,000 pesos, taking them to Laguna Province and then to Anda's headquarters in Pampanga. He also transported the treasure carried from Mexico, amounting to more than 2.5 million pesos (far above the official *permiso* of half a million pesos in the galleon trade, it will be noted) on the patache *Filipino*, which had eluded the British and made port in Palapag, Samar. This treasure was transferred to smaller vessels and taken first to Camarines and then to Maúban in Tayabas Province on the east coast of Luzon, where it was unloaded and transported under constant threat of British attack to Pampanga. He was put in charge of the provinces of Laguna, Batangas, and Tayabas; purchased wheat, other foodstuffs, and arms for Anda; sent vessels with messages and orders to other islands; and helped the Zamboanga garrison.

His wartime service cost him dearly. His Manila home was pillaged by the British. His son-in-law was caught and died in occupied territory, though not before having taken note of enemy troop dispositions and sent this intelligence across the lines. Salgado also paid spies out of his own pocket, especially one (apparently a woman) in the executive palace in Manila. He lost 360,600 pesos on a huge galleon captured by the British, the two-thousand-ton *Santísima Trinidad*, on cargo he had shipped on commission from various participants in the trade.

But the more subtle and longer-term costs came from the antipathy he provoked among those of his contemporaries who worked under the British, namely, two judges and the atttorney general, Viana. The latter did not commit treason, as Salgado claimed, but his pliable conduct stood in contrast to Salgado's strong patriotic stance. This antipathy would dog Salgado's attempts to gain royal favor in the future, as his enemies rose to high official positions, and he never received the patent of nobility that he sought.

After the war, Salgado turned to indigo, on which he had experimented with Norton Nicols in 1760. On the basis of samples sent to the court in 1766 and of a favorable analysis, he was given a tract of fallow and wooded land in Calauan, Laguna, and a monopoly over indigo production for fifteen years. Guatemala indigo set the standard for the Spanish possessions, and although Salgado knew little about the process he went ahead, operating by trial and error. Two problems he had to overcome were how to minimize the lime content of the native liquid indigo (sometimes called indigo mud), used locally and for export to China in jars, and how to accelerate the precipitation of solids in mixing tanks from four to five days to a matter of hours.

Salgado began in 1774–75 to clear the land and build installations. He was required by his enjoyment of monopoly rights to send 150 *arrobas* annually to Spain. But his first harvests were poor, and his many activities distracted him from properly supervising his overseer, who wasted large amounts of seeds in improper planting. The friars of adjacent parishes also opposed Salgado's project for reasons that are not clear.

One of Salgado's distractions in 1775 was his proposal to mine copper deposits on the island of Masbate, for which again he sought the assistance of his friend Governor Anda. Of the many concessions requested by Salgado, Anda among other things authorized him to bring twelve founders and one collier from China; gave him ordnance, arms, and munitions for defense against Moro raiders; and authorized the building of two forts. Anda's measures were approved by the Spanish court in 1777, and Salgado prepared a fleet of five ships to transport men, supplies, and arms. But by then Anda had died in office, royal officials procrastinated until the favorable sailing season was past, and Salgado abandoned the project.

The lack of a friendly presence in the governor's palace would also affect his indigo project. The able but headstrong José Basco y Vargas, of whom more will be seen, took office in 1778. While he favored economic development projects, he was also extremely sensitive, and Salgado antagonized him by sending cinnamon samples to Spain without informing him. It was downhill from there. He seized on Salgado's failure to remit the 150 *arrobas* of indigo annually as proof of his incapacity and lack of effort. He claimed that in the six years of Salgado's monopoly he had hardly produced a dozen *quintals* to send as samples and had set his sights on building himself a beautiful estate with cattle, trees, plantings, and crops for his personal interest while sending to Spain promises, excuses, and papers. Basco considered Salgado's monopoly prejudicial to the natives and the Crown.

Salgado defended himself by pointing to his installations, including pools, troughs, mixing tanks, and buildings; by claiming that the enterprise was fully functional; and by stating for the record that he did not keep his methods a secret but was interested in diffusing knowledge so that the product would become of general manufacture after the expiration of his monopoly. He went so far as to ask in one petition that Viana, sitting on the Council of the Indies as the count of Tepa, refrain from attending sessions in which his case was being discussed. It was to little avail. Basco branded him an audacious, captious, and restless spirit, opined that lawsuits and gambling left him little time for rest, and scornfully counseled that he should abstain from airy projects and enjoy his twilight years. Salgado's monopoly was annulled by a royal decree of June 20, 1781.

In the meantime, Basco had encouraged an Augustinian, Fr. Matías Octavio, to teach indigo cultivation to the inhabitants of the town of Tambobong (Malabon), including Chinese mestizos who controlled the trade in native liquid indigo. The friar had apparently picked up some pointers from a former assistant of Salgado's. The first samples sent to Spain in 1781 received an unfavorable rating, but those sent the following year were better, and a royal decree in 1785 suggested to the governor that he encourage cultivation by the natives of a better quality of indigo. Apparently Father Octavio continued to make improvements, and by 1789 indigo growing had spread to other provinces. It is probably fair to say that Salgado pioneered the preparation of indigo paste and Father Octavio improved, developed, and extended the industry. It is also probable that Octavio's system was more socially beneficial since it relied on the efforts of small cultivators rather than large estates.

Even while his indigo project was meeting with difficulties, Salgado was involved in another line of cultivation, namely, cinnamon. He had known something of Norton Nicols's efforts on Mindanao, and in 1774 he sent for thirteen plants from the commander of the Zamboanga garrison for transplanting to his Calauan estate. In 1778, he wrote of his hope that in eighteen or twenty years the cinnamon trees would have multiplied sufficiently to supply all of Spain, assuming of course that he would receive all necessary help in transporting trees and seeds from Misamis and Zamboanga. But when a shipment of two hundred plants arrived Salgado was denied the twelve he had requested from the governor, who planted all of them in the palace garden, where the soil was unsuitable and most of the plants died. A later shipment of over a thousand plants and many seeds was distributed among several persons, with Salgado again pointedly excluded. On his own estate, he lost large quantities of seeds due to lack of knowledge and initially positioned the plants in a location where the east wind blew the blossoms down. But he was learning from experience.

Basco in the meantime undertook his own initiatives in cinnamon culture. Seven Dutch sailors in 1779 escaped from the captivity of Moro raiders and went to Zamboanga, where the garrison commander, on the unfounded supposition that since they were Dutch they must know something about cinnamon culture, sent them to nearby mountains to look for the plant. With the specimens they gathered, they were sent to Cavite the following year. Basco proposed that the Consulado finance its development. The Consulado assigned two commissioners from the Company of the Major Guilds to undertake tests and inquiries. One of the commissioners was Salgado, who reported that the cinnamon had a bitter taste, showing that its gum had not been removed completely and thus was commercially uncompetitive with that from Ceylon.

Basco, however, had persuaded the Dutchmen to remain for twenty-five pesos a month, and the Consulado could derive the financing from the *avería* tax assigned to it. Salgado proposed further that the Major Guilds and Ustáriz companies be asked to contribute. However, the work of the Dutchmen in Mindanao was worthless. The Consulado lost nine thousand pesos and decided to give up the project. Royal orders, influenced by more favorable appraisals reaching Basco, were received as late as 1785 encouraging cinnamon culture, but they came after the Zamboanga enterprise had been abandoned.

Meanwhile, Basco in 1781 ordered Salgado to furnish him with complete information on everything pertaining to cinnamon culture, especially the method for removing its gum. Salgado made the required report but omitted the information on method. A second decree angrily repeated the previous request, and Salgado answered with a long report, again leaving out the memorandum on method with the excuse that it had already been sent to the court. Samples accompanying the report were sent to the Economic Society, which returned an unfavorable report.

Salgado found an ally in Juan de Cuéllar, a botanist sent to the Philippines by the Royal Philippine Company. He was impressed with Salgado's plantation and estimated in 1787 that it had six hundred trees ready to be cut, more than three thousand small ones, and two seedbeds with two thousand plants. The new governor, Felix Berenguer de Marquina, received a royal decree ordering him to promote Salgado's plantation, making use of Cuéllar's knowledge and securing the cooperation of the directors of the Royal Philippine Company.

Cuéllar reported in 1789 that Philippine cinnamon belonged to the same species as that of Ceylon but with a difference in gum content owing to different soil types. The specimens he collected were sent to Spain and analyzed. They represented a great improvement over earlier ones, but the old problem remained: Salgado's cinnamon contained too much gum, or viscous matter.

This report gave rise to a royal decree ordering the intensification of cinnamon culture, and the governor was told to give Salgado whatever help he needed. Salgado asked for a loan of thirty thousand pesos to come in equal parts from the Consulado and the Royal Philippine Company, payable in three years. But, although by July 1791 there were already 590,382 trees growing on the estate, they temporized. Under pressure from the governor, they finally agreed to lend five thousand pesos a year each for three years, with Salgado mortgaging his estate to them, the loan to be repaid with the proceeds of the first cuttings. In 1791, the first shipment of any importance, consisting of three boxes containing 293 pounds of cinnamon, was sent to Spain. Salgado was not only borrowing money but selling jewelry and property to keep the project going. Cuéllar did everything possible to help. But a new analysis made in Spain in 1792 declared the new specimens inferior to the previous ones and so lacking in essential oils as to be worthless. And there were still no known methods of removing the gum. Cinnamon cultivation diminished yearly and was finally abandoned by the nineteenth century. Salgado and Cuéllar also attempted to grow nutmeg from about 1788, but an analysis made in Spain in 1790 was unfavorable.[14] The old dream of growing spices in the Philippines died hard.

There is little doubt that Salgado displayed the initiative and pioneering spirit characteristic of entrepreneurs. But his dependence on official favors and concessions, probably reflective of the age he lived in, left him vulnerable to the vagaries of personal relations (Governors Obando and Anda were friendly, Arandía and Basco were not). He also seemed to be lacking in constancy, as if he were interested in identifying and launching projects but found it tedious to keep them going over the long term. Put differently, he was an entrepreneur in need of a manager. He stopped operating the Santa Inés mine and then declined to resume work when the circumstances changed in his favor, he desisted from his Masbate copper project in the face of one season of official contrariness, and he gave up indigo processing when the industry was opened to competition, missing out on the growth of a product that became a major export item.

Despite his losses, he seemed to have ample investment funds. It is puzzling that his losses should be so well documented but that so little has survived about his sources of funds. Since he was a galleon trader, it can be surmised that this was the main source, and this reinforces the impression that profitability was still to be found more in that trade than in the economic development projects that were so assiduously encouraged.

Governor Basco

If Salgado was the outstanding private sector personality in the late-eighteenth-century Philippine economy, Governor José Basco y Vargas (1778–87), his adversary, occupied the corresponding niche in the public sector. He was described as diligent, zealous, just, and impartial. But he was also the epitome of eighteenth-century enlightened despotism, and in the face of obstinate opposition to his progressive ideas he at times reacted in an authoritarian manner, with excessive violence and an inability to listen to any opinion other than his own.

As he was simply a frigate captain who was addressed as "Sir" (*Usted*), the judges of the Audiencia over whom he was to preside, who were addressed as "Your Excellencies" (*Señorías*), regarded him with some disdain, clashed with him, and even plotted to unseat him. Confident of the king's support, he seized and shipped off to Spain the regent, dean, and attorney general. Some low-ranking personnel were sent to Mexico aboard a galleon that was never heard from again. One possible reason for the Audiencia's hostility was Basco's decree of July 1778 allowing the return of the Chinese to Manila.

Basco's economic activity falls roughly into three categories: overall policies, specific projects, and institution building. His underlying ideas seem to have been the attainment of economic autonomy in order to mitigate the uncertainty of foreign supply and fiscal independence in order to eliminate reliance on the Mexican *situado*. He thought it necessary to establish a secure and inexhaustible commerce based on domestic production and to achieve a firm union among the industries of Spain, the Philippines, and the American possessions. This would result in a reciprocal circulation of goods and specie, obviating the resort to foreign countries that carried off Spanish treasure. The Philippines should prohibit the shipment to Spain of goods, especially cotton, not produced in the islands, and it should also exclude from entry foreign cotton clothing so as to increase domestic production.

Basco's policies were contained in a "General Economic Plan" of April 17, 1779, and the complementary "A Friendly Reminder" of September 1 of that same year. He sought to encourage agriculture and industry by offering prizes to those who excelled in cultivating cotton, mulberry trees, and spices such as cloves, cinnamon, pepper, and nutmeg; to those who established factories for the processing or production of silk, porcelain, hemp, linen, and cotton; to those who produced inventions useful to the state; and to those who distinguished themselves in the sciences, the liberal arts, and the trades. He distributed instructions on the methods of cultivating and processing cotton, silk, sugar, and other products. He also proposed reforming the galleon trade's *boleta* system by having the *boletas* sold by royal authority to genuine merchants at one hundred pesos each. This was not strange, as he stated frankly that "our decline has come from the airy [i.e., insubstantial] trade of the Acapulco ship . . ."

Since his proposals were met with a deafening silence, he established as the vehicle for the propagation of his ideas the Real Sociedad Económica de Filipinas along the lines of similar societies established in Spain and somewhat akin to the Society for the Encouragement of Arts, Commerce, and Manufactures founded in England in 1754. The royal order of the previous year recommending its formation provided for convening citizens of the greatest authority, wealth, and talent from among the most learned churchmen, military officials, and other persons of recognized ability to form a society of "selected people capable of producing useful thoughts."

In his inaugural address on May 6, 1781, he soared to flights of rhetoric uncharacteristic of one so deeply immersed in the workaday world. The society seems to have owed its existence largely to his initiative and drive, for it was most active for about two years, and when he left in 1787 it fell into a prolonged period of suspended animation, not to revive until 1819, when it added the phrase Amigos del País—friends of the country—to its name. The society did, however, reveal its roots in the Enlightenment by taking up the cudgels for the native Filipinos in 1782 against the resident Spaniards, who were perceived to be transients with short-term perspectives. Of Basco's specific projects, mention has already been made of his failure to encourage cinnamon culture and his support of Fr. Matías Octavio's successful projects in indigo.

Basco's earliest project in agriculture was an attempt to grow flax and hemp for linen weaving in 1778–79. He imported the first seeds and had them planted in northern Luzon, Pampanga, Laguna, Batangas, and the vicinity of Manila. The seeds arrived spoiled, and few plants germinated. Basco ordered more seeds from Mexico, but when the plantings failed again he had to admit defeat.

In 1781, Basco turned his attention to pepper, which grew wild in the country and should have been easy to propagate. He issued instructions for its cultivation to the civil and ecclesiastical authorities and the Consulado and promised to purchase all the pepper presented to him in the next five years at twenty pesos per *picul*. He offered to distribute free seeds and established prizes for the one who would grow the most pepper and the first five persons who harvested pepper of superior quality and quantity in good time. The rewards would take the form of tribute exemption, cash, or the grant of certain distinctions.

The idea was first to meet domestic demand and then to export pepper to other Spanish provinces. It was estimated that even if it were sold at half a real per pound the gain would amount to 300 percent. But development was slow and opposed by the merchants, who considered it "of little worth and value." Intendant Carvajal consulted the botanist Cuéllar, who opined that Laguna was the province best suited for its propagation. (Indeed, the friar of Majayjay was reported to have sown seventeen million plants.) Cultivators who followed his advice got excellent results, and in 1788 the Royal Philippine Company was able to purchase some pepper and sign contracts with the natives. At a later time, however, they tired of the painstaking care required in its cultivation and turned to coffee. This may have represented the workings of opportunity cost in the form of gains from the coffee crop.

In 1782, the Economic Society undertook the encouragement of silk-worm culture and silk weaving, and the following year mulberry trees were brought from China for propagation. The governor pressured each town to devote a measure of land to mulberry trees, and each native was to plant a certain number of the trees around his house. In Camarines, four million trees were ordered planted. The Royal Philippine Company also entered the picture, and between 1788 and 1790 its ships carried small amounts of raw and woven Philippine silk.

But in many cases the value of the final product did not cover the cost of the venture, whether because of poor harvests or the use of Chinese labor, which was more costly than local labor. Even when costs might have been covered, historical accounts clearly indicate the work-ings of opportunity costs: even if the land devoted to mulberry trees were given over to the lowly *camote* (sweet potato), in Philippine society the food of last resort in times of want, it was perceived to yield more than silk culture.

It was in connection with agriculture that Basco made another effort to reform the allocation system of the galleon trade. To encourage large-scale indigo cultivation, he proposed that the Consulado grant a share in the galleon in proportion to the capital invested in indigo factories. This was flatly rejected. His successor, Felix Berenguer de Marquina, made an even more radical proposal to replace the *boleta* system and auction off the lading space on the galleon, with the Royal Company permitted to bid. But this met the same fate.

In the mining sector, Basco undertook to revive the Santa Inés mine. Four Spanish residents put in a bid in 1779 to develop all the mines in the country under a contract with a set of thirty-one stipulations. Basco found them so onerous, with the price of iron higher than if it had been procured abroad, that he decided to have the government itself undertake the devel-opment of the mines. Santa Inés ore would be transported five or six leagues on the backs of carabaos to the ironworks at San José de Oogong (Uugong). Within a year, production was at a peak in Santa Inés, and the Spanish foremen and native workers discovered the Chinese process of refinement and were able to turn out plows, *carajais,* and bullets.

Since direct government administration of the project was a tempo-rary expedient, Basco considered the proposal of María Isabel Careaga, already a contractor for the wine revenue, which consisted of twenty-two conditions. These he found unacceptable, but Careaga then offered to work the mine as a claimant subject to the pertinent regulations provided that she was not dispossessed of the mine unless the government itself decided to work it. She undertook to pay the government for all the equipment and metal tools in the mine and foundries and for all expenses she incurred while operating the mine.

Basco awarded Careaga the lease in 1781. In June 1783, she went over Basco's head to the Crown and asked permission to ship two thousand *piculs* of iron to Acapulco yearly; to exempt from statute labor all the mine workers, whether natives, (Chinese) mestizos, or other nationals; that the exemption remain for life for those who had worked for three years; that she be authorized to bring in the needed Chinese masters and skilled workmen, even if they were non-Christians; and that they not be subject to any order of expulsion that might be passed in the future. These conditions, which had been rejected in the Philippines, were granted by Madrid on December 26, 1783.

At the same time, the Angat iron mines discovered by Salgado were being operated by another Manila resident, Lorenzo Buicochea. Even adding this mine's output to that of Santa Inés was not sufficient to meet domestic demand in Basco's opinion, and the actual yield of both mines was below their capacity, possibly owing to Careaga's advanced age and her need for an active manager and Buicochea's lack of capital. But Careaga turned the mine over to her son-in-law, Count Jose Avilés. There were six foundries in Morong making bombs, grenades, and bullets, leading to a small industrial boom in the town.

Whatever Basco's opinions of the adequacy of output, during his term Manila was the arsenal of Mexico's Pacific coast. Acapulco's newly built Fort San Diego was equipped with cannons made in the Philippines, and the Department of San Blas was furnished a packet boat, the *San Carlos*, alias *Filipino*, constructed in Cavite. Various letters sent by Basco to Intendant José de Gálvez show that between 1781 and 1785 Manila supplied Fort San Diego with six cannons of caliber twenty-four, five of caliber six, eight of caliber four, and two fourteen-inch mortars.

Basco made his greatest mark in the field of public finance with a series of revenue measures. He instituted or placed on a new footing government monopolies in palm wine and areca nuts. In 1780, it appears that the privilege of selling these articles of common consumption was farmed out at public auction to contractors. The palm wine monopoly applied only to certain regions, not to the whole country, and it yielded 45,200 pesos, while areca nut revenues were 15,765 pesos. Both were placed under direct government administration, and in 1809 the proceeds were 221,426 and 48,610 pesos, respectively. Licenses to operate cockpits were also sold at auction, and the proceeds in 1780 were 14,000 pesos. With the extension of licensing to more provinces, revenues reached 40,141 pesos in 1810. Gunpowder manufacture was also made a government monopoly.

But the most famous measure for achieving the Philippines' fiscal independence was the tobacco monopoly, decreed in Manila on May 5, 1781, and extended to the rest of the country on March 1, 1782. This was to prove the most effective and lasting measure initiated by the industrious governor. It was to endure a century—an institutional longevity perhaps second only to that of the galleon trade—and most of its history is properly bound up with a later period than the one covered here. It did not assume importance in the country's foreign trade until about the third decade of the nineteenth century, and as late as 1818 there were no recorded exports of tobacco. During the first three or four decades of its existence, its importance was primarily fiscal, and it became the major source of revenue for the Spanish government in the Philippines.

Under this system, the planting of tobacco was prohibited in all except certain specified regions, which in Tomás de Comyn's time (1810) were Gapan (then in Pampanga Province), Cagayan, and Marinduque. Within these areas, tobacco culture was rigorously supervised from the seedling stage to the delivery of mature leaves to the government stores. This supervision grew increasingly oppressive over time, as the growers were accountable not only for the number of plants but even for the number of leaves expected from each plant. They could not consume their own product but had to buy cigars from the factories of the state. Ill-paid lawmen were needed to enforce compliance with the strict regulations, subjecting the growers to exactions and vexations. In a few provinces, however, the growing of tobacco was permitted for local consumption only.

Enforcement of the three monopolies—tobacco, palm wine, and areca nuts—required setting up inspection stations along the principal waterways, which were the country's main avenues of internal communication. At these stations, boatmen often would simply give the inspector a portion of their wares to avoid additional vexations, thus raising the price of the product going to the city and even causing frequent shortages of staple articles. Replacing old inspectors with new ones only showed that the latter were as corrupt as the former.

It is small wonder that the imposition of this system, coming after a time when all had been free to grow their own tobacco, an item of general consumption, was obstinately resisted by the people, and the well-meaning governor had to summon all his "circumspection and constancy" to put it into effect. An indirect effect was the beginning of agricultural specialization, since the tobacco-growing regions could no longer grow their own food but had to import it from elsewhere in the country.

In terms of revenue, however, it proved immediately effective. In 1782, its second year of existence, the Philippines was able to remit 150,000 pesos to Spain. Before Basco's term was over, another 300,000 pesos had been sent, and by 1795 the cumulative total reached 1,971,696 pesos from a colony that had previously been a drain on the royal treasury. Tobacco consumption was constantly on the rise, and, despite widespread smuggling and evasion provoked by the severity of the regulations, revenue from the monopoly generally rose over the years. Net proceeds were 44,698 pesos in 1782, 227,519 pesos in 1785, 257,665 pesos in 1790, 322,497 pesos in 1795, and 516,401 pesos in 1800.

Wearied by his struggles with hostile local interests, Basco resigned from office in 1787. Two events of commercial significance bracketed his term. The first was the regulation of *libre comercio* of October 12, 1778, which opened the trade of the Indies to several Spanish ports besides Cádiz and Seville and allowed other sources of Asian textiles to supply Mexico. This was a blow to the galleon trade.[15] The other event was the establishment of the Royal Philippine Company, to which we now turn.

The Royal Philippine Company

What at the time seemed to be the biggest event in Basco's administration was the creation of the Royal Philippine Company in 1785, the culmination of several earlier efforts and projects (such as a company founded in 1733) that had come to naught in the first flush of the Bourbon revival.[16]

In the same month that the *Asunción* returned to Cádiz on the last voyage of the royal naval line from the Philippines, the Caracas Company— the Real Compañía Guipuzcoana de Caracas—was refused a renewal of its monopoly. This had been foreseen, and at the company's general meeting on May 6, 1784, the influential Frenchman Francisco Cabarrús, a director of the company who had long favored establishing a company to trade directly with the Philippines, proposed the formation of such a company. Although not all stockholders favored the idea, the king's willingness to subscribe 1 million pesos and make an interest-free loan of 1,200,000 reales vellon (60,000 pesos) out of the funds he kept with the major guilds showed his determination to establish direct trade with the Philippines. Three days later the general meeting accepted the idea.[17]

The royal decree authorizing the creation of the Royal Philippine Company—the Real Compañía de Filipinas—was promulgated on March

10, 1785. It provided for the liquidation of the assets of the Caracas Company and the transfer of the net proceeds to the Philippine Company, although apparently the new company was subrogated to the creditors of the old company. The governing board was composed of three directors of the Bank of Havana, two of the Bank of the Guilds, one of the Bank of Seville, and two from among the general stockholders. The company's charter was to last for twenty-five years beginning on July 1, 1785.

The company's capital stock was set at 8 million pesos divided into 32,000 shares worth 250 pesos each. The king subscribed 1 million pesos for himself and his children in addition to the shares he held in the Caracas Company. Municipalities and Spanish American Creoles were also invited to invest, but much of the issue probably went to shareholders of the dissolved company, as they were instructed to exchange their paper for equivalent stock in the new company. In total, 155,059 shares were applied for, although only one-fifth of that number could be issued.[18]

The objectives of the company were broad and far-reaching and amounted to establishing contact among the various Spanish colonies and between those colonies and the motherland. It was to stimulate Spanish trade with Asia and expand that of the Philippines by taking advantage of the direct route from East Asia to Cádiz. Preferably it was to go from Spain to Spanish America and thence to the Philippines to pick up Philippine and other Asian goods, returning always via the Cape of Good Hope since it was not permitted, at least initially, to make voyages from Asian waters to the Americas. An unstated objective was to place the Spanish import trade from Asia in Spanish hands so that foreigners would not monopolize the profits from it.

Its principal purpose, however, repeated in various articles of its charter (especially articles 13, 40, and 50) was to stimulate the economic development of the Philippines. To this end, it was encouraged to trade in the products and manufactures of the archipelago. Article 40 made Philippine goods shipped on its vessels duty free at both Manila and Cádiz. Under article 50, the company was required to invest 4 percent of its net annual profits in the encouragement of Philippine agriculture and manufactures.

The next three articles were infused with the spirit of the Enlightenment. Articles 51 and 52 required the company to provide free passage on its vessels to the Philippines to artisans and professors of mathematics, chemistry, and botany; the artisans were also to be provided with the tools of their respective trades. Article 53 provided that up to one-third of the crews on the ships could be natives of the Philippines, regardless of color, origin, or status, and they were to be treated and promoted according to merit in the same manner as European sailors.

Unlike the British and Dutch East India Companies, the Royal Philippine Company could not maintain armies, make treaties, or declare war. It was required by article 33 not to interfere in the politics of the nations with which it traded and to maintain amicable relations with them.

To balance these obligations, the company was conceded certain privileges, chief among them a monopoly of the direct trade between Asia and Spain. It was conceded the right to send annually two thousand tons of merchandise to Venezuelan ports (a privilege held over from the dissolved Caracas Company) and eight hundred tons to Mexico. It also enjoyed certain other tariff and import concessions in Spain.

The suspicions of the Manila merchants, chronically fearful that their monopoly of the Acapulco trade would be broken, were addressed in several articles. Article 43 confirmed the monopoly of the Acapulco trade as a prerogative of the Manila merchants "for the present"—hardly a reassuring formulation. The company could not take any interest in that trade, and any goods it shipped from Mexico on the galleon had to pay the same nonpreferential rates as ordinary cargo. Additional safeguards for the Acapulco trade were the requirement that all return trips from Asia must sail via the Cape of Good Hope and the prohibition against shipping to the Americas from Asia. Article 42 gave the Manila merchants the same right conferred by article 31 on the company, allowing it to undertake trading ventures to "China and other parts of Asia"; in effect, this repealed the two-century ban on Spanish subjects trading on their own in Asian countries. Manila merchants were conceded the right to use up to one-fifth of the lading space on the company's vessels' return trip to Cádiz to encourage them to take part in this trade. Three thousand shares of the company's stock were reserved for disposal among the natives and residents of the Philippines. Finally, the company's Manila governing board was to include a representative of that city's interests besides the governor, the intendant, two directors, the director of the Patriotic Society, and the treasurer-accountants.[19]

Use by the new company of the Cape of Good Hope route provoked a protest from the Dutch Estates General, which, under prodding by the Dutch East India Company, claimed on July 22, 1786, that that route had been barred to Spain by the treaties of Munster and Utrecht. This was followed by a long and bitter exchange of notes. The Dutch tried to enlist French and British support, but Spain could count on the Bourbon family compact to keep France in line and Britain feared that Holland's real motive was to justify building up a naval force in the East Indies. In any case, Spain prepared two fighting fleets and vigorously rejected, on October 31,

1786, the claims of the Dutch, whose opposition thereafter fell apart. Despite the apparent advantages of the company, British diplomats in Madrid did not disguise their doubts about its financial viability.[20]

Despite its name, it would be erroneous to take a purely Philippine-centric view of the company. It had substantial holdings in the Americas, and its directors were the same as those of the predecessor Caracas Company. Its efforts in the Philippines were limited and did not determine its global results. This is made clear by an overview of its voyages in the first years of its existence, when it was most active. Exports to the Philippines to 1789 were 28 percent of its total trade and produced only 1 percent of the gross profit. Imports from Asia were 29 percent of total trade and yielded 21 percent of the gross profit. On the other hand, exports to the Americas made up 31 percent of its total trade (of which only 2 percent consisted of Asian goods) and yielded 63 percent of the gross profits, while imports from the Americas were 12 percent of total trade and yielded 15 percent of the gross profit. Thus, the American trade accounted for more than three-fourths of the gross profit on less than half of the investment. This skewed profit pattern was attributed to the requirement that company ships acquire all their Asian goods in Manila; it was represented that this routing accounted for 24 percent of the selling price of Chinese goods in Spain and 44 percent of that of Indian goods.

At the company's first stockholders meeting, which finally adjourned in 1793, official approval was secured to bypass Manila in the Asian trade and lift the requirement to invest 4 percent of profits in Philippine economic development. There was even a proposal to dissolve the company, but this was rejected by a commission appointed at the general meeting because it would result in the loss of 75 percent of the capital and the state would have to assume at great sacrifice the task of Philippine economic development. The company also petitioned the Crown to allow it to share in the galleon trade, again showing where the real profits lay, but this was rejected.

After 1789, the company's activity began to decline, and this can be seen in its shipping ventures. Prior to that year, twenty-nine voyages had been completed, of which twenty were in the American trade and nine with Manila; a tenth vessel was expected. Before 1790, the number of ships dispatched to Manila was twelve, but between that year and 1817 only twenty more voyages were made to Asia, not all of which called at Manila. One estimate is that between 1785 to 1820 only sixteen direct voyages were made between the Philippines and Spain by company ships.

Despite the preponderance of Chinese and Indian goods in the cargoes to Spain, there were small quantities of Philippine items. In 1788, one ship carried 1,100 pounds of indigo, 113 pounds of silk, 180 *quintales* of raw cotton, 700 *quintales* of *sapan* wood, and 150 pieces of Philippine textiles. The following year two ships included in their cargoes 22,975 pounds of indigo.[21]

The company's total purchases of Philippine goods by 1788 were 156,386 pesos, and it had an additional 258,362 pesos in stores and warehouses. By 1790, its gross profits amounted to 9,597,350 pesos. The cumulative total of the funds used in its operations was 23,488,400 pesos, including loans raised in Holland, Spain, and the Indies, amounting to 1,779,250 pesos, and advances and help from the government, amounting to 1,655,042 pesos. It had sent to Spain Chinese, Indian, and Philippine goods worth 6,238,598 pesos and on to the Americas 262,182 pesos worth of the same goods. Total profits during the first five years of its existence were estimated at 802,582 pesos (an annual average of 160,517 pesos or about 2 percent of the original capitalization, which, as Azcárraga remarks, could hardly have been cause for congratulation to the shareholders and management).[22]

It did undertake for a while the task of stimulating agriculture and manufactures in the Philippines, helped by Basco's Economic Society. Part of the plan presented at its first general meeting called for placing twenty million reales vellon in Manila (one million pesos), of which twelve million would be sent from Spain and eight million raised from loans at 5 percent in Mexico or the Philippines from the *obras pías*. These funds were to be used to make advances to cultivators for new plantations or improvements, at 6 percent if secured and 8 percent if unsecured. It would also make loans to manufacturers and artisans to procure raw materials, make advances for wages, and so on.[23]

In its agricultural operations, the company took up the ongoing efforts that have already been mentioned. Indigo had been easy to encourage, with only small advances made to producers to purchase utensils for processing the crop into paste. Philippine indigo exports between 1786 and June 30, 1802, were 31,224 *quintales* (1 *quintal* = 100 Spanish pounds), of which 6,328 were exported by the company, 5,999 by individual nationals, and 18,897 by foreigners. This was in addition to 46,452 *quintales* of liquid indigo taken by the Chinese in the same period.[24]

Sugar also proved an easy and rewarding business. When the company came to the Philippines, sugar was, after rice, the most common crop, but exports were scanty. These were usually transported in "Armenian" ships (probably British vessels in disguise) to Madras and then only in years of great abundance. A total of 860 *arrobas* (1 *arroba* = 11.5 kilograms) was exported to Spain in 1786, and two years later 9,663 *arrobas* were sent to China, the Asian coast (probably India), and Spain. Governor Felix Berenguer de Marquina reported sugar exports for 1789 at between 40,000 and 50,000 *piculs* (1 *picul* = 63.262 kilograms). From 1786 to 1802, Philippine sugar exports totaled 267,634 *piculs*, of which 8,045 were by the company, 24,137 by individual nationals, and 235,452 by foreigners.[25]

The overwhelming proportions of these crops' exports taken by foreigners—60.5 percent of the indigo and 88 percent of the sugar—probably indicated that they were commercially competitive and in little need of special incentives. The company's share was noticeably minor.

The third crop to claim the company's initial attention, pepper, was tried in various provinces, but only in Tayabas, where it was aided by the governor, Don Miguel de San Agustín, "who is an Indian, a man of commendable merit," did it have any significant results, with 272,180 pounds gathered by July 1802.[26]

Cotton, the fourth crop to claim the company's attention, was also tried with little success except in the textile-producing region of Ilocos. There the company concentrated its efforts, offering numerous inducements to the Ilocanos to produce cotton and thus spurring the extension of cotton culture and the opening of new lands. Although in fourteen years the only complete harvest was that of 1796–97, Ilocos came to be considered the most agricultural and industrious region in the country, greatly reinforcing its long-standing position as the supplier of cotton to Manila and the rest of the country.

Juan de Cuéllar, the botanist who was the only scientist brought to the Philippines under the pertinent provision of the company's charter, was sent there as provincial governor by Governor Rafael María de Aguilar in order to encourage the production of cotton textiles. The company, which had dispensed with his services as botanist in 1794, was asked to name him its factor in that province. In December 1797, Governor Aguilar named Cuéllar superintendent of the sailcloth factory in Sarrat and of all others that might be established subsequently. The following year Cuéllar proposed a general distribution of lands to the inhabitants so that they might grow cotton, but this was not legally possible. In 1798, cotton cultivation was extended by him into Pangasinan. In 1799, the Ilocos harvest was poor, but the Royal Navy in the Philippines purchased the total output of sailcloth. Cuéllar is believed to have died in 1801. The company's purchases of cotton to December 1795 were 8,291 *arrobas* and 16,165 textile pieces; from 1796 to 1802, they were 37,000 *arrobas* and 32,042 textile pieces that it had ordered manufactured.

Separately, the same sources record company purchases of Ilocos blankets and textiles called *mantalones* and *terlingas*, despite the fact that they were more expensive than those of Bengal, in order to introduce them into the export trade, and the company claimed that demand for them rose, as did prices, but it also said that improvements were needed such as increased capital and more modern instruction. Azcárraga, with the wisdom of hindsight, criticized the fruitlessness of these efforts, alleging that the company's directors should have known that European countries were seeking outlets for their own manufactures in exchange for tropical products and that the company would have been well advised to concentrate on the latter.[27]

The company's ventures in cinnamon and silk shared the fate of others that have already been mentioned. The company's attempts to grow cinnamon in Laguna and Tayabas, apparently by taking charge of Salgado's plantation, were failures owing to the unsuitability of the soil. As for silk, the company sought to help the project of then governor Carlos Conely of Camarines by making heavy advances, offering prizes, and buying up all the silk offered to it for sale despite the virtual certainty of initial losses. The project seems to have been given up in 1798, although there were at that time 4,485,782 mulberry trees in thirty villages. The company was apparently scared off by poor returns; in Camarines, on an outlay of 7,488 pesos, it got only 967 pounds of silk, and in Tondo, on an outlay of 7,257 pesos, it got 116 pounds.[28]

The company claimed that there was hardly any phase of economic activity in the Philippines in which it had not taken part, including iron mining in Morong. The amount of cash advances is difficult to calculate because the returns were in kind, but up to June 1802 advances written off amounted to 2,300,473 reales vellon (115,024 pesos), which represented the cost to the company of encouraging agriculture and industry in the Philippines.[29] It may be noted that this was slightly smaller than the volume of the return cargo on one of the guilds' shipments on the galleon of 1780.

If the company's efforts at economic development had rather mixed results, two indirect initiatives in trade had longer lasting effects, although not necessarily in the company's interest alone. The first move was to use foreign commission merchants as intermediaries in its operations, apparently in line with article 71 of its charter. Thus, although foreigners theoretically could not set up business houses in the Philippines, they seem to have been able to do so as agencies of the company or as representatives of

83

firms with which the company dealt. There are indications that they also traded on their own account and made business contacts for foreign merchants coming to Manila.

As early as 1787, La Perouse mentions finding a French merchant named Sebir residing in Manila. When Nathaniel Bowditch entered the port in 1796 as supercargo on Elias Haskett Derby's *Astrea*, he resided at the home of a Philadelphian named John Stuart Kerr, who seemed to be discharging consular functions for visiting Americans while carrying out his business transactions there. That same year Kerr also acted as the customs agent for the *Abigail* (captained by Christopher Thornton) from "Rodesilan," as the Spanish records called Rhode Island, signing a customs entry that showed a payment of a little over 291 pesos in duties on a cargo that included seven hundred pounds of butter, hemp rope, alembics, sheets of lead, iron of various kinds, anchors, bullets and grapeshot, European plows, and an assortment of carpentry tools and supplies such as mallets, chisels, scrapers, adzes, gouges, augers, nails, and hinges. The English firm that was permitted to establish itself in 1809 and was reputed to be the first of its nationality in the Philippines was also one of the company's intermediaries.[30] These were the harbingers of the foreign merchants who would play a key role in Philippine foreign trade long after the company was gone.

Bowditch's visit was made possible by the company's other trade initiative, namely, the opening of the port of Manila to world commerce in 1790. Previously, Manila had been closed to European shipping, except for the Portuguese, who exercised a right inherited from the days when the Crowns were united (1580–1640). The company's charter, under articles 29 and 30, opened Manila to Asian shipping in 1785, but this merely legalized the prevailing practice and there was no marked increase in general commerce or in that of the Philippine Company. In 1787, the minister for the Indies gave special instructions to officials in Manila to admit Portuguese vessels and those of native Indian princes that included in their cargoes goods of other Europeans in India.

This also did not affect the volume of the India-Philippines trade because it merely legalized the status of European captains of such ships. As was seen earlier, the "country trade" with the Philippines had been carried on by English ships flying the flags of Asian states or Portugal, with up to six layers of deception employed to keep up the pretense—the *garde-pavillon*, the consigner, the shipowner, the proxy owner (usually in Macao), the supercargo, and the consignee in Manila. (Some of these roles might have been played by the same person, reducing the layers of deception.) But the indirect route used and the involvement of so many people meant increased costs, with the need to pay off officials at both Macao and Manila. Similarly, Spanish traders going to India arranged to use the Portuguese flag.

It was to everybody's interest in the trade to facilitate it by reducing these costs—the galleon traders to get cargoes for Acapulco, the company to get cargoes for Cádiz, and the English in India to get silver for their China ventures (although the Manila traders opposed the company out of sheer antagonism). For the English, trade with Manila ranked second only to the China trade in their operations east of the Bay of Bengal.

The company's petitions to open up Manila, ostensibly traceable to dissatisfaction with the goods brought by Asian traders and with the galleon-linked cargoes procured by Manila merchants on the Asian mainland, were finally granted by the Supreme Council of State on which sat both Viana and Basco. By a decree of August 15, 1789, European ships were permitted to enter Manila during a three-year period starting September 1, 1790, in order to bring Asian goods; European goods were excluded. The three years were extended to seven, but the extension appears to have become indefinite in practice until Manila became de jure an open port. Unlike the previous concessions of 1785 and 1787, which merely ratified existing practices, the new decree represented a positive move toward liberalization of Manila's port regulations, and the English "country trade" should have gotten the most from it.

Ironically, neither the British Indian merchants nor the company benefited immediately from the decree, although activity in the port of Manila rose after a few years. The Nootka Sound crisis of 1789–91 impelled both Spain and Great Britain to make preparations for war. In the meantime, all foreign-flag vessels were expelled from Manila in December 1790, and, although the situation eased, the port stayed officially closed. However, English ships continued to call under their own colors.[31]

For the company, the decree backfired in the Philippines. Alleging that it had neglected one of its important obligations, which was to supply the country with European products, the authorities sought to fill the resulting commercial vacuum by allowing a flood of European imports (supposedly excluded by the decree) of better quality and lower price than those brought by the company. For instance, the *Astrea* in 1796 carried a cargo of Madeira wine. There was a time-consuming exchange of representations and recriminations, in the course of which the company's monopoly of imports from Europe was shown to be illusory. Perhaps this was one of the "contrarieties" devised by local interests hostile to the company.[32]

In truth, the company was not in a position to do much of anything. Its initial financial weakness drove it into debt, and by the early 1790s it was almost paralyzed by its global debts, internal bickering, continuing hostility in the Philippines, and disputes in Spain. Trading with India through the Philippines was claimed to have added 45 percent to the cost of goods in Cádiz, so direct trade with India became part of the rehabilitation effort. A royal commission, again including Viana, met in 1796 and confirmed the company's right to sail to India directly. But after the first ship sailed war broke out with Britain, with which an almost continuous state of war would exist until Napoleon's invasion of 1808 except for a break in 1802–4. During those wars, the trade between the Philippines and India was maintained from the Danish enclaves at Serampore and Tranquebar and the Portuguese enclave of Santo Thome. But the company itself suffered heavily from the capture of its ships, including one that had to be ransomed for 400,000 pesos and another captured with cargo worth 200,000 pesos. Direct trade with Spain, of course, became highly risky.

Wartime hazards prompted development of a method of payment that would assume great importance in the future. The proceeds of cargoes sold in Manila were taken to Canton, only a short crossing away, and the silver was used to purchase bills of exchange on India issued by the Canton Committee of the English East India Company. The ships could then take on freight for India or the East Indies. Safety was the primary concern because there were also disadvantages. The committee never issued sight bills, and few time bills were for less than three months, tying up an investor's capital until the bill's maturity. Furthermore, a rise in demand for bills at Canton would send down the rate of exchange. When peace returned, therefore, payment of the proceeds of cargoes reverted to the transport of specie.[33] But the use of bills instead of cash was another harbinger of future events.

Also of aid in the company's rehabilitation was the right of direct trade between Spain and Canton and Manila and Lima, both granted in 1793. The Lima line expanded Philippine trading contacts and helped the company because, unlike the general run of its ventures, this one was quite lucrative. As in the Acapulco trade, the upper limit on the value of the cargoes was similar. About four-fifths were Chinese products—raw and unmanufactured silks, and so on—and the rest were Bengali cloth and spices. The Peru cargoes had a tariff advantage over those of Acapulco, as they paid only an 18 percent ad valorem duty, compared to 33 percent at Acapulco. The export tax on specie, however, was 6 percent at both ports. The Lima trade was not without its losses (one ship was lost in 1798 and at least two others were captured by the English in 1806) or its quirks (in 1801, the company ship inexplicably put in at Acapulco instead of Lima, thus aggravating the glut of products in Acapulco).[34]

Despite the rehabilitation effort, the company was pulling in its horns. In 1793, its managing board decided to dissolve the Manila directorate and replace it with a simple factory or agency run by three men. This was opposed, to no avail, by Governor Aguilar.

In 1802, the factors purchased for the company's account Salgado's estate at Calauan, proposing to continue the plantings begun by him (consisting of indigo, cinnamon, pepper, coffee, and other crops), but the Madrid directorate disapproved the expense and compelled the factors to refund the amount as well as the sums invested in implements and works. The reason given was that the company's financial state dictated that it must limit itself to commercial activities. With this event, all the company's efforts to promote the Philippine economy came to a halt. It even abandoned its practice of making advances and limited itself to buying at appropriate prices domestic products that came on the market.[35]

The company would drag on for another thirty-two years, but aside from a few trading voyages it would have little further to do with the Philippines, and a discussion of its activities outside the country need not be taken up here. Suffice it to note that its factor in India, sent with the idea of promoting direct voyages to Spain, arrived at the outbreak of war in 1796 and had his hands full simply staying out of trouble. The factors in Canton employed their official time and facilities to participate in the growing opium trade. Finally, the company's quasi-public nature left it susceptible to government pressure to undertake unprofitable ventures. It was under-capitalized (among other reasons, because the hostile Manila merchants had refused to subscribe the shares reserved for them) and debt-ridden. As late as 1805, it was still paying off debts incurred by the defunct Caracas Company.[36]

It was given a new charter in 1803, but this was effectively nullified by war with Great Britain in 1804 and Napoleon's invasion in 1808. Direct trade with Spain, dangerous since 1796, now became impossible. During the various wars, especially the Mexican War for Independence, it advanced money to the government, of which 2.4 million pesos were still outstanding in 1820; the government was doing little about it beyond inviting its creditors to subscribe to the consolidated public debt. Its former monopolies had been thrown open during the war, rendering them illusory, and its textile import privileges drew an increasing clamor from domestic Spanish manufacturers, leading the Cortes in 1820 to put an official end to them.

In thirty-five years, the company had declared dividends amounting to 32 percent, or a little less than 1 percent annually, representing a total of about 2.5 million pesos, mostly paid before 1803. Its balance sheet at the end of 1819 showed that its capital and liabilities, amounting to 8 million pesos, exceeded its assets by about 1.3 million pesos, and of the assets fully 60 percent were receivables while inventories accounted for another 28 percent. The return of absolute monarchy in 1823 restored its privileges on paper. But Spain's American empire was nearly gone, and war and internal politics had destroyed the company beyond resurrection. A royal decree of September 6, 1834, ordered its demise;[37] with the extinction of its privileges, Manila became de jure what it had been de facto for four decades, an open port.

A Brief Appraisal of the Eighteenth-Century Transition

The inauspicious end of the ventures, mostly state sponsored, initiated in the period under review (roughly 1765–1815, or from the end of the Seven Years' War to the end of the Napoleonic Wars) has tended to draw attention to the failures and shortcomings of both projects and policies. These shortcomings were many. The state was a looming presence and in its reformist mode was a force for economic progress. But precisely because of its large role, the effects of errors were also magnified. Private ventures came to depend excessively on the grant of official favors such as monopolies and fiscal concessions, which might promote profitability and development but gave scant regard to the efficiency attainable through competition. Reformist zeal also translated into self-righteousness, leading in some instances to a stubborn insistence on unsound projects.

In a protectionist milieu, it was easy to fall into the error of identifying technical with economic feasibility. In some cases, costs exceeded market prices. Even when they did not, opportunity costs tended to eliminate many objects of official attention and direct economic activity to those more commercially viable. For the latter, it would seem that special incentives were not really essential, and (as in the cases of indigo and sugar) it was the private foreign merchants who made up much of the market for them. Ironically, the transshipment-based galleon trade, despite official efforts to bring about its demise, continued to be more profitable than the state-sponsored development projects, and both the guilds and the Royal Philippine Company tried to take part in it, successfully in the former case and unsuccessfully in the latter.

On the positive side, when all the undertakings are considered together the cumulative effect is seen to be considerable. It was in this period that the Philippines broke the mold of commercial tradition, began expanding and diversifying its trade, and took its first organized steps to develop its natural resources. It was this period of government-sponsored enterprise that paved the way for the workings of private enterprise in the nineteenth century. The actual changes were perhaps not great—for example, Philippine commerce continued to be predominantly a transshipping operation until the end of the Napoleonic Wars—but the groundwork was laid for the changes that occurred later, and the Royal Philippine Company played a constructive part in laying much of this groundwork.

In the field of trade, direct contact with Spain was established, for the first time in 240 years, by naval frigates, and it was maintained by the Philippine Company. Contact with the Americas was broadened by the historically hazy San Blas trade and the company's expeditions to Peru. The Acapulco galleon monopoly had become eroded. The freedom to initiate trading voyages to other Asian ports instead of passively waiting for Asian (or Asian-based) traders to come to Manila was granted the Manila merchants and the company's agents. The admission of non-Asian foreign vessels and agents further broadened the country's trading connections. And the coming of foreign merchants introduced a new element that was to prove of extreme importance in succeeding decades. A further augury for the future was the first tentative use of bills of exchange in transferring funds through Canton.

A quantitative estimate of the effect of this period's initiatives on Philippine foreign trade is not easy to make in view of the scattered data. Imports at 1,185,807 pesos in 1785 and 5,329,000 pesos in 1810 do not permit the conclusion that trade increased four and a half times because most intervening years are missing and the available figures for customs duties show wide variations from year to year, exhibiting at least an irregular cyclical pattern.[38]

In the field of economic development, Basco's tobacco monopoly meant fiscal independence from Mexico, which enabled the Philippines to subsist on its own resources during the Napoleonic Wars and the disintegration of the Spanish Empire in the Americas. The monopoly was also responsible for the most conspicuous (though not the first, which may have been Salgado's textile factory) implementation of the factory system in the Philippines, as represented by the government-run cigar and cigarette factories built as part of the operation of the system.[39]

An export trade in native products was for the first time consciously stimulated by means of shipments on the naval frigates, by the encouragement of the Royal Economic Society, by innovators and entrepreneurs like Salgado and Fr. Matías Octavio, and by the Royal Philippine Company. Two of the products would become important in the nineteenth century: indigo (for a while) and sugar (to the present). An effort was also made to stimulate and keep alive native manufactures, especially textiles. And the combined effect of the tobacco monopoly and the domestic operations of export producers, including the company, was the start of agricultural specialization in the Philippines. Previously, most regions had grown what they consumed, but now certain areas began to concentrate on the planting of given crops and to depend on other areas for items of consumption. This made for greater internal trading and marked the country's progression in the direction of an export economy.

Finally, the company foreshadowed the commercial operations of foreign firms in the following decades. Its practice of making monetary advances, probably the first such advances on a large and organized scale, placed ready money in the hands of native Filipinos and laid the economic foundation for the rise of a native middle class. The profits of trade no longer went predominantly to a few privileged Spaniards and Creoles in the galleon trade but also to native producers of export crops in many areas of the country. These Filipinos were to form the educated, aspiring class that was increasingly to demand reforms and liberal government, and finally national independence, in the nineteenth century.

After
the Galleons

Part 2

The Rise of Domestic Exports
in the Nineteenth Century
and Associated Changes

The Philippines was developed considerably during Spanish rule,

and especially during the nineteenth century,

as Spain gradually let down the bars to external trade

and the entry of foreigners into shipping, hemp and sugar buying,

and the lines of internal commerce

upon which internal development was dependent. . . .

He who studies Philippine history with care will learn

to be less contemptuous of the present state

of industrial development in the Philippines

and of the present social status of the Filipinos.

—JAMES A. LEROY (1905)

Overleaf: A print of nineteenth-century Manila from M.C.L. Domeny de Rienzi, *Oceanie au Cinquième Partie du Monde*, vol. 1 (Paris; Fermin Didot Frères, Editeurs, 1836).

CHAPTER 4

Foreign Trade in the Nineteenth Century: Levels, Commodities, and Geographic Distribution

From the commercial point of view the Philippines is an Anglo-Chinese colony with a Spanish Flag . . .

—*Carlos Recur (1879)*

In this and the next chapter, the course of Philippine foreign trade in the nineteenth century will be reviewed and several features connected with it will be examined for the light they may throw on changes occurring in the country's economy. It will be seen that from a fairly varied assortment of exports, if at low levels, in the first quarter of the nineteenth century a trend soon emerged toward greater concentration on a few exports, and two commodities—sugar and abaca—accounted for more than half of exports by midcentury and for two-thirds to four-fifths later. Together with two other items—tobacco and coffee—they made up late in the century as much as 90 percent of total exports.

In the decade and a half before midcentury, this trend was helped along by external events, government policies, and trade practices. The abolition of slavery in the West Indies and the consequent fall in sugar output there stimulated the Philippine sugar trade in the mid-1830s. Spain allowed leaf tobacco to be exported for the first time

93

in 1837, and American merchants instituted more competitive trading conditions in abaca in 1848, as will be seen. Just after midcentury, the Australian gold rush of 1851 increased the demand for Philippine exports, especially sugar.

At the same time, certain exports that had started strongly early in the century lost their ranking. Indigo, once the leading export item, fell unevenly but steeply in a long contest with aniline dyes, and rice changed from a major export to an import item. Minor products were marginalized, either by losing their relative importance or by falling in absolute value. On the import side, one commodity group, textiles, assumed a substantial share of the total from the first years for which statistics are available, accounting for one-third to three-fifths of total imports until the third quarter of the nineteenth century. These pushed the domestic home-weaving industry into decline.

Concurrently, there was up to a point an increase in the geographic concentration of trade. Britain, the United States, and China were the main trading partners. Contrary to standard colonial patterns, the Philippines was not economically complementary to the metropole, Spain, which took only a minor share of its foreign trade.

The combined effect of the commodity and geographic concentrations of trade made the country economically dependent on a few products and trading partners. Over time, certain major domestic needs came to be filled by the import trade rather than local production. Such changes, it will be argued, indicated a transformation of the country from a subsistence economy, largely self-sufficient for its ordinary needs and wants, to an agricultural export economy, concentrating on the production of a few cash crops for sale in the markets of the world and depending for its economic viability (and the provision of a good part of its basic necessities such as food and clothing) on foreign trade instead of direct local production. These considerations constitute the starting point for identifying and investigating the agents through which the changes occurred.

End of the Mexican Trade and the Crisis of Manila's Commerce

Even before the end of the eighteenth century, fundamental changes were taking place in the currents of Asian trade that would affect the role of Manila and with it the state of Philippine trade in general. Manila's position as the predominant port in East Asia, established by the galleon trade and fed for more than two centuries by commercial flows from Fujian and the Bay of Bengal, began to erode. Reference has already been made to the fall in demand for the galleons' cargoes in Spanish American markets and the rise in prices in the sources of supply. More threatening to this position was the rise of new trade flows involving new commodities between Canton and Europe, which reduced or eliminated the need for specie movement. With the industrial revolution, Britain sent textiles to India in exchange for opium and opium (which China tried to ban in 1800) to Canton in exchange for a commodity quickly coming into favor, namely, tea.

This resulted partly from the growing prosperity of the British middle class and partly because tea, as the only available item of general consumption that did not compete with home manufactures, benefited from the Commutation Act of 1784, which lowered tariffs on it from 100 to 12.5 percent. The East India Company concentrated its purchases on tea, although the traditional trade in silk, porcelain, and lacquered goods continued, increasingly carried on by private merchants, and in its last years tea was its sole export from China, providing its entire profit and about 10 percent of England's total revenue.

Thus, the Pacific-oriented silk-for-silver trade of Fujian was overshadowed by the European-oriented tea-for-opium trade of Canton, which superseded Manila in preeminence in the Southeast Asian trade during a period that straddled the turn of the century. In a letter to a correspondent written in November 1813 (during the war of 1812), the firm of Bryant & Sturgis in Boston gave instructions that if a vessel could not get into China for a cargo of tea it should be given funds to call at Manila to load indigo, sugar, saltpeter, or anything else of value. "Indigo will pay well under any circumstances, but Teas, sir, Teas are [the] no [sic] plus ultra of Mercantile profit . . . ."[1]

With the end of the Napoleonic Wars, a new and better era seemed to dawn for the foreign commerce of the Philippines. When peace was made in 1814, it was stipulated that ports in the colonies that still remained under certain restrictions would be opened to the ships of all nations and that European aliens would be allowed to settle in those ports. This put an end of the exclusive limitations that had characterized the European colonial system, which Spain was the last to abandon. The concession given in 1809 to an English firm to establish itself in Manila, probably due to the Spanish Cabinet's close ties with the English after 1808, was thus made applicable to all foreign westerners.[2] (It has already been noted that western merchants began operating in Manila in the late eighteenth century in connection with the activities of the Royal Philippine Company.)

It was necessary to secure permission in every case in which a foreign business wished to establish itself in Manila, but this requirement seems to have had only a slight deterrent effect. Within a few years, as will be seen, several foreign merchants had settled in Manila and were trading actively. Completely free access to the city by ships of all nations was likewise theoretically impossible while the privileges of the Philippine Company were maintained, but this does not seem to have caused any particular difficulty to foreign ships wishing to enter the port, partly because the privileges were largely concerned with the direct trade between the Philippines and Spain and partly because the company had in practice long since ceased to enjoy certain other privileges.

At the time of the Congress of Vienna, therefore, the prospect for Philippine foreign trade, with the major powers at peace, was not unfavorable, in part because the long-standing trade with Mexico was expected to continue and three elements had at least the potential to participate in it: state-sponsored enterprise, in the form of the Philippine Company; the Manila merchants, who had fallen heir to the trade route of the recently suppressed Acapulco galleons; and the newly admitted foreigners.

Events conspired, however, to remove the first two elements within a few years. The confirmation in 1814 of the company's 1803 charter was little more than a dead letter, and its attempts to resume trading suffered from the encroachments of others on its privileges. The withdrawal of these privileges by the Spanish Cortes in 1820 dealt it a death blow; any voyages undertaken after this were no more than the last feeble gasps of a moribund organization.

The Manila merchants, who took over the trade with Mexico and other points in Spanish America with the suppression of the Acapulco galleon trade (decreed in 1813 and accomplished in 1815) seem to have begun with a fairly favorable outlook. The company was on the wane, and they had contacts both in Asia and Spanish America and a trade of sizable proportions involving the flow of large amounts of goods and specie, although considerably less than in the best days of the galleons. To Acapulco they sent a corvette in 1814, two frigates in 1815, a frigate and a brigantine in 1816, two frigates and a brigantine in 1818, and a frigate in 1820.[3]

The situation seemed to be that the ports of San Blas, Guayaquil, and Callao were open to private traders from Manila, there was an export quota of 500,000 pesos, and the distribution of licenses under this quota was a function of the Consulado. Comyn's oft-cited figures for 1810[4] and the official statistics for 1818[5] permit a glimpse into this trade and a comparison with earlier years.

It is immediately apparent that there was a serious decline in the level of the trade with Mexico (the 1818 report lists three vessels as going to Acapulco, although the designated Mexican terminus was San Blas). Total trade with New Spain in 1810 had a median value of 3,325,000 pesos, consisting of 2,225,000 in imports and 1,100,000 in exports. In 1818, the values were only slightly more than a quarter of their 1810 level, 26.86 percent to be exact. Total trade with Mexico then amounted to 892,979 pesos, of which 356,157 represented imports and 536,822 exports. (Even if for any reason the 1818 figures are understated by half, the level would still be far below that of 1810.)

The importance of the Mexican trade relative to the country's total trade also seems to have declined due to a shift in the import component. In 1810, the Mexican trade accounted for 32.84 percent of total trade; this had been reduced to 20.62 percent by 1818. Moreover, its relative importance in the import and export components was reversed. In 1810, it accounted for 41.74 percent of total imports and 22.94 percent of total exports; in 1818, it accounted for only 11.4 percent of total imports but rose to 44.53 percent of total exports.

Another difference was that, whereas in the previous year there had been an import balance (as in most years of the galleon trade) of 1,125,000 pesos, in 1818 there was an export balance of 180,665 pesos. This may have been due to the fact that the new private trading arrangement was just getting under way and that the rising value of the cargoes sent as this trade developed exceeded the proceeds from the sales of earlier cargoes. Pointing to this conjecture are heavy imports in the same year from India, China, and Macao, most of which, if earlier practice is any index, were destined for reexport to the New World. These imports amounted to 2,136,606 pesos, or 68.37 percent of total imports; India alone accounted for 1,421,904 pesos or 45.5 percent of total imports.

In one main aspect, however, the Mexican trade in 1818 was similar to that of an earlier era. It was still overwhelmingly a transshipping operation. Of exports to Mexico amounting to 536,822 pesos, 482,116 pesos, or 89.81 percent, were reexports of Asian goods and only 54,706 pesos, or 10.19 percent, were native Philippine goods, all textiles. In fact, all of the country's reexports were accounted for by this trade. Of imports from Mexico amounting to 356,157 pesos, 327,312 pesos, or 91.9 percent were in specie and 28,845 pesos, or 8.1 percent, were in goods.

The Mexican trade accounted for the major portion of the trade carried on national vessels (practically synonymous in those early days with that carried by local merchants). Practically all their exports—536,822 out of 551,465 pesos or 97.34 percent—were sent to Mexico, the remaining 2.66 percent (representing 14,643 pesos) going to Macao, India, and the capital of the then independent sultanate of Sulu, Jolo (in that order of importance). A goodly portion of the import trade on national vessels—356,157 of 936,827 pesos or 38 percent—was also accounted for by the Mexican trade. Thus, of total trade amounting to 1,488,292 pesos carried on national vessels, 892,979 pesos, or 60 percent, were accounted for by the Mexican trade.

The local merchants in 1818 therefore enjoyed a large share in the country's foreign trade. National vessels accounted for 1,488,292 pesos out of a total trade of 4,330,965 pesos or 34.36 percent. Their share of the import trade was 936,827 out of 3,125,315 pesos or 29.98 percent; of the export trade, it was 551,465 out of 1,205,650 pesos or 45.74 percent. And, as has been suggested, there seem to have been good prospects for an increase.

Two features connected with the export trade to Mexico deserve more than a cursory glance. The first is that native Philippine textiles formed a part of it and constituted 4.54 percent of total Philippine exports in 1818. This seems to indicate a continuing Spanish interest in encouraging the Philippine textile industry, the presence of a market for Philippine textiles in Spanish America, or both. The other is that the portion of trade in the hands of domestic merchants was primarily a transshipping business, and the maintenance of this sizable share seems to have been dependent on the market for Asian reexports in the Americas. Outside of the native textiles mentioned above and the small cargoes sent to neighboring countries, they seem to have had little interest in developing any significant native exports. They might have begun to do so if the transshipping business had continued long enough for them to build up some surplus investment funds.

But there was never an opportunity to put this to the test, for Manila's days as an entrepôt in the Asian-American trade were numbered. The standard of revolt had been raised in Spanish America, and the wars of independence in the colonies had reached their final phases. These disturbances in themselves would have been enough to disrupt the trade between the newly independent countries on the one hand and Spain and her remaining colonies on the other.

But the body blow that was dealt the Manila-Mexico trade was a specific incident, although it was connected with the general movement for independence. In February 1821, Agustín de Iturbide, then a royalist officer, later to be proclaimed emperor of Mexico, and still later to be shot for treason (all in a space of less than four years), seized the proceeds of the sales of the Manila frigate *Santa Rita* in Chilpancingo while they were being conveyed to San Blas in order to pay his troops and meet other expenses. Paul Proust de la Gironiere, the French doctor-entrepreneur who had married a rich widow in Manila, describes the distress occasioned by this incident to himself and his wife, whose entire fortune was tied up in the venture. Overnight, investors in the Mexican commerce were ruined. In 1822, the brigantine *El Feliz* arrived at Acapulco to claim the money seized by Iturbide, without success. Early accounts (including Gironiere's) gave somewhat exaggerated estimates of the amount seized, but recent research places it at 525,000 pesos. Moreover, it appears that, once Mexican independence had been achieved, official provisions were adopted to repay what may have been Mexico's first recognized external debt. Whether this was ever fully accomplished is in doubt, as in 1831 there was still a claim for 100,000 pesos from just one Manila merchant.[6]

The days of the flourishing entrepôt trade were over. In 1825, the only commerce with Mexico consisted of 7,352 pesos' worth of specie imports, and 48,151 pesos' worth of exports, of which only 30,573 went to Acapulco, the rest going to a sparsely populated "outer province" (*provincia exterior*) called California.[7] This represented a trade of 55,503 pesos, or only 6.22 percent of the 1818 level and 1.67 percent of the 1810 level.

The blows that befell the Philippine Company and the merchants of Manila in 1821 took them out of serious contention for leadership in the foreign commerce of the Philippines, and the initiative passed to the hands of the foreigners, who were to hold it for the balance of Spanish rule (and, indeed, well into the twentieth century). The Spanish government continued to be interested in encouraging Philippine commerce, and a royal order of March 7, 1820, granted duty-free entry for ten years to Philippine products taken to Spain in national vessels.[8] However, at this time the Manila merchants did not seem to have much interest in the trade with Spain. They had never made much use of their lading privileges on the Philippine Company's ships. The wealthier ones had probably been crippled by Iturbide's seizure. And such of them as were interested in the direct trade with Spain ran into the company's privileges, even as it was winding up its affairs, and had to secure the consent of the liquidators to make their shipments.[9] It is ironic that the company's privileges should have caused such difficulties for Spanish nationals while they seem not to have bothered the foreigners.

Still another restriction on Philippine commerce, besides the legal inability or practical unwillingness to send ships to Europe, was that licenses issued to vessels of Philippine registry for the Asian trade required them to return directly to Manila from their destinations. This occasioned the loss of many opportunities to carry goods from one Asian port to another. This practice was finally eliminated during the term of Governor Pascual Enrile, first by an order granting Philippine vessels sailing permits for up to two years without requiring them to state their ports of destination and second by giving Philippine vessels the freedom to navigate freely wherever they pleased. This was confirmed by a royal order of July 17, 1834.[10]

But the local merchants never regained their former standing. John Wise, a young English merchant, reported from Manila in 1837 that "compared with the size and trade of the place, the Spanish merchants are few in number and their transactions small; the principal are to China and the islands to the southward and in produce at this place." Half a decade later, Sinibaldo de Mas gave his opinion: "The old merchants of Manila are not versed in this mode of operations [foreign trade by bills of exchange] for their only schooling was received in the Acapulco galleon trade; the young ones in general lack funds, connections and an enterprising spirit."[11] And toward the midcentury mark a former Belgian consul to Manila wrote:

> The Spanish firms established in Manila have for the most part only very limited capital and many of them, in order to maintain themselves or to undertake any ventures, have to resort to the funds of the religious corporations (obras pias) which they borrow at 5 percent annually. The business of these firms consists in the claying of sugar and the purchase of export products which they procure by means of agents whom they have in the provinces; others devote themselves exclusively to equipping the vessels which navigate regularly to China and Singapore.[12]

There were a few Manila merchants who continued to be active in certain lines down to the end of the period under study, and some of them will be mentioned in a later chapter. But Spanish efforts to link the island colony more closely to the mother country by means of increased trade were based on the delusion that this trade could be built up in competition with that carried on with other parts of the world.

This was unrealistic for several reasons. The first is that navigation was dangerous for Spanish vessels in the South Atlantic in the decade of the 1820s because it was infested with South American corsairs. The second is that Spain lagged behind the more active and industrial countries in terms of purchasing power and therefore was not as flourishing a market for Philippine goods. Even that portion of Philippine exports which it took, consisting mostly of tobacco, was not taken in free competition on the open market but by the agency of a government monopoly. The third reason is that Spain itself was racked with the intermittent Carlist Wars and almost constant civil dissension during much of the nineteenth century, which not only further reduced its ability to buy Philippine exports but also severely limited its capacity to participate in the Philippine import trade until fairly late in the century. Vicens Vives remarks that intolerance, dogmatism, pride, and sectarianism produced a continuous atmosphere of civil war, which from 1808 to 1876 consumed the country and paralyzed its economic development. The fourth reason is that two of the major commodities that the Philippines exported—sugar and tobacco—were available in better quality from sources much closer to home, Cuba and Puerto Rico.[13] It is little wonder, then, that policies designed to foster Spanish-Philippine trade had little effect for a long time.

Change in the Nature of Philippine Trade

The same events that led to the collapse of the trade with Mexico brought about a change in the nature of Philippine trade—from the commerce of a mere entrepôt to one consisting largely of native products. In 1810, the median value of imports was 5,330,000 pesos, but only 900,000 pesos' worth, or 16.89 percent, became available for local consumption. Of exports, with a median value of 4,795,000 pesos, only about 500,000 pesos' worth, or 10.4 percent, consisted of native products; almost nine-tenths of the export trade was made up of reexports.[14] In a total trade amounting to 10,125,000 pesos, therefore, only 1,400,000 pesos, or 13.83 percent, represented imports for domestic use and local exports.

In 1818, the situation was a transitional one. Of total exports of 1,205,650 pesos, local products accounted for 723,534, or 60 percent, and reexports from China and Asia accounted for only 482,116, or 40 percent.[15] This was quite a sizable proportion, however, and had the Mexican trade continued it might have increased, although not at its former level. Iturbide's seizure eliminated any such possibility, and by 1825 it is safe to surmise that the bulk of Philippine exports consisted of native goods.

The proportion of imports figuring in the entrepôt trade in 1818 cannot be specifically stated. A rough estimate would place them at around 43 percent or about the same proportion that the entrepôt trade occupied among exports. This figure was arrived at by comparing the figures for imports from India and China (including Macao) for 1818 and 1825 on the assumption that the figures for the latter year represent imports largely for domestic use. Subtracting their value from the corresponding figures in 1818 gives the value of imports that were earmarked for the reexport trade. The value of specie imports was subtracted in the one case in which it appeared (imports from China in 1825), primarily to show more clearly the movement of commodities but also because such imports probably arrived on British or American ships (the Chinese did not bring money into the Philippines but rather took it away). The result was the following:

Value of Commodity Imports (pesos)

Year	From China	From India
1810	1,150,000	1,150,000
1818	714,702	1,421,904
1825	624,843	179,535

Imports from both India and China totaled 2,136,606 pesos in 1818 and only 804,378 in 1825. The difference, 1,332,606 pesos, can be taken as representing the magnitude of imports for the entrepôt trade in 1818.[16] It should be stressed again that this is no more than a rough estimate.

It will be noticed that, whereas there was a continuous decline in imports from China, those from India in 1818 increased by 23.64 percent over their 1810 level. This may have been because Indian goods had come into greater esteem than those from China. The Philippine Company said as much in 1813.[17] It should be remembered that it had not yet received its quietus of 1818, and therefore part of the Indian goods may have been imported for its account. However, the China trade was more solidly grounded, and after the Mexican entrepôt trade was gone China imports in 1825 fell by only 12.57 percent whereas India imports fell by 87.37 percent. (Contributing to this result was the destruction of India's home textile industry by British imports.)

Turning to more general developments, it will be seen in table 1 that there was a steep decline in the value of the Philippine foreign trade between 1810 and 1825, the level of trade in the latter year being only 28.21 percent of that in the former. The decline seems to have been more severe in exports, which fell to 20.98 percent of the 1810 level, than imports, which fell to 34.71 percent.

Hidden behind these figures, however, was a trend of great importance, namely, a continuous rise from 1810 in the value of domestic Philippine exports. Abstracting from monetary movement, and on the assumption (supported by internal evidence in the statistics) that Philippine exports from 1825 on consisted largely of local products, the trend is clear from the following figures.

	Value of Domestic Philippine
Year	Commodity Exports (pesos)
1810	500,000
1817	529,273
1818	723,534
1825	843,834
1827	1,093,610
1828	1,475,034
1829	1,397,623
1830	1,497,621

These figures show that 1818 exports of native goods were almost 45 percent greater than in 1810, while 1825 exports were 16.63 percent above their 1818 level, which by 1828 had more than doubled.[18]

The export trade in domestic Philippine products, an outstanding feature of the Philippine economy until recently, was finally under way. Azcárraga called it the beginning of "the true prosperity of the Philippines." It took place in a crucial decade, that of the 1820s, which saw the establishment in Manila of several western firms, many of which were shortly to attain great importance (some will be mentioned in a later chapter), and the beginning of western dominance in Philippine foreign trade. In fact, it was no accident that the two trends—the rise in native Philippine exports and the beginning of western dominance in Philippine commerce—should have coincided, for the westerners from the beginning showed much more interest in purchasing local products than had the Manila merchants or the Spaniards (with the possible exception of the Philippine Company). In

1818, their ships carried 65 percent of the total trade—70 percent of the imports and 54 percent of the exports. More significant, however, is the fact that they carried the vast bulk of the native exports; of 723,534 pesos' worth of such exports, they carried 654,185 pesos' worth or 90.5 percent. They carried no reexports. By 1825, they were carrying 74 percent of the total trade—77 percent of the imports and 68 percent of the exports.[19]

The 1818 exports, while they showed the increased relative importance of native products, also showed the undeveloped state of domestic agriculture. The leading export item was white birds' nests, to the value of 301,568 pesos, which exceeded the combined value of exports of sugar, indigo, hemp, cordage, coffee, and rice, all of which were to figure prominently in the country's export trade in later years. More than half the total value of domestic exports consisted of such items (most of them requiring little processing) as birds' nests, bêche-de-mer, wax, tortoiseshell, seashells, dried shrimp, and sharks' fins, almost all of which were destined for the China market.[20]

A comparison of 1818 exports of certain products with those given by the Philippine Company for an earlier period suggests that 1818 may have been a year of depressed agricultural exports. Although domestic products had attained in that year a relative importance they had not had since the advent of Spanish rule, there are indications that the absolute level of certain exports, and perhaps of total domestic exports, was below that of the heyday of the company. This is not surprising, as the company had by this time ceased operations in the field of direct encouragement of agriculture and manufactures for a decade and a half, and the western merchants, who were just beginning to familiarize themselves with the country, had not yet begun large-scale operations in earnest.

Philippine sugar exports in the fifteen and a half years between 1786 and mid-1802 showed an annual average of 17,267 *piculs* (Azcárraga claims that sugar exports in 1782 were 30,000 *piculs*, and it has been seen that Governor Berenguer de Marquina reported sugar exports of between 40,000 and 50,000 *piculs* in 1789); by 1818, these had been reduced to 14,405 *piculs*. Liquid indigo exports, an item in the China trade, had decreased in the same period from 2,997 *quintales* yearly to 1,105. Indigo, however, showed an increase—the only commodity to do so; from 2,014 *quintales* annually in the earlier period, it had risen to 3,200 *quintales*. It should be borne in mind, however, that figures for the earlier period include the years in which production was first stimulated, and it is reasonable to surmise that annual exports in the later years of that period were above average. The increase, therefore, may not be as great as the figures indicate in this case, and conversely the decrease may be greater in the case of the other commodities. It should be noted in connection with indigo that it was a product much sought after by foreign merchants (e.g., Bowditch procured some during his 1796–97 visit), which may account for its holding up quite well relative to other commodities. The same was true of sugar, which nevertheless suffered a decline. In the case of cotton, the annual average export during the five and a half years between 1796 and mid-1802 (assuming that all the company's purchases of it were exported) was 1,223 *piculs*; this had declined to 1,176 *piculs* by 1818 (1 *picul* = 63.262 kilograms; 1 *quintal* = 46.009 kilograms).[21]

	Annual Average	
Commodity	1786–1802	1818
Sugar (*piculs*)	17,267	14,405
Liquid indigo (*quintales*)	2,997	1,105
Indigo (*quintales*)	2,014	3,200
Cotton (*piculs*)	1,223*	1,176

*Annual average, 1796–1802

After 1818, the trends followed by the various products diverged. Cotton seems to have reached its peak early in the following decade, when in one year more than 5,000 *piculs* were exported to China. The 1825 report mentions cotton and sugar as the country's two principal exports. After that, it suffered a decline. In 1846, cotton exports were 2,174 *piculs*; in 1847, 1,924 *piculs*; in 1856, 80 *piculs*; and in 1864, 101 *piculs*. By 1867, they were so insignificant that they did not merit a separate listing in the annual customs report.[22] It was a doleful ending for one of the Philippine Company's favored exports.

Indigo exports evidently attained their highest quantity levels late in the decade of the 1820s; in 1829 and 1830, they were 16,237 and 19,062 *quintales*, respectively. They were never to reach these levels again. In those same years, sugar reached new peaks, with 120,274 and 138,387 *piculs*, respectively, and was on its way to attaining much higher export levels.[23] And a new product was beginning to appear that would also attain great importance in later years—abaca (Manila hemp). Exports in 1818 were 261 *piculs*; in 1824, 2,864 *piculs*; and in 1830, 17,292 *piculs*. On the basis of comparative market prices given by González and Moreno, the indications are that in 1830 indigo ranked as the first export, with sugar, rice, and abaca following in that order.[24]

The outlines of the future were becoming clear, and in 1878 it was possible for Del Pan to write that the situation created from 1825 to 1830 was the same as that which prevailed in his time.[25] Although this was not strictly accurate when applied to the whole economy, as will be seen in the course of this study, it was true enough as regards the general conduct of foreign trade. The qualitative transformation from an entrepôt to a domestically based trade had been completed by 1830 and perhaps even as early as 1825. Commerce was recovering from the shambles of 1821, and an active trade in native exports was under way. Changes in foreign trade for the remainder of the century were largely to be changes in degree rather than kind.

This, however, did not preclude larger economic and social changes. The very solidity of the foundations of the new trade made it the channel through which such changes exerted their leverage on the country. In order to see what these were, and to understand them, an examination of certain features of Philippine foreign trade in the nineteenth century is in order.

The Course of Foreign Trade in the Nineteenth Century

The rise of foreign trade in the Philippines after the low levels plumbed in the 1820s may be seen in table 1. Unfortunately, the statistics are fragmentary before the middle of the century, but enough are available to sketch the main outlines of the picture. The progression shows a gradual rise during several cyclical movements in the first two decades or so after 1830. It is not, however, until 1855 that the level of 1810 is once again attained—almost half a century after Comyn's time. After that year, there is a saltatory rise, and the lowest level of total trade after that is higher than the highest level reached before. After some fluctuations in the 1860s, there is another saltatory rise late in that decade and early in the next one, which is partly obscured by the strange hiatus in the official statistics for the years 1868–71. The previous phenomenon repeats itself: the lowest level of total trade after this saltatory rise is higher than the highest reached before then. While there are ups and downs—two fairly sustained declines occurring in 1872–76 and again in 1880–87, although the last one is much milder and takes place at a consistently higher level—the overall trend remains upward until 1895, following which there is a steep downturn until 1896,

TABLE 1
Foreign Trade of The Philippines, Selected Years, 1810-1897 (in pesos)

Year	Total Trade	Imports	Exports	Balance
1810	(10,125,000)ª	(5,330,000)	(4,795,000)	–(535,000)ᵇ
1817	(4,594,226)	(3,157,783)	(1,436,443)	–(1,721,340)
1818	4,330,965	3,125,315	1,205,650	–1,919,665
1825	2,856,044	1,850,032	1,006,012	–844,020
1827	(2,142,370)	(1,048,680)	(1,093,690)	(45,010)
1828	(3,490,280)	(1,052,760)	(1,537,520)	–(415,240)
1829	(3,512,847)	(2,052,949)	(1,459,898)	–(593,051)
1830	(3,320,158)	(1,740,585)	(1,579,575)	–(161,012)
1831	2,434,157	1,249,148	1,185,009	–64,139
1835	(5,932,250)	(3,158,709)	(2,773,541)	–(385,168)
1836	–	–	(2,965,113)	–
1837	4,016,897	2,060,145	1,956,754	–103,389
1838	5,604,524	2,710,456	2,894,068	183,612
1839	4,827,467	2,153,247	2,674,220	520,973
1840	4,320,336	1,844,424	2,475,942	631,518
1841	5,619,731	2,252,997	3,368,734	1,113,737
1842	5,929,676	2,856,095	3,073,580	217,484
1843	5,113,480	2,191,685	2,923,795	732,110
1844	6,551,704	3,301,312	3,242,392	–56,920
1845	6,955,541	3,934,824	3,020,717	–914,107
1846	5,612,460	2,639,493	2,972,967	333,474
1847	6,558,072	3,429,931	3,126,141	–303,790
1848	6,124,970	3,149,163	2,978,807	173,356
1849	6,167,136	2,443,215	3,723,921	1,280,706
1850	6,751,316	3,178,249	3,573,067	393,818
1851	7,473,608	3,301,334	4,172,274	870,940
1852	8,967,646	3,951,333	5,016,313	1,064,980
1853	9,783,206	4,004,530	5,778,676	1,774,146

ª Figures enclosed in parentheses indicates those derived from sources other than official Philippine customs reports, even if such sources claim to be citing official publications. This is simply to indicate the difference in derivation of such figures, and does not involve any judgement as to the relative reliability of the statistics. Figures in this table derived from other than official sources are those for 1810 (Comyn), 1817 (Pardo de Tavera and John White), 1827-1830 (Meyen), 1835 (De Mas), 1836 (John Wise), 1868-1869 and 1871 (British Consul), and 1896-1897 (Foreman). All except Comyn and the British Consul claim to be citing official customs data. For the year 1870, see note 'd'.

ᵇ A minus sign after a figure in this column indicates an import balance; no sign indicates an export balance.

Table 1 *Continued*

Year	Total Trade	Imports	Exports	Balance
1854	9,036,267	3,756,344	5,279,923	1,523,579
1855	10,710,549	4,773,399	5,937,150	1,163,751
1856	16,092,571	6,959,254	9,133,317	2,174,063
1857	21,803,120	9,907,299	11,895,821	1,988,522
1858	15,193,195	5,798,720	9,394,475	3,595,755
1859	15,354,428	6,271,560	9,082,868	2,811,308
1860	18,248,955	8,739,474	9,509,481	770,007
1861	18,213,690	10,148,160	8,065,530	−2,082,630
1862	16,042,532	6,941,735	9,100,797	2,159,062
1863	17,521,281	7,465,063	10,056,818	2,591,755
1864	21,558,610	10,901,584	10,657,026	−244,558
1865[c]	19,401,570	8,938,261	10,466,309	1,531,048
1866[c]	19,947,157	8,855,895	11,091,262	2,235,367
1867[c]	18,593,829	7,590,427	11,003,402	3,412,975
1868	–	–	(11,771,668)	–
1869	–	–	(14,013,108)	–
1870[d]	(27,794,799)	(12,396,836)	(15,198,263)	(2,601,727)

Continued next page

[c] The original figures for these years are carried in *escudos*, of which there were two to a peso. This fact is noted in *Statistical Bulletin No. 3 of the Philippine Islands* (without giving, however, the peso equivalent of the *escudo* figures) but not in *Census of 1903*, where the original data are carried as if they had been given pesos. All foreign trade values for these years in all the table where they appear in *Census of 1903* are therefore double what they should really be, and users of this source should exercise due care in referring to them.

[d] The figures for these years are taken from Cavada's *Historia*, which reproduces the results of the Spanish Statistical inquires of 1870. The figures of this year given in both *Census of 1903* and *Statistical Bulletin No. 3* seem unduly high and probably were derived from less reliable secondary sources; it has seemed advisable to avoid using them in this study. A rough sort of check on Cavada is provided by English consular calculations of export values, which are of the same order of magnitude as his, as are Tornow's.

Note: Compilers of Spanish-Philippine trade figures have customarily excluded the operations of the Customs bonded warehouse (deposito mercantil). Releases for the domestic market in 1853 were about 6 per cent of current imports, while total transactions were less than 0.5 per cent thirty years later. The early Customs reports (1851-55) contain internal unresolved inconsistencies. The totals were corrected in the 1856 revision, but this leaves individual items in doubt. For example, imports from Singapore in 1854 are given as 291,901 pesos in one table, and 219,961 pesos in another table of the same report, thus resulting in two different totals, neither of which corresponds to the revised total given in the 1856 revision.

Table 1 *Continued*

Year	Total Trade	Imports	Exports	Balance
1871	–	–	(13,317,681)	–
1872	38,593,797	22,163,142	16,430,655	5,732,487
1873	36,740,365	13,217,836	23,533,529	10,304,693
1874	31,007,231	13,704,254	17,302,977	3,398,723
1875	31,135,628	12,216,153	18,920,475	6,705,322
1876	26,824,958	11,987,162	14,837,796	2,830,634
1877	35,870,347	19,522,897	16,347,450	3,175,447
1878	34,703,409	17,285,792	17,417,617	131,825
1879	36,804,466	18,028,739	18,776,727	746,988
1880	48,910,095	25,459,810	23,450,286	–2,009,525
1881	45,350,538	20,771,531	24,579,007	3,807,476
1882	41,926,430	21,255,096	20,675,534	–579,762
1883	47,675,989	21,295,262	26,380,727	5,085,465
1884	43,919,074	21,243,241	22,672,833	1,426,592
1885	43,713,755	19,160,070	24,553,685	5,393,615
1886	45,791,630	20,073,595	25,721,032	5,647,434
1887	42,787,337	17,530,198	25,257,139	7,726,941
1888	47,301,753	21,208,482	26,293,271	5,084,789
1889	59,907,801	24,980,832	34,926,969	9,946,137
1890	46,003,190	19,789,636	26,213,554	6,423,918
1891	48,547,318	21,642,246	26,906,102	5,262,886
1892	51,780,116	23,803,547	27,976,569	4,173,022
1893	62,101,836	25,913,870	36,187,966	10,274,096
1894	61,708,056	28,558,072	33,149,984	4,591,912
1895	62,054,525	25,398,798	36,655,727	11,256,929
1896	(45,950,042)	(17,740,010)	(28,210,032)	(10,470,022
1897	—	(16,350,328)	–	–

Sources: Tomas de Comyn (translated by W. Walton), *State of the Philippine Islands* (London, 1821); T.H. Pardo de Tavera, *Biblioteca filipina* (Washington, 1903); J. White, *History of a Voyage to the China Sea* (Boston, 1823); Yldefonso de Aragon, *Estado que manifiestan la importacion y exportacion 1818* (Manila, 1820); *"Estado que manifesta el numero de buques"* 1825; F.J.F. Meyen, *Reise um die Erde* (Berlin, 1835); *Cuadro general del comercio exterior de...Filipinas...1856*; Sinibaldo de Mas, *Informe sobre el estado de las Islas Filipinas en 1842* (Madrid, 1843); *Centenary of Wise and Company in the Philippines, 1826-1926*; *Statisitical Bulletin No. 3 of the Philippine Islands,* 1920; Census *of 1903, Vol. IV*; British Consular Reports, 1868, 1870, 1871; Agustín de la Cavada, *Historia geografica, geologica y estadistica de Filipinas* (Manila, 1876); J. Foreman, *The Philippine Islands, 2d. ed.* (New York, 1899).

the year of the Philippine Revolution. The highest level, reached in 1893, was about twenty-nine times the lowest level, plumbed two generations earlier in 1827.

The movements described by the figures for total trade are generally followed by those for exports and imports. The former, however, follow an upward trend more consistently than the latter; in fact, exports continue to rise in those years in the 1880s when imports are falling.

The balance of trade before the mid-1830s shows a preponderance of imports; after the mid-1830s, export balances become the rule. The mid-1840s are the last period in the nineteenth century in which any sustained import balances appear. Not too much, however, should be made of these balances, as the trade figures randomly include specie movement and therefore the balance is composed partly of equilibrating factors that act to bridge the gap between exports and imports rather than widen it.

The upward course of Philippine commerce in the nineteenth century is reflected in the ever-increasing tonnage entering Philippine ports for the external export and import trade, as may be seen in table 2. In the late 1830s and early 1840s, shipping tonnage clusters around the fifty-thousand-ton level. Two decades later, it is three times as high, and by the last decade of the century it is eight or nine times as high. (Certain extreme values in the early 1880s are ignored in accordance with the caveat attached to table 2.)

The curious saltatory movements exhibited by the foreign trade figures in the mid-1850s and the late 1860s coincide with certain important events that affected Philippine commerce during those periods. The first of these events was the opening of three additional Philippine ports to foreign commerce in 1855. Previous to that, Manila was the only port open for external commerce, the only exceptions being in connection with the rice export trade, as will be discussed later. By a royal decree of March 31 and an order of the insular government of September 29, the ports of Iloilo, Sual, and Zamboanga were thrown open to general foreign commerce (the last one had previously been a port of call, a "refreshment stop," for whalers). It is difficult to say whether this provoked the saltatory movement of the time. Chroniclers of the event, such as Azcárraga and Sir John Bowring, the former governor of Hong Kong, report that for the first three or four years the results were disappointing, and Jagor avers that up to March 1859 not one of them had been entered by a foreign vessel, although he says nothing about ships of local registry. Azcárraga, however, reports a fair amount of activity in Sual by 1857. The sluggish response reinforces the thesis that the ports were opened as the outcome of a struggle among

TABLE 2
Foreign Trade Shipping Movement in Philippine Ports
Selected Years, 1818-1897

| Year | Entered | | Cleared | |
	Number of Ships	Total Tonnage	Number of Ships	Total Tonnage
1818	55	-	61	-
1824	70	-	71	-
1825	91	-	91	-
1826	99	-	100	-
1827	82	-	79	-
1828	98	-	92	-
1829	119	-	123	-
1830	111	-	111	-
1831	115	-	117	-
1832	136	-	132	-
1833	137	-	141	-
1837	134	48,779	135	47,095
1838	129	35,847	141	38,763
1839	154	41,950	147	42,319
1840	187	56,578	188	57,706
1841	177	55,945	190	60,489
1842	149	46,869	162	50,226
1843	183	58,550	185	59,222
1844	235	78,672	286	76,100
1846	162	51,233	168	56,017
1847	181	62,732	172	58,467
1851	195	75,374	204	79,808
1853	194	84,750	208	86,590
1854	209	94,862	201	93,061
1855	245	140,154	233	123,198
1856	253	137,076	230	142,575

Continued next page

interest groups and that this happened before the export traders were ready to use them. Another port, Cebu, was opened shortly afterward, by a royal decree of July 30, 1860, and the first foreign vessels to enter it were apparently two English ships in 1863.[26]

Another series of events clustered around the other saltatory movement in the late 1860s and early 1870s. A more liberal tariff was

Table 2 *Continued*

	Entered		Cleared	
Year	Number of Ships	Total Tonnage	Number of Ships	Total Tonnage
1857	234	138,399	234	141,316
1858	273	169,437	234	143,995
1859	217	135,892	240	153,253
1860	174	139,063	229	134,177
1861	221	122,805	216	120,563
1862	235	151,583	227	146,082
1863	297	162,224	292	163,386
1864	262	115,757	277	125,070
1865	342	155,532	347	153,675
1866	278	146,286	283	150,792
1867	269	147,120	282	149,738
1872	320	199,072	300	185,073
1873	351	210,793	305	184,549
1874	341	217,169	342	213,325
1875	349	257,221	313	224,075
1876	311	221,800	311	224,538
1877	355	251,657	346	244,887
1878	447	304,358	448	305,938
1879	458	317,069	478	325,695
1880	542	449,927	325	459,412
1881	722	627,272	604	550,018
1882	371	253,421	375	271,998
1883	440	261,371	435	783,250[a]

Continued next page

[a] This extreme value is of dubious authenticity. Whereas the average tonnage in other years of this period is between 700 and 900 tons, the average resulting from this figure is 1800 tons per vessel. The disturbing item consists of 27 ships going to Barcelona with a supposed total tonnage of 603,131 (*Estadistica general*, 1883, p. 177), which would result in an average of 18,633 per vessel. The error may have been one involving the correct placing of digits; 50,000 tons is a much more plausible figure than 500,000 for 27 vessels.

ordained in 1868 and put into effect in 1869 (this will be discussed more at length later). In the latter year, the Suez Canal was opened in the Middle East, which reduced the traveling time to Europe from the three to six months to about a month, and sailings were more frequent.[27] Presumably, there was a reduction in insurance premiums for

Table 2 *Continued*

Year	Entered		Cleared	
	Number of Ships	Total Tonnage	Number of Ships	Total Tonnage
1884	450	328,855	449	318,794
1885	390	314,808	364	303,667
1886	398	316,249	404	333,264
1887	438	359,999	435	345,350
1888	415	383,117	413	388,164
1889	418	419,336	398	388,449
1890	339	334,420	348	357,585
1891	401	387,025	401	404,936
1892	471	517,554	447	484,374
1893	359	392,373	360	411,084
1894	330	397,335	271	358,233
1896	228	357,409	224	347,241
1897	252	385,523	247	360,868

Sources: Yldefonso de Aragon, *Yslas Filipinas* (Manila, 1820); "Estado que en virtud de lo mandado en el articulo 4o de la Real orn de 13 Enero de 1834 se fra de los Buques que han entrado y salido en las islas Filipinas desde el año de 1824 hasta el de 833 con espresion de Naciones procedencias i destinos." Aduana de Manile *legajo* 1830-39, PNA; Sinibaldo des Mas, *Informe sobre el Estado de las Islas Filipinas en 1842*; Jean Mallat, *Les Philippines* (Paris, 1846), II; Jules Itier, *Journal d'un Voyage en Chine* (Paris, 1848); Joseph Lannoy, *Iles Philippines* (Brussels, 1849); "Balanza general," 1847"; *Balanza General*, 1851, 1853; *Balanza mercantil*, 1854, 1855, 1857-1862, 1864-1865; *Estadistica mercantil*, 1867, 1876, 1878, 1879; Jimeno Agius, *El comercio exterior de Filipinas; Estadistica general*, 1880-1894.

ships sailing to Europe. In 1874, the Spanish government began to grant subsidies to its shipping industry, which helped domestic ship-owners in the Philippines.

There were also trends of a more general nature at about the same time. Steam navigation was coming into greater use. Shanghai and Hong Kong were growing in importance in the East Asian trade, the Meiji era had just gotten under way in Japan, and French rule was being extended over Indochina. There was therefore a greater concourse of European vessels in the Far East, especially after the piercing of the isthmus of Suez and the greater speed of steamships had cut the sailing time to Asian waters so drastically. According to Recur, there were about 1,000 European and

American ships plying East Asian waters around 1860; by 1879, this figure had grown to 11,000. Trade in the same period rose from 50 to 400 million pesos. Some of this increased activity in trade and navigation was bound to affect the Philippines.[28]

There were also elements of a monetary nature. For most of the early and middle nineteenth century, the silver peso had been worth more than the gold dollar and had maintained a fairly stable value. There seems to have been a period of appreciation in the late 1850s and a mild fall thereafter to the late 1860s. Then came the plunge. In 1874, gold and silver could be exchanged at par. After that, silver depreciated rapidly, and by the end of Spanish rule it was worth less than half its face value in gold.[29] A complicating factor was the bimetallic character of the Philippine currency. A more detailed view of currency and exchange will be given later.

While depreciation would tend to make exports cheaper and imports dearer, its restraining effect on the latter did not appear to be very great. Although the rate of increase of imports in the 1880s lagged behind that of exports, by 1895 both had just about doubled their 1875 levels. The improvements and economies achieved in European-Asian navigation during the advent of steam, the opening of the Suez Canal, and the increase of trade with East Asia probably served to cushion the effects of silver depreciation on imports, as did the liberalization of tariffs. The increasing value of exports, the growth of population, and a continuing influx of foreign capital in the last two decades of the century (the Manila-Dagupan railroad, for example, was built by a British firm), together with a growing diffusion of liquid wealth in the rising class of Filipinos, must have contributed to keeping up the level of import demand. Probably working in the same direction was the increase in Spain's military establishment toward the last years of its rule in an effort to defuse increasing Filipino disaffection.

Further on, attention will be called to other significant developments that were contemporaneous with the second saltatory movement of Philippine commerce in the nineteenth century and with the cluster of events that occurred at the same time. At this point, a closer look at the composition of trade is warranted.

The Commodity Composition of the Export Trade after 1830

Certain features of the composition of trade deserve notice. Since the import trade was dominated by textiles, to which a separate section will be devoted, only the export trade will be discussed here.

114

Principal Products and Their Movements

During the period under scrutiny (1830–95), the products that figured most prominently among Philippine exports (excluding gold and silver) were sugar, abaca (raw and manufactured), coffee, indigo, tobacco
(leaf and manufactured), dyewoods, and rice. These were the mainstays;
other products were of relatively minor importance. Rice will receive more
extended treatment in a separate section due to its importance and its
shifting position in the country's trade; the present discussion will therefore revolve largely about the other six products (eight if manufactured
abaca and manufactured tobacco are considered separately).[30]

Divergent trends were exhibited by the various commodities. Sugar
and raw abaca enjoyed the most consistent progress, exhibiting an upward
trend to the end of the period. The first rose from an export value of
1,066,628 pesos in 1840 to a high of 16,914,980 pesos in 1893; the latter rose
from 322,396 pesos in 1840 to a high of 14,516,717 pesos in 1894. Coffee
showed the same trend until 1889; from 64,844 pesos in 1840, it rose to
2,474,210 pesos at its peak in that year. (The peak year in quantity exports,
however, was 1883, with 7,662,789 kilograms compared with only 200,514
in 1840). At one time, some was even exported to Brazil—46 kilograms,
worth 10 pesos, in 1867. The industry suffered from the ravages of plant
disease and insects late in the century, and the mortal plunge in the export
figures shows the destruction that overtook it within the space of less than
half a decade. Manufactured tobacco also showed a general increase, although its progression was less steady; from a level of 392,730 pesos in
1840, it rose to 2,265,764 pesos in 1895.[31]

Leaf tobacco showed a rise that was interrupted several times and
moved in a somewhat jagged and abrupt manner. Starting in 1837, the first
peak seems to have been reached in 1857, after which time there was a fall
to 1860. Another rise began then, with its peak in 1870. This cycle slid into
a trough on the eve of the abolition of the government's tobacco monopoly
in 1881 (except for a rather large quantity exported in 1879). After a temporary rise in 1882 and a fall in 1884, tobacco exports finally seemed to enjoy
a steadier progression to higher export levels. It is well to remember that
this was about the time that the Compañía General de Tabacos de
Filipinas, a Spanish firm that took over much of the tobacco trade, began
operations. The value of leaf tobacco exports rose from 116,190 pesos in
1840 to 2,163,292 pesos fifty-five years later.[32]

Manufactured abaca, on the other hand, showed a downward trend
over most of the second half of the century, spread over two cyclical move-

ments (ignoring the extreme values of 1889 and 1890, which seem improbable). There is evidence pointing to a rising trend before 1850. Exports amounted to 3,400 pesos in 1818, 6,831 pesos in 1836, 62,440 pesos in 1847, and 140,905 pesos in 1854.33 It seems to have enjoyed its best years in the late 1850s and early 1860s, after which time there was a decline. There was another brief upsurge in the late 1870s and then a resumption of the descent to insignificance; from the 1860 peak of 326,730 pesos, it fell to only 43,019 pesos in 1894. (The activities of American entrepreneurs in connection with this particular commodity will be discussed in a later section.) Apparently it was more profitable to sell the raw product to factories abroad than to manufacture goods from abaca at home.

Indigo, it has been stated, saw its largest quantity exports in 1829 and 1830. But in 1829 it was reported that Prussian blue had been used successfully in England as a much cheaper substitute, and this affected the indigo trade thereafter. Levels for the rest of the century were lower, and the movement of indigo exports was extremely jagged. It seems to have alternated between boom and bust periods without going anywhere in particular. There seem to have been exceptional peaks in 1844, 1855, 1866, 1877, 1888, and 1892 and exceptional troughs in 1858, 1873, 1883, and 1894. Spasmodic revivals of the industry seem to have taken place in the mid-1850s, the mid-1860s, the middle and late 1870s, the late 1880s, and the early 1890s. Competition from Bengal and Java indigo and aniline dyes apparently worked havoc on exports of this product, but the discredit into which aniline dyes later fell brought about the upsurge of the late 1870s and early 1880s. Some idea of the extreme instability of the movement of indigo exports may be gathered from the fact that the highest value in the second half of the nineteenth century, 241,540 pesos, and the lowest, 12,338 pesos, occurred in successive years, 1857 and 1858.[34]

The most marked cyclical movement is exhibited by dyewood exports. There is clearly traceable a cycle in 1837–53 and another in 1853–63. The period from 1863 to 1895 may be looked on as one extended cyclical movement broken up into minor jags. This product apparently reached its export peak in the 1870s. Its lowest value, 4,631 pesos, was registered in 1863 and its highest, 345,989 pesos, fifteen years later. Its export value in 1895 was only 26,907 pesos.[35]

Average Values of Principal Exports

The average unit value of exports of the four principal products—sugar, raw abaca, leaf tobacco, and coffee—also showed divergent trends, as may be seen in table 3. Sugar, total export values of which showed an upward trend until the end of the Spanish regime, exhibited a general declining trend in its average unit values, which indicates that quantities exported rose at a faster rate than the total value of the exports. There were a few years of high prices in the late 1850s and 1873, when the peak unit value of 160.78 pesos per metric ton was reached. However, by 1895 it had declined to its lowest level, 34.58 pesos per metric ton. As the only principal export experiencing sluggish long-term price trends, it was arguably the major beneficiary of the depreciation of the silver peso beginning in the 1870s.

Raw abaca, on the other hand, showed a rising trend spread over several rather symmetrical cyclical movements. From a low point of 46.29 pesos per metric ton in 1847, it reached a peak of 196 pesos per metric ton in 1889. Evidently, demand for this product grew more rapidly than the supply; the value figures for exports exhibit a faster rate of increase than do the quantity figures.

Unit value figures of coffee exports showed a rising trend over most of the nineteenth century until the blight of the coffee plantations around 1890. The only prolonged break occurred in 1880–86, when quantity exports attained their peak without a corresponding increase in the value figures. From 117.93 pesos per metric ton in 1846, coffee rose to 433.51 pesos in 1891, probably the last normal year in the Philippine coffee trade. The progression to a peak of 590.20 pesos per metric ton in 1894 probably represented scarcity prices that people were willing to pay, and the plummeting of the export unit value to 41.16 pesos per metric ton in the following year probably reflected the destruction of the coffee trade and the deterioration in quality of what little coffee remained.

The movement of unit values of leaf tobacco exports is extremely erratic, as might have been inferred from the quantity and value series. In the second half of the century, there seems to have been a rising trend to the early 1870s, followed by a period of extreme movements, after which there was a decline in the early 1880s and relative stability after that. The stability may have occurred because the private tobacco trade paid more attention to quality than had the government monopoly, which was more intent on revenue from quantity sales and sent to Spain, with half the freight paid by the Manila treasury as a fiscal contribution, 135,000 *quintales* of low-grade tobacco. The questionably low figure for the second half of the century, 13.65 pesos per metric ton, was registered in 1879, and the following year saw the high figure of 885.51 pesos per metric ton, which gives some idea of the instability of that particular period.[36]

Trade figures are taken from Spanish customs reports, and the practice of mixing official prices with appraised values blurs the sharpness of the statistics, which are better taken as reasonable estimates than exact numbers. In the nature of things, this was more likely to apply to imports than to exports, but it is useful to check the export unit values against random price quotations.

Manila: Current Prices of Selected Exports
in Various Years, 1818-1876
(Pesos)

Commodity (unit)	1818	1820	1830	1840	1850	1875 (June)	1876 (Nov.)
Sugar (picul)	7.00	8.00	6.94	5.00	4.375	2.50-4.625	3.125-5.25
Abaca (picul)	4.00	-	5.00	3.875	6.00	7.00-9.50	6.375-6.875
Abaca rope (picul)	6.85	-	4.50	7.00	10.50	12.50-13.00	11.50-12.00
Coffee (picul)	6.60	16.00	6.00	15.75	14.875	22.00-25.00	19.00-20.50
Indigo 1st cl. (quintal)	60.00		80.00	130.00	64.00	50.00	45.00	35.50-36.00
2nd cl. (quintal)			60.00	85.00	56.00	28.00	20.00-25.00	26.00-29.00

Sources: Gonzalez & Moreno, *Manual*, p. 238; *Anuario 1877*, p. 79; Aragon, *Estado...1818*; A. Scarella, "Manila Price Current 17th February 1820," ECPRIHS. For a detailed series on sugar prices see Larkin, *Sugar*, p. 52; for abaca, see Owen, *Prosperity without Progress*, p.52.

The quotations show the general upward tendency in abaca prices, a substantial increase in coffee prices, a steep fall in indigo prices, and a downward drift in sugar prices. Since sugar was in first or second rank among exports throughout the century, this must have resulted from technological improvements in sugar production, especially as regards the efficiency of extraction and techniques of refining. Abaca, on the other hand, was more dependent on price movements than technological improvements for its prosperity.

The Relative Importance of Various Products in the Export Trade

The different exports were of varying importance at different times (gold and silver movements excluded). It has been seen that in 1830 there is evidence to indicate that indigo ranked first, sugar second, rice third, and abaca fourth. By 1836, according to John Wise's report, sugar had assumed primacy in the export trade, a position it was to retain throughout most of the century; rice was second, abaca third, and indigo fourth.[37] A new and important product was added to the Philippine export trade when early in 1837 the export of leaf tobacco was permitted[38] (the export of cigars had been allowed as early as the 1820s, and John Wise puts them fifth in importance). This propelled tobacco (leaf and manufactured) to second place in the Philippine export trade for most of the years in the 1840s for which some figures are available, namely, 1840–42, 1844, 1846, and 1847. Abaca was in third place in those years except for 1840 and 1841, when it seems to have enjoyed a slight resurgence, and 1844, when rice and tobacco outranked it. Fourth place was occupied by indigo in 1842; abaca in 1840, 1841, and 1844; and rice in 1846 and 1847.[39]

In the next decade, abaca (raw and manufactured) displaced tobacco from second place and even gave a foretaste of what it would do at the end of that century and the beginning of the next by temporarily displacing sugar from first place in 1855 and 1858. Tobacco settled into third place, which it was to occupy with only minor interruptions for the next four decades. In the half century, between 1846 and the Philippine Revolution, these three products occupied the top three places among Philippine exports, with only occasional exceptions.

Occupation of fourth place was settled a little later. Rice was fourth in 1855 and 1856, but it gave way to indigo the following year, the last time it was to figure among the four top exports. Then in 1858 there emerged a vigorous newcomer in the leading export ranks—coffee. Rice was to figure in fourth place again in 1860 and 1865, but aside from these interruptions coffee was the fourth-ranking export from 1858 to 1891—fully a third of a century. In fact, it even displaced tobacco from third place in 1877, 1881, and 1887.[40]

For about three decades, from the late 1850s to the late 1880s, then, the four main exports of the Philippines were sugar, abaca, tobacco, and coffee, in that order. Occasional shifts in rank other than those already noted occurred in 1863, when tobacco reoccupied second place, and 1866, 1867, 1870, and 1884, when abaca occupied first place.

119

Philippine sugar received a boost from the emancipation of slaves in the West Indies and the consequent decline of production there. Early in 1834, Captain B. Lockwood wrote to Edward Carrington in Providence, Rhode Island, that sugar in Manila was up to 5 to 5.25 dollars (Mexican) and sugar holders thought prices in Europe would remain high owing to the emancipation. British demand rose for Philippine sugar, and the Foreign Office appointed William Farren in 1844 as the first British consular agent in Manila. One of his duties was to certify that sugar going to Britain was the product of "free labour." When in that year British duties were reduced on "free-grown" sugar, Manila sugar prices rose immediately by 10 percent, but this rise was not sustained. Although exports rose, prices were paradoxically flat or declining, probably reflecting a drop in world sugar prices owing to reduced processing costs.

TABLE 3
Average Unit Values of Sugar, Raw Abaca, Leaf Tobacco and Coffee Exports of the Philippines, Selected Years, 1840-1895 (pesos per metric ton)

Year	Sugar	Raw Abaca	Leaf Tobacco	Coffee
1840	63.23	63.23	163.01	323.39
1841	63.23	63.23	163.01	158.07
1846	49.06	48.64	243.67[a]	117.93
1847	50.22	46.29	480.29[a]	121.77
1854	44.04	115.78	177.31	160.87
1855	43.54	114.19	176.38	184.05
1856	70.05	113.73	197.41	170.88
1857	116.18	90.77	217.34	157.46
1858	77.57	84.89	217.35	199.81
1859	76.67	77.30	215.70	189.35
1860	66.70	67.52	157.73	200.49
1861	64.81	59.00	175.39	197.42
1862	54.37	57.85	308.65	214.09

Continued next page

[a] includes manufactured tobacco

TABLE 3 *Continued*

Year	Sugar	Raw Abaca	Leaf Tobacco	Coffee
1863	61.73	70.04	271.00	264.89
1864	73.83	90.18	418.97	277.22
1865	64.83	105.75	332.78	220.97
1866	69.52	128.80	305.51	245.79
1867	55.76	125.63	299.07	239.67
1870	65.71	187.88	363.60	139.61
1873	160.78	128.98[b]	516.71	348.47
1874	59.93	113.21	464.38	345.42
1876	56.72	102.10	576.17	293.58
1877	71.54	91.48	174.25	316.76
1878	67.78	87.30	576.28	322.98
1879	58.80	95.68	13.65	288.04
1880	62.97	105.34	885.51	363.35
1881	59.40	149.68	441.23	172.36
1882	59.39	149.70	388.18	208.28
1883	61.43	153.55	423.10	168.50
1884	56.31	140.45	443.79	195.35
1885	50.72	124.03	264.10	179.30
1886	48.54	115.04	190.54	189.25
1887	46.56	142.50	194.00	423.10
1888	52.78	134.37	186.42	323.28
1889	54.20	196.00	209.13	397.85
1890	60.92	178.39	182.17	431.33
1891	53.11	156.69	178.88	433.51
1892	44.86	142.61	186.96	467.14
1893	64.75	133.95	222.24	579.87
1894	52.10	150.44	200.69	590.20
1895	34.58	118.23[b]	215.06	141.16

[b] Includes manufactured abaca

Sources: Manuel Azcárraga, *La Libertad de Comercio en las Islas Filipines* (Madrid, 1871); Sinibaldo de Mas, *Informe sobre el estado de las Islas Filipinas en 1842* (Madrid, 1843); Joseph Lannoy, *Iles Philippines*, (Brussels, 1849), appendix; *Balanza general*, 1847; *Balanza mercantil*, 1859; Agustín de la Cavada, *Historia geográfica, geológica y estadistica de Filipinas* (Manila, 1876); *Statistical Bulletin No. 3 of the Philippine Islands, 1920*; *Census of the Philippine Islands, 1903*.

But a fresh boost came from Australia in 1851 at a time when loadings were brisk. "In this state of the market," reported Russell & Sturgis, "news arrived from Sydney of the discovery of Gold in great abundance in that vicinity, and apparently a number of orders were received by various parties, principally for Sugar. This circumstance caused an immediate advance in prices asked by dealers . . . higher prices than has ever before been the case."[41]

Then, in the late 1880s, sugar lost its primacy, and beginning in 1887 it yielded it to abaca, which was to occupy first place for almost a generation with the exception only of the years 1892 and 1893 (and perhaps 1896, for which no official figures are available). While this was taking place, destruction overtook the coffee industry, and in 1892 copra assumed fourth rank—the first step on the road that was to take it to first place after World War II.[42]

In the half century preceding the Philippine Revolution, there is reason to believe that the commodity pattern of the export trade became more concentrated. The four highest-ranking exports, whatever they were in any particular year, made up between 68 and 72 percent of exports in 1842, 1844, and 1846–47; in 1840 and 1841, they were around 83 percent. In 1855, the figure rose to 93.98 percent; a decade later, it was 78.87 percent; a decade after that, it was 94.33 percent; in 1885, it was 84.37 percent; and in 1894 it was 93.65 percent.

Table 4 shows the proportion of exports accounted for by sugar, abaca, tobacco, and coffee from 1840 to 1895. The total percentages of the four products range from 56 to 95 percent. Up to 1866, there is no year in which the total exceeds 87 percent. From 1867, however, the total percentages do not fall *below* 87 percent except in five out of the twenty-five years for which data are available. It will be seen in table 4 that this increase in relative importance is due to the two ranking exports, sugar and abaca, since tobacco and coffee decline in relative importance after 1870.

Two comments should be made on table 4 and the data it contains. The first is that, since coffee is taken to represent the fourth-ranking export, the combined percentage total for the four top products is understated in those years in which coffee ranks below fourth place. For the relevant period (1840–95), these years are 1840, 1842–47, 1855–57, 1860, 1865, and 1892–94. The figures for the 1840s, 1855, 1865, and 1894 have already been given. The rest are as follows: 1856, 82.22 percent; 1857, 82.17 percent; 1860, 80.38 percent; 1892, 93.68 percent; and 1893, 94.15 percent.[43]

This does not affect the argument adversely. On the contrary, it strengthens the impression that there was an increase in product concentration in the export trade between the 1840s and the 1890s. Over the whole period, the argument can be rephrased slightly by stating that before 1867 the four top-ranking exports exceeded 87 percent of total exports in only two out of the eighteen years for which data are available (1854 is not counted, as data for certain exports are not available). From 1867, the statement stands that they never fell below 87 percent except in five of the twenty-five years for which data are available. Obviously, the modal values are higher in the later period. The argument that the two top-ranking exports, sugar and abaca, show a relative increase in the later period is also unaffected by the changes in detail.

The second comment on table 4 is somewhat more serious. Since gold and silver movement is included in the Philippine foreign trade statistics for most of the nineteenth century, a heavy outward movement of specie would, by accounting for a good percentage of total export value, drive down the percentage credited to commodity exports proper. This is in fact what happened in some years. In 1858, exports of gold and silver coin were 22.4 percent of total exports, and in 1861 they were 10.45 percent; in 1890, silver coin exports were 9.88 percent.[44] If the same phenomenon were present in the early years, the argument postulating a growing product concentration of exports would be seriously impaired.

This is not so, however. In 1846, specie exports were only 2.73 percent of total exports; even adding gold dust, the figure reaches only 7.67 percent. In 1847, the percentages are even less; coin exports take up only 1 percent of total exports and together with gold only 4.63 percent. In each case, there is a margin of more than 20 percent of total export value that is accounted for by commodities other than the four ranking exports and gold and silver movement. In later years, the margin is much less.

While this does not do away with the disturbing effect of specie movement, which in some years is lumped together with the movement of gold and silver in bars, dust, decommissioned jewels, and the like, it does support the view that there was an increase in concentration in the product composition of the Philippine export trade in the last half century before the Revolution and behind that quite probably a growing specialization in the production of export crops for the Philippine economy as a whole.

The Geographic Distribution of Trade

The geographic distribution both of individual commodities and of trade as a whole serves, like the commodity distribution of trade, to point to certain elements of change as well as stability in the country's external

TABLE 4
Sugar, Abaca, Tobacco, and Coffee Exports, 1840-1895
(percentages of total exports)

Year	Sugar	Abaca (Leaf and Manufactured)	Tobacco (Raw and Manufactured)	Coffee	Total
1840	38.54	14.38	18.39	2.34	73.65
1841	32.98	11.94	23.75	1.49	70.16
1842	27.11	13.68	20.14	3.72	64.65
1844	28.72	10.44	14.22	3.35	56.73
1846	34.44	13.04	18.50	2.87	68.85
1847	37.29	12.59	18.40	3.37	71.65
1854	33.07	24.18	17.11	2.16	76.52
1855	26.83	43.62	13.66	1.70	85.81
1856	38.61	29.78	15.53	2.24	86.16
1857	36.19	23.37	20.52	1.62	81.70
1858	22.73	24.75	17.32	3.12	67.92
1859	38.52	21.79	20.63	3.32	84.26
1860	40.93	22.24	11.71	1.91	76.79
1861	37.41	20.40	14.18	5.11	77.10
1862	37.00	22.56	16.39	2.77	78.72
1863	31.44	21.49	27.31	3.08	83.82
1864	31.20	25.38	17.58	4.69	78.85
1865	29.01	24.58	17.47	3.94	75.00
1866	25.88	30.35	20.14	3.77	80.14
1867	28.42	33.91	20.85	4.87	88.05
1870	30.63	33.21	22.95	2.76	89.55
1873	58.24	22.46	9.65	4.59	94.94
1874	35.11	28.27	20.00	5.70	89.08
1875	48.88	20.51	18.47	6.47	94.33

Continued next page

commerce. With respect to individual commodities, only exports will be discussed here, since imports (as mentioned previously) were so dominated by textiles that this group of commodities will be considered apart.

In connection with the geographic distribution of commerce, certain statistical peculiarities about Philippine foreign trade data in the nineteenth century should be borne in mind in connection with an important component, the China trade, and also with the British and American shares. Hong Kong and Singapore are lumped together under British pos-

Table 4 *Continued*

Year	Sugar	Abaca (Leaf and Manufactured)	Tobacco (Raw and Manufactured)	Coffee	Total
1876	49.91	27.71	8.02	7.50	93.14
1877	53.77	21.86	7.61	8.75	91.97
1878	47.34	24.64	11.89	4.50	88.37
1879	41.21	20.64	7.17	5.95	74.96
1880	48.65	23.37	10.56	7.95	90.53
1881	50.47	36.72	3.28	3.90	94.37
1882	43.22	33.78	12.73	5.64	95.37
1883	45.83	28.97	11.25	4.87	90.92
1884	30.33	31.78	8.00	6.49	76.60
1885	42.18	27.02	11.18	3.99	84.37
1886	34.90	21.78	9.99	5.27	71.94
1887	31.66	42.11	8.02	8.29	90.08
1888	32.32	41.86	12.62	7.73	94.53
1889	35.45	40.81	8.79	7.08	92.13
1890	33.72	34.77	11.46	7.37	87.23
1891	27.29	49.64	10.30	4.58	91.81
1892	40.54	36.03	13.23	2.27	92.07
1893	46.63	34.72	10.94	0.47	92.76
1894	33.11	43.92	9.53	1.07	87.63
1895	32.22	34.62	12.08	0.07	78.99

Sources: Manuel Azcárraga, *La Libertad de Comercio en las Islas Filipines* (Madrid, 1871); Sinibaldo de Mas, *Informe sobre el Estado de las Islas Filipinas en 1842* (Madrid, 1843); Jean Mallat, *Les Philippines, II* (Paris, 1846); Jules Itier, *Journal d'un Voyage en Chine* (Paris, 1848); Joseph Lannoy, *Iles Philippines* (Brussels, 1849), appendix; *Balanza General*, 1847; *Balanza Mercantil*, 1859; Agustín de la Cavada, *Historia geográfica, geológica y estadística de Filipinas* (Manila, 1876); *Census of the Philippine Islands*, 1903.

sessions or British East Indies in the years 1873–87. Before and after that period, Hong Kong is included under the China trade, which in scattered years occasionally included trade with Cochin China and Japan.

The case of Hong Kong, however, is the most serious one because, being a port of transshipment, its trade represented not only commerce with China but also part of that with the United States and European countries. In those years in which it is included under China, therefore, the percentage of trade going to China is obviously overstated; conversely, in those years in which it is separated from the China trade, that trade is understated. In any case, some understatement of the proportion accounted for by the United States occurs, and to a lesser extent this is also true of trade with other countries using Hong Kong as an entrepôt.[45] It is pointless to dwell on the fact that this shifting from one category to another mars the statistical homogeneity of the geographic distribution of commercial data.

Singapore, another large entrepôt, presents similar problems. Much of the trade carried on with it was actually trade with England, other European countries, and India. The proportion of Philippine commerce carried on with England is therefore somewhat understated, as is that with other European countries (except perhaps Spain), which, being much less, is not as damaging to the statistical clarity of the picture. Trade with India completely disappears behind the Singapore screen, although the evidence is that it was quite small by this time.

One reason for these peculiarities is that these two great ports were termini for shipping coming from both Europe and America, in which Manila figured to a much lesser extent. A considerable portion of the trade of the Philippines with other countries, therefore, was carried on through these two places in national bottoms engaged in transshipments to or from foreign vessels. This applied with special force to imports, for Spanish laws gave national bottoms a favorable tariff differential during most of the nineteenth century, with the result that by and large the majority of imports was carried in national bottoms.

The bulk of exports, on the other hand, went out in foreign ships, which preferred entering Manila harbor in ballast to unloading even a single article of importation, which would have subjected them to heavier port dues than those exacted from foreign vessels entering in ballast. As Hong Kong developed, there appears to have emerged a difference in freight charges in its favor, and efforts were made to get Manila traders to ship via that port. But, although this was done occasionally, direct shipments were preferred, especially in the sugar trade, because the breakage in bags and loss in weight of sugar were feared to be heavy and were estimated to exceed the difference in freight.[46]

Individual Exports

One element of stability emerging from an examination of the data for individual commodities is the large role played by Great Britain and the United States. These were the most consistent buyers of the country's exports; furthermore, their purchases were directed toward the ranking exports, sugar and abaca. In 1847, they took 27.38 and 27.86 percent, respectively, of sugar exports; ten years later, they took 19.13 and 17.86 percent; and in 1873 they took 46.42 and 33.81 percent. In the 1880s, the United States surpassed Great Britain in importance in this branch of exports. The British share was 14.91 percent in 1883–87 and 25.1 percent in 1888–92, and the American share was 66.11 and 40.27 percent, respectively. By 1895, however, Great Britain had recovered its supremacy, with 38.99 percent, while the United States had only 17.42 percent. But "China" was listed as having taken 28.19 percent, part of which probably went to the United States.

Great Britain and the United States also played a preponderant role in abaca exports. The American sponsorship of the industry was evident in the overwhelming share of exports of this commodity that went to the United States until late in the century, when Britain took the lead. The American share was 82.11 percent in 1847, 73.52 percent ten years later, 50.6 percent in 1873, 50.4 percent in 1883–87, 26.86 percent in 1888–92, and 32.52 percent in 1895. The British share was 12.65 percent in 1847, 25.17 percent ten years later, 39.27 percent in 1873, 28.07 percent in 1883–87, 46.2 percent in 1888–92, and 31.32 percent in 1895. The decline in the share taken by the United States seems accountable by the rise in the British share until the 1870s; then rising exports to the British East Indies and "China," which included portions of both the American and British trade, obscure the picture. In 1895, for instance, "China" accounted for 32.83 percent, the United States for 32.52 percent, and England for 31.32 percent. It is quite possible that the United States may have been the leader in that year; Hong Kong transshipments to it probably exceeded those to Europe. In that same year, Japan took 1.29 percent of abaca exports.

The United States also accounted for the major share of the indigo trade. In 1847, its share was 67.66 percent, ten years later it was 77.43 percent, and in 1873 it was 39.08 percent. But by then the industry was in a parlous state and indigo had ceased to rank as a major export.

One more element of stability was the overwhelming share of leaf tobacco exports going to Spain, attributable in most years to the government's monopoly of the marketing of this product. In 1847, Spain took 47.8 percent (including manufactured tobacco in this year); ten years later, 85.57 percent; in 1873, 86.73 percent; in 1883–87, 77.44 percent; in 1888–92, 78.46 percent; and in 1895, 66.58 percent.

Other products and countries showed elements of change. Early French interest in coffee, through such men as Gironiere, seems reflected in

France's preponderance in coffee exports before the midcentury mark. In 1846, the French share was 88.23 percent and the following year 67.8 percent. Australia occupied second place, with 9.31 and 28.17 percent, respectively. However, ten years later the French share had declined both absolutely (from 71,446 to 7,201 pesos) and relatively (to 2.76 percent). Australia became the leading Philippine coffee market, with 46.17 percent, followed by the United States with 19.23 percent, "China" with 18.67 percent, Spain with 6.67 percent, and England with 5.39 percent. In 1873, England had assumed the lead, with 49.85 percent, followed by France with 12.72 percent and the French East Indies with 12.3 percent. The United States' share had declined to 6.22 percent and Spain's to 6.11 percent. In the next decade, however, Spain assumed the commanding position in coffee exports. In 1883–87 and 1888–92, its share was 46.31 and 49.86 percent, respectively. In the death throes of the coffee industry, Spain still took a good share, with 43.17 percent in 1895, although first rank was assumed by "China," with 50.23 percent.

Australia occupied an important place for a few years. Besides taking first place in coffee exports in 1857 and second place in 1846 and 1847, it was first in sugar exports in 1847 and 1857 and second in 1846. It was first in rope exports in 1857 and second in 1847. In the seven-year period 1845–51, the quantity of sugar shipped to Australia (955,798 *piculs*) was, according to the commercial accounts, almost as large as the combined total sent to Great Britain and continental Europe (983,396 *piculs*) and far greater than that shipped to the United States (559,829 *piculs*). From the early 1860s on, however, it declined in importance in the Philippine trade.

Before then, Australia seems to have taken an important portion of certain minor processed exports such as cordage, cigars, and hats. For certain years around the midcentury mark for which official figures are not presently available, or where commodities are not geographically segregated in the official customs reports, commercial circulars give some idea of its importance for certain commodities. In 1850, it took nearly half of the exports of hats (9,350 out of 19,025); in 1853, a little over half (37,057 out of 72,584); in 1854, a great majority (57,164 out of 71,424); and in 1855 nearly 40 percent (8,000 out of 21,050). In the latter two years, it also took a large share of cordage exports: 9,750 *piculs* out of 18,088 in 1854 and 9,527 *piculs* out of 23,367 in 1855. It also took a good portion of cigar exports: 34,290 mil out of 79,311 in 1853, 33,999 mil out of 100,267 in 1854, and 26,172 mil out of 86,304 in 1855. By 1872, cigar exports to Australia were down to 2,930 mil and in 1873 to 4,860 mil.

Another frontier area, California, also took a number of minor Philippine exports at that time (in addition to the main staples of the trade): cordage, cigars, hats, maize, garlic, rice (into the 1860s and 1870s), and, most unexpectedly, chicken eggs. A total of 55,450 eggs were sent there in 1850 and 131,400 the following year (out of total chicken egg exports of 184,347 sent to destinations such as Spain, England, Germany, the U.S. East Coast, Cuba, China, Australia, the Dutch East Indies, Singapore, and Oceania). The eggs appear not to have been salted (ducks' eggs, listed separately, are specified as salted) and may have been preserved for the long trans-Pacific voyage by methods known in Mexico such as immersion while still very fresh, preferably the day they were laid, in melted goat's fat just before cooling (if for a few months) or in a 10 percent lime solution (if for more than a year). This unusual spillover from the California Gold Rush reached Philippine poultry farms, and apparently it was worth somebody's while to gather, prepare, and ship the eggs. Even at 75 cents per hundred (apparently an "official" price), the amounts were small: a little over 1,500 pesos for the total, of which just under 1,000 pesos represented sales to California. By 1853, the item had disappeared from the customs returns, either because the egg trade was unremunerative or because closer sources of supply were found.[47]

While rice remained an export, most of it went to China, but there were years in which other markets were supplied. In 1847, for instance, China took 38.95 percent, England 22.74 percent, and Cuba 20.24 percent. High-grade white rice was favored in California.

Manufactured goods fared in different ways. Textiles will be discussed in the appropriate place. The decline of abaca rope has already been mentioned. Early American interest in it is reflected by the United States' top-ranking share in rope exports in 1847, with 40.27 percent. In the following decades, however, the United States was more interested in the raw product and took only an infinitesimal proportion of rope exports, although in 1890 it found itself temporarily in first place again, with 50.81 percent. Manufactured tobacco, on the other hand, fared quite well, and after the extinction of the tobacco monopoly it seems to have acquired greater stability and somewhat increased importance relative to leaf tobacco exports.[48]

The relative importance of various countries in Philippine commerce in the nineteenth century becomes clearer when data on the geographic distribution of total trade as a whole are examined (tables 5 and 6), despite the problems raised by the transshipping trade in Singapore

and Hong Kong. The preponderant part played by the United Kingdom, the United States, and China comes to the fore. Spain remained
in a minor role, although it was able to legislate itself into importance
toward the end. The relative importance of the various countries was
different in the export and import trades, so that separate treatment of
these is necessary.

Total Exports

Before 1850, judging from the scattered data at hand, leadership in
the Philippine export trade changed hands several times. In 1818, when
the country was still under the influence of the entrepôt trade with Latin
America, Mexico occupied first place, with India, the United States, China,
and France (in that order) following far behind but still accounting for sizable shares of the trade. In 1825, after the destruction of the entrepôt trade
with Mexico, the number one export market was China, followed by
Spain, India, the United States, and Macao, in that order. The differences in
level were not very great and point to a fairly well distributed export trade
(although it should be remembered that this was a year of exceptionally
low exports). However, around this time Macao exercised the same effect
on the data concerning the distribution of trade that Singapore and Hong
Kong were to exercise later. Undoubtedly much, perhaps most, of it was part
of the China trade, but there were probably sizable proportions accounted for
by England and the United States, the two countries most active in the Canton trade, and perhaps also India. Some understatement of the Chinese,
American, Indian, and British shares was therefore likely in this year.

In 1846, the export trade already showed signs of more modern conditions. England took the lead, followed by China, the United States,
Spain, and Australia. The differences between the various shares were
greater than in 1825. The following year, the United States foreshadowed
the state of things to come by charging into the lead, with Australia, England, China, Spain, and Singapore following in that order. Between 1847
and 1851, the U.S. share of Philippine exports jumped from 26 to 39 percent. It was perhaps not a coincidence that this followed the introduction
of more competitive practices in the abaca trade in 1848, as will be seen
later. The United States maintained a share above 30 percent for the rest of
the decade.

In the second half of the century, the United States was the most
consistent leader. It was number one in twenty-two out of thirty-nine
years for which data are available. It lost this primacy in two periods: in

TABLE 5.a
Geographic Distribution of Philippine Exports
Selected Years, 1818-1894
By Region
(percentages of total exports)

Year	Europe	Asia	Australasia
1818	13.80	28.84	-
1825	28.61	49.82	-
1841	50.22	24.51	4.78
1842	34.70	31.24	13.48
1844	34.43	41.82	4.30
1846	44.16	28.46	11.48
1847	34.63	20.53	16.79
1851	30.17	15.25	14.61
1853	19.74	19.89	14.65
1854	36.88	11.84	10.20
1855	34.92	23.86	10.52
1856	37.42	11.78	13.58
1857	33.91	17.26	22.71
1858	31.20	35.61	10.41
1859	42.31	18.42	14.78
1860	29.99	29.03	8.82
1861	39.45	27.66	15.44
1862	48.94	19.21	15.09
1863	36.91	48.58	-
1864	42.74	29.31	3.80
1865	34.77	34.90	4.30

Continued next page

the early 1860s, coincident with the War between the States, and again early in the 1890s, following the failure a few years before of the second of the two influential American business houses that went down in successive decades.

Great Britain ranked next as a customer for Philippine exports. It was first in twelve years and generally ranked second except for a few years during the mid-1880s.

"China" and the British East Indies vied for third rank in importance. "China" was first in four years and the British East Indies in one. China's relative importance as a Philippine export market seems to have

Table 5.a *Continued*

Year	Europe	Asia	Australasia
1866	57.16	28.97	-
1867	43.65	20.91	3.25
1873	50.32	16.38	-
1874	44.37	21.70	3.22
1875	53.51	11.83	3.33
1876	38.12	19.91	0.96
1877	41.38	19.97	0.18
1878	34.52	31.65	1.51
1879	33.95	38.86	1.12
1880	30.90	23.89	0.79
1881	42.46	19.41	0.57
1882	45.95	17.11	0.75
1883	33.96	19.45	0.98
1884	35.07	29.40	0.89
1885	29.15	29.92	-
1886	36.57	50.29	-
1887	24.03	29.48	-
1888	35.79	28.40	-
1889	35.29	27.77	0.34
1890	38.65	42.97	-
1891	53.13	21.26	0.05
1892	42.84	39.99	-
1893	54.86	26.02	0.21
1894	38.69	29.62	7.73

declined from what it was in the 1820s. Even in the years in which it is inflated by the Hong Kong trade, it usually ranks below the United States and Great Britain and comes to the fore only occasionally. When it is reflected that most of the trade listed as going to the British East Indies had Great Britain as its ultimate destination, and in 1873–87 also the United States, and when furthermore it is considered that the China trade except in 1873–87 contains within it part of the trade going to the United States and to a lesser extent to Great Britain, the important position of the two English-speaking nations stands out even more prominently.

Spain all through the century took a moderate percentage of Philippine exports, largely in the form of tobacco, for which it was the principal outlet. Its percentage share was modally between 8 and 12 percent. The

TABLE 5.b
Geographic Distribution of Philippine Exports
Selected Years, 1818-1894
By Country
(percentages of total exports)

Year	United Kingdom	China[1]	Br. East Indies[2]	United States	Spain
1818	5.01	9.37	-	10.74	-
1825	4.87	16.71	1.94	13.87	15.26
1841	23.67	14.35	5.00[3]	20.47	20.61
1842	16.62	21.29	7.43	19.37	17.63
1844	15.59	30.63	1.93	18.79	13.14
1846	25.52	21.48	4.01	15.17	12.62
1847	14.77	14.08	4.62	25.89	10.99
1851	15.66	10.16	2.83	38.75	10.70
1853	8.34	15.51	3.74	45.40	9.82
1854	27.52	9.40	1.33	41.04	8.00
1855	19.61	20.00	2.75	30.34	12.21
1856	22.16	9.17	1.04	36.94	14.16
1857	17.64	10.98	5.33	25.92	14.89
1858	18.30	27.78	3.33	22.75	11.16
1859	23.83	13.98	2.06	24.38	15.35
1860	24.85	22.07	4.98	31.35	4.30
1861	32.23	20.90	3.45	17.10	5.37
1862	35.02	15.00	1.35	16.30	12.30
1863	24.50	36.33	11.05	14.42	11.34
1864	36.92	25.91	1.92	24.14	4.95
1865	20.33	30.60	2.82	24.83	12.83

Continued next page

[1] Includes Hong Kong except in 1873-1887
[2] Includes Hong Kong in 1873-1887.
[3] Two thirds of the 'East Indies.'

level of its share in 1825, when it granted duty-free entry to Philippine products, was surpassed in only five years during the remainder of the century. In 1841, its share was a respectable 20.61 percent, undoubtedly reflecting the recently authorized start of leaf tobacco exports, but this declined until the mid-1870s, then shot up to a high point the following decade. Later it dropped again but to a level higher than that of the 1870s.

133

Table 5.b *Continued*

Year	United Kingdom	China[1]	Br. East Indies[2]	United States	Spain
1866	28.95	18.08[4]	9.07	32.59	7.43
1867	30.96	16.98[4]	2.94	29.80	11.20
1873	40.17	0.89[4]	14.19	33.11	8.02
1874	35.06	0.34	19.63	30.72	9.31
1875	43.97	0.22	11.14	31.33	9.54
1876	34.72	0.46	18.85	41.01	3.40
1877	37.33	0.03	19.26	38.46	4.05
1878	28.79	0.89	29.21	32.32	5.73
1879	27.70	0.54	37.61	26.07	5.50
1880	25.89	0.17	21.75	44.42	4.75
1881	38.01	0.28	18.54	37.56	4.45
1882	33.81	0.07	16.42	36.20	12.13
1883	23.15	0.05	19.31	45.62	10.81
1884	16.87	0.15	28.80	34.64	18.19
1885	13.93	0.27	29.21	40.93	14.68
1886	9.63	0.26	26.93	33.14	26.77
1887	14.60	0.33	27.66	46.48	9.08
1888	23.46	19.18	8.49	35.81	12.06
1889	26.11	22.98	3.65	33.47	8.75
1890	27.69	34.88	5.44	14.91	10.69
1891	42.82	15.91	3.97	21.02	9.95
1892	33.25	30.15	8.22	15.15	9.60
1893	44.79	21.89	2.31	13.47	8.65
1894	26.21	20.41	5.09	22.27	8.61

[4] Including Cochinchina and Japan, not separately reported.

Sources: Yldefonso de Aragon, *Estado que manifiestan la importacion y exportacion 1818* (Manila, 1820); *Estado que manifiesta el numero de buques...1825*; Jean Mallat, *Les Philippines, II* (Paris, 1848); Jules Itier, *Voyage en Chine* (Paris, 1848); Joseph Lannoy, *Iles Philippines,* appendix (Brussels, 1849); *Balanza general del comercio de las Yslas Filipinas....1847, 1851, 1853*; *Balanza mercantil de la renta de aduanas*, 1854; *Census of 1903*, Vol. VI; *Statistical Bulletin No. 3 of the Philippine Islands, 1920*.

The Australasian trade, which was of some importance in the late 1850s (reaching second place in 1857), fell after 1862.

Philippine exports seem to have been most concentrated in a few countries in the mid-1860s, and perhaps also in the next two decades, al-

TABLE 6
Geographic Distribution of Philippine Imports
Selected Years, 1818-1895
(percentages of total imports)

Year	U.K.	China[1]	Br. East Indies[2]	United States	Spain	Germany
1818	2.88	12.79	-	11.66	-	-
1825	18.78	27.16	7.15	10.42	4.64	-
1841	52.58	12.65	2.53	19.22	5.86	-
1842	20.55	13.22	18.40	12.34	5.24	-
1844	18.66	43.18	18.79	5.66	5.67	-
1846	4.35	42.27	33.74	4.73	9.97	-
1847	18.23	34.41	34.32	2.59	4.64	-
1853	26.39	35.13	27.22	.91	5.95	-
1854	55.13	27.20	10.11	.64	6.19	.04
1855	52.65	22.91	16.85	.68	3.98	1.64
1856	36.10	45.65	6.85	4.01	4.11	-
1857	34.88	38.80	9.74	3.78	8.59	1.14
1858	62.72	14.84	6.04	.75	7.64	2.01
1859	39.73	29.68	11.87	1.04	14.94	.22
1860	59.04	21.77	4.83	4.36	6.94	1.74
1861	67.37	20.99	5.06	.67	4.95	-
1862	40.69	30.37	4.63	1.28	15.80	3.48
1863	33.64	46.01	6.80	1.86	8.35	.95

Continued next page

[1] Includes Hong Kong except in 1873-1887
[2] Includes Hong Kong in 1873-1887.

though the shifting of Hong Kong to the British East Indies in 1873–87 precludes any definite conclusion on that point. The years of lesser concentration in the second half of the century seem to have been the late 1850s.

Imports

Imports seem to have been concentrated in a fewer number of countries than exports, but the shifting of Hong Kong between different categories seems to have more markedly affected the statistics on geographic distribution in the second half of the century. The early years are of course

Table 6 *Continued*

Year	U.K.	China[1]	Br. East Indies[2]	United States	Spain	Germany
1864	32.75	50.56	3.46	1.32	7.92	1.96
1865	42.50	42.60	3.04	1.71	5.30	3.11
1866	57.47	30.72[3]	4.80	.94	3.76	.06
1867	56.07	32.44[3]	2.47	.38	4.33	1.78
1873	26.96	2.96[3]	60.61	.24	3.82	1.69
1874	25.36	3.62	62.26	.52	3.22	.98
1875	25.09	3.74	61.28	1.16	5.24	2.15
1876	26.05	12.08	53.16	.66	5.01	1.85
1877	24.60	6.35	58.12	.77	4.92	1.60
1878	24.17	8.04	54.59	.77	4.37	1.27
1879	17.73	6.20	67.34	1.22	4.38	1.85
1880	25.02	3.01	64.13	1.93	3.27	1.12
1881	28.65	3.00	53.83	4.17	7.39	2.63
1882	31.11	2.49	44.34	7.27	10.76	3.21
1883	27.17	2.30	55.63	4.68	3.64	1.17
1884	27.86	3.49	38.67	2.15	4.74	7.00
1885	43.16	2.53	29.76	.80	9.19	6.62
1886	34.19	3.12	33.51	2.71	9.08	7.38
1887	36.06	2.89	29.16	2.99	14.18	3.83
1888	45.84	20.96	6.44	2.96	4.22	5.59
1889	30.64	23.68	10.93	3.96	5.61	7.52
1890	35.44	23.99	15.62	3.32	6.91	1.14
1891	30.50	21.04	10.79	2.07	20.10	1.86
1892	31.83	18.57	6.05	1.28	26.95	3.23
1893	26.73	14.08	1.00	6.02	32.13	7.84
1894	24.74	16.11	1.55	2.55	36.80	6.51
1895	21.68	16.78	1.36	4.07	36.59	7.75

Sources: same as Table 5.
[3] Includes Cochinchina and Japan, not separately reported.

free from this distortion, but there is in 1818 and 1825 an analogous problem, though of lesser magnitude, which is presented by Macao.

Far in the lead in the import trade in 1818 was India; most of this, it has already been pointed out, was probably destined for reexport to Mexico. Far behind India, but occupying sizable shares, came China, the United States, Mexico, and Macao. The distortion introduced by the last-named trade was probably not enough to alter the above rank-ing, as it would tend to understate the shares provided by China and the United States, which were already in the second and third ranks and even with the addition of Macao did not come close to the Indian share.

In 1825, China had moved to first place, England to second, and Macao to third; the United States had fallen to fourth and India to fifth. Singapore occupied sixth place and Spain seventh. Eliminating Macao and distributing its share to other countries would most likely result in the same ranking, as the three countries that would gain the most from such a procedure are those that were already in the lead.

After a spurt that carried over into the early 1840s (currently there are no comprehensive data on what happened between 1825 and 1840), the United States became a minor factor in the Philippine import trade. Following that spurt, it never enjoyed much of a commodity trade in im-ports. In the early years, American imports consisted mostly of specie, rep-resenting imports of capital rather than goods. In later years, whenever its share exceeded 3 or 4 percent, this was due to imports of specie and textiles if before 1880 and imports of mineral oil, wheat flour, wines and spirits, and textiles if after that date. (The statistical effect of Hong Kong should be kept in mind, however.)

The data for the half-century before the Philippine Revolution con-tain elements of ambiguity, but the evidence points to England and China as the most important countries in the Philippine import trade until the last few years.

In 1846, the five top-ranking countries were, in the order of impor-tance, China, Singapore, Spain, the United States, and England. In the fol-lowing year, a somewhat similar picture emerged, except that England had moved up to third place, Spain had dropped to fourth, and the United States had fallen to fifth. Since much of the Singapore trade represented transshipments from England, it is possible that England was in second place in the former year and first in the latter.

After the midcentury mark, England's importance became quite clearly marked. It ranked first in eighteen of the thirty-nine years for which data are available. The fact that the British East Indies accounted for a fair proportion of the Philippine import trade (first place in 1873–84 with the inclusion of Hong Kong) bolsters England's claim to leadership in the Philippine import trade, since the trade through Singapore, as has been pointed out, presumably consisted in large part of transshipments from the United Kingdom. There were also probably Indian goods in

137

these transshipments, but it is impossible to tell in what proportion, as this trade had declined rather steeply from its levels in the second decade of the century.

"China" came next to England in importance, ranking first in six years and probably second in most others, since in those years in which Hong Kong is lumped in with it no other country (except England, which ranked above it) came near it, except in the last few years.

Spain furnished a moderate share of Philippine imports; the average percentage in most years would be between 7 and 10. It enjoyed two spurts in the late 1850s and early 1860s and two more in the 1880s and then made a spectacular climb in the 1890s coincident with the introduction of the nationalistic tariff of 1891. In the last three years for which there are detailed data (1893–95), Spain seized the leadership in the Philippine import trade, displacing England and finally attaining what many nationalistic Spanish writers and officials had so long desired. This represented one of the few instances in which Spanish public policy in the Philippines attained its objectives. It was the only time in its three and a third centuries in the Philippines that Spain enjoyed primacy in any branch of Philippine commerce, and it was not to enjoy it long, for this was the eve of the Revolution and the Spanish-American War. Even so, Spain was in 1893 and 1894 only in the second or third rank as far as total trade was concerned (imports and exports combined). In the former year, England had 37.26 percent of total Philippine trade and Spain only 18.42 percent, and China ranked slightly ahead of it. In the latter year, the respective English and Spanish shares were 25.53 and 21.66 percent. It is quite possible that England was still in the front rank in the import trade in 1893, if its share hidden by the Hong Kong and Singapore trade is taken into account, but this seems less likely in the two succeeding years, when Spain's margin of advantage became more decisive. What happened in the export trade in 1895, and in the total trade in 1896 and 1897, is unknown because official data are not available. What is indubitable is that Spain had in a few years managed to lift itself to a position of importance in Philippine commerce.

Other countries were of considerably less importance. Germany appears to have come up in the 1880s, when its share of Philippine imports rose. The French East Indies showed a definite increase in the last two decades, reflecting the start of regular yearly net imports of rice into the Philippines.

The Philippine import trade seems to have been most concentrated in a few countries in the 1860s and less so in the second half of the century.

Further Comments

Two further comments on both exports and imports should be added. The first is that the geographic classification of tables 5 and 6 (based on that used in the *Census of 1903*, vol. 4) answers adequately the taxonomical requirements of the figures starting in 1841, but it does not do so for 1818 and 1825, when the residual categories (especially "Asia") contain items that do not figure importantly in later years. This in itself is an indication that certain conditions of trade changed significantly between 1825 and 1841. Between these two years, probably in the late 1820s or early 1830s, lies the beginning of the modern pattern of trade for the Philippines.

The second comment is that, although the problem presented by the trade with Hong Kong makes impossible any exact estimate of the course of the China trade, there is reason to believe that China's commerce with the Philippines declined in relative importance in the latter part of the nineteenth century. For the early years, the evidence points to a rise in relative importance. On the export side, the Chinese share rose from 9.37 percent in 1818 to 16.71 percent in 1825 and 21.48 percent in 1846; on the import side, it rose from 12.79 percent in 1818 to 27.16 percent in 1825 and 42.27 percent in 1846. The Hong Kong trade in 1846 was probably not enough to cause a serious distortion in the figures.

At about this time, however, forces were already in play that were to diminish the relative share accounted for by China. The most important, of course, was the increase in the relative importance of other countries, notably England and the United States. The English and American merchants who developed the country's export trade, mainly sugar and abaca, found the majority of their market outlets elsewhere than in China; the English merchants who imported Manchester textiles captured a large portion of the Philippine market from both local and Chinese textiles.

There were other factors. The rice trade with China seems to have been quite vigorous from the 1820s to the early 1850s, when there was a brief interruption. As will be seen later, after 1870 the Philippines ceased to be a rice-exporting country. Certain commodities much sought after by the Chinese also did not maintain their export levels. White birds' nests, for instance, which with a value of 301,568 pesos had in 1818 constituted 25 percent of Philippine exports, fell to only 13,094 pesos in 1847, 6,974 in 1856, and 3,000 in 1864. Bêche-de-mer, with a value of 54,384 pesos, had made up about 4.5 percent of total exports in 1818. Though the value rose to 60,411 pesos in 1847, 85,255 pesos in 1856, and 92,389 pesos in 1873, this was much lower than the rate of growth of exports as a whole, and by 1892 bêche-de-mer was down to only 48,277 pesos, falling below even its 1818 level.[49]

The Second Hirschman Index

A statistical index measuring the geographic concentration of foreign trade of small or weak nations has been developed by Dr. Albert Hirschman, the second of three indices constructed in connection with world trade studies. The index is computed as follows. A country's exports to other countries can be expressed as percentages of total exports. These percentages are squared, and the squares are summed. The index number for exports is the result of extracting the square root of this sum. An analogous operation with import data will yield the index number for imports. The significance of the index is best expressed in Dr. Hirschman's own words.

> As an index of concentration of a country's trade, it varies directly with the concentration of the total trade and with the concentration of any part of this trade. It should therefore be considered as expressing the degree of *oligopoly, or oligopsony existing in a country's external market, monopoly being considered as a limiting case of oligopoly.*[50]

A brief glance at some of Hirschman's findings and procedures as applied to twentieth-century data is in order.

For the purposes of this index, colonies are regarded as separate from the mother country. However, when one country is completely annexed by another, as in the Austrian Anschluss of 1938, the annexed territory is considered part of the annexing power. For residual categories ("other countries"), the assumption was made that the countries comprehended thereunder each took 0.5 percent of a country's total exports (or imports). This was done to avoid the statistical upward bias that would result if the residual percentage, in cases where it was quite large (say, 5 percent), were squared as a whole (in this example, 25) instead of adding the squares of 0.5 percent (in this example, 10 x 0.25 = 2.5).

As a practical proposition, an index of 20—the average value for England, which had the greatest spread in its trade relations—would be the lower limit, whereas the highest reached is Ireland's export index for

1925, at the level of 97. (The theoretical upper limit of 100 would represent a case of complete monopoly or monopsony.) Hirschman seems to regard 40 as the dividing line between high and low levels of trade concentration; countries registering index numbers above 40 are considered to have a highly concentrated trade.

A high geographic concentration of exports was found to be correlated with a high commodity concentration. The export index for small countries with a relatively high foreign trade concentration tended to be higher than the import index, presumably because they specialized in the production of a few products for certain markets and imported a great variety of goods. Since the exports of industrialized countries are more diversified than those of agricultural countries, the former register low geographic concentration and commodity concentration levels, contrary to the experience of the latter.[51]

Turning to the computation of the second Hirschman index for Philippine foreign trade data in the nineteenth century, certain similarities with and divergences from the above features should be called to attention. The separation of colonies from their metropolitan rulers presents no problem; they are carried separately in the trade data. The annexation of territories also is treated in the manner suggested by Hirschman. The only major instance of this is the transfer of California from Mexico to the United States. Before 1846, it is considered a part of Mexico; after that, it is combined with the United States, although the original data in some years carry it separately. This was of practical application only in the year 1825. When an independent country becomes a colony but remains separately listed, no statistical effect ensues; thus, to consign trade with Cochin China and Tongking in 1818 under the classification French East Indies is not, historically speaking, strictly accurate, but since no statistical advantage would be gained by a separate listing of these regions in earlier years in the underlying statistical series, it has been deemed advisable to lump them under a heading applicable only later in the century.

Hirschman's device of dividing residual categories into components of 0.5 percent or fractions thereof, however, has not been generally followed. For most years, the percentages involved are small, and in most of the cases checked they did not amount to more than one or two countries. To have followed Hirschman here would have introduced a slight and unnecessary downward bias in the index. Where these percentages are large, an attempt to identify the component countries has been made, and the index was computed on the basis of these percentages rather than on an arbitrary assignment of a given value spread over the residual percentage. This experience suggests that, for a small country with limited commercial connections and accounting for only a minor share in total world trade, to follow Hirschman's way of avoiding an upward bias in the index might very well result in the injection of the opposite type of statistical bias, although the effect is probably not great in either case. The results of the computations for the Philippine case in the nineteenth century are presented in table 7.

Following Hirschman's criterion of 40 as the dividing line between low and high geographic concentration, it is evident that the Philippines falls into the latter category, the export and import indices dipping below the 40 level only twice each in the forty-seven years for which data are available. However, contrary to Hirschman's experience, the level of the import index remains consistently above that of the export index except in 1842 and in eight years toward the end of the century. The possible reasons for this are several. The first is that Philippine imports were dominated by textiles, which (after an initially strong showing from the United States) came predominantly from one source, England, throughout most of the period covered. This might suggest that, for countries just emerging from a subsistence economy, with low consumption standards and local production of consumer goods still in competition with hypothetical imports, the existence of high commodity and geographic concentration in the import trade is not surprising, as the most enterprising country in the import field would tend to dominate the import trade. Hirschman's data are for the present century, when these conditions were no longer operative in many countries. Second, although major Philippine exports were few in number, there was competition between two great trading countries, England and the United States, for its two top exports, sugar and abaca, and its third- and fourth-ranking products, tobacco and coffee, found markets in Spain and elsewhere. These factors tended to raise the level of the import index and lower that of the export index.

Hirschman's finding of a correlation between increasing commodity concentration of exports and increasing geographic concentration seems borne out by the trend of the index between 1825 and 1867. After the latter year, an important reservation must be entered. Comparison of the index up to 1867 is impossible with that for later years until 1888 because, with the shift of Hong Kong to a different classification in 1873–87, the series temporarily loses its statistical homogeneity. The index numbers for that decade and a half are not comparable with those for earlier and later years; they do not, however, totally lose all usefulness because they are still comparable within that period. When the data be-

TABLE 7

Hirschman Indices of Geographic Concentration of Foreign Trade of the Philippines, Selected Years, 1818-1895

Year	Imports	Exports	Year	Imports	Exports
1818	31.2	50.1	1873	66.6	54.7
1825	40.0	33.0	1874	67.5	51.6
1841	57.8	41.0	1875	66.0	56.0
1842	36.2	40.7	1876	60.7	57.1
1844	51.8	41.8	1877	63.7	57.1
1846	55.5	41.0	1878	60.6	52.6
1847	52.2	39.4	1879	70.1	53.8
1851	-	47.0	1880	69.0	56.1
1853	52.2	51.9	1881	61.7	56.8
1854	62.6	52.0	1882	55.8	53.6
1855	60.0	46.8	1883	62.4	52.3
1856	58.9	48.3	1884	49.6	51.4
1857	53.9	43.2	1885	53.9	54.2
1858	65.5	43.4	1886	49.8	51.4
1859	53.2	42.8	1887	62.8	56.8
1860	63.6	47.1	1888	52.0	49.2
1861	71.0	45.4	1889	33.2	49.5
1862	53.6	47.6	1890	47.2	48.7
1863	58.0	48.8	1891	44.8	51.6
1864	61.0	51.6	1892	46.8	49.2
1865	60.6	47.0	1893	43.5	52.7
1866	65.4	48.7	1894	48.1	42.3
1867	65.0	47.8	1895	47.0	-

Sources: see Tables 5 and 6

come comparable to the earlier years from 1888 on, the import index is at a lower level, suggestive of a greater variety of imports and coincident with the increasing share provided by Germany and with Spain's concentrated drive to occupy the leading position in the Philippine import trade. The import index for 1889–95 is at a lower level than in any other comparable year except 1825 and 1842. The export index, on the other hand, seems to have risen slightly (except for 1894) from its mid-1860 levels. This would be in line with the positive correlation found by Hirschman between increasing commodity concentration and increasing geographic concentration.

For the noncomparable years 1873–87, two remarks will suffice. One is that the import index remains above the level of the export index except in three years. The other is that the import index exhibits a declining trend, while the export index holds fairly level. Both of these trends are compatible with the level of the index that emerges in 1888 in comparison with 1867.

An even more serious flaw in the data than the temporary loss of statistical homogeneity is provided by the sizable transshipping trade through those perennial spoilers, Hong Kong and Singapore. Hirschman refrained from computing the index for countries (like Paraguay and Venezuela) where transshipments played a large part.[52] Since the main currents of Philippine trade are known, however, such restraint, while it might have exhibited caution, was not strictly necessary, provided the various qualifications to the data are kept in mind.

To recapitulate the various biases introduced by Hong Kong and Singapore: Singapore overstates the share going to itself and as such gives an upward bias to the index; both understate the share going to the United States and Great Britain, the two most important countries in Philippine trade, and as such give a downward bias; and Hong Kong overstates the China trade for about half a century, thus introducing an upward bias, except in 1873–87, when its removal from the China trade understates the China share and gives a downward bias to the index, which, however, may be counterbalanced by the upward bias resulting from its addition to the Singapore component. On the whole, the downward biases probably outweigh the outward biases, and the level of both indices should be higher, not by much in 1818 and 1825 (when the analogous problems raised by Macao are somewhat less serious), slightly more in the 1840s, and still more in later years. The amplitude of the movements of the index is probably due to the influence of the two great ports of transshipment.

All these, however, do not completely vitiate the index. From what is known, the relative position of the export and import indices would remain unchanged. The import index would still have the higher level, as there is nothing in the export trade to compare with England's preponderant position in the import trade until the last few years. The overall trends of the index in comparable years also correspond to what is otherwise known about Philippine trade, especially the rising trend from 1825 to 1867, indicative of an increase in the degree of oligopsony and oligopoly in the country's markets and sources of supply.

A word is in order about the correlation between the level of the index and the level of trade. Low levels of the index seem to be associated with low levels of trade in the early years. The index goes down in 1825, which is the lowest level reached during the century except for the import index of 1889. This coincides with the fall in commerce attendant on the ruin of the Mexican trade and with the readjustment of Philippine trade to new conditions. From then until 1867, the index shows an overall upward trend, which again corresponds to a general upward movement in Philippine commerce. It is not possible to follow the correspondence from here on, but there would seem to be little correlation after that. If the export index remained fairly level or even went up slightly, this failed to reflect fully the great increase in exports that continued practically to the end of the Spanish regime. And if the import index declined, as seems to have been the case, this ran counter to the general, if somewhat unsteady, rise in imports to the eve of the Revolution. The trends after 1867, if they have been accurately gauged, indicate a slight rise in the degree of oligopsony in the country's export trade and a fall in the degree of oligopoly in its import trade.

The positive correlation between commodity and geographic concentration seems to have existed most markedly between 1818 and 1867, concomitant first with the end of the Mexican entrepôt trade and then with the half century beginning in the 1820s that can be looked on as the formative period of Philippine trade and the Philippine economy as it was when Admiral Dewey's guns spoke on May Day in 1898 and as it has remained in many essentials down to recent times. It is to important developments in this formative period that our attention now turns.

CHAPTER 5

Textiles and Rice
as Indicators of Economic Change

In view of the importance of clothing and food in daily life and the paucity of data on such other items as nontradables in the period under study, the place of these articles in the foreign trade of a country can be indicative of the economic pattern existing therein. Heavy importers of these goods, for instance, must be presumed to be heavy exporters of other goods—specie in the case of a gold- or silver-producing country, manufactured goods in the case of an industrialized country, or raw materials in the case of an agricultural or mining country. (Under modern conditions, the exports may take the form of services—tourism in countries with scenic or cultural attractions or such services, for example, as go with the Panama and Suez canals.) In the previous chapter, consideration of textile imports and rice exports was deferred in favor of fuller treatment, which will now be undertaken.

The agricultural character of the Philippine economy and its exports has been noted. What will now be called attention to is the type of goods for which these exports were exchanged. At first, they were predominantly textiles. Later they were also to include food, but textiles were to continue occupying a large share of the Philippine import trade to the end of the century (and, indeed, down to modern times).

Textile imports were dominated by the British, and such imports drove domestic Philippine textiles into decline despite Spanish efforts to

146

protect and even encourage the industry. Only after the nationalistic tariff of 1891 did Spanish textiles succeed in wresting leadership in the trade from the British, but by then Spanish rule was nearing its end.

Rice imports characterized the last three decades of the nineteenth century, but before then rice had been an export, particularly to China, with heavy shipments continuing into the mid-1860s. Rice prices generally followed price trends in China, but the Spanish authorities followed a policy of price moderation, with rice exports banned during times of high prices in order to protect consumers. In 1855, definite trigger prices were announced, and shortly thereafter rice imports were allowed freely. The policy of price moderation, judging by the maintenance of prices below the trigger price, was on the whole quite successful, although modal prices toward the end of the century were higher than in earlier years but still generally below the trigger price. Price moderation was not, however, synonymous with price stability, as prices fluctuated freely below the trigger price. The turning point in the rice trade is identified as the early 1870s, and the factors behind this development appear not to be limited to price movements but encompass disruptions in the pattern of village productive relationships, as smallholder cultivators experienced a reduction in supplementary household income from the decline of domestic textiles.

The Position of Textiles in Philippine Foreign Trade

It has been seen how the influx of Chinese textiles for the galleon trade brought about the early decline of certain sectors of the native textile industry. However, native textiles continued to be made on home looms in many parts of the country and in such quantities that the Royal Philippine Company and the government made efforts to stimulate them not only for the benefit of domestic consumers but also for export. Part of the former prosperity of the Ilocos region seems to have been based on the planting, processing, and weaving of cotton. Although the company incurred losses in its ventures with Philippine textiles, its operations had some effect, and in 1818 native textiles made up 4.54 percent of total exports, ranking fourth among the domestic items (after birds' nests, indigo, and sugar).

It is not easy to estimate the position of textiles in Philippine commerce in that or earlier years insofar as they met local needs and consumption. Although they made up a part of the country's export trade, they were also imported in some quantity not only for reexport to Acapulco, San Blas, and Lima but also for local use. Much of the domestic consumption was furnished from local looms, but Comyn in his time spoke of "great supplies of goods annually imported into the country, for the purpose of making up the deficiencies of the local manufactures."[1] With the end of the entrepôt trade, shipments from India diminished, although a minor trade was carried on in Bengal cloth for domestic consumption. This came to an end with the coming of inexpensive textiles from Europe.[2]

In the same decade that saw the end of the transshipping commerce to the Americas, renewed efforts were made to stimulate native textiles. In 1824, a prize was offered by the revived Royal Economic Society for blankets woven domestically, and a surtax was requested on those imported from China as well as on certain China silks. It was calculated that certain kinds of blankets imported from China amounted to 40,000 pieces annually, while the potential output of looms in Batangas, Taal, Bauan, Balayan, Tambobong, and Las Piñas was 1,215,435 pieces. In fifteen years, Chinese blankets ceased to enter the country in their former quantities. This was not due to the competition of native looms but of American cotton textiles, an eventuality foreseen by neither the Chinese nor the Economic Society.[3]

This was a foretaste of what was increasingly going to happen during the remainder of the Spanish period. Toward the midcentury mark, Lannoy wrote:

> From time immemorial the natives of the Philippines have known the manufacture of different kinds of textiles suited to their needs. This industry, entirely domestic, falls to the lot of the women; it has greatly lost its importance due to the suppression of the Acapulco trade and the moderate prices of the cloth from Europe, prices which permit the Indian to clothe himself suitably on an outlay of a few reals.[4]

There could be little doubt as to the outcome of the competition between factory-made textiles and those produced on local cottage looms, despite the efforts of the Spanish government to protect the Philippine textile industry. In fact, Lannoy recommended that the government reverse its stand and force the Filipinos to abandon an industry that had no future, owing to the competition of foreign goods of a similar nature, and devote themselves entirely to agriculture.[5]

English textiles seem from an early stage to have dominated the import market (despite some initial competition from New England), which is not surprising in view of Great Britain's head start in factory output and also the fact that, as Mac Micking reported, "the import trade of Manilla is almost entirely in the hands of the British merchants established there, so far as the great staple articles of manufactured goods are concerned . . ."[6] Their exact proportion to total imports is impossible to specify because so much was transshipped to Spanish vessels at Singapore in order to take advantage of tariff differentials favoring national bottoms. In 1847, for instance, 51.07 percent of cotton textile imports was listed as coming from Singapore, 26.04 percent from Britain, and 20.56 percent from China. A quarter of a century later, in 1873, 67.25 percent of such imports came from the British East Indies (including Hong Kong in that year) and only 32.29 percent from Britain.[7] Yet every indication points to Britain as the main supplier of textiles. Consul Ricketts reported to the British Foreign Office from Manila for the year 1870 that cotton and linen goods, iron, coal, and machinery came principally from Great Britain. British interest in the Philippine market is shown in the following passage from his report:

> The native textures usually worn are either made from the fibre of the Musa textiles [sic] or, from that of the piña; the former are most in use among the poorer, the latter among the richer, portion of the inhabitants.
>
> The piña stuffs are being gradually superseded by articles of European manufacture, but the Abaca stuffs are still preferred by many to anything that has as yet been introduced into this country.
>
> When it is considered that some three-fourths of the inhabitants outside Manila, are in the habit of dressing in garments one part of which is of European and the other of native fabric, it is evident that there is still room for some expansion in this branch of our commerce.[8]

Later that same decade, Recur made an estimate in another fashion, saying that certain native textiles were composed of three parts piña to one part cotton.[9]

The effects of Britain's profound interest in the textile trade are apparent from the value of textile imports over the years (tables 8 and 9). In the half century before the Revolution, the value of textile imports increased more than ninefold. This was true as well of by far the biggest items in textile imports, cotton textiles. The ninefold increase was much more rapid than the rate of growth of the population, which only doubled in the same period.

The importance of textiles in the import trade in the early years is brought out by their ratio to total imports. Textiles constituted more than half the value of imports in 1846 and 1847; in the former year, they were

TABLE 8
Philippine Textile Imports and Their Ratio to Total Imports
Selected Years, 1844-1895

Year	Value (pesos)	Percentage of Total Imports
1844	1,471,939	44.47
1846	1,349,349[1]	51.12
1847	2,042,999[1]	59.56
1856	2,786,541[2]	40.10
1857	3,489,320[2]	35.22
1864	3,601,589	33.04
1865	4,215,105	46.12
1867	4,613,431	60.78
1876	5,831,241	48.65
1878	6,744,058	39.00
1879	5,125,224	28.42
1880	9,025,238	35.41
1881	6,971,777	33.54
1882	8,104,397	38.11
1883	9,060,591	42.52
1884	6,937,532	32.65
1885	7,516,004	39.20
1886	6,829,099	34.02
1887	5,460,454	31.47
1888	9,654,431	45.52
1889	7,494,744	30.23
1890	6,504,581	32.86
1891	8,337,115	38.51
1892	9,283,114	38.98
1894	10,712,663	37.50
1895	8,725,315	34.36

[1] Includes all cotton manufactures.

[2] Approximate. Textile import figures for these years were not consolidated. Some minor items may have been missed in making the present compilation.

Sources: Jules Itier, *Journal d'un Voyage en Chine* (Paris, 1848); Joseph Lannoy, *Iles Philippines*, appendix (Brussels, 1849); *Balanza general* 1847; *Cuadro general*, 1856; *Balanza mercantil*, 1857, 1864, 1865; *Estadistica mercantil*, 1867, 1876, 1878-1880; *Estadistica general*, 1890, 1892; Society of Jesus, *El Archipielago Filipino*, I, 312.

TABLE 9

Philippine Cotton Textile Imports and Their Ratio to Total Imports
Selected Years, 1844-1895

Year	Value (pesos)	Percentage of Total Imports
1844	1,400,127	42.31
1846	1,010,841[1]	38.30
1847	1,647,889[1]	48.04
1864	2,418,220	22.18
1865	2,620,804	28.68
1867	3,163,791	41.68
1873	4,859,796	36.77
1874	5,303,736	38.70
1875	4,213,969	34.50
1876	4,810,578	40.13
1878	5,890,991	34.07
1879	4,484,473	24.87
1880	7,934,639	31.13
1881	6,057,266	29.15
1882	6,586,048	30.98
1883	7,529,992	35.34
1884	5,656,625	26.62
1885	6,279,861	32.76
1886	5,804,612	28.92
1887	4,626,387	26.66
1888	8,547,461	40.30
1889	6,780,559	27.35
1890	5,554,369	28.06
1891	6,082,754	28.10
1892	7,923,119	33.27
1893	8,662,072	33.42
1894	9,272,487	32.47
1895	7,557,262	29.75

[1] All cotton manufactures.

Sources: Jules Itier, *Journal d'un Voyage en Chine* (Paris, 1848); Joseph Lannoy, *Iles Philippines*, appendix (Brussels, 1849); *Balanza general*, 1847; *Balanza mercantil*, 1864, 1865; *Estadistica mercantil*, 1867, 1876, 1878, 1879, 1880; Ramon Gonzalez Fernandez and Federico Moreno Jerez, *Manuel del Viajero en Filipinas* (Manila, 1875), p. 207; *Anuario Filipion para 1877*, pp. 71-72; *Estadistica general*, 1881-1894; Society of Jesus, *El Archipielago Filipino*, I, 312.

51.12 percent and in the latter 59.56 percent. The respective percentages for cotton textiles alone in these years were 38.30 and 48.04. Despite the lower percentages found in the next two decades, the importance of textiles in the Philippine commodity import trade may not have diminished by much because these were years with comparatively heavy inward movements of specie, which tend to diminish the relative importance of the commodity trade. In 1856, gold and silver in coins, bars, and dust made up 38.53 percent of total imports; the following year, gold and silver coin made up 41.36 percent; in 1864, gold and silver of all kinds made up 33.36 percent; and in 1865 they made up 14.67 percent. These figures compare with specie imports amounting to only 6.07 and 8.08 percent, respectively, in 1846 and 1847. Where the ratio of specie imports to total imports is low in later years, as in 1867, when it was only 1.26 percent, the ratio of textiles to total imports shoots up to about the level of the 1840s; it is 60.78 percent in that year.[10]

After 1870, however, the somewhat diminished relative importance of textiles in the import trade seems to be no longer in doubt. Holding inward specie movement constant (at, say, the 1846–47 level), an informed guess would put the modal values of the ratio of textiles to total imports before 1870 at around 55 percent; after 1870, the modal values are only between 35 and 40 percent. This is not to be wondered at because these were the years in which regular net imports of rice became the rule rather than the exception (as will be seen in the next section), and the low ratios of the last two decades (in 1879, 1884, 1887, and 1889) correspond to years of heavy rice imports.[11] The last two decades also saw increasing imports of wheat flour, coal, mineral oil, and metals, which can be regarded as somewhat increasing the diversification of the import trade. Still, the absolute value of textile imports rose, and they remained the most important item in the Philippine import trade. An analogous argument can be formulated, mutatis mutandis, for the case of cotton textile imports alone.

In the meantime, native textiles lost ground in the country's foreign commerce relative to foreign textiles, although for a while there was an absolute rise in the value of textile exports. From 54,706 pesos in 1818, the value of native textile exports rose to 72,649 pesos in 1846, 108,901 pesos in 1856, and 157,278 pesos in 1864, which seems to have been a peak year. The almost threefold increase since 1818, however, was much slower than the rate of growth of total exports or of total trade, and soon the trend was reversed. In 1867, native textile exports had declined to 36,666 pesos, and by 1890 they amounted to only 10,455 pesos. Part of the reason for the increase in textile exports around the middle of the century was the export of a coarse abaca cloth called *medriñaque* that was used for baling cotton and for lining, of which a large part was exported to the United States. This trade seems to have reached its peak in 1856 when it accounted for more than two-thirds of the value of Philippine textile exports. By 1864, it had declined to such a level that it was no longer listed separately in the annual customs return.[12]

Equally instructive are figures on the exports of distinctively Philippine textiles, *piña, jusi,* and *sinamay* (table 10). In the mid-1840s, their export level was between 22,000 and 28,000 pesos. In the next decade, this fell to between one-sixth and one-ninth of the mid-1840s level. After 1873, it fell below the 1,000 peso mark more often than not, and by the mid-1880s it had declined to such a point that the item either disappeared completely in some years or was so insignificant that it did not merit a listing in the annual customs reports.

Although native textiles continued to be important items of use in people's daily lives and in the industry of some regions—Recur in the 1870s reports forty thousand looms on the island of Panay alone, and continuing imports of cotton twist to the end of the century attest to its use in

TABLE 10
Textiles (Piña, Jusi and Sinamay) Exported From the Philippines
Selected Years, 1844-1890

Years	Value (pesos)	Years	Value (pesos)
1844	22,791	1867	3,674
1846	26,131	1868	—
1847	28,292	1873	1,142
1854	3,678	1874	2,669
1855	3,349	1875	805
1856	1,378	1876	3,175
1857	709	1877	3,350
1858	4,979	1878	845
1859	6,675	1879	485
1860	6,533	1880	1,655
1861	6,214	1881	720
1862	4,598	1882	3,021
1863	3,713	1883	551
1864	2,949	1888	638
1865	2,445	1890	202
1866	9,709		

domestic manufacturing—there is little doubt that they had declined in relative significance in both the country's trade and domestic use and manufacture since the days of the Philippine Company and the first two or three decades of the nineteenth century. Furthermore, the imported cotton twist cannot invariably be looked on as an addition to the country's manufactures since in many cases it replaced local cotton twist and drove domestic enterprises to the wall. Recur lamented the lack of incentives and prizes in the cotton manufacturing industry.

By the 1880s, native textiles were in a sad state. As British Vice Consul Shelmerdine reported from Iloilo in 1887:

> During the last five years the native industry in the manufacture of cloths has declined very much, and is now not of half the importance that it was. This change has been brought about by the importation of cotton goods to take the place of the native manufactures. . . .
>
> A few years back a quantity of cloths were exported from this district to other parts of the islands, and in fact the chief and almost only industry of this district, before it was opened up for sugar growing, was the weaving of various kinds of cloth called "piña", "sinamay", and "jusi", besides which a garment called a "patadiong", made of coloured cottons, and used by the women here as the "sarong" is used in Java, was manufactured in large quantities.
>
> This "patadiong" has now been almost altogether superseded by the importations from Glasgow, but the industry still continues to a small extent, and these native hand-woven goods are preferred by the natives when rich enough to afford them, although their cost is twice that of imported goods.

The social costs of this decline may have been considerable, for, by Shelmerdine's own account, "in some of the villages nearly every cottage, however poor, will contain a loom." If, as seems certain, there was a rise in the aggregate income level of the region with the start of heavy sugar exports, it was quite unlikely for the beneficiaries of this new development to be the same people who suffered by the decline in the textile industry. There was therefore probably some redistribution of income, away from small weavers and toward sugar planters and workers and away, also, from women toward men. The hypothetical increase in "utility" represented by the imported textiles was called into question by British Vice Consul Cadell in Cebu, who reported the same year:

154

The clothing of the poorer class of natives is made of hemp and aloe fibres—very durable materials—and it is doubtful whether the natives would be the gainers by exchanging their present excellent fibre shirts for cotton imitations, which would probably not wear nearly so well, whilst the finer qualities of fibre cloth are only required in small quantities.[13]

In its decline, the Philippine textile industry appears to have contracted into two main geographic areas, southern Panay (around Iloilo) and Ilocos (largely around Bangar and Namacpacan, now called Luna, in La Union). This may be inferred from the exhibitors at the Philippine Regional Exposition of 1895 in Manila. Of the approximately 290 exhibitors in section 4, group 6 (textiles), with an identifiable geographic provenance, 128 were from Iloilo and 22 from Antique, indicating that southern Panay accounted for more than half of the exhibits. The only other large cluster came from La Union, with 55 exhibits. Together with Ilocos Norte (12 exhibits) and Ilocos Sur (6 exhibits), Ilocos accounted for more than a quarter of the exhibits. Of the 290 geographically identifiable exhibits, nearly 60 were put up by women, one of these being Miss Patrocinio Gamboa of Jaro, Iloilo, who in a few years would become a heroine of the Revolution.[14]

The final chapter in the textile trade in the nineteenth century was not without its ironic overtones. British textiles, heavy imports of which had since the 1820s been relegating native textiles to a decreasingly important role in the country's economy despite government protection, were themselves given stiff competition, in the last quinquennium for which figures are available, by Spanish textiles with the aid of the tariff of 1891. By that time, apparently, the Spanish government had decided, in addition to the somewhat futile protection until then accorded to domestic Philippine textiles, to favor the products of its own looms, and this time Spain was, with the help of the tariff, in a position to deliver the goods due to the industrialization of Catalonia.

The figures tell the story in the case of the most important item, cotton textiles (table 11). In the ten years from 1883 to 1892, the value of Spanish cotton textile imports into the Philippines had risen more than twenty-one times, and by 1895 they were half again as great as the 1892 figure.

The percentage figures attest to the same trend. Occasional high figures in the 1890s evidence the ad hoc efforts then made to favor national manufactures. But the real spurt came when all the ad hoc imports were systematized in the tariff of 1891. From contributing only between 1 and 2,

TABLE 11
Value of Philippine Cotton Textile Imports From Spain
and Their Ratio to Total Cotton Textile Imports, 1883-1895

Year	Value (pesos)	Percentage of Total Cotton Textile Imports
1883	99,307	1.32
1884	100,971	1.79
1885	167,294	2.49
1886	354,772	6.11
1887	134,146	2.90
1888	136,614	1.60
1889	828,699	12.22
1890	349,119	6.29
1891	1,317,464	24.95
1892	2,116,978	26.72
1894	3,898,543	42.04
1895	3,219,559	42.60

Sources: *Estadistica general*, 1892; Society of Jesus, *El Archipielago Filipino*, I. 305-606, 312-313.

and occasionally 6, percent of Philippine cotton textile imports, Spain's share in 1891 rose to 24.95 percent. The following year it was 26.72 percent, by 1894 it had climbed to 42.04 percent, and in 1895 it was 42.6 percent. The tariff of 1891 was strikingly successful for Spain in this respect and may even have forced the British to erect a modern textile mill in 1897 in Manila, which Victor Clark visited in the middle of the following decade.[15] The Revolution and the American conquest of the Philippines prevented Spain from enjoying the full benefit of the new tariff. They may also have aborted the start of the modern Philippine textile industry, as the British mill apparently did not survive the duty-free entry of American goods under the new administration, as in fact it was not expected to do.

The Position of Rice in Philippine Foreign Trade: From Export to Import

Less ambiguous than the place of textiles in Philippine commerce was that of rice. It was definitely an export until the 1850s, it was predominantly an export from then until about 1870, and it was definitely an import from the 1870s until the end of the Spanish period (and down to the present day, despite recurrent campaigns to reattain self-sufficiency in rice).

Its movement in foreign trade is one of the most important indications of change in the Philippine economy in the nineteenth century, as it is the single most important item in all Filipino family budgets and an article of general consumption among all classes. The Spaniards referred to it as the bread of the natives.[16] As a food item, and as an agricultural product, it ranks as a consumer good par excellence.

The significance of the movement of rice in the foreign trade of the Philippines does not seem to have been properly appreciated down to the present time. Furthermore, there was a tendency to classify it as an import at a date somewhat earlier than is justified by the available data. Thus, the *Census of 1903* says: "In 1857 import duties on rice were abolished; since then and for some years prior thereto, the deficiency in home production has been made good by importation, although small quantities have been occasionally exported."[17] This is accompanied by a table showing rice imports since 1854 and their ratio to the total value of imports in each year. No indication is given, however, of the magnitude of rice exports in those years.

The same statistical procedure is followed in *Statistical Bulletin No. 3* and *Monthly Summary of the Commerce of the Philippine Islands* for December 1904, where various tables list rice imports from 1855 on but there is no indication of rice exports in any year. Del Pan also gives 1857 as the year when Philippine rice exports ceased.[18] Only Tornow seems to have realized that rice exports continued well into the 1860s: "Formerly, in 1850 to 1860, or even later, rice was exported from the islands, but the quantity gradually decreased until exportation ceased altogether, and finally the grain began to be imported . . ."[19]

The Rice Trade in the Early Nineteenth Century

The Spanish authorities in the Philippines followed what might be called a policy of price moderation through food security, in recognition that rice was not merely a trade item but one with sociopolitical aspects; for example, in 1830 the local inhabitants of Tondo and Binondo made representations to the government about the rising price of rice. As expressed in a commercial report, rice was obtainable through the year at prices that never varied much within a range of 1.5 to 2 pesos per *picul*, but when its price exceeded a certain level the government stopped its exportation until the next crop was harvested.[20]

This had been criticized early in the nineteenth century by Fr. Joaquín Martínez de Zúñiga in the following words:

> Rice, if there were freedom to export it without obstacles to merchants, could be taken to China and become a branch of commerce. Some think that the exportation of rice would cause famine, and it is so untrue that the contrary would happen. The *indios* now plant no more rice than they consume among themselves, and if a harvest is lost they suffer famine. If exportation were permitted, much more would be planted than is consumed annually in the islands; in time of shortage the price would rise, as a result of which merchants would be unable to export it, and all that had been earmarked for trade would in this case cover the deficiency in the harvest, and the famines that destroy the provinces would not be suffered.[21]

The good friar was thinking ahead of the civil authorities, but he did not go far enough. Demand in China was not sufficiently predictable to form a stable basis for long-term export production. Philippine rice exports were largely dependent on the magnitude of rice shortages in China and of surplus production in the Philippines, and their level fluctuated widely from year to year without any clearly discernible secular trend, as is shown in the quantity figures for Philippine rice exports for 1831 and 1837–56 carried in the *Cuadro General* for 1856. Greenberg termed speculations in rice as "spectacular but spasmodic" but also noted that the rice trade in the 1830s was so large that Jardine, Matheson & Co. set up Otadui & Co. in Manila practically as a branch to engage in it in association with an American, John Shillaber.[22]

The instability in the rice trade was reflected in commercial operations. On a rice cargo sent in 1832 by Russell & Sturgis to Olyphant & Co. in Canton, "we were afraid an inevitable loss would follow, but a period of unfavorable weather has raised the price of Rice to a profit of 20 a 30 cts. per picul."

Since rice exports were made on the basis of individual permits, possession of an unused permit enabled some merchants to circumvent the export ban in times when it was in place. "Rice is prohibited and has been for the last year, but I think I can succeed in getting about 3000 piculs of rice and paddy (which an old spanard [sic] told me today he had permission to ship) at a high price," wrote Capt. Benoni Lockwood early in 1834. Toward the end of that year, Russell & Sturgis reported that the coming crop would be very large and opined that exports would soon be allowed.

Commercial intelligence in the region was good, and price signals were transmitted rapidly and set off the movement of transport. In June 1833, rice prices in China were high (three dollars per *picul*) and rising, and Olyphant & Co. reported from Macao: "There are a great number of Junks waiting here to procure Cargoes to carry up to the North and East, where the people are said to be almost entirely destitute of provisions."

Prices in the Philippines generally moved in sympathy with those in China. "The price has risen in China and consequently here . . ." reported Russell & Sturgis in the middle of 1835 from Manila. In 1848, it reported: "The news of a short crop in China has sustained prices just as they were beginning to decline from the high rates which have been maintained for more than a year past. . . . The crop about being gathered is abundant; but if there is a scarcity in China, prices will keep up." (Prices at the time were from 1.375 to 1.5 pesos per *picul*.)

But there were times when price trends diverged, and these presented traders with opportunities for making handsome profits. At the end of 1835, the Philippine rice crop was so abundant that prices were low and declining, at 13 to 13.25 *reales* (or 1.625 to 1.66 pesos) per *picul*. Apparently the ships in port were in a monopsonistic position and could hold off buying until prices went to (they hoped) less than 13 *reales*. By waiting a week, they could save four or five cents per *picul*, which would more than pay for their demurrage. If prices were to rise in China, "there will be money made by those who are here to take advantage of it," exulted Captain Lockwood. His cargo of nearly 6,000 *piculs* was sold in Canton at $2.30 per *picul*, which (after deducting expenses for "chops," "shroff," and commission) netted $13,341.22. This represented a profit of roughly sixty cents per *picul*. In addition he sold a small amount of paddy (130.83 *piculs* at $1.50) in Macao to B. Barretto, netting after expenses $181.09.[23]

If Chinese demand for Philippine rice was unstable, there was another demand that showed more constancy, although it may have been a minor factor. American and other foreign ships engaged in the Canton trade either called at Manila for rice on the way to China or made side trips for the commodity instead of lying idle awaiting cargoes of tea and silk off the Chinese port (as will be seen again later in this study). As many as six such voyages a year could be made. In a detailed account of Manila's trade in 1829, Russell & Sturgis reported that rice was raised very abundantly throughout Luzon and "is taken very frequently by American vessels in order to avoid payment of Cumsha and measurement in China." But it was necessary to seek specific permission to export, and this could frequently occasion "the most vexatious delay." At this time, an export prohibition could be imposed on the general grounds that the crop was not sufficiently large. On September 3, 1855, price triggers were announced; rice exports would be permitted while the price did not exceed 2.25 pesos per *cavan* in Manila and 1.75 in the provinces.

When foreign demand for Philippine rice was high, it could tax the resources of the coasting trade and cause problems for other export goods. "The price of Rice has been so high of late in China, and consequently here," reported Russell & Sturgis in 1844, "that most of the Provincial craft usually employed to bring up Hemp here have loaded with Rice, and we find it quite difficult to supply the active demand for the former article."[24]

The position of rice in the export trade is somewhat more easily gauged in those years for which value figures are available. Rice exports were of some significance for the Philippines into the third quarter of the nineteenth century. John Wise's figures for 1836 consign rice, accounting for over 25 percent of the total value of exports, as the number two export. In 1846, rice accounts for about 6 percent of exports and is number four in rank. In 1847, it retains the same rank and constitutes 3.6 percent of exports. In 1856, it again holds the same rank with 4.3 percent, and in 1857 it slips to fifth place with 2.15 percent. The years 1858 and 1859 are deficit years (as will be explained below), but in 1860 rice is back in fourth place with 1.91 percent. In 1864, it is up to 4 percent but remains in fifth place. In 1865, it regains fourth place with 7.7 percent of total exports. This seems to be the last year for which data are accessible in which rice is of some relative importance in the Philippine export trade.[25]

The Transition Period

More revealing, especially with reference to the moot question of when rice ceased to be an export and became an import, are figures for the *net* movement of rice, whether inward or outward, in the country's foreign trade. Only the transition period 1851–76 need be covered here, since there is no question of rice being an export before that and an import afterward.

Going back to the Philippine customs returns themselves, it is possible to form an idea of what the net movement of rice was. Although data for all years were not readily available at the time of writing (the statistical hiatus years 1868–69 and 1871–72, when no reports were published because of a bureaucratic mix-up), the evidence points to a preponderance of net rice exports before 1871. From 1851 to 1870, data on rice exports are available for sixteen years. Of these, only two show net imports of rice; the other fourteen show net exports (table 12). For most of this period the sta-

TABLE 12
Philippine Rice Exports and Imports, Selected Years, 1846-1876

	Rice Exports		Rice Imports		Balance	Balance
Year	Quantity (kgs.)	Value (pesos)	Quantity (kgs.)	Value (pesos)	of Rice Trade (quantity in kgs.)	of Rice Trade (value in pesos)
1846	10,016,155	176,406	-	-	10,016,155	176,406
1847	5,490,445	113,873	-	-	5,490,445	113,783
1851	651,619	15,751	(3)	15,198	-	553
1853	17,393,232	368,387	152	100	17,393,081	368,287
1854	9,100,698	167,607	4,584	290	9,096,114	167,317
1855	19,162,843	586,189	1,025	65	19,161,818	586,124
1856	12,516,543	352,428	29,285	209	12,487,258	352,219
1857	4,491,670	234,566	2,856,456	183,938	1,635,214	50,628
1858	1,234,985	62,224	5,457,486	342,013	-4,222,501	-279,789
1859	1,310,540	51,380	2,623,484	90,634	-1,312,944	-39,254
1860	10,083,948	432,937	8,729	588	10,075,218	432,349
1861	3,902,813	144,668	72,232	3,097	3,830,581	141,571
1862	1,786,921	102,503	27,517	1,566	1,759,404	100,937
1863	(1)	(2)	(1)	(1)	+?	+?
1864	9,382,298	337,368	488,796	21,912	8,893,502	315,456
1865	21,974,086	827,907	258,656	11,714	21,715,430	816,193
1866	3,017,000	(3)	371,000	15,513	2,646,000	?
1867	2,036,696	72,198	479,804	18,999	1,556,892	53,199
1870	2,323,136	473,945	704,203	404,671	1,618,933	69,274
1873	13,215	396	7,316,388	218,459	-7,303,173	-218,962
1874	54,827	2,667	10,842,000	488,224	-10,787,000	-485,557
1875	1,524,855	34,587	2,910,467	93,569	-1,375,612	-58,982
1876	3,571,931	80,127	239,539	6,196	3,332,392	73,931

(1) The 1863 Customs report carries no figures whatever for rice exports and imports, and paddy exports of only ps. 48,500, although it is known from commercial correspondence that the rice trade was active that year, particularly exports from Sual.
(2) Azcárraga says rice exports this year from the Port of Sual alone amounted to 496,000 pesos. It was probably a net rice exporting year, therefore.
(3) Figure not given.
    Sources: See Tables 1,2,3 and *Balanza mercantil de las Islas Filipinas*, 1863.

tistical evidence decisively points to rice as an export. The country at that time still seemed quite capable of providing for its own basic food needs.

The initial year of the period, 1851, was one in which rice exports were prohibited for most of the year, from at least February until mid-December. At the same time, some rice cargoes from Singapore were permitted by special order for the use of the army and prison contractors. In February, April, and August, rice prices ranged from 1.625 to 1.875 pesos and even 1.9375 pesos per *cavan*. By mid-December, the old crop was quoted at from 1 to 1.125 pesos, with the new crop only 12.5 to 19 cents higher than that. Despite the export ban and the importation through Singapore, it was a year of a small net export largely because of shipments to Cuba and to a lesser extent California. There were also some exports of paddy (unhulled rice), mostly to China.

The Cuban shipments reflected the momentum of a movement noted in the late 1840s, when, in the absence of demand from China or Europe, extensive purchases for Havana kept rice prices high. In October 1847, two ships carried 700 tons to Havana, and in February 1848 three ships carried another 1,350 tons. At that time, prices ranged from 1.50 to 1.625 pesos per *cavan*.

At the end of 1852, with prices between 1.125 and 1.375 pesos per *cavan*, there were delays in getting export permits, but purchases were made for California at 2.25 pesos per *cavan*, probably for the high-grade white variety favored in that market. The following April a price rise in China caused great activity in Manila, and there was a considerable net export, but prices remained at the 1.25 peso level.[26]

After a period of fluctuations, something new appeared in 1858–59: for the first time, there were considerable net imports. In October 1857, Java rice was reported sold at between 2.43 and 3.25 pesos per *cavan* in silver (which at the time commanded a 19 to 20 percent premium). But it was not a purely sellers' market. The following month some of the imported grain was shipped on to Amoy. In April 1858, a ship returned to Hong Kong with an unsold cargo of Siamese rice, having been unwilling to take 2.50 pesos per *picul* in gold. Domestic rice was selling at 2.62 to 2.65 pesos per *cavan* in silver (which then commanded a premium of 12.5 to 13 percent). In August, there was even a repatriation of previously exported Pangasinan rice, which was sold for 2.59 pesos per *picul* in silver. By September, large amounts of foreign rice had sent prices down. By October, rice merchants were finding it difficult to sell at retail "except at great sacrifice from the late high cost." By November, Java rice fetched only 2.15 pesos per *picul* in gold. A year later, although 1859 as a whole was a deficit year, eight to nine thousand *cavan*s of Philippine superior white rice were sent to Havana at 2.75 to 3 pesos per *cavan* in silver (with silver at a 10 percent premium).

The net imports of 1858–59 were facilitated by the 1856–57 dispositions declaring the rice trade free.[27] This crisis was both an adumbration of what would come after 1870 and an aberration from preceding trends. The failure even to approach this level of imports again until the 1870s reinforces the argument for considering rice an export until 1870. The argument is further strengthened when it is noted that until the opening of the port of Sual to general commerce in 1855, and perhaps after that, the amount of rice exports was understated because much of the article was loaded directly from ports in rice-producing regions of the country by local vessels without figuring in the annual customs returns from Manila. The rice-exporting ports from the early part of the century were Currimao in Ilocos Norte, Salomague in Ilocos Sur, Sual in Pangasinan, Pasacao in Camarines, Sorsogon in Albay, and Capiz on the island of Panay. The first three were the more important because they were nearer to the Chinese market and because they were outlets for regions that produced the best rice. In 1854, Russell & Sturgis reported that vessels bound for China had taken thirty thousand *cavans* "and exports to that quarter are large from the Northern Provinces direct." Mac Micking reported Ilocos rice to be of the best quality, being heavier than that of other regions per unit of volume. (A *cavan* of "fine white" rice weighed 133 lbs.; "good & common," 129 to 130 lbs.; and "ordinary" (*pinagua* or *pinawa*), 126 to 128 lbs.) In his time, at the midcentury mark, he listed the country's rice granaries as Ilocos, Pangasinan, Bulacan, Capiz, Camarines, and Antique.[28]

On the level of Philippine rice exports, the following is Mac Micking's testimony:

> The quantity of rice and paddy shipped to China from the provinces cannot be ascertained with any degree of exactness; what goes from Manila is very small, because, before arriving there, it has, by its transport expenses, added to the price at which it is obtainable in the districts where it is produced, which, of course prevents its being shipped from the capital. At a guess, however, I should suppose that about a million cavans, each of which, one with another weighs about a China picul, or 133 1/3 lbs., is an average yearly export, should the Government not prohibit the article from being exported for a longer period than usual, which is annually regulated by the scarcity or abundance of food in the country.[29]

The rice trade in the 1860s continued to exhibit the usual ups and downs. In August 1860, rice in Hong Kong was reported to be in fair demand with prices rising. But on November 14 rice was reported as "very dull." Only eleven days later, the local (China) rice crop prospects dimmed and prices went up ten cents a *picul*.

The November 14 Hong Kong price quotations are of interest because they show how Philippine rice compared with that from other countries.[30]

Rice Prices in Hong Kong, November 14, 1860
($ Mex per picul)

Siam	1.80 to 2.00
Arakan	1.80 to 1.85
Java	2.10 to 2.25
Saigon	2.25 to 2.40
Pangasinan	2.25 to 2.30
Ilocos	2.30to 2.40

The rice from different places was of varying quality, with Ilocos rice (as Mac Micking had indicated) ranking high. Bearing all this in mind, Philippine rice appeared competitive, as shown by the substantial net exports of 1864 and 1865 (table 12).

The destination of Philippine rice, however, was no longer limited to South China. Manila merchant A. V. Barretto and Sual merchants Arrechea & Co. and Jose Bosch in 1863 made several shipments to the "northern ports" of Chinhae, Ningpo, and Shanghai. The Ningpo market was characterized as variable and subject to sudden fluctuations. Rice cargoes were insured at a uniform price of $2.50 per *picul*, but actual market prices could differ. For example, in Ningpo on August 5, 1863, Manila rice was quoted at $2.90 per *picul* and no. 2 quality at $2.80. At Hong Kong on September 3, white Sual rice was quoted at $2.25 to $2.50 per *picul*, with no stock on hand. On January 8, 1864, rice was quoted in Ningpo at $2.92 to $3.10 per *picul*, and a sale was made later that month at $3.07 per *picul* ex-warehouse. But in August the Ningpo rice was down to $2.86 per *picul*.

Rice prices in Hong Kong in 1864 were up from 1860 levels, and Philippine rice appeared to hold its relative position. Bangkok rice was quoted at $2.40 to $2.50, Manila at $2.65 to $2.85, and Bengal at $3.00 to $3.15 per *picul*. In fact, the net rice exports of 1865 were the largest on record in terms of both quantity and value (table 12). Manila rice was still being quoted in Amoy in mid-1869.[31]

The Turning Point and the Reasons for It

After 1870, however, the picture changed. From 1873, when figures again became available following the statistical break of 1871–72, until

1880, only one year (1876) showed net rice exports. They seemed to have been negligible from 1877 on, and net annual imports became the rule. The port of Sual, opened in 1855, closed less than three decades later for lack of business.

In assigning a turning point to the rice trade, then, the best choice seems to be the early 1870s rather than the mid-1850s. The most logical time to specify as the turning point seems to be 1871–72. Before 1871–72, there were two years of net rice imports, but the article was on balance an export; after 1871–72, there was one year of net rice exports, but the article was on balance an import.

Various reasons have been assigned for this change in the position of rice in the foreign trade of the Philippines. According to Del Pan, the liberalization of the rice trade, the extension of the tobacco monopoly to the Ilocos district, and the availability of Saigon rice were the principal causes. He writes:

> Until 1856 some rice was exported, in good years, to China. This export in some years exceeded half a millions *cavans*, all from Pangasinan and Ilocos. But since 1857, when this trade was declared free, and coincident with the creation of tobacco collections in Ilocos Norte—a measure which converted a region yielding much good rice into a producer of the worst kind of tobacco—the country does not export grain, as much because it harvests only what it needs for consumption as because it would not be able to compete in price with the rice of Cochin China despite its superior quality.[32]

Serious flaws can be pointed out in this argument, however. The statistical evidence adduced previously invalidates his dating of the change. It will be remembered that rice continued to be an export for a decade and a half after the date he gives. The export level he estimates is only half that calculated by the shrewd Scot, Mac Micking, who was active in the rice-exporting era and was much more intimately connected with business affairs. The extension of the tobacco monopoly to Ilocos (which, incidentally, may also have brought about the decline in cotton culture) is more important and will be taken up later. And he omits the entrance of Zambales into the rice trade.

In addition to the two regions he cites, namely, Ilocos and Pangasinan (with Ilocos rice selling at higher prices due to superior quality), Zambales rice began to be commercially quoted in 1856 practically on a par with that of Ilocos. But this addition to the trade did not stave off the crisis of 1858–59, and whatever addition to exportable stocks took place did not last long because around 1863 Ilocos disappeared from the commercial quotations. Zambales itself dropped out, too, after late 1874, leaving Pangasinan as the sole supplier to the export trade until that trade petered out.[33] Were local factors affecting supplies? This can only be answered by using local histories.

The loss of one rice-producing region would have meant little in a country where there were other rice-surplus regions and where new lands were being opened and agricultural production was on the increase, *provided this increase were in basic food crops* (which gives a clue as to where the answer might lie). As for competition from Saigon rice, it is one thing to explain why the export trade ended, but it is another to explain why an export should suddenly turn into an import, and a heavy one at that (8.68 percent of total imports in 1878, 15.65 percent in 1879, 15.27 percent in 1884, 13.02 percent in 1886, 13.44 percent in 1887, 12.7 percent in 1888, and 21.2 percent in 1889). In any case, the year he mentions (1857) probably was not affected by Saigon rice; in the years before the 1870s, the only recorded rice imports from Cochin China were 273 metric tons worth 7,600 pesos in 1859. There is no record of further rice imports from that region until 1873, when the first heavy imports of Saigon rice are carried in the trade figures. (Transshipments through Hong Kong may of course have been hidden in previous years, especially in the two years before 1870 when Cochin China was lumped in with China, but these could not have been very heavy in view of the low level of rice imports then.) The argument that liberalization of the external rice trade *caused* heavy rice imports confuses a necessary with a sufficient condition. What has to be explained is not a temporary and reversible dislocation but a chronic shortage of a basic food staple, which had been under cultivation for hundreds of years, in a country where people were accustomed to its culture and new lands were being put under cultivation. The things mentioned by Del Pan undoubtedly had some influence, but they do not seem to go to the heart of the matter.

Tornow takes a slightly different view. He writes:

The blame lies with the miserable administration of the country. The planters can no longer compete with Rangoon, Saigon, and Bangkok, where the authorities know how to meet the farmers when necessary, and where the ships are not exposed to endless chicanery, such as is practiced by the Manila customs-house officials. For this reason most foreign vessels are careful to steer clear of the latter port . . .[34]

This, however, does not explain why ships that steered clear of Manila when picking up rice did not steer clear of it when unloading rice or picking up sugar and hemp. It would be getting nearer to the bottom of things to say that population increase had something to do with this phenomenon. Corpuz estimates that the annual growth rate of the population from 1805 to 1850 was 1.8 percent. But from 1850 to 1903 this had slowed to 1.2 percent, owing to natural calamities and cholera and smallpox epidemics. Doeppers, using a different time frame, estimates average annual population growth from 1840 to 1870 at 1.7 percent but from 1870 to 1905 at only between 0.9 and 1.0 percent. Despite the slowdown in the population growth rate, and in the presumed increase in total consumption, there was no return to net exports of rice.[35]

In any case, population increase *by itself* explains little unless a change is assumed in the pattern of production of the country. If the pattern of production remained the same, an increase of population in a country with new and fertile lands coming under the plow would simply mean proportionally greater subsistence production. New lands did come under the plow, but they were not devoted primarily to rice. Even lands that were formerly devoted to its culture were diverted to other crops, and so was the labor formerly employed on it. This diversion seems to have been the main factor behind the changes in the movement of rice in foreign trade.

Recognition of this is found in the following passage in the *Census of 1903*:

> For many years surplus crops were produced and the grain was exported in large quantities, but as the production of more profitable crops, such as hemp and sugar, increased, the cultivation of rice diminished, and from becoming an article of export it changed to one of importation, as the population and their food requirements increased. . . . It may be said that, as a rule, the falling off in the production of rice has not resulted in any great loss to the population, except when resulting from drought or locusts, as that portion of land and labor formerly devoted to its cultivation was subsequently used for the production of more profitable crops.[36]

The same point is made, approached from a somewhat different angle, emphasizing the strategic role of foreign trade, by González and Moreno:

Production of this cereal has diminished notably in the country for lack of the incentive of the Chinese market, which has been supplied more abundantly and more cheaply with rice from Cochin China since the French established themselves at Saigon. Nowadays grain is not exported, and when the price of the most common variety reaches two pesos, rice comes in from the outside to contain a further rise. The lands which used to provide the surplus production in years of good harvests have been planted to sugar and other crops, since the benefits from them are evident to the inhabitants. The towns which are exclusively rice producing are considered the poorest and most backward.[37]

This is certainly a logical and plausible explanation and, though it contains almost the same elements as Del Pan's, it sets forth the main factors in sharper focus as well as clarifying the role of the mechanisms of foreign trade in helping to bring the change about. It was not simply a case of needs outstripping production but a diversion of factors of production to more lucrative employment.

The role of foreign trade had of course started much earlier than this time (the 1870s); the first step was to establish a nexus with an external market for local products, including rice, which had hitherto been grown for subsistence. This seems to have happened early in the century. Then came a period of production of this commodity both for subsistence and for export, which for those times was a fortunate coincidence. After this came the decline of the external market and the fall in demand of this product, while demand for other crops held firm and even rose, which, through the foreign trade mechanism, helped bring about the diversion of factors of production to other crops. These were not subsistence products but crops in which foreign merchants were interested for the world market, like sugar, abaca, and coffee, and whose production thus had an advantage over that of rice.

This of course meant an increase in the agricultural specialization of the country and was undoubtedly one of the reasons behind the growing commodity concentration of Philippine exports and the increase in relative importance of the two ranking products, sugar and abaca. It is unnecessary to belabor the point that developments in the foreign trade sector were already having important repercussions in the internal economy (including subsistence production), which was beginning to change in reaction to external forces.

Some idea of the diversion of factors of production to export crops and the increase in internal agricultural specialization can be gleaned from several accounts. Bowring, who visited the Philippines in 1858, paraphrases a British vice consular report on one aspect of internal trade:

> The paddy exported [from Panay] is chiefly conveyed in small schooners (*pancos* and *barotos*) to the neighboring islands of Leyte and Samar, and also to Camarines and Albay, in exchange for hemp and cocoa-nut oil (the latter obtained in Leyte), which are either brought to Iloilo for sale or taken on to Manila, When prices at Manila leave a sufficient margin (which they generally do throughout the year), some amount of paddy goes in that direction, forming a portion of the cargo of the vessels leaving for the capital.[38]

From this it can be gathered that the former rice-exporting provinces of Camarines and Albay have had to turn to other regions for their food supplies.

The German naturalist Jagor, who visited the country only four months after Bowring, confirms this in his comments about those provinces: "The production [of hemp] in many provinces had reached the extreme limit; and a further increase . . . is impossible, as the work of cultivation occupies the whole of the male population . . ."[39] It is noteworthy that these observations were made before the definitive loss of the China market for Philippine rice, which indicates that the diversion of factors of production from this line, while it was helped along by that event and its subsequent repercussions in the foreign trade sector, had in fact been initiated by trading in the other export crops and the capital advances made by the foreign firms to encourage their culture. In other words, the initial impulses came not so much from a fall in demand for one product as a rise in demand for others.

Victor Clark wrote that "the labor expended on export crops, valued at what the laborers receive for their production, is furnished by possible rice-crop labor and leads to a deficit in the latter."[40] Like Jagor, Clark put his finger on the real constraint, labor, which was in limited supply whereas land was plentiful.

It is equally instructive to compare the area under cultivation devoted to different crops in 1870 and 1902. The absolute figures probably mean little because the statistics were collected by different methods and therefore are not strictly comparable. The diminution in cultivated area that they show may be illusory, although it is actually not improbable, as several years of revolution, war, and natural calamities had intervened around the turn of the century. But the proportions are revealing. In 1870, rice took up 48.35 percent of the area devoted to crops; in 1902, the ratio of rice land to total cultivated area had gone down to 45.58 percent. It was a slight but noticeable reduction, especially since in 1870 the transformation of the Philippines into an export economy was already in the process of completion. More significantly, the area devoted to the four leading export crops was 26.56 percent of the total in 1870 and had climbed to 36.1 percent in 1902.[41] Together with the decrease in the proportion devoted to rice, this increase in the percentage devoted to exports argues a greater degree of dependence on the export trade by the economy.

Contemporaries, however, seemed to be unaware of the change that was occurring in the position of rice in the economy around the mid–nineteenth century. In 1855, the Spanish government, in an access of optimism, opened the rice port of Sual to general foreign trade, not foreseeing that rice would decline vis-à-vis other exports, that in less than two decades it would become an import, and that Sual was doomed to vegetate in provincial obscurity.

Sir John Bowring, writing of the liberalization of the rice and paddy trade, said: "I found that the emancipation of these important articles from all custom-house interference had been attended with the best results, by regulating and assimilating prices, without any detriment to native production . . ." Elsewhere, commenting on the prospects of the rice trade for the island of Panay, he wrote:

> The paddy shipped from Iloilo is chiefly drawn from the vast plains of Dumangas, Zarraga, Pototan, Santa Barbara and Barotac-viejo. Were a large portion of the land brought under cultivation, the increased surplus of this grain, would be available for export to China, in which foreign vessels might be employed as they frequently are at Sual, in Pangasinan; and it may not unreasonably be surmised that, in the course of time, ships frequenting the port of Iloilo, and proceeding to China, will naturally take part of their cargoes in rice, and thus give a further impetus to its cultivation . . .[42]

Don Manuel Azcárraga, noting a great increase in exports in the period 1850–70, said of rice:

> Only in rice is it noted that exportation has decreased in the years 1858 and 1859, although it has increased afterward in 1860. This

small decrease has not affected the general increase in the volume of exportation of the country's products, since undoubtedly this is due to the fact that some provinces have devoted themselves more in recent years to sugar cane, oil or some other article because of the immense profit which these products give them. In any case, the benefit which the Islands have received from the decree of free importation and exportation of rice in 1856 . . . has been to leave this branch of commerce to the working of the individual interest, as it should be, so that should there be a great harvest it would be easy and expeditious to take the cereal for sale in neighboring markets, with great advantage to the producer; and when, far from having a surplus, it should be scarce in the Islands, it would be equally easy to bring it from other countries, so that this aliment of such necessity may always maintain a fair price. And we believe that the native, under these conditions, will always return to the cultivation of this grain, because it is well known, and because, as we have said, it is his principal sustenance.[43]

Neither Sir John nor Don Manuel, both excellent observers, scholars, and men of affairs, proved to be good prophets. The vast plains that the former saw were devoted to sugarcane instead of rice under the stimulus of demand and capital advances from foreign firms, and the expected rice exports to China never materialized. A market report from Iloilo at the end of 1867 specifically reported: "There have been no foreign exports, all our surplus having been consumed in Manila and the neighboring provinces."[44] Azcárraga, writing later, seems to have seen more clearly what was going on, but his apparent belief in a frictionless and reversible economic mechanism led him to surmise that the principal food crops would always be produced in sufficient amounts. The same assumption seems to have been held by the French doctor J. Montano, who made an official visit to the Philippines in 1879–81. He writes of rice as follows:

> In years of drought, the Philippines do not produce the quantity necessary for local consumption; the difference has to be sought in importation, which heavily burdens the resources of the colony; but, in normal years, needs are more than fulfilled, and the exportation of rice is considerable.[45]

When he visited the country, of course, rice exports were already past history, but such is the persistence of human patterns of thinking that it was still considered a possible export product, and shortages were attributed to exogenous causes such as droughts instead of more fundamental economic changes.

Finally, there are the following comments by W. Gifford Palgrave, Her Britannic Majesty's consul in Manila in 1876:

> Eight million natives, more or less, inhabit the Philippines; and of this vast aggregate the principal, almost the only sustenance, morning, noon, and eve is rice. And what famine is, how frequent, how disastrous, how overwhelming among a rice-subsisting population, the annals of Madras, Orissa, Ceylon, Bengal, have too often taught us. A calamity that, it would seem, no foresight can avert, to which no remedy can suffice. And yet, in the Philippine Archipelago, scarcity even is of rare occurrence, famine unknown; in the worst of years hardly a sack of grain has to be imported; in average seasons the land has enough for her children, all swarming as they are, and to spare. More still, after deducting the entire vast extent of soil and amount of labour devoted exclusively to this one staff of local life, enough remains of both to supply the export trade with a yearly equivalent of four to six million sterling in sugar, coffee, hemp, tobacco, and all the other varied products of tropical agriculture . . .[46]

Palgrave predicted that this idyllic-sounding state of affairs would come to an end with the advent of European capital and enterprise, which would upset the balance of production in the country. What he does not seem to have realized is that his fears had already come to pass: foreign capital and enterprise had already transformed the pattern of production and had oriented the country's economy toward foreign trade.

In the context of the times, and from the point of view of raising aggregate income, this was not necessarily considered an evil, for apparently there was more to be gained by raising export crops. Victor Clark wrote:

> Undoubtedly it is for the interest of the Philippines that the islands should be made self-supporting in the matter of rice production, providing this can be done without lessening the export crops. Compared with each other, the latter are probably more profitable for all parties concerned than the former.[47]

The *Census of 1903* reported:

This condition [rice importation] is likely to continue indefinitely, it being more profitable to raise other crops, particularly hemp. The proceeds derived from the sale of hemp from a given amount of land will purchase much more rice than could be grown on the same area, and as long as this remains true the islands will undoubtedly depend to a large degree on importations of the grain.[48]

Elsewhere it delivered the judgment that "the falling off in the production of rice has not resulted in any great loss to the population . . ."[49]

Evaluation of the Outcome

The cheerful optimism of these views can stand some scrutiny since the areas producing export crops were not necessarily those that used to grow rice and the putative benefits were not spread evenly. Two aspects will be examined here, namely, the maintenance of moderate prices and the effects on what Palgrave, in a fit of bucolic nostalgia, called "all the equable balance of property and production, of ownership and labour, that now leaves to the poorest cottager enough, and yet to the total colony abundance to spare."[50]

It has been noted that the policy of periodic export bans, and later of liberal importation, had for their objectives the maintenance of the prices of the common varieties of this important staple under 2.00 to 2.25 pesos per *cavan*.

Table 13 tracks prices of ordinary grades of rice from 1806 to 1883. Although there are gaps in the series, it appears that the policy by and large attained its objective, with the exception of two years in the late 1850s, four in the mid-1860s, and three in the late 1870s. Consumers did benefit.

But by the 1870s there were multiple references by both Del Pan and González and Moreno to rice-producing areas, prosperous and fortunate in earlier times, as being poor and backward. While the 1883 price did not differ much from that forty or fifty years earlier, ten-year averages of median prices show those of 1874–83 to be about 25 percent higher than those for 1844–53. This represents an average annual increase of less than 1 percent annually, but the average hides wide price fluctuations. If rice prices were kept moderate, did this prejudice rice producers? Was this the principal cause of their poverty or was it the wide cyclical swings? It is tempting

TABLE 13

Prices of Rice, Ordinary Grades, Selected Years, 1806-1887 (Pesos per Cavan)

Years	Ranges	Median	Year	Ranges	Median
1806	2.00	2.00	1856	1.375-2.56	1.97
1818	1.35	1.35	1857	1.75-3.50	2.63
1820	1.125	1.125	1858	1.25-3.875	2.56
1824	1.14 -1.25	1.20	1859	1.25-2.75	2.00
1826	1.31-1.50	1.41	1860	1.72-2.66	2.19
1827	1.25-2.00	1.63	1861	1.375-2.25	1.81
1829	0.75-1.00	0.875	1862	1.00-2.125	1.56
1830	1.375	1.375	1863	1.00-2.00	1.50
1831	1.02-1.14	1.08	1864	1.81-3.00	2.40
1833	1.48-1.82	1.62	1865	2.375-2.75	2.56
1834	1.14-1.80	1.49	1866	2.375-3.00	2.69
1835	1.46-1.62	1.54	1867	1.875-3.00	2.44
1837	1.37-1.50	1.44	1868	1.00-2.375	1.69
1839	1.69-2.00	1.85	1869	1.25-1.88	1.57
1840	1.375-2.25	1.81	1870	1.375-2.25	1.81
1841	1.50-1.625	1.56	1871	1.625-1.875	1.75
1842	0.875-1.14	1.01	1872	1.76-2.375	2.07
1843	1.02-1.37	1.20	1873	1.365-2.56	1.96
1844	1.19-1.69	1.44	1874	1.25-2.375	1.81
1845	1.37-1.59	1.48	1875	1.375-1.625	1.50
1846	1.48	1.48	1876	1.125-2.50	1.81
1847	1.25-2.50	1.875	1877	1.95-3.625	2.78
1848	1.25-1.625	1.44	1878	2.50-3.50	3.00
1849	1.19-1.625	1.41	1879	2.05-3.00	2.525
1850	1.31-1.81	1.56	1880	1.50-2.25	1.875
1851	1.00-1.94	1.47	1881	1.50-2.00	1.75
1852	1.07-1.625	1.35	1882	1.625-1.875	1.75
1853	1.125-1.75	1.44	1883	1.50-1.88	1.69
1854	0.90-1.625	1.26	1886	1.99-2.41	2.20
1855	1.125-2.80	1.96	1887	1.81-2.16	1.985

Sources: Renouard de Sainte Croix, *Voyage*; Estado....*1818*; Edward Carrington Papers, RIHS; *Price Current Manila*, March 13th, 1824; *Manila Price Current*, various dates 1826-67, 1829; Gonzalez & Moreno, *Manual del viajero en* Filipinas; Russell & Sturgis, *Prices Current of Exports at Manilla*, various dates 1831, 1833-35, 1843; *Precios Corriantes de Manila*, various dates 1839-1841; *Manila Prices Current*, September 1st, 1842; *New Weekly General Price Current*, Manila, vaious dates, 1843-1846; *Shipping Intelligence*, Manila, various dates, 1851-1855; Circular Letters, various dates, from Fred. Baker & Co., Ker & Co., Peele, Hubbell, & Co, Russell & Sturgis, J.M. Tuason & Co.

to theorize along these lines, but the truth is a great deal more complicated, involving structural elements, as will be seen in two cases.

The first, described by McCoy, is the old rice and textile area of southern Panay, where almost half the potential female labor force was estimated to be employed in the textile industry. The introduction of manufactured British textiles led to the decline of native weaving. It became apparent that in the overcrowded weaving towns the small farm parcels and poor agricultural conditions were unable to support their large populations without the income from women's handicrafts. A migration to sparsely populated Negros ensued, where the entrepreneurship and capital displaced from the weaving industry found a new outlet in the expanding sugar economy.

But with the diversion of factors of production to the export sector, the region lost the ability to feed itself. Food shortages occurred after 1870, starvation was mentioned in a British consular report of 1878, and there were recurrent famines.[51] Apparently, the most important element for impoverishment was not so much price fluctuations as the loss of supplementary household income.

The second case is that of Ilocos, especially the province of Ilocos Norte, already identified as the source of the best rice in the trade. The town of Paoay in that province may be taken as representative of the region. In 1807, a former French cavalry officer, Felix Renouard de Sainte-Croix, visited it and described it as one of the largest in the province, with a population of eighteen thousand. Between the town and the mountains to the east lay the most fertile soil, planted to cotton in great quantities and of a superior quality. From this was woven beautiful cloth, which in ordinary weeks produced an income of two thousand pesos. He also found there the best bread he had ever tasted, much better than that of Manila, presumably from the local wheat, of which Ilocos (along with Tayabas) produced the best kind. This was a town, he rhapsodized, that managed its business well. How many cities in Europe, he exclaimed, would think themselves happy to have even half of what Paoay had?[52]

Nearly forty years later, Joseph Lannoy, a Belgian businessman and consul in Manila, described the basis of the prosperity in Ilocos as a kind of rational agriculture involving rice and cotton, which were both annuals and were planted on the same ground in the same year at different seasons.[53] For those times, this represented a continuous use of land, a relatively stable level of annual income, and a fairly advanced degree of regional economic diversification.

At midcentury, the Ilocos provinces were characterized as agricultural, commercial, and above all industrial, with their inhabitants excelling in common textiles, of which they manufactured all kinds from their cotton harvests. To the Manila markets they sent great quantities of rice, wheat, sugar, raw and manufactured cotton, wax, sugar vinegar, dyewoods, hides, bovine and equine cattle, and textiles of various kinds.[54] This must have been the economic base for the massive stone churches that are strung out along the length of the Ilocos coast. The eighteenth-century Paoay church, which (along with Santa Maria's down the coast) has merited listing among UNESCO's world heritage sites, with its size (about sixty by three hundred feet) and its huge buttresses, is probably the supreme example of Philippine earthquake baroque.

By 1870, the picture had changed. Ilocos Norte's population had declined from 157,559 in 1850 to 150,947, and its commerce was of scant importance, with only three *pontines* (schooners) and eight minor craft employed therein. The town of Paoay was down to 10,503 inhabitants. Ilocos Sur's population in the same period had fallen from 192,272 to 179,305, and it had become a net importer of rice. Del Pan characterized it as very populous and very poor; as for Ilocos Norte, it was equally poor and even more backward.[55]

What had happened? Del Pan's view, attributing the decline to the imposition of the tobacco monopoly, has already been noted. He overstates his case, however, when he adds that Ilocos Norte had abandoned rice culture because it had been compelled to grow tobacco. In 1870, the value of rice grown there was 659,427 pesos or about three-fourths of the total value of all agricultural products in the province. The tobacco crop was worth 206,562 pesos or only 23.5 percent of the total. This was nearly double the value of tobacco production of the rest of the region, broadly defined. In Ilocos Sur, rice made up just over 70 percent of the value of agricultural output, while tobacco accounted for only 5 percent.[56]

According to Ahujas, the monopoly, which in Luzon had the exclusive right to trade in tobacco, actually came to Ilocos by a circuitous route. Agents of the monopoly around the years 1841–43 had conducted intrusive searches of persons and homes in Ilocos and Pangasinan. To avoid these vexations, and after an abortive compromise, the people petitioned for exemption from the monopoly in their area and for the freedom to plant tobacco for their own consumption in exchange for certain monthly payments. The freedom to plant for themselves, however, was also a duty to grow for the monopoly, and the chiefs of tobacco collections visited more vexations on the people such as indirectly ordering the cutting of nontobacco plants like cotton and sugarcane.

This may explain the reduction in rice production in Ilocos and consequently the national shortfall. But abolition of the tobacco monopoly was decreed in 1880, only six years after Ahujas wrote, effective in 1882,[57] and yet there was no return to previous patterns of cultivation. Tobacco remained, rice did not revive, and the outmigration continued. Something else must have been involved.

It is possible to hypothesize a broader scenario. Since Ilocos had previously been characterized as above all industrial, a process similar to that which overtook Iloilo's textile industry can be envisioned. Competition from imported textiles cut the demand for domestic textiles, home industries and cotton growing declined, and household income was reduced. The dual cropping system described by Lannoy broke down as the demand for cotton evaporated. Cotton growing had disappeared in Ilocos Norte by 1870, and in Ilocos Sur it amounted to only 1 percent of the value of the rice crop. Ilocos was also a grower of indigo, which was likewise in decline. Indigo production in Ilocos Norte in 1870 was a minuscule one-fourth of 1 percent of the total value of agricultural output, while in Ilocos Sur it was a little better at 10 percent.[58] The smallholders' parcels were insufficient to maintain the population, and the Ilocano migration, already under way, accelerated. The crucial element was not just the substitution of one crop for another but the disappearance of supplemental household income, which could not be made up for even with favorable agricultural prices. Monocropping was not the answer to rural poverty.

Recent research has explored the possible nexus between mortality rates among the peasantry and the spread of commercial agriculture. Rising mortality rates in the nineteenth century and the increasing frequency and intensity of mortality crises are thought to be connected with the expansion of commercial agriculture and the substitution of export crops for locally consumed food crops, even after allowing for the spread of communicable diseases.

It is recognized that commercial agriculture can be associated with rising living standards when it takes place in labor-short areas or when it is accompanied by transfers of technology and increasing unit productivity. But in the Philippine case the most significant aspect of commercialization was identified as the erosion of traditional landholding arrangements.[59] Put differently, it was not estates that made commercial agriculture possible but commercialization that facilitated the formation of estates.

There are still no categorical conclusions, but based on what has been seen in this section investigators along this line of research would do well to broaden their horizons. The shift of factors of production, especially labor, in this case may explain the change in the pattern of cultivation, but the lack of improvement and even deterioration in the lot of substantial sectors of society seem to have resulted from the fall in supplemental, especially nonagricultural, household income.

A Resume

The nineteenth century was a fateful one for the Philippine economy, and the period 1820–70 was especially significant for the changes that overtook the country. The nature of its foreign trade changed from being largely a transshipping operation to a commerce that involved the exchange of the country's products for goods that filled the domestic needs of the people. The value and quantity of both exports and imports rose greatly from the 1820s until the end of the century after having suffered an initial diminution following the termination of the entrepôt trade with Mexico.

The commercial sector also showed indications of economic change, which came about largely through the mechanism of foreign trade and the injection of foreign capital and enterprise in the export business. There was an increasing commodity concentration of exports about the middle of the century, which became more marked after 1870. There was an increasing geographic concentration of trade up to about 1870. Textiles accounted for the bulk of imports, and with these heavy importations the native textile trade declined. And rice changed from an export to an import crop around 1870. Both trends had significant social and demographic repercussions.

To recapitulate, the Philippines was a rice-exporting country until 1870. The preceding twenty years may be regarded as a transition period, during which for the first time there were recorded net rice imports in two years in the late 1850s, although these were followed by the largest recorded net exports ever in the mid-1860s. After 1870, rice became an import item.

The reasons were various, although much was due to the shifting of productive factors, especially scarce labor, into export crops. But the mechanisms were circuitous and involved demographic shifts. In rice-producing Iloilo, the decline of the home weaving industry under the impact of imported textiles cut household incomes and the ability of the populous towns to support their inhabitants, leading to a migration to sparsely settled Negros, where under the influence of capital and entrepreneurship, also displaced from the traditional weaving industry, they went into the rising sugar export industry, being financed by foreign merchants. In Ilocos, the introduction of the tobacco monopoly in 1857 partially diverted productive factors from rice culture and accelerated outmigration, but when the monopoly was lifted twenty-five years later there was no return of these factors to previous cultivation patterns. The ratchet effect may have come about because Ilocos, having like Iloilo a substantial home weaving industry, underwent a similar experience, compounded by the fall in derived demand for cotton, which had been dual cropped with rice. The policy of price moderation maintained throughout the period meant that there were no special price incentives for rice culture. Although moderate domestic prices should have helped in external markets with the depreciation of silver from about 1874 on, the depreciation did not help in the principal market, China, which also had a silver-based currency. Aggravating the trend toward impoverishment was the concurrent fall in the external demand for indigo, another regional crop.

Until 1870, it would not have been inaccurate to characterize the Philippines as having a subsistence economy, largely dependent on its own domestic production for the provision of basic needs and exporting only its surplus. But after this what emerged in the last quarter-century of the Spanish period was what might be termed an agricultural export economy—one specializing in the production of a few export crops (mostly primary goods sent to the metropolitan countries to be processed) in return for which it received manufactured goods and even its own basic necessities in food and clothing.

The transformation can be said to have begun in earnest in the 1820s, in the first years in which the country's foreign trade came to rely predominantly on domestic exports rather than transshipped goods and with the first heavy imports of factory-made textiles. It continued with a gradual concentration in both the commodity pattern of exports and the geographic pattern of trade. And it was essentially completed in the 1870s when rice definitely passed into the category of imports.

This turning point derives added significance from its being coincidental with other economic events—the opening of the Suez Canal, the liberalization of tariffs, the start of monetary depreciation, the granting of Spanish shipping subsidies, an increase in trade and navigation in Asian waters, and a saltatory rise in the level of foreign trade (which probably derived from all these factors). It was also coincidental with historical events of larger significance. The execution of three Filipino martyr-priests, Burgos, Gomes, and Zamora, in 1872, is generally regarded as the starting point of Filipino nationalism.[60] The next three decades were to see what was probably the first great modern flowering of Philippine art and letters, an outburst of intellectual activity and agitation, and the events that culminated in 1896 in the first national revolution in Asia. The factors that brought about the economic change must now be considered.

CHAPTER 6

Factors Behind the Growth
of the Export Economy

Presssure and Plantations

The Philippines was not unique in Southeast Asia in undergoing an economic transformation from a subsistence to an export economy in the nineteenth century. Under the impact of rising world demand, the same thing was happening all over the region, and the general factors behind this trend have been well summarized by Karl Pelzer.

> Whereas during the sixteenth, seventeenth and eighteenth centuries the various European nations active in Southeast Asia had, on the whole, limited themselves to trading and the acquisition of high-priced nonbulky commodities, such as spices, the economic policy of the nineteenth century called for large quantities of bulky goods, such as sugar, fibers, oil seeds, coffee, and copra. Since the peasantry of Southeast Asia, almost without exception, raised only subsistence crops and had only limited surpluses, it became necessary for the colonial powers to increase agricultural production. This was done in two ways: (a) through the application of pressure on the peasantry to produce for export and (b) through the development of large-scale plantation agriculture.

From 1830 to 1870 the peasants of Java were forced to cultivate crops and turn them over to the government in order to meet
their tax obligations. In other areas the introduction of taxation
to be paid in money forced the peasantry to raise crops for sale.
In one way or another the political and economic penetration of
Southeast Asia during the nineteenth and twentieth centuries
replaced the traditional subsistence and barter economy by a
money economy. This was, of course, a slow process that began
in different places at different times. But as various regions became linked with the outside world, people gave up the old pattern of raising crops only for family consumption and began to
cultivate export crops. In some instances this meant that they increased the production of traditional food crops, for example, rice
or coconuts; in other instances they began to cultivate crops that
had been introduced by the Europeans.[1]

When the Philippine case is examined closely, however, it becomes
evident that Dr. Pelzer's generalizations, while they might hold for most
of the Southeast Asian region, do not hold (except perhaps with severe
qualifications) for it. In the crucial half century between 1820 and 1870,
both factors mentioned by Pelzer—pressure on the peasantry and large-
scale plantation agriculture—were more noticeable for their inconspicu-
ousness than for their effectiveness. Toward the end of the century, the
second factor probably increased in importance and may have been responsible for the great increase in exports at that time. But by then the
transformation of the Philippines into an export economy was complete,
and what look like, for instance, sugar plantations after the middle of the
century seem to have been more a response to the export trade than a cause
thereof. Larger agricultural units certainly helped to raise production in
later years, but they cannot have been the initial factor.

The matter warrants a closer look. With regard to pressure on the
peasantry, certain examples that might be classed under this heading (e.g.,
the tobacco monopoly) have been referred to in earlier chapters. Plausible
instances may be detected in the days of the Royal Philippine Company,
when, it will be remembered, payment of tribute in kind was permitted to
those raising cotton and manufacturing certain textiles and assumption of
tribute payment by the company was made under certain conditions in the
case of pepper farmers. But those are perhaps better classed as inducements than as pressure. What is most noticeable about these early attempts to induce the production of certain export items is that, where

they did not end up in absolute failure, as in the case of pepper, they met with only limited and temporary success, as in the case of cotton and textiles.

Much more successful was the scheme that really was a case of pressure on the peasantry and was the nearest thing to the forced culture of Java that occurred in the Philippines, namely, the tobacco monopoly, which propelled the product to the third-ranked (and for a time second-ranked) place among Philippine exports. Even here, however, the case is not completely unambiguous. For one thing, the motivation behind the scheme was not primarily commercial but fiscal. It has been seen that it was originally instituted to free the Philippines from dependence on the *situado,* or Mexican subsidy; there are suggestions that Governor Basco, observing the newly won independence of the thirteen American colonies, foresaw the same occurrence in Latin America and wished to prepare the Philippines for that contingency.[2] There is the fact, already noted, that exports of cigars did not occur until the 1820s and leaf tobacco exports until 1837, which were four and five decades, respectively, following the founding of the monopoly. Its long duration was due primarily to its fiscal importance; as late as the budget of 1868–69 for the central insular government, it accounted for 6,714,500 pesos out of receipts totaling 11,924,826 pesos, or 56.3 percent.[3] The proportion of the country's population brought directly under it was only around 10 percent and probably never exceeded 15 percent.[4] While it held an important rank in the country's export trade, it only occasionally reached or surpassed 20 percent of total exports (see table 4), and as time went on it was increasingly overshadowed by sugar and abaca. (Day draws closer parallels than are warranted by the actual facts to the much more comprehensive culture system in Java.)[5]

It can be argued with reason that the motivation behind the scheme was of little importance as long as its working did tend to force increased production for export. This may be true. But so partial a phenomenon as this was, while of some importance in the country's economic and social landscape, and while it may have helped push the country in the direction of an export economy, falls far short of being the main factor in setting the trend in motion. It seems clear that pressure on the peasantry, even if the term is stretched to include official inducements, cannot have been the main reason for the country's economic transformation.

The development of large-scale plantation agriculture has even less claim to consideration in this connection, at least in the period 1820–70, for the simple reason that there were few properties that could be dignified by the term *plantation.* It has been seen how the Spaniards tended to congregate in Manila to engage in the galleon trade and left the land largely in the hands of the native Filipinos. The preponderant testimony is that, in the period under consideration, the Philippines was largely a land of smallholders. There were some large properties, as has been noted, in the form of endowments to religious and charitable corporations, and there was also a tendency for Chinese mestizos to accumulate landed property in the course of their trading and financial operations through *pactos de retro* or *retroventa* (defined in Philippine law as conventional sales with the right of repurchase).[6] While these two factors may have contributed to sporadic popular discontent, which was to cumulate in later years, they were not enough to destroy the country's character of individual small ownership, at least during the half century that has been termed in this study the formative period of the Philippine economy as it existed until recently.[7]

In any case, what is more important than ownership in this matter is the question of the individual unit of cultivation. There is even more reason to believe than in the case of ownership that this was small and that there were few instances in which centralized scientific management existed, even in the cases in which large ownership might have made this a possibility. There were no counterparts in the Philippines to the West Indian sugar estates or the cotton plantations of the southern United States and little resemblance to the methods of control resorted to by planters and the governments of Malaya and Indonesia. In fact, the usual complaint was that the small size of farm holdings made it impossible to introduce modern methods of agriculture and retarded the growth of production and the country's material progress.

Some observations made at different times will serve to show the peasant character of Philippine cultivation in the period under study: Mac Micking at the midcentury mark said the following:

> There are very few people in the colony who are possessed of the capital necessary to start a plantation on a large scale. . . .
>
> However, should plantations on a large scale ever be carried on in these islands with an equal degree of facility, science, care, and attention, and with the improved machinery now employed in sugar estates in Jamaica and elsewhere, there can be little doubt that the productions of the islands will be greatly increased, and it will do good so far; but whether it would tend to improve the condition, or increase the comforts of the people, now so independent of care for a livelihood, appears to be more than doubtful; in other respects, it would do them good, by stimulating their energies. At present there

are no large plantations on the islands, although two or three of small size exist, none of which are understood to be sufficiently remunerating to offer any inducement to invest money in a similar manner. . . .

The whole of the productions of the islands are raised by the poor Indian cultivators, each from his own small patch of land, which they till with very simple, though efficient implements of agriculture.

With the existing high prices of labor, there is, however probably nearly as much surplus produce available for exportation as there would be for years to come, under the system of large plantations and dear labour. Because the present occupiers of the land . . . are certain to expend far more labour on their own land, and to bring it to a much higher degree of cultivation, than it would suit the purpose of a large planter to do. . . .

These reasons make me loath to see the present system of small holdings changed, which would sever old and respectable ties, and would force the present independent Indian cottage-farmer to seek employment from the extensive cultivator, and, without getting more work out of him, in the course of a year, would lower him in self-respect, and in the many virtues which that teaches, without deriving any correspondent advantage to society.[8]

Palgrave, who must have made his observations while serving as British consul in 1876, had almost the same things to say.

All are distinguished by the peculiar absence of one feature, rarely missed elsewhere in the colonial tropics, namely large estates. Rice lands, cane lands, coffee lands, hemp lands alike, all are divided and subdivided; and however vast the green carpet of cultivation may be in its total extent, the irregular patches that make it up are not less infinite in number than capricious in shape. . . .

Large proprietors, in the accepted signification of the phrase, are rare in the Philippines, where "every rood of ground maintains its man"; and little room accordingly is left for the expansion of single estates. Little room, and, luckily, as we shall see, for the prosperity no less than for the happiness of the "natives," little agglomerated capital. Spanish capitalists here are none; and other European proprietors of land and field, from a variety of causes useless here to discuss, none worth mentioning also. Mestizos, that is half-breeds, generally of Chino-Malay origin, are the most bulky estate-owners;

and the lands and fortunes they not rarely amass into one seldom hold together beyond a life-time, but some obey the Eastern law of subdivision between heirs, and fall asunder. The far greater part of the soil is in the hands of the Malays themselves, who, easily contented, and not much given to anxieties about fortune-making and the future, till each his little plot, and make their bargains for disposing of the produce with the Chinese or semi-Chinese middlemen; by whom again it is transferred wholesale to European, chiefly British merchants, and so reaches the coast and the cargo ships.[9]

The condition seems to have held as late as the beginning of the American regime. According to the census of 1903, out of total farm area of 2,827,704 hectares, 2,137,776, or 75.60 percent, were held by owners. Of farms numbering 815,453, 658,543, or 80.76 percent, were held by owners. There were, of course, regional differences in distribution; for example, in the province of Bulacan in central Luzon, there were about three times as many farms held by tenants as by owners. The average size of farms for the whole country was 3.47 hectares; the average area of the cultivated portion of farmland was 1.59 hectares. It is instructive to notice that, outside of sparsely settled areas like Mindanao, Mindoro, and the Mountain Province on Luzon, the average size of farms was largest in the two sugar-producing provinces of Negros Occidental and Pampanga, where they were 25.47 and 10.54 hectares, respectively.[10] These figures suggest a correlation between the size of landholdings and sugar production.

It seems clear, therefore, that neither pressure on the peasantry nor the development of large-scale plantation agriculture was primarily responsible for transforming the Philippines from a subsistence to an export economy. Other factors will have to be examined, and it will be useful first to turn to Spanish commercial policy in the Philippines, a review of which will at the same time provide a helpful background for events in the commercial sphere during the nineteenth century.

Spanish Commercial Policy in the Nineteenth-Century Philippines

Several threads run through the somewhat tangled skein of Spain's commercial policy in the Philippines beginning in about 1830. Some of the aims sought, while theoretically harmonious, were in practice contradictory. The main objectives that it is possible to discern seem to have been the following:

1. Expansion of Philippine trade
2. Development of internal Philippine resources
3. Closer communication with Spain by means of trade
4. Protection and encouragement of Philippine industry
5. Favored treatment of Spanish goods
6. Encouragement of national (Spanish and Philippine) business
7. Encouragement of national (Spanish and Philippine) shipping

The contradictions will be immediately apparent to anyone conversant with the situation. The development of internal Philippine resources and the expansion of Philippine trade were bound to be hampered by the desire to encourage national business and shipping and protect Philippine industry. This was so because local and Spanish capital was scanty and much of the progress made by the country would of necessity have to come about through the activities of foreign firms and the investment of foreign capital, of which the Spanish government was chronically suspicious. The desire to draw the Philippines and Spain closer by means of trade, which represented a tendency toward what was sometimes called *asimilismo,* or the merging of Spanish and Philippine interests, while theoretically unobjectionable, was practically unrealistic, as Spain's low purchasing power, retarded economic development, and chronic political turmoil made it a poor market for most Philippine exports except tobacco, while Spain in turn was unable to provide the Philippines with any really significant items of importation except wines and liquors and certain foodstuffs, most of which were consumed by the Spanish population in the Philippines rather then by the Filipinos. The execution of policy was quite frequently thrown into confusion by what might be called an ideological struggle between the liberals, who advocated free trade, and the conservatives, who stood for protectionism and nationalism. Bureaucratic inefficiency and corruption often complicated the picture and served to defeat well-meant policies.

What emerged in practice at any given moment, therefore, often represented a compromise between divergent trends, and it was the plaint of many that the Philippines could have achieved a greater degree of internal development and a much faster expansion of exports except for the obstacles interposed by the Spanish government. A subsequent observer has remarked that "the government failed to adjust its commercial policy to the new conditions which confronted it and to the end of Spanish dominion continued to hamper the trade it should have been its care to foster."[11] Java was often held up as a shining example of what might have been accomplished in the Philippines, whose economic progress was deemed relatively slow. In view, however, of the consideration of balanced growth as distinguished from the growth of only one sector of the economy (in this case the agricultural export sector), this may not have been an unmixed evil, or possibly not an evil at all.

Some of the commercial effects of the tobacco monopoly have already been noted. The opening of additional ports to general commerce after the middle of the century has likewise been noted. Not least among the factors that brought this about was the introduction of steam navigation in 1848, which finally gave Spain naval superiority over Moro raiders and made the Visayan Islands safe for navigation. There was also, of course, a mercantile demand for easier access to productive regions and a move for greater liberalization of trade, as illustrated by Sinibaldo de Mas's report of 1855.[12] Some other moves made by the Spanish government deserve to be noted here.

Indultos de Comerciar

One feature of Spanish local administration could have been construed as pressure on the peasantry. This was the institution of *indultos de comerciar,* which will be described below. In an oblique allusion to the Dutch system in Java, Tarling called it "a sort of culture-unsystem."[13] Under the Laws of the Indies (bk. 2, title 6, law 26; title 16, law 54; bk. 5, title 2, law 5), provincial governors (*alcaldes*) were prohibited from trading. For the privilege of violating this prohibition, however, a royal order of July 17, 1754, prescribed the *indulto de comerciar,* a fine paid in advance by the officeholder.

Since the governor was not given a salary commensurate with the duties and dignity of his office, he often took advantage of the privilege of trading to make his fortune. It has been noted that this provoked the hostility of some governors toward the factors of the Royal Philippine Company, whom they looked on as rivals, and was one of the reasons behind the company's failure. The system also gave rise to other abuses. In a falling market, the governors could refuse to receive articles previously contracted for; in a rising market, they could hold the seller to the contract price and reap all the profits themselves. The small cultivator under their jurisdiction had little redress against them, and it was not uncommon for them to amass fortunes rapidly. Tarling quotes a trader as writing that "the Alcaldes have power over the natives to induce them to bring so much of the Rice to them as they wish to buy . . ."

The bases for establishing the salaries, bonds, and *indultos* were not always clear. The highest salaries were reserved for men serving at mili-

Annual Salaries of Heads of Provinces, Annual Amount of Fine Paid to Trade, and Value of Bonds Filed with the Ministry of Finance

Province	Annual Salary (pesos)	Fine for Trading (peso/ reales/ granos)			Value of Bond (pesos)
Albay	600	125	0	0	8,000
Antique	600	0	0	0	5,000
Bataan	300	63	0	8	3,000
Batanes Is.	360	0	0	0	0
Batangas	600	130	0	0	6,000
Bulacan	600	100	0	0	8,000
Cagayan	600	225	0	0	4,000
Calamianes	600	300	0	0	2,000
Camarines Norte	600	0	0	0	1,500
Camarines Sur	600	170	0	0	8,000
Capiz	300	130	0	0	6,000
Caraga	600	300	0	0	4,000
Cavite	2,000	0	0	0	0
Cebu	600	180	0	0	8,000
Ilocos Norte	300	125	0	0	8,000
Ilocos Sur	600	125	0	0	8,000
Iloilo	600	200	0	0	10,000
Negros Island	600	80	0	0	4,000
Laguna	600	137	0	0	8,000
Leyte	300	125	0	0	5,000
Marianas	1,800	0	0	0	0
Mindoro	1,000	80	0	0	2,000
Misamis	600	80	0	0	3,000
Nueva Ecija	1,200	0	0	0	2,000
Nueva Vizcaya	1,500	0	0	0	2,000
Pampanga	300	241	7	4 2/5	8,000
Pangasinan	600	250	0	0	10,000
Samar	600	125	0	0	5,000
Tayabas	600	90	0	0	6,000
Tondo	300	0	0	0	20,000
Zambales	600	40	0	0	3,000
Zamboanga	2,000	0	0	0	0

Source: *Almanaque Filipino*, 1834, pp. 158-160; *Guia de Forasteros*, 1845, pp. 237-238; Montero y Vidal, *Historia General*, III, 71- 72.

tary posts such as those at Cavite and Zamboanga, which moreover paid no fines, making them the best remunerated posts. High salaries were also paid in new or frontier provinces like the Marianas, Mindoro, Nueva Ecija, and Nueva Vizcaya. The highest bonds were posted for populous provinces with the greatest revenues (Tondo, Iloilo, Pangasinan). But if the highest *indultos* were to be paid for the provinces with the most promising trading prospects, supposedly showing these to be the most desired posts, that is not apparent from the facts, which indicate that the highest *indultos* were in fact paid by those serving the sparsely settled frontier provinces of Calamianes and Caraga. And nine provinces had no *indultos* attached, supposedly because they had no trading activity; plausible for some (Batanes, the Marianas), this beggared belief for others (Cavite, Tondo).

George Santayana's maternal grandfather, José Borrás, was named governor of Mindoro in 1845, but for politico-bureaucratic reasons was unable to assume it and had to settle for a much lesser position.

The system was too unfocused to constitute pressure on the peasantry to produce specifically for export, and on the other hand it was more a hindrance than a stimulus to trade on the incentives side since the governors did not take kindly to competition. The system was finally abolished by a royal decree of September 23, 1844 (title 3, article 45), and a *cédula* of October 3, 1844.[14]

The *indultos de comerciar* were not the only system that might provoke abuses in gubernatorial office. Labor service on public works (*servicio de polos*) could be diverted to personal service on the governor's property. And as long as the tobacco monopoly was in existence there was an invitation to arbitrariness in the bonus given by the central insular government for each bale of tobacco produced in a given province. For instance, it was reported that a governor in an abaca-producing province ordered the planting of tobacco and gave verbal orders to cut down the abaca plantings; the result was a loss in abaca production without a corresponding gain in the output of tobacco, whose cultivation the people refused to undertake.[15] It was the viciousness of such measures, striking at the very livelihood of the people, that swelled the public outcry against the monopoly, with the more enlightened Spanish officials joining in the protest. This finally brought about the decree in 1880 that ordered its termination.

The Economic Society

It was seen earlier how the Royal Economic Society of the Philippines, founded by Governor Basco, went into a protracted period of suspended animation after the termination of his incumbency. It was revived in 1819, with its name lengthened to the Real Sociedad Económica de Amigos del País de Filipinas—the Royal Economic Society of Friends of the Country of the Philippines—and began a new period of activity in 1822 with capital of thirty thousand pesos.

It was a semipublic body composed of private individuals and government officials and with certain public functions of a consultative nature. For example, around the middle of the century a druggist named Jacobo Zóbel imported some distilling apparatus, which the customs authorities taxed at the full rate. Zóbel, however, claimed reduction of and exemption from certain imposts on the ground that the importation of such machinery was for the general public benefit and as such was entitled to certain privileges by law. The case was sent to the Economic Society for adjudication, and a verdict favoring Zóbel was returned.[16]

The main activities of the society were multifarious and add up to an impressive catalogue. Anything of an economic or scientific nature was deemed within its legitimate sphere of interest; in this, it resembled the learned societies of the eighteenth- and nineteenth-century Enlightenment in Europe. Some of its activities have a modern look to them. As early as 1823, the society was encouraging technical training by contributing 250 pesos a year for a professorship in agriculture, establishing a school of drawing, and agreeing to send a trainee to India to learn how to dye certain textiles. The following year it underwrote the training of eight Filipino dyers. In 1840, it contributed 500 pesos toward the publication of Father Blanco's classic *Flora de Filipinas*, and in 1846 it agreed to send Filipino youths to study mechanics abroad. The following year it gave 500 pesos to the support of the university, and in 1865 it agreed to make a monthly contribution toward the upkeep of the Botanical Gardens (which, it may be noted in passing, continued in existence until World War II).

Mechanical improvements also attracted attention. In 1823, the society agreed to order three rice-hulling machines from the United States. Six years later, it received such machines from the Economic Society of Cádiz. Spindles from the United States were ordered in 1826. A decade later, one of its members, Eulogio de Otaduy, introduced steam-powered rice-hulling machines on a large scale. In 1843, a steam-powered machine for quilting abaca was imported, and in 1850 the introduction of new methods and machinery in the sugar industry was proposed by a member.

As an incentive to worthy projects, the society offered and awarded prizes for several things—canal building (1823); blankets woven locally in imitation of Chinese imports (1824); coffee culture (1837, 1838, 1846, and

1847); inventing a machine to card abaca (offered 1823; a prize of two thousand pesos was given ten years later to Cándido López Díaz for inventing a machine to clean the fiber); studies regarding the extraction of abaca fiber from all species of the *musa* plant; cotton growing (1862); good house building (1865); and good cattle and textiles for local use at the Batangas fair of 1866. It made and published studies and memoranda on numerous topics—indigo (1826); coffee (1827, 1874); opium (1833, 1848, 1849); a paper factory (1825, 1835); tea (1834); coal (1834); silk (1835); public and vacant lands (1839); sugarcane (1844, 1874); population and the protection of agriculture (1845, 1854); a museum (1850); clay and pottery (1851); the free export of rice (1851, 1855); the opening of ports (1852; in 1855, it congratulated the government on the opening of Iloilo, Sual, and Zamboanga); the sending of youths to Europe for mechanical studies (1856); a steamship corporation (1856); methods of procuring birds' nests in the Calamianes (1856); uniform weights and measures for the Philippines (1858); two annual rice crops (1858); an agricultural school (1862); provision of a water system for Manila (1862); reduction of duties on imported wheat flour (1864); establishment of a quarantine station in Manila Bay (1865); cacao and abaca (1874); and swamp drainage.

It lent the weight of its opinion to public policy projects, and also expended sums to make Philippine products better known abroad and to introduce new plant varieties in the Philippines. It supported the government's plan to establish a bank (1829) and a savings institution (1868) and appointed a commission to study the project to establish an agricultural bank (1874). It assigned money for the purpose of experimenting with the importation of certain birds to fight the locust plague (1849, 1850, 1852). It sent Philippine articles to London in 1850 for exhibition purposes and received prizes for them in 1853 and 1858. It imported American cottonseed in 1841 and distributed it locally; it did the same with Egyptian cottonseed in 1862. In 1855, it offered the government 20 percent of its capital without interest for the purpose of improving public buildings; the money was delivered two years later.

Craftsmen and farmers were given special attention. In 1863, the society donated five hundred pesos for the earthquake relief of artisans and farmers. Four years later, it allocated a similar sum for the replacement of plows, hoes, and farm implements lost by farmers in Ilocos in a disastrous flood.[17]

An evaluation of the effect of the society's activities is difficult. A glance at the list of its activities shows that some of them had the effect of fostering the entrepreneurial function of innovation. Others were in the nature of what nowadays would be called social overhead, for example, educational projects that seemed to claim a large share of its attention and effort. The society met with success in some of its projects—prizes for coffee culture, for instance, of which more later. In others, however, such as its attempts to encourage cotton growing and textile weaving, it found itself fighting forces more powerful than itself.

In view of what is known about other factors in the country's economic life at that time, it is perhaps not unfair to conclude that, while it did have some effect on production and output, its direct influence on such matters was not very great. Its influence on public policy was possibly more important. And it must be credited with a share in the higher level of education existing in the country at the end of the century in comparison with the early decades. In any case, its interest in encouraging economic development in the Philippines extended over the whole range of economic activities and was not limited to the agricultural export sector alone. And its role in the country's transformation into an agricultural export economy can at most have been only an auxiliary one.

Spanish Tariff Policy in the Philippines

An obvious subject to examine in any consideration of foreign trade is a nation's tariff system. Reference has been made previously to the various duties levied at different periods before 1830. In brief, these consisted of import duties amounting to 15 percent on all goods from Mexico (except wines, which paid 5 percent more), 6 percent on all Chinese imports and 3 percent on all other imports, and export duties of 10 percent on all Chinese and other Asian goods reexported to Mexico and 3 percent on all other products.[18] The coming of the Philippine Company introduced variations, in that Spanish and Spanish colonial goods imported on company ships were duty free, as well as Philippine exports sent to Spain by the same conveyance. Spanish public policy continued the duty-free admission of Philippine goods into Spain in the decade 1820–30, although by this time the company's operations had dwindled to insignificance.

The new directions taken by Philippine trade in that fateful decade made necessary an overhaul of the archipelago's tariff system, and a royal order of April 6, 1828, created a tariff board to draw up a new schedule of duties. The board was to be guided by three purposes: (1) to increase the revenue of the public treasury, (2) to encourage and protect especially the country's agriculture and the arts, and (3) to encourage an expansion in both national and foreign commerce.[19]

Basically, each article was subject to four rates of duty, and the classifications and ordinary ad valorem rates of import duty were the following:

1. National goods on national vessels—3 percent
2. National goods on foreign vessels—8 percent
3. Foreign goods on national vessels—7 percent
4. Foreign goods on foreign vessels—14 percent

The policy of favoring national goods and national shipping is evident at a glance, and for certain items the differential enjoyed by national products was increased. The rates in classes (3) and (4) above were raised to 40 and 50 percent, respectively, for footwear; some items of ready-made clothing; wines and liquors (except champagne) and vinegar; foodstuffs such as beans, lentils, raisins, fruit, peas, chickpeas, noodles, dried and preserved seafood, pickled radishes, sweet potatoes, onions, sweets and candy, and nuts; bolos (machetes); and copper for containers. Lower, but still protective, differential rates on classes (3) and (4) were prescribed for Indian textiles, which paid 15 and 25 percent, respectively, except for certain Madras textiles, which paid 20 and 30 percent. Paper in the same two classes paid 8 and 16 percent. Diamonds and jewels, however, had a tariff advantage, paying only 1 and 2 percent. Duty-free entry was accorded machines of all kinds of common utility, chalices and other religious articles, breeding mares, seeds for vegetables and flowers, paper for drawing plans, cotton twist (in red, yellow, rose, and green), teakwood, gold, and silver. Prohibited were rum, pocket pistols, gunpowder, tobacco of any kind, wheat flour, Spanish books printed outside of Spain, and foreign primers of instruction.[20]

The special differentials point to the various national items that the Spanish government wished to favor. These were Spanish wines and liquors, sweetmeats and certain foodstuffs, Philippine textiles (and the Philippine dye industry), palm wine, tailoring, shoemaking, metal manufactures, (e.g., bolos made from ore from the Angat iron deposits), tobacco, and wheat. In some cases, the items singled out for higher tariffs were specified as those imitating some Philippine product, for example, Baliuag skirts. Other items come as a surprise to modern observers—wheat, for example, which it is easy to forget nowadays was grown in the provinces of Ilocos, Tayabas, and Laguna as late as the middle of the century.[21]

The rates of export duty were classified, somewhat like those on the import side, as follows:

1. For Spain on national vessels—1 percent
2. For other countries on national vessels—1.5 percent
3. For Spain on foreign vessels—2 percent
4. For foreign countries on foreign vessels—3 percent

Manufactured tobacco was export duty free, as was abaca for three years. Gold and silver shipped to Spain were also duty free. For foreign countries, silver coin paid 8 percent, silver bullion 6 percent, gold coin 3 percent, and gold ingots and dust 0.5 percent.[22]

Discrimination (or protection) against foreign goods was achieved not only by tariff differentials but also by setting arbitrarily high official values on goods that came predominantly from abroad. Once a certain value had been set for an article, it was likely to stand, and this in effect converted the ad valorem duty into a specific one.[23]

The tariff went into effect January 1, 1832. As was natural, the tariff schedule underwent slight modifications by means of administrative ruling or government decree over the years. The duties on imported wines and spirits were raised, following the import classification above, to: (1) 10 percent, (2) 25 percent, (3) 30 percent, and (4) 60 percent. Export duties on abaca were raised to: (1) 1 percent, (2) 1.5 percent, (3) 2 percent, and (4) 2 percent. Rice was export duty free on national vessels, 3 percent on foreign vessels bound for Spain, and 4 percent on foreign vessels bound elsewhere. In 1857, its importation was made duty free. Abaca rope remained export duty free. In 1855, many official prices were changed.

In 1860, there were some amendments meant to update it, consolidate certain items under cognate classifications, reflect minor changes in policy, or simply change the official prices used in calculating duties. The inclusion of coal from Europe, India, and Australia was in recognition that the age of steam navigation had begun. The various separate textile items were grouped together into a special textile schedule, and certain items protecting specific domestic products (like Baliuag skirts) were absorbed into more general classifications, with, however, higher rates for foreign textiles than before (40 and 50 percent in classes [3] and [4] as against 15 and 25 percent previously). There seems to have been a policy of encouraging a transshipment trade from contiguous oceanic countries for China in, for example, rattan, sea slugs, tortoiseshell, and birds' nests, as is shown by the low 2 percent rate of import duty and 0.5 to 1 percent rate of export duty.[24]

The protective features of the tariff came in for some comment, most of it adverse, from observers with free-trade sympathies. Azcárraga classed as prohibitive the rates on wines and liquors and observed that tailoring and shoemaking had made no progress despite the protection accorded footwear and ready-made clothing and that the Chinese were the principal beneficiaries since they controlled the majority of the tailoring and shoemaking establishments.[25] Bowring makes the same observation, calling the Chinese "mere birds of passage in the country" and adding that the protective duty encouraged the Chinese to become manufacturers rather than the agricultural laborers who were desired as a matter of public policy. The low quality of shoes was in addition a menace to public health, as they did not keep out rain and mud. "So runs the round of folly and miscalculation," concludes Bowring.[26]

Mac Micking's reflections take a more philosophical turn:

A dark complexioned beauty is never improved by a yellow dress; and any woman at all old or ugly looks hideous indeed when dressed in that colour. Apparently the Government were not ignorant of this when they imposed a heavy duty on blue, purple, or white articles of dress, and allowed yellow and other colours disliked by the natives to come into the country on the payment of a less duty. They have even gone the length of allowing yellow cotton twist of foreign manufacture to be imported duty free.

Truly this was very cunning of them—this apparent liberality to a foreign nation, ignorant that the colour would scarcely ever be used. Its affected moderation would most certainly tend to stop any complaints which might be made about the high duties imposed on our manufactures into the colony.[27]

The protective devices embodied in the tariff of 1832 had some effect. Most of the imports came in national vessels to take advantage of the tariff differentials, while the exports, for which the duty rates were of less consequence, were taken away in foreign bottoms. But there were evasions from the beginning, and the advantage enjoyed by national vessels was put to use only between the two British ports of transshipment, Singapore and Hong Kong, and Manila. The statistical consequences of this have already been seen. The objective of encouraging a national carrying trade between Europe and the Philippines was therefore largely unmet, as foreign shippers preferred to send goods to Singapore and Hong Kong and have the Spanish ships pick them up from there. To discourage this practice, the government imposed a surtax of 2 percent on goods originating west of the Cape of Good Hope that were carried on national vessels from

Hong Kong and a surtax of 1 percent on such goods coming in national vessels from Singapore.

There were other evasions. For example, the yellow cotton twist that was admitted duty free under the theory that no one would import it because of its unpopular color actually was used to circumvent the duties on white cotton twist. Foreign suppliers took to coloring their twist with removable yellow dye, which could easily be washed off by the consignee in the Philippines.

There were some instances of successful encouragement—for example, of tobacco exports and for a time abaca rope. But there is little reason to suppose that these would not have flourished without an exemption from export duties. The country's other major exports made great strides independently of Philippine customs preferences in response to economic forces much stronger than government tariff policy made in Manila and Madrid.

By and large, the government's protectionist features and its attempt to give shape and direction to the Philippine economy were ineffective. Outside of the fragmentary successes just mentioned, its failures were numerous. It failed to save native textiles and wheat or to improve native palm wine, ironmongering, tailoring, and shoemaking. The reasons are perhaps obvious. Little capital was being invested in these industries, and few improvements were being introduced. The Chinese, who controlled some of them, were transients who had no thought of long-range investment. They gave of their labor and their skill, reaped whatever profits were to be made (including the monopoly profits made possible by the high tariffs on certain items) and returned to their homeland to retire.

The tariff of 1832, with the noted modifications, endured for more than a generation, remaining in force until 1869. Thus, it covered the major part of the half century 1820–70, when the Philippines grew to become an export economy. From what has been seen of it, its effect on that trend could have been (like the Economic Society's) at best only auxiliary, and it is even possible that it may have had an opposite effect and served to retard the process rather than accelerate it. The contradiction in Spanish policy between expanding trade and encouraging economic development and favoring local interests over the foreigners who were, for much of that time, the only ones in a position to bring about both objectives (as they eventually did in their own way) could not be resolved without inconsistencies and evasions in practice. In any case, tariff policy cannot have been the main force behind the emergence of the Philippine export economy.

Later Tariff Policy

The tariff reforms that occurred around the time of the opening of the Suez Canal and formed part of the cluster of events that was mentioned several times in the previous chapter may have helped, by their liberal tendency and in conjunction with other historical developments, to bring the process to completion at that time instead of during a later period. For this reason, and to complete the picture of tariff policy in the Philippines to the close of the Spanish period, it will be instructive to take a cursory look at subsequent legislation in this sector of public policy.

Royal Order no. 1071 of November 21, 1860 authorized the customs authorities to introduce improvements in the Philippine tariff system. With the advent of liberal constitutional government in Spain in 1868, the first of a series of reforms was ordered, effective the following year. A few excerpts from Minister López de Ayala's decrees will suffice to show the liberal tendency underlying the reform.

> New rules . . . facilitate trade and consequently lower the cost of living. . . . The motives [for tariff reform] . . . are no other than the faithful application of sound economic principles for the growth of native production and the encouragement of commerce, removing whatever obstacles there existed to this development. . . . The economic ideas of the undersigned are liberal in the fullest sense of the word . . .[28]

The 1869 tariff changed several features of that of 1832. The major reforms were the abolition of all export duties and the reduction of the tariff differential enjoyed by goods carried on national vessels. The rates on goods carried in national bottoms remained as before, but the rate on Spanish goods carried in foreign bottoms was reduced from 8 to 5.5 percent and that on foreign goods imported on foreign carriers from 14 to 10.5 percent. These represented a 50 percent cut in the differential between the old rates and the standard rates of 3 and 7 percent. Furthermore, this was but one step toward the complete abolition of the flag differential within a period of two years.

There were other changes. The surtaxes on foreign cargoes coming on national vessels from Hong Kong and Singapore were abolished. The "official values" of certain items, on which ad valorem rates were computed, were reduced. Colored cottons were no longer carried as a separate customs item due to the evasion (described above) of the attempted protection of native white cloth. This was an example of the reduction of the protectionist features of the tariff system, concerning which the overseas minister said:

> The Government has taken account of the fact that the inconveniences of exaggerated protection are greater in that Archipelago, because products peculiar to it have no need of it; because the greater part of goods similar to those produced in other neighboring countries and even to those of Europe are meant exclusively for domestic consumption, without growing in importance, in spite of being protected, due to their scantiness and their prices, which do not permit them to compete . . .[29]

The principle of protection was being eroded. Those were the days when liberals could still speak with a clear conscience of the complete abolition of customs duties as at least an eventual possibility without having to think of "escape clauses" for special interests.[30]

There were other provisions of an administrative nature such as prescribing the use of the metric system in customs procedures and the fusing of several charges into one impost. Encouragement of shipbuilding and navigation was continued by means of premiums paid for locally constructed vessels and a rebate of customs duties on materials used in construction.

In other respects, however, certain features of the old tariff continued with only slight changes. Special tariff advantages were enjoyed by practically the same goods as before—textiles, footwear, ready-made clothing, certain sweets and foodstuffs, paper, and so on. The free list was also similar, with white rice, coal and coke, wheat flour (perhaps at the instance of the Economic Society), and building stones added. Foreign goods enjoying a tariff advantage (partly in order to encourage trade with China) included birds' nests, bêche-de-mer, mother of pearl, pearls, potatoes, and wheat besides the diamonds and jewels of the 1832 tariff. Tobacco paid a specific duty.

Before two years had passed, another tariff reform was decreed, effective July 1, 1871. Except for the restoration of export duties on certain articles, the new tariff represented a continuation of the liberal trend in Spanish legislation at the time. Minister Moret, in the covering decree, said that "absolute freedom of trade" was an indispensable condition for the progress of the Philippines, the development of its wealth, the growth of its industry, and a reduction in the cost of living, thereby attracting colonists. He added that he would go so far as to recommend the abolition of duties but for two considerations: the needs of the public treasury and the desire to link Spain and the Philippines closer together by means of preferential trade. All thought of protectionism was disclaimed, and the new duties were said to be strictly for revenue purposes. As in the 1869 tariff, it was stated that no decrease in revenue was expected to result from the lower rates of duty because a higher level of trade was expected.[31]

The tariff of 1871, from a liberal point of view, represented a backward step from that of 1869 in prescribing a return to export duties. This was no doubt motivated by the needs of the public treasury and the impending abolition of the tobacco monopoly. However, the new export duties were levied only on what were considered the leading exports—indigo (solid and liquid), abaca (raw and manufactured), rice, sugar, coffee, and dyewoods. All others were deemed so insignificant as to be not worth the bother. (It is interesting to note, in connection with the argument in the previous chapter about the position of rice in Philippine commerce, that it was still considered one of the country's leading exports at this time.) The rates were changed from ad valorem to specific duties.

The rest of the 1871 tariff represented a progression along the liberal road embarked upon two years previously. As in the case of export duties, most import duties were specific rather than ad valorem, and their maximum rate converted to an ad valorem basis did not exceed 10 percent. The number of classifications in the tariff was reduced, and goods falling outside these classes could be imported freely.

Two new features deserve to be noted in connection with customs duties. The flag differential, which was due to expire by virtue of the 1869 tariff, was abolished, but it was revived in a different form so as to provide for its more gradual extinction. The 1871 tariff, instead of prescribing a rate directed against foreign carriers, gave a tariff reduction, gradually diminishing over eight years, in favor of Spanish vessels. Thus, foreign goods shipped in national bottoms enjoyed a 25 percent tariff reduction between July 1, 1871, and June 30, 1873: 20 percent in the next two years, 15 percent in the two years after that, and 10 percent in the final two years of the prescribed eight-year period. The distinction between raising rates for foreign vessels and reducing them in favor of national carriers is at best a tenuous one, but it did represent a difference in basic approach, and the diminishing preference accorded Spanish shippers was in line with the trend toward equalization.

Of a more ambiguous nature was the other important disposition with respect to customs duties, namely, the exemption of Spanish goods shipped on Spanish vessels from payment of all tariffs. By interpretation, this was held to apply to all Spanish goods shipped from Spain in Spanish vessels even if they were subsequently transshipped to foreign carriers. It was more liberal in the sense that it removed obstacles to at least a part of the country's foreign trade; it was less so in that it was a step away from equal treatment of all nationalities. In any case, it set an important precedent that was followed till the end of Spanish rule in the Philippines.

The 1871 tariff also recognized that rate reduction alone would not necessarily mean freer trade, and it prescribed administrative measures such as the simplification of customs procedures, the abolition of consular registers, and the admission of goods on open consignment. The Manila authorities were given the power to open new ports to foreign trade besides the five already in operation (Manila, Iloilo, Cebu, Zamboanga, and Sual). Premiums for shipbuilding were abolished, but exemption from the import duty on shipbuilding materials was continued along with other incentives related to navigation.[32]

Azcárraga praised the reform in no uncertain terms as being a decided step in the right direction. However, he also found things to criticize, among them the fact that reciprocal free entry was not extended to Philippine goods in Spain.[33] Some tariff concessions were granted to Philippine products; by the terms of the Spanish tariff approved on July 12, 1869, Philippine goods paid only one-fifth of the regular duties in Spain.[34] Had the trade between the two countries been of a more significant proportion, the point might have loomed larger; as it was, it made little difference one way or the other.

Of almost equal importance with the tariff of 1871 was a new law relating to the admission of foreigners to Spanish overseas possessions passed by the Cortes on May 19, 1870, and decreed in the Philippines on September 10 of the following year. Earlier in the century, royal permission had been necessary for foreigners to set up in business in the Philippines; later this permission was given by the governor. Now, however, during the high-water mark of nineteenth-century Spanish liberalism, foreigners were given the right to acquire real and movable property and pursue freely any industry or profession for which no Spanish professional degree was necessary.[35] This made it much easier for foreigners to establish themselves in the Philippines. However, the firms that were most influential in shaping the course of Philippine trade had by then been in existence for a long time, and the quantitative effects of the liberalization may have been more important than its qualitative effects.

The 1871 tariff was amended slightly in 1874, apparently because Madrid felt that the Manila authorities had been overenthusiastic in putting articles on the duty-free list. Minister Balaguer reminded them that "only those articles are free of duty which serve to promote the moral and material interests of those islands." Some rates were also changed, but the basic outline of the 1871 tariff stood for two decades.[36]

The modifications that took place in Hispano-Philippine tariff relations over the next few years came about largely through individual laws. Tobacco was added to the list of goods paying export duties with the abolition of the tobacco monopoly in 1880. Beginning in 1882, products from Cuba, Puerto Rico, and the Philippines were admitted duty free into Spain, but certain commodities were excepted: spirits, tobacco, sugar, cacao, chocolate, and coffee—a list that included three of the Philippines' four ranking exports. These were subject to tariff duties diminishing by 10 percent yearly, so that by 1882 their entry into Spain would be free of duty. Philippine goods received preferential treatment in that they paid only one-fifth the rate paid by Cuban and Puerto Rican products. An administrative ruling in 1886, moreover, had the effect of classifying Philippine sugar as duty free if taken to Spain on national ships. Thus, the reciprocity desired by Azcárraga was being gradually attained.[37] In 1887, sugar was declared exempt from export duty in the Philippines.[38] Exempted from import duty at about the same time were materials for the construction of the Manila-Dagupan railroad and the Manila-Caloocan trolley line, in conformity with the government's policy of promoting the country's development.[39]

Thus far the modifications had continued the trend toward the liberalization of trade, which had been in consonance with major European liberalizing moves as exemplified in the repeal of the British Corn Laws in 1846, the abandonment of the British policy of monopolizing colonial trade, the virtual abandonment of British tariffs on manufactures, the Cobden-Chevalier treaty of 1860, and similar treaties concluded by France with most European states, including Spain. But in the late 1870s a protectionist backlash set in, from which Spain was not exempt.[40]

A royal order of July 25, 1885, began what developed into a move in the opposite direction by decreeing a consumption tax on imports of wine, spirits, beer, cider, vinegar, cheese, lard, preserved foods, and sweetmeats.[41] This tax was computed separately from other duties but was collected at the customs house. It is open to question whether to consider it a tariff or an internal revenue tax in the light of modern usage. In practice, it amounted to a surcharge on the original duty; but since those days countries have experimented with internal revenue taxes on imports, sales taxes payable in advance, internal revenue taxes from which domestic goods are exempted, and similar devices designed to circumvent international agreements on tariff reduction (some examples may be seen in the U.S. Agricultural Adjustment Act), and this particular consumption tax probably belongs in that twilight zone between tariffs and internal revenue taxes in company with them.

Then came a series of additional surcharges in quick succession. A 50 percent surcharge on import duties was imposed in August 1889. A consumption tax on rice and industrial alcohol and spirits was decreed. And loading and unloading taxes began to be collected in 1890. There was also a surtax in Manila for harbor improvements. The pendulum was swinging away from the liberalism of the 1870s (as might have been expected after the restoration of the monarchy in 1876), which culminated in the protectionist and nationalistic tariff of 1891.

This tariff was apparently motivated by the unsatisfactory results of the piecemeal legislation of the preceding years, especially since some of the imposts that were not clearly duties were applied to Spanish goods, which went against the protectionist grain of the Madrid government. Three reasons were given for the new legislation: (1) the need for more public revenue, (2) the desirability of protecting Spanish and Philippine commerce and industry, and (3) improved conditions in the Philippines compared with the 1870s. The covering decree also mentioned that Spain could not isolate itself from the worldwide trend toward a "prudent protection" of national interests nor ignore the need to widen Spanish markets in order to counter moves made by other countries. The Philippines was said to offer a fertile field for development and an assured future for Spanish interests, with proper legislation that would also stimulate Philippine interests, establish local industries, exploit natural products, and attract Spanish capital. The monopolization of commerce by foreigners was deplored.[42]

The new tariff fused several of the previous charges into one import duty, abandoned all ad valorem duties and made them specific, exempted Spanish goods imported in Spanish vessels from payment of duties, increased the protection given to Spanish and Philippine products, and reduced and practically abolished the free list.[43] Export duties were eliminated, but a loading tax was levied, not only on exports but on coastwise trade (one peso per thousand kilograms on exports and half that rate on internal shipments). This provoked such an outcry from merchants that the tax had to be suppressed and changed, and export duties were again imposed in 1893.[44]

The effects of this tariff on imports in general and textile imports in particular have already been noted, and part of the increased industrial activity of the period may be at least partially attributed to it. There is no doubt that it raised the overall tariff level and the degree of protection. A comparison of this tariff with the old one (including the 50 percent surcharge) shows that, out of more than three hundred classifications, only about one-tenth that number enjoyed rate reduction. The duties on most other classes of goods went up, and a few remained the same or were not comparable because they were changed from ad valorem to specific duties. In addition, thirty-six classes of goods formerly on the free list (including machinery) were made dutiable.[45]

The movement of the average tariff level in the Philippines in the latter part of the nineteenth century is shown in table 14. Its computation follows the most simple definition, namely, the ratio of import duties collected to the value of total imports. It is only a rough measure of the degree of protection since a really prohibitive duty would, by its very effectiveness, tend to take itself out of the computation and a sizable free list would tend to lower the level. It is, however, often used in modern tariff discussions, and it is therefore instructive to inspect its trend, which is seen to be on the whole upward for the half century before the Revolution, with the sharpest interruption coming in the liberal years of the early 1870s. The sharpest rise clearly occurs in the 1890s. Insofar as other charges were levied on imports, the figures in table 14 understate the tariff level; since, however, the other taxes were often computed on a different basis, it was deemed advisable for the sake of statistical homogeneity to include only import duties proper. The understatement is not serious except in the years 1890, 1891, and 1893, and even so the secular trend is not affected, although the rate of increase of the last spurt is. Adding the 50 percent surcharge, the consumption tax and the unloading tax in these three years results in the following increases in tariff level: 1890, from 7.37 to 12.74 percent; 1891, from 11.95 to 14.39 percent; and 1893, from 13.58 to 15.06 percent, which makes it the peak for the century.

When the free list (of Spanish goods) is separated from the value of total imports, the tariff level of course rises. Plehn calculates that for 1894 the tariff level on this basis was 16 percent as against 12.94 percent for total imports. A war tax of 6 percent ad valorem was imposed in 1897, it may be noted here. Computing the tariff levels on the basis of dutiable imports alone would be tedious owing to the nonsegregation of certain classifications and to sometimes divergent figures. However, a tentative estimate on this basis for 1874 results in an import tariff level of 7.52 percent as

TABLE 14
Average Rates of Import Duty for the Philippines
Selected Years, 1844-1895

Year	Import Duties (pesos)	Imports (pesos)	Average Rate[1]
1844	162,090	3,301,312	4.41
1847	186,249	3,429,931	5.43
1855	283,034	4,773,399	5.93
1856	316,268	6,949,254	4.55
1857	393,717	9,907,299	3.97
1858	347,383	5,798,720	5.99
1859	328,388	6,271,560	5.24
1860	565,091	8,739,474	6.47
1861	679,917	10,148,160	6.70
1862	398,341	6,941,735	5.74
1863	402,772	7,465,063	5.40
1864	521,538	10,901,584	4.78
1865	566,144	8,935,261	6.34
1866	568,848	8,855,895	6.42
1867	521,344	7,590,427	6.87
1868	618,025	(2)	-
1869	529,924	(2)	-
1870	622,315	12,596,536	4.94
1871	782,336	(2)	-
1872	684,286	22,163,142	3.09
1873	869,961	13,217,836	6.58
1874	938,666	13,704,254	6.85
1875	907,748	12,215,153	7.43
1876	933,725	11,987,162	7.79
1877	1,332,626	19,522,897	6.83
1878	1,202,488	17,285,792	6.96
1879	942,565	18,028,739	5.23
1880	1,643,346	25,459,810	6.45
1881	1,850,642	20,771,531	8.96
1882	2,139,558	21,253,096	10.07
1883	1,716,035	21,295,262	8.06
1884	1,563,919	21,246,241	7.36
1885	1,430,493	19,160,070	7.47

Continued next page

[1] Ratio of import duties to total imports, in percent.
(2) No Data

Table 14 *Continued*

Year	Import Duties (pesos)	Imports (pesos)	Average Rate[1]
1886	1,393,104	20,073,595	6.94
1887	1,158,058	17,530,198	6.61
1888	1,856,941	21,208,482	8.76
1889	2,081,685	24,980,832	8.33
1890	1,458,312	19,789,636	7.37
1891	2,587,151	21,642,246	11.95
1892	3,493,258	23,803,547	14.68
1893	3,519,109	25,913,870	13.58
1894	3,231,442	25,398,798	12.72

Sources:Jules Itier, *Journal d'un Voyage en Chine* (Paris, 1848); *Balanza general* 1847, *Cuadro general* 1856; *Balanza mercantil*, 1857-1861; *Estadistica general*, 1891-1894; Society of Jesus, *El Archipielago Filipino*, I, 314.

against 6.85 percent for total imports, showing a contrast between the liberal 1870s and the protectionist 1890s.

The average rate of export duty is not as important a concept since this impost was levied primarily for revenue purposes. Table 15 shows that the average export duty level in the years 1855–65 was higher than in the two succeeding decades, although the absolute amount collected in the latter period (except 1869–71) was generally higher than in the former. There was an increase in the mid-1880s. From 1890 on, the situation is complicated by the loading tax, which in some years included internal trade as well as exports. However, this much can be said: the reduced level in 1890 is illusory, but that in subsequent years is not, though it may be overstated; and the rise in 1894 and 1895 is also real, though somewhat understated. For comparison, a tentative estimate of the average export duty level for 1874 shows it to be 1.98 percent of dutiable exports against 1.41 percent of total exports.[46]

Banking

The expansion of trade could not have taken place unaccompanied by an expansion of credit facilities, and it is worth looking briefly into Spanish efforts in this field to see if they might have been the propelling force behind the country's economic transformation.

TABLE 15
Average Rates of Export Duty for the Philippines
Selected Years, 1844-1895

Year	Export Duties (pesos)	Average Rate[1] (percent)
1844	870	0.03
1847	337	0.01
1855	127,582	2.15
1856	178,901	1.96
1857	243,297	2.13
1858	164,862	1.75
1859	188,531	2.33
1860	181,530	1.90
1861	152,994	1.90
1862	173,683	1.90
1863	199,506	1.98
1864	209,996	1.97
1865	226,715	2.17
1866	188,481	1.70
1867	185,441	1.69
1868	184,396	1.57
1869	81,531	0.58
1870	—	0.00
1871	84,877	0.64
1872	235,651	1.43
1873	217,531	0.92
1874	243,201	1.41
1875	267,846	1.42
1876	280,020	1.89
1877	266,301	1.63
1878	277,944	1.60
1879	281,792	1.50
1880	367,488	1.61
1881	432,507	1.76
1882	323,240	1.56
1883	435,281	1.65
1884	419,455	1.85
1885	700,509	2.85
1886	620,541	2.41

Continued next page

Table 15 *Continued*

Year	Export Duties (pesos)	Average Rate[1] (percent)
1887	570,829	2.26
1888	597,947	2.27
1889	574,882	1.65
1890	354,027	1.35
1891	25,546	0.09
1892	—	0.00
1893	314,931	0.87
1894	630,439	1.90
1895	729,369	1.99

[1] Ratio of export duties to total exports.
Sources: See Table 14.

Before doing so, it should be noted that in the last half century of the Spanish period three commercial banks were established—the Banco Español-Filipino de Isabel II in 1852 (authorized in 1851); the Chartered Bank of India, Australia, and China in 1872; and the Hong Kong and Shanghai Banking Corporation in 1875.[47] The last two were branches of the British banks of those names already operating in the Far East. They undoubtedly had much to do with the increased commercial activity in the country in the last quarter century of Spanish rule, but since this came after the transformation to an export economy had been completed they need not be considered here.

This leaves the Banco Español-Filipino, which exists to this day under the name Bank of the Philippine Islands and claims to be the first bank established in the Far East. As in the case of the Economic Society, it was of a quasi-public nature and had as its patron the governor of the islands, representing the monarch. Of the two thousand shares of capital stock, worth a total of four hundred thousand pesos, one thousand shares were purchased with funds of the venerable *obras pías*, which were now under government regulation, and of the *cajas de comunidad* (reserve funds made up of proceeds of local taxation) and were declared inalienable and nontransferable. The remainder was made available for purchase by the general public.[48]

The quasi-public nature of the bank may have been a necessity dictated by the scantiness of local capital and the government's control of the *obras pías*; it exposed the institution to the delays and exactions that attached to such a status. The founding of the bank, for example, had apparently been an idea of long standing. As early as a royal order of April 17, 1826, members of the *obras pías* were asked their opinions regarding the feasibility of establishing "a public bank." Among those petitioned was the Economic Society. Even before the replies were in, which took until 1829, a royal order of April 6, 1828, ordered the establishment of a public bank. A dilatory process then was set in motion. Files were sent to the Tariff Board and continued to be sent as late as 1837.[49] It was not until August 1, 1851, that the bank was created and May 1 of the following year that its first transaction was made.[50]

The bank's first operations were limited to discounts and exchange because the government took until 1854 to approve its bylaws and empower it to issue notes and because all of its capital had not yet been received.[51] Even after its founding, it was called upon to render unusual services. In 1864, for example, at a time when a top-heavy bureaucracy had caused government expenses to outrun revenues, the public treasury tried to borrow 200,000 pesos from it without interest or a set time limit (those were the days, it should be recalled, when it was still considered bad form for governments to fall in arrears in their budgets). It took a royal order from Madrid to call the Manila authorities to order and to authorize at most a reduction in the interest rate on the loan. The Bank Board on August 18, 1864, conceded the treasury a rate of 6 percent instead of the going rate of 8 percent, and the loan was made six years later.[52]

The bank seems to have been very conservatively managed. In its first annual report, its principal point was that, despite the fact that it had not fulfilled the most optimistic hopes and had reported no great profit, sound management had enabled it to maintain its capital intact and declare a dividend of 6 percent.[53] Four years later, the annual report was still talking about having incurred no losses or suffered a diminution of capital in five years of operation. It did complain about a lack of profits, slow business, and a monetary "crisis," as shown by an inward monetary movement of over three million pesos.[54]

This is far from the imaginative and daring conduct one is accustomed to associate with credit institutions in times of economic expansion, although for its part it must be said that its conservative management is probably what has enabled it persist to the present day and declare dividends from the earliest years ranging from 6 to 21 percent.[55] It also, by the mere fact of its existence, was of public service in increasing the facilities available to commerce and bringing into circulation hoarded savings; in its first ten months of operation, its current accounts amounted to 1,394,847 pesos.[56]

But the available evidence indicates that the Banco Español-Filipino could at best have been only an auxiliary factor in the country's transformation due to the fact that it was established three decades after the start of the predominance of native goods in the export trade and to its conservative management. Its contribution along these lines probably came through its extension of credit and other facilities to the foreign merchants who had subscribed to some of its capital stock and who made use of part of this credit to extend credit on their own account to local producers. But they had been doing this with their own funds even before the establishment of the bank, and priority in banking operations must be credited to them. Tornow wrote that

> 1851 saw the establishment of the Banco Español Filipino; but by reason of bureaucratic formalities and strict limits imposed transactions were much impeded. . . . Up to 1860 and still later, banking transactions were therefore done almost wholly through two large American houses.[57]

There were also local financial houses. The earliest ones were said to have been founded by Paris-educated Dámaso Gorricho and Francisco Rodríguez, the Anglicized Filipino Quaker whose austere dress must have been a unique sight in the Manila of the 1830s. Whether or not these houses deserve to be called banks is a moot point. Gorricho's was simply a moneylending concern, and Rodríguez conducted his business as a companion to the British and American houses. Whatever the case, Rodríguez is credited with having organized the first Filipino financial institution, which was followed by another founded by Mariano Tuason.[58] When the Banco Español-Filipino was founded, a Tuason (José María) was its first manager.[59]

Spanish interest in the banking sector continued to the end of the regime. Demands for an agricultural banking system were voiced in the 1870s and projects for its establishment discussed, but nothing practical came of them because of the old and thorny question of proper land registration and titulation,[60] without which land could not be used as security for loans.

It is clear, however, that neither the quasi-official Banco Español-Filipino nor any of the local financiers was the main force behind the country's commercial progress in the period under discussion. Neither were the other facets of Spanish policy—the activities of the Economic Society, the *indultos de comerciar*, or the workings of tariff policy—the last of which, referred to as "une tarification vicieuse et arbirtraire" by one writer,[61] may have actually been a hindrance rather than a stimulant to commerce, although the others undoubtedly were the latter.

Foreign Merchants and the Consequences of Their Advent

It seems clear from an exploration of the alternatives—plantations, pressure on the peasantry, and government policy—and from the available evidence that the major role in the expansion of Philippine commerce and the transformation of the Philippine economy in the nineteenth century was played by the foreign business houses that had established themselves there after the end of the Napoleonic Wars. These houses not only dealt in merchandise but went into the banking business as well.[62] They formed the main nexus between the Philippine economy and the currents of world trade. The rising demand of the western world for raw materials was transmitted by them to the country in which they operated. The increased productivity and industrialization of Europe and the United States was likewise reflected in their role in importing large quantities of manufactured goods. As Le Roy writes:

> The presence of foreign traders, introducing agricultural machinery and advancing money on crops, was the chief stimulus to the opening of new areas of cultivation, the betterment of methods of tilling and preparing crops for the market, and the consequent growth of exports; indeed, one may almost say that certain American (United States) and English trading houses nurtured the sugar and hemp crops of the Philippines into existence. And the pioneer work in this respect was done before the opening of the Suez Canal brought the Philippines into vital touch with Europe by means of steam navigation—American influence being then, in fact, already on the wane. . . Hence, the opening of the Suez Canal only gave a new turn and a great acceleration to a movement that, as regards Philippine internal development, may more logically be dated from 1815, the year of the last voyage of the galleon.[63]

All the available testimony points to the preponderance of the British and Americans in the foreign trade of the Philippines, as might have already been inferred from its geographic distribution. For example, Mac Micking wrote around the midcentury mark:

Nearly the whole of the produce of the Philippines is exported from Manilla by the foreign merchants resident there, none of the Spaniards being engaged in commerce to anything like the same extent as the foreigners are; the few British and the two American houses doing an immensely greater amount of business than the whole transactions of all the Spanish merchants, numerous though they be.[64]

At the end of Spanish rule nearly half a century later, the same situation prevailed, except that the Americans had disappeared.

The larger houses—those controlling the exporting and importing business—are in the hands of the English, Swiss, Spanish, Germans and French, of importance in the order named. Many of these establishments are successors of American houses which in former years controlled the commerce of the Philippine islands. We were of the first commercial importance in the Asiatic cities twenty years ago, at Hong Kong, Shanghai, and Manila, but gradually yielded to the English, Germans, and Chinese, the same factors that must be met at this time. These foreign houses export the sugar, hemp, indigo, and tobacco of the Philippines, and their market is with Europe and the East. This is so because the products of the islands are more easily and cheaply delivered there, and also because the wares of the Orient are most eagerly received in exchange . . .[65]

A quantitative estimate of the relative importance of foreign and Spanish (i.e., domestic) houses was attempted by Max Tornow, a German merchant, on the basis of customs duties (import and export) paid in the last three years of Spanish rule. He gave the following figures.

	1895	1896	1897
From foreign houses	$2,818,900	$3,106,100	$3,322,500
From Spanish houses	$361,400	$425,900	$903,000
Total	$3,180,300	$3,532,000	$4,225,500

According to Tornow's calculations, the foreign houses paid 87 percent of the duties in 1895, 88 percent in 1896, and 73 percent in 1897.[66] It should be borne in mind, however, that Spanish goods enjoyed preferential customs treatment at this time.

The Chinese, as they did in so many other countries in Southeast Asia, occupied (and still occupy) a strategic position in the country's trade; at that time, it was as intermediaries between foreign western merchants and domestic suppliers and consumers. "Practically all the retail and much of the wholesale trade of the Philippines is in the hands of the Chinese," wrote Victor S. Clark in 1905. Elsewhere he remarked: "Commercially they form a connecting link between Europeans or Americans and the natives . . ." Max Tornow stated flatly: "The retail and intermediate trade is done by the Chinese . . ." Samuel W. Belford was more specific:

> They [the Chinese] are the middle-men between the producer and the exporter, as well as between the consumer and the importer. They control those lines of business that involve daily contact with the people, whose wants they know and with whom there is a certain community of interest . . .[67]

Besides acting as wholesalers and retailers, some Chinese also traded abroad directly on their own account, as may be seen in customs records in the Philippine National Archives, but in the period under study their importance does not appear to have been large.

The coming of the foreign traders and the opening of the country to foreign trade affected not only the country's economy but also its social and political life. The British vice consul in Iloilo reported in 1858 that

> a very marked change has taken place in the dress and general exterior appearance of the inhabitants of the large pueblos. . . . In the interior of the houses the same change is also observable in the furniture and other arrangements, and the evident wish to add ornamental to the more necessary articles of household uses . . .[68]

A native middle class was rising, a class that had the means to study, reflect, and enjoy the amenities of life. The members of this class, according to Pardo de Tavera,

> gave a proof of their intelligence and of their aspirations by sending their children to Manila to be educated, buying furniture, mirrors, articles of luxury for their homes, and persons; buying pianos, carriages, objects imported from the United States and Europe which came their way, owing to foreign trade.[69]

In the matter of piano imports, the annual customs reports show that in the five-year period 1856–60, 163 pianos with a value of 40,970 pesos were imported; in the four-year period 1891–94, the number had increased to 1,685 pianos with a value of 210,625 pesos.[70]

The effects of commercial prosperity in the coffee capital of the country, Lipa, Batangas, have been graphically described by a contemporary Filipino writer:

> The American millionaires of approximately the same period had nothing over their Philippine counterparts in the matter of rococo splendor. The wealthy Lipeños washed their faces in silver basins and ate from gold plates. Their women wore slippers heeled with gold and embroidered with diamonds; and their children were attired in the fashions of Victorian England. When they rode through the Villa in their stylish carriages, servants ran ahead to bid the common folk to make way. If they deigned to walk on the street, they were sheltered from the sun by servants bearing parasols. A favorite sport of Lipa's young blades then was to toss their diamond rings into the darkness and then search for them by the light of burning bank notes.
>
> The pious shuddered at such wanton ostentation; and when, toward the end of the 1880s, the pest finally descended on Lipa's coffee trees, many felt it to be indeed a deserved visitation of God's wrath.[71]

The effects of the acquisition of ready money by the native middle class were not limited to nouveau riche patterns of behavior of an ostentatious sort; there were deeper consequences culturally and politically. "The fructifying effect of commercial prosperity on culture," continues the above account, "was to be revealed in the generation of Batangueños that succeeded the coffee millionaires—the generation that produced Mabini, Apacible, the school of Batangueño writers that dominated the newspaper field in the 1900s, and—of course—the Kalaws."[72]

The cultural effects were not confined to the coffee regions but were widespread, and they occurred as a general movement, a flowering of Philippine art, letters, and culture that was to carry over into the first decades of the American period. There were painters like Lozano, Hidalgo, and Luna, the latter two of whom won prizes in Europe. There were the novels of protest written by Rizal and political tracts by Del Pilar and López Jaena. There were poets like Fernando Ma. Guerrero and Cecilio Apóstol and scholars like T. H. Pardo de Tavera, the lawyer-economist Sancianco, the military strategist Antonio Luna, and a galaxy of other lights, major and minor, who clustered about the quickening movement of the times. As one of the signs of the epoch, Italian opera companies began to visit Manila annually from 1867 on, even before the Suez Canal was opened. Even earlier, non-Hispanic western influences at a more popular level had begun to have an impact. In 1856, Henry Sturgis Grew described a child's funeral cortege as "preceded by a band of music playing lively airs, among them several American ones such as 'Camptown Walls' [undoubtedly Camptown Races], 'O Susana' etc."[73] (In the Philippine countryside, children's funerals feature "happy" music on the reasoning that children, being sinless, go straight to heaven, a reason for rejoicing.)

The rise of the native intelligentsia and Spain's repressive political policies were bound to culminate in an outburst of no mean proportions. Pardo de Tavera describes how this process was linked with commercial progress:

> Freedom of trade was bound to bring capital and active people from the outside of the archipelago. Capital would be of use to develop production and, naturally, consumption, and exportation. Persons who came freely brought new ideas, new methods, new moral and intellectual needs, without the support of privileges which served for exploitation, so that such men had to influence favorably the general progress of the Filipinos. . . . Freedom of trade brought about the development of agriculture which had already been initiated by the Real Compañía. . . . Wealthy citizens would come to Manila, make purchases, become acquainted with the great merchants who entertained them in their quality as customers, whose trade they needed; they visited the Governor General, who would receive them according to the position that their money gave; they came to know the justices of the Supreme Court, the provincials of religious orders; they brushed up as a result of their contact, with the people of the capital and on returning to the pueblo they took in their hearts and minds with them the germ of what was subsequently called subversive ideas and later *filibusterismo*. . .

> Already the "brutes loaded with gold" dared to discuss with their curate, complain against the alcalde, defend their homes against the misconduct of the lieutenant or sergeant of the constabulary police; such people were starting to emancipate themselves insensibly as a consequence of this economic independence. Their

money permitted them effectively to defend questions involving money first, then those of a moral nature—they were actually becoming insolent, according to the expression of the dominators; in reality they were beginning to defend their rights.[74]

This was not all. The increasing wealth of the Filipinos was reaching into the very social life of the villages. The *cabeza de barangay* system was beginning to break down. This was a survival of pre-Spanish tribal organization. *Cabezas de barangay* were heads of clans or villages, and when the Spaniards came a transformation analogous to what happened to the European nobility took place: the *cabezas* were converted into tax collectors and local public officials, and thus a military class became an administrative one. As long as there were no radical economic changes and no great differences in levels of income, these men enjoyed great prestige in their communities and were addressed by their compatriots with the title Don. When, however, the increasing profitability of export crops and trade and widening differences in income levels made it possible to acquire prestige without going through an onerous term of service as a *cabeza*, the institution became obsolete. Persons of wealth did not wish to become public officials, and nonentities were elected as *cabezas*. These in turn elected from among their numbers the *gobernadorcillos* or *capitanes* (heads of municipalities). These formed, theoretically, the native upper class, but the reality was far from that. The *cabezas* were responsible for tax collection, and when it became possible for Filipinos to travel about freely without passports the *cabezas* had difficulty finding the tributants under their jurisdiction and had to make up from their own pockets what they were unable to collect. This worked while their personal fortunes held out, but when these were exhausted the alternative was prison. By the 1870s, there were numerous *cabezas de barangay* in Philippine jails.[75]

As the native middle class grew in importance, its sense of political injustice was exacerbated by the harsh methods by which the Spanish colonial administrators sought to smother discontent. Even Peninsular Spaniards resident in the Philippines began to make common cause with the native born. And when the Revolution broke out sons of Spaniards, Frenchmen, and Chinese marched to battle together with Filipinos of Malay racial stock.

These political, social, and cultural events are beyond the proper scope of this study. It is needless to say that freedom of trade and the entrance of foreign merchants were not the only factors leading up to them. The educational innovations instituted by the Jesuits upon their return in 1859 and

216

the temporary triumph of liberalism in Spain in 1868–76 are just two of the other factors that led to the transformation. But they have been sketched in at this point to indicate the effects to which the opening of the country to commerce and the coming of foreign merchants made a substantial contribution. The reasons why these merchants came to the country, the forms of business organization they adopted, the methods they employed, some of the personalities involved, and examples of various facets of their entrepreneurship have yet to be scrutinized. Their examination will occupy the balance of this study.

After
the Galleons

Part 3

Entrepreneurial Aspects

For the great mass of transactions that make up the commerce

of nations in the capitalist epoch it is clear, however,

not only that the stage has at any time been set for them

by the cyclical process of evolution, but also that priority in the mechanism

of economic relations between nations belongs not to trading but to finance.

It would be truer to say that modern commodity trade

followed and complemented capital transactions than that

the latter arose out of and complemented commodity trade.

Selling presupposes lending or "capital export" in other forms,

and commerce develops within environments first created

and incessantly reshaped by entrepreneurial and capitalist ventures.

-JOSEPH A. SCHUMPETER (1939)

Photographs overleaf: (1) Narciso Padilla (*top, left*), Filipino businessman and lawyer, active c. 1820–1865; (2) Paul Proust de la Gironière (*top, right*), a French agricultural entrepreneur, active c. 1820–1860; (3) Robert MacMicking (*bottom, right*), British merchant (1826– c. 1907); (4) Jose Ma. Tuason (*bottom, left*), Filipino businessman and banker (d. 1856); (5) Jonathan Russell (*center*), American merchant (1825–1875). *Inset*: an indigo factory. *Sources*: (1) Cultural Center of the Philippines Archives; (2) *Aventures d'un Gentilhomme Breton aux Iles Philippines* (Paris: Au Comptoir des Imprimeurs-Unis, Lacroix-Comon, 1855); (3) *Sydney Mail*, 24 June 1908; (4) Tuason family; (5) Heirs of John J. Russell.

CHAPTER 7

Conceptual and Technological Considerations

Conceptual Notes

Interest in entrepreneurial questions stems in part from a dissatisfaction with mechanistic theories in the explanation of economic phenomena and especially economic change. On this score, Schumpeter wrote:

> Practically all the economists of the nineteenth century and many of the twentieth have believed uncritically that all that is needed to explain a given historical development is to indicate conditioning or causal factors, such as an increase in population or the supply of capital. But this is sufficient only in the rarest of cases. As a rule, no factor acts in a uniquely determined way and, whenever it does not, the necessity arises of going into the details of its *modus operandi*, into the mechanisms through which it acts.[1]

Gustav Cassel had expressed much the same sentiment somewhat earlier and indicated where to look for the mechanisms of change:

> The factors of production, however, do not flow spontaneously in the direction marked out for them by prices. They must be directed by human activity, as is done when the entrepreneur buys factors of

production, uses them in cooperation, and sells the products of his enterprise. Thus the pricing of factors of production is, in general, in the hands of the entrepreneurs, and is effected by their work.[2]

Many would welcome this line of inquiry as indicating a restoration of human values to what is, after all, a social science and as asserting the importance of the individual personality in an increasingly impersonal world.

In any event, it is not hard to discern in the Philippine case in the nineteenth century examples of results that could not have been uniquely determined by such conditions as rising world demand, population growth, and other global forces. The most striking instance that meets the eye is the case of abaca. There was no reason to suppose before the 1820s that this product would one day become one of the country's leading exports and would for a generation enjoy the primacy in the export trade. It was practically unknown in the currents of world trade, and therefore its coming into use cannot be explained solely or even primarily by a demand for it. The intervention of human agency is clearly indicated.

Such an outcome is what Schumpeter has called creative response, something outside the range of existing practice, in contradistinction to adaptive response, which simply is an adjustment of the economy to a change in its data in the way that traditional theory describes. This creative response has at least three essential characteristics according to Schumpeter. The first is that (assuming full possession of all relevant facts) it can always be understood ex post but practically never ex ante, that is, "it cannot be predicted by applying the ordinary rules of inference from the pre-existing facts." The case of abaca seems to be such a phenomenon. The second is that creative response has a long-run and irreversible effect on economic and social situations; once it has occurred there is no turning back, no link to "might have beens." Third, the frequency of occurrence of creative response, its intensity, and its success or failure have obviously something to do

> (a) with quality of the personnel available in a society, (b) with relative quality of personnel, that is, with quality available to a particular field of activity relative to quality available, at the same time, to others, and (c) with individual decisions, actions and patterns of behavior. . . . Accordingly, a study of creative response in business becomes coterminous with a study of entrepreneurship.[3]

222

In such a study, however, according to the same author, "theories of past economists relative specifically to entrepreneurship will not form a very firm support for future investigations of facts. New hypotheses and the marshaling of factual data, old and new, must proceed together."[4] Whom he includes among "past economists" is not certain, but the statement is slightly ironic coming from one of the modern giants of economic theory, especially one whose own work is full of fruitful suggestions for the economic investigator.

It is true that there is no such thing as *the* modern theory of entrepreneurship. But in empirical research it is not a good idea to attempt to fit all the observable facts into a rigid theoretical mold. What can be done is to use theory as a researcher's toolbox, as Schumpeter himself has elsewhere recommended,[5] to see what particular circumstances to watch for in an inquiry into concrete situations. There will of course be facts that will fit no preconceived theory or whose importance will be evident without the need of any more elaborate theoretical apparatus than is provided by common experience and common sense. But certainly a study will be the richer from being able to draw both from scholarly theory and from common sense.

In this, as in almost any other attempt to coordinate theory and reality, there arises the old and thorny problem of bridging the epistemological gap between a theoretical concept and a concrete fact. Entrepreneurship is no exception. Attempts to define it range all the way from the specific Schumpeterian concept of innovation to a rather general conception of the entrepreneur as "the person or group that makes business decisions; and of entrepreneurship as decision-making in the sphere of business."[6] And, although the entrepreneur is generally regarded as an agent of change, the suggestion has been made that he might also be the promoter of stability.[7]

This is, however, not the occasion to discuss theoretical definitions and refinements. That change occurred in the case under study has already been demonstrated, and that entrepreneurship or business leadership (be it called what it may) played a substantial part in bringing that change about seems clearly indicated by an examination of the possible alternatives and by the testimony of informed observers. What can be done here, therefore, is to set forth the concepts that will prove most useful in studying the methods employed by entrepreneurs in their mercantile operations, the institutional forms through which they conducted their business, and such personal qualities as are known about some of them that might throw more light on their actions and on the results of these actions.

Since the function of entrepreneurship, as isolated after successive theoretical refinements from J. B. Say to Schumpeter, in real life inheres in actual people who perform functions other than entrepreneurship, it will be well to utilize concepts that enable one to distinguish the different functions in real persons without having to resort to idealized personages. For this purpose, it is helpful to start from terminology in which the term *business leader* denotes the entrepreneur of actuality, a distinction suggested some time ago by Fritz Redlich. This business leader is conceived of as performing some combination of three main functions in the world of economic reality: those of capitalist, manager, and entrepreneur. As capitalist, he would provide the funds for the enterprise. As manager, he would supervise the internal affairs of a business. As entrepreneur, he would decide larger questions related to the place of his business unit in the economy and society. The distinction between management and entrepreneurship is analogous to that between tactics and strategy. In dynamic theory, that is, as related to economic growth or economic development, Redlich would add the adjective *creative* to each of these terms, but in this study this refinement will de dispensed with as a superfluity since the situation described is a dynamic one and there need be no confusion about the terminology being applied to a static theory.[8]

The business leader or entrepreneur in reality may fuse in his conduct two or more of the above functions. He may be both entrepreneur and capitalist. Or he may be both entrepreneur and manager without being the capitalist. He may be merely a manager, but under modern conditions this would make him a highly paid employee at best, while if he were only a capitalist and nothing more he would merely be a stockholder or perhaps a banker.

Not only are the functions conceptually different, but any one of them may be distributed among a number of persons rather than concentrated in one person alone. This is clearly true about the function of capitalist, but it may also be true of that of entrepreneur, which may be discharged by several men in one organization. It might even be exercised by a man or men outside the organization, if such a man or men were of the power and position of, say, J. P. Morgan.

To the entrepreneurial function corresponds an entrepreneurial return, which in Redlich's schema is imputed directly to entrepreneurship rather than being a surplus over costs, as in alternative theories. (The writer, however, prefers the latter approach.) The entrepreneurial return need not show up as a profit, nor need it go to the entrepreneur. Where the entrepreneur is an employee, the entrepreneurial gain may go to the capitalists in the form of higher returns; where he faces strong labor unions, it may go to the workers in the form of higher wages or benefits. In both cases, there is "exploitation" of the entrepreneur for the benefit of nonentrepreneurial groups. Schumpeter describes entrepreneurship as follows:

> The entrepreneur and his function are not difficult to conceptualize; the defining characteristic is simply the doing of new things or the doing of things that are already being done in a new way (innovation). . . . It should be observed at once that the "new thing" need not be spectacular or of historic importance. It need not be Bessemer steel or the explosion motor. It can be the Deerfoot sausage.[9]

The innovations introduced by entrepreneurs may take many forms. They may be new ways of combining factors of production in order to improve a product or produce it more cheaply or even to turn out a new product. They may therefore be new or better ways of organizing business units. Innovation may also be displayed in the opening up of new markets, the development of new sources of supply, the securing of greater financial resources, and the cultivation of good relations with the public authorities and the community at large.[10] Redlich would also include among creative entrepreneurs those who introduce into a country or a line of trade some new device or product already existing elsewhere. This, of course, is on the borderline between innovators and imitators, but Redlich points out that the first followers of a creative entrepreneur are themselves creative, though to a lesser degree.[11]

Some additional comments should be made about the concepts set forth above. The first is that innovation and invention are not necessarily coterminous since an invention does not become an innovation until it assumes economic significance. However, many inventors have in practice been entrepreneurs.[12]

The second is that the innovations, the new combinations of factors introduced by entrepreneurs, if successful, produce a surplus over costs, which is entrepreneurial gain. The surplus may come because costs are lower or because people are willing to pay more for an improved product or a new commodity. This entrepreneurial gain, a residual over costs in Schumpeterian theory—although Redlich, as has been seen, suggests its direct imputation to entrepreneurship as a factor of production—has three features deserving of notice. The first is that in a fairly competitive system the gain is temporary because as imitators copy the innovation prices come down, costs go up, or both. The rate of speed of imitation varies from case to case, but it is through this process that the improvement becomes more widely distributed to the mass of consumers. A high rate of imitation may therefore seem socially beneficial, except that it might discourage entrepreneurial effort if it is too rapid, and society seems to recognize this by legislating patent and copyright laws. The second feature is that, because it stems from innovation, entrepreneurial gain has in the initial stages the character of a monopoly profit. The third feature is that in Schumpeterian theory entrepreneurial gain does not consist of the current return on the enterprise but of an increase in the value of the assets of an enterprise—in short, in a capital gain. It is in this way that industrial fortunes are typically created.[13]

The third comment is that in Schumpeterian theory the entrepreneur uses capital as the kingpin in the changes he is making. To put it colloquially, he "parlays" the capital available to him into control over the other factors of production.

This leads to the fourth comment, which is that, in theory at least, the provision of capital is not one of the elements of entrepreneurship. The provision of capital, as pointed out above, is a separate function. Therefore, the entrepreneur *as such* is not the risk bearer.[14] If his enterprise fails, it is the capitalists—banks or stockholders, for example—who suffer financial adversity. He, too, may suffer if he has invested money or pledged his assets as collateral, but this happens in his capacity as capitalist. And he may conceivably suffer also if he stops drawing remuneration from a bankrupt company, but this happens in his capacity as employee or manager.

The fifth comment is that innovation very often involves destruction of existing institutions or situations, which is necessary in order for the innovation to make headway. This exhibits what Redlich calls the daimonic nature of entrepreneurship and what Schumpeter calls creative destruction.[15]

The sixth comment is that the crude profit motive is usually not enough to explain entrepreneurial activity. The general desire to find a gainful occupation is of course always present, but it falls short of explaining this particular form of activity. Schumpeter suggests dynastic ambition, a desire for success itself, and a creative joy in getting things done as some of the more important entrepreneurial motives.[16] Certainly there are a host of others.

CONCEPTUAL AND TECHNOLOGICAL CONSIDERATIONS

The seventh comment is that entrepreneurship appears, not in an even distribution over time, but in swarms or clusters. This is "because the appearance of one or a few entrepreneurs facilitates the appearance of others, and these the appearance of more, in ever-increasing numbers."[17]

The suggestion has been made that economic development is possible only by means of a frontal attack of this type, in which the momentum of a whole general trend makes possible the success of individual enterprises, which in different circumstances might have little effect on a country's economic growth and might even fail altogether. Under contemporary circumstances, it has been suggested that the only way such a frontal economic assault can take place in low-income (or developing) countries is for the government, which can draw on resources beyond the reach of any individual or group, to undertake the function of entrepreneurship itself, as was done by the Japanese government in the Meiji era.[18]

Enough has been reviewed to help guide us through the historical archives, and it is time to leave theory and return to history.

Terminological Distinctions

The word *entrepreneur* has a restricted theoretical meaning as well as a looser, more general one. In the latter sense, it refers to an actual person and may be considered synonymous with *business leader* or even *businessman*. In the following discussion, the meaning will usually be clear from the context; more often than not it is the more general denotation that will be used. Where the narrow sense of the word is employed, the fact will be indicated if it is not clear from the context.

Another distinction is that between foreign and domestic enterprise. There is no question in the case of British, American, French, Chinese, or other nationals who were obviously foreigners. The question enters in the case of Spanish firms and merchants. Some of them are clearly from outside the country. For example, the Tabacalera company of the 1880s (extant to this day) was capitalized in Spain and has its head office in Barcelona. But other Spanish merchants identified themselves to such an extent with the Philippines, as will be seen shortly, that they must be considered domestic.

A differentiation along ethnic lines is not very fruitful because of the frequent intermarriages between Filipinos, Spaniards, and Chinese. There *were* ethnic distinctions, in some cases institutionalized, but no hard and fast color line. Two Englishmen four decades apart bore witness to this. Bowring wrote:

I found a kind and generous urbanity prevailing,—friendly intercourse where that intercourse had been sought,—the lines of demarcation and separation between ranks and classes less marked and impassable than in most Oriental countries. I have seen at the same table Spaniard, mestizo and Indian—priest, civilian and soldier. No doubt a common religion forms a common bond; but to him who has observed the alienations and repulsions of *caste* in many parts of the Eastern world—caste, the great social curse—the blending and free intercourse of man with man in the Philippines is a contrast well worth admiring.[19]

Frederic Sawyer, an English engineer of long residence in Manila, wrote at the turn of the century:

The islands were badly governed by Spain, yet Spaniards and natives lived together in great harmony, and I do not know where I could find a colony in which the Europeans mixed as much socially with the natives. Not in Java, where a native of position must dismount to salute the humblest Dutchman. Not in British India, where the Englishwoman has now made the gulf between British and native into a bottomless pit.[20]

It must be remembered that at that time distinctions that might be valid in the present would be difficult to make. The Filipino nationality had yet to be formed by the Reform and Propaganda Movement, the Revolution, and the struggle for independence. In any case, most of the Filipinos of that era (then referred to as *indios*) were engaged in agriculture, home industries, or local administration and did not enter into large-scale commercial ventures until perhaps the latter part of the century. These fell to the lot of mestizos, Spaniards, and Chinese. Of these groups, the first must certainly be classified under domestic enterprise; nowadays most of them are Filipino citizens. Of the Spaniards, there were two distinct groups: the Peninsulars, or those born in Spain, and the Filipinos, or those born in the Philippines. The latter—the Azcárraga family being one of the more prominent—must also be bracketed with domestic enterprise. And of the former there were some who identified themselves so prominently with local interests that they must be considered domestic rather than foreign. It should also be borne in mind that the children and descendants of foreigners, most notably of Spaniards and Chinese, often felt the Philippines to be their rightful home and supported the reform movement at the end of the century.

228

In the discussion that follows, then, the distinction between domestic and foreign enterprise will not be drawn along ethnic lines but according to whether the interest of the parties involved was or was not identified root and branch with the Philippines. By this criterion, not only the native born, whether of Filipino, mixed, or Spanish parentage, but also such of the foreign born as had clearly thrown in their lot with the country will be considered as falling under the classification of domestic enterprise. This would, as will be seen later, be fully in accord with the spirit of inclusivity in the 1899 Malolos Constitution. Three examples will serve to demonstrate how one has to steer his way through these distinctions.

The first is the Barretto family, of Portuguese and Indian descent. Somewhere in their lineage is a sixteenth-century viceroy of Goa (Francisco), whose main claim to historical fame is that he once clapped the poet Camoens in the local jail and exiled him for writing satirical verses that did not, as the saying goes, amuse him. (The immortal *Lusiads* were believed to have been partly written during his confinement.)[21] Of the Manila Barrettos, one (Luis) was born in Bombay in 1785, moved to Calcutta, and settled in Manila, where he married a Spanish lady in 1815. Two others (the half-brothers Bartolomé Antonio, or B. A., and Antonio Vicente, or A. V.) were born in Macao and also settled in Manila around 1846, merging quite comfortably into Manila society. A fourth (Enrique, son of B. A.), was born in Manila. As early as 1818, the Barrettos maintained trading connections with the New England Perkinses in Canton.[22] A Barretto was associated with Thomas T. Forbes during the latter's business operations in Manila in the mid-1820s.[23] Half a century later, some Barrettos figured in the bankruptcy proceedings of the American firm of Russell & Sturgis.[24] And in 1890 Enrique Barretto founded the firm that is at present considered one of the most solid businesses in the Philippines, San Miguel Brewery[25] (now called San Miguel Corporation). Just to complicate the terminology, at midcentury B. A. Barretto & Co. was listed as a British firm, in part perhaps because the firm was founded with the support of Jardine Matheson. A touching little item in a Canton trade paper in 1849 announced the death in Manila at age five years and four months of Bartholomew, "the only son of B. A. Barretto, Esq., late of Macao."[26] There can be little doubt that the Barrettos should be regarded as domestic Filipino entrepreneurs considering their long-standing local presence.

The second is the Roxas (or Rojas) family. They are descended from a doctor who came from Mexico late in the eighteenth century. There was considerable intermarriage with Filipino families. They undertook several ventures in the nineteenth century, including mining and distilling. Domingo Roxas was identified at midcentury as one of the largest and most progressive sugar planters in the country as well the owner of a gunpowder factory in Laguna. In the last decade of the century, a Roxas (Francisco) lost his sanity in a Spanish dungeon and his life before a firing squad on January 11, 1897 (victimized by forged evidence planted by some revolutionaries) a few days after the national hero, José Rizal, and another Roxas, Pedro, a friend of the national hero, had his property embargoed for rebellion. By an ironic twist of events, the Roxases of the direct male line retain Spanish citizenship, while many of their relatives descended from female Roxases have assumed either Filipino or American citizenship. But there can be no doubt that they should be classified as domestic entrepreneurs.[27]

The third is the Tuason family. Local lore has it that they are descended from a Chinese named Son Tua, from whom they derive their family name. From 1756 until 1783, the first Tuason identifiable in print, Antonio, served as governor of Chinese mestizos and a colonel in the urban militia, contributing to the expenses of the navy and the royal treasury and arming and maintaining a large number of soldiers during the war with the English (1762–64). He also contributed to the reconstruction of various churches and public offices. For his services, he was given a patent of nobility by a royal *cédula* of February 21, 1783, with the title of Caballero Hijo-Dalgo, and the following year a coat of arms. Retana calls him the first Filipino not of Spanish origin to merit such a distinction. He was reported to have made his fortune in the galleon trade and was reputed to have been the richest man in the country.

On August 20, 1795, the king confirmed the *mayorazgo* (a trust left in perpetuity and with the prerogative of primogeniture) established by Antonio Tuason (recently deceased) in favor of his son Vicente Dolores Tuason, in consideration of the services rendered by Antonio and the payment of a half-annate of 8,800 reales. The *mayorazgo* covered certain urban properties and chattels and the extensive haciendas of Santa Mesa-Diliman and Mariquina acquired at auction in 1794 from the holdings of the then-suppressed Jesuit order. Significantly, in the instrument of entail Antonio Tuason referred to "the evanescence of the great family fortunes which have existed in these Islands on account of their not having been entailed," echoing the Jesuit procurator Fr. Jose Calvo's 1753 observation that not a single hereditary estate had been founded since the coming of Spain to the Philippines.

Armed with his father's fortune and patent of nobility, Vicente Dolores Tuason in 1800 put in the highest bid (12,200 pesos) for a seat on the city council. But the Spaniards united to frustrate Tuason's bid, claiming that it was improper to have a Chinese mestizo as a councilor, or *regidor*, of a Spanish city (although the patent of nobility had made the Tuasons Spaniards by royal decree) and that Tuason continued to follow Chinese customs and deal socially and commercially with the Chinese. They offered to make up jointly the difference between the next highest bid and Tuason's. The governor-general sided with them and gave the post to the next highest bidder, prompting Tuason to take the case to court in Madrid. The final outcome of the case remains unknown.

The Tuasons' drive to obtain social parity may have been slowed, but it was not stopped, and by dint of education, business activity (of which more will be seen later), and intermarriage they attained not only the parity that they considered their due but even social and commercial prominence. By the mid–nineteenth century, a Tuason had become the first manager of the Banco Español-Filipino, and Azcárraga describes J. M. Tuason & Company as a Spanish firm.[28] Up to the middle of the twentieth century, the more numerous and influential branches of this family retained Spanish as the language spoken at home. Again, there can be little question as to their identification with the domestic scene.

If the first Tuasons in the dim historical past had begun as small traders, artisans, or even laborers, like so many Chinese immigrants, their case serves to indicate the existence of not only racial but social mobility in Philippine society. It may be noted that none of the main branches of the families cited here has gone into politics, with the exception of a Barretto who became a provincial governor, and one wonders who is being referred to as a member of "the traditional blue-blooded oligarchy" (whatever may be meant by *blue-blooded* in a Philippine context) seen by some American scholars as holding the political reins in the country before the Magsaysay administration.[29]

One feature in connection with Filipino enterprise should be noted here, although it is at present not possible to point out specific examples. This is that very often a woman—a wife, mother, or sister—was the guiding spirit behind an enterprise, although their male relatives might figure officially as the businessmen in the case. This is apparently a Philippine tradition of long standing, and it was reinforced by Spanish laws protecting the woman's property in a marriage. Foreman notes this with thinly disguised disapproval:

231

The Spanish laws relating to married persons' property are quaint. If the husband be poor, and the wife well-off, so they may remain, notwithstanding the marriage. He, as a rule becomes a simple administrator of her possessions, and, if honest, often depends on her liberality to supply his own necessities. If he becomes bankrupt in a business in which he employed her capital or possessions, she ranks as a creditor of the second class under the "Commercial Code." If she dies, the poor husband, under no circumstances, by legal right (unless under a deed signed before a notary) derives any benefit from the fact of his having espoused a rich wife,—her property passes to their legitimate issue, or—in default thereof—to her nearest blood relation. The children might be rich, and, but for their generosity, their father might be destitute, whilst the law compels him to render a strict account to them of the administration of their property during their minority.[30]

When the poor husband was a Spaniard of pliant disposition and the well-to-do wife a Filipina of the opposite temperament, the result could be a hilarious sort of countercolonialism, as exemplified by the Espadaña couple in Rizal's famous novel *Noli Me Tangere*.

At this point, much of the background against which entrepreneurial activity took place in the nineteenth-century Philippines has been sketched. Certain social features were noted in previous chapters, and Spanish commercial policy was discussed in chapter 6. Reference has also been made to the restrictions under which the foreigners operated until 1870. In this connection, it should be noted that the severity of the law and official policy was probably compensated for by the generous hospitality of both Filipinos and Spaniards, and a foreigner could expect friendly personal treatment regardless of what the official policy might be. Perhaps a modern parallel can be found in the contrast between U.S. immigration laws and the welcome that is often accorded foreigners in private American homes.

One last major point shall be made here. The Philippines historically was a Christian country with long-standing connections with the western world; its rising class looked to Europe as the fountainhead of modern thought and material progress. There existed, therefore, a predisposition to include western items of consumption in household expenditures, and this no doubt facilitated the capture by foreign entrepreneurs of the Philippine market for textiles and made it a good outlet for other western goods. As early as 1856, the British consul reported that Philippine trade with

Great Britain had exceeded British trade with several European states, with any single African port or state, and with Mexico, Colombia, and Guatemala. The foreign merchants themselves, by demonstrating the luxuries and conveniences that they brought with them, further contributed to the increasing demand for western commodities.[31] The competition that western goods, especially textiles, offered domestic and other Asian textiles was therefore not only price but also prestige competition, which may help explain why a modern textile industry did not arise early in the Philippines (like it did in India).

CHAPTER 8

Early Foreign Contacts
and the Establishment of Merchant Houses

This and the following chapters will point out the salient features of entrepreneurship in the nineteenth-century Philippines and will give more extended treatment to those cases for which the material justifies it. They will not attempt to cover entrepreneurial activity exhaustively, nor will they be a continuous narration of the business events of that period. Features of theoretical interest will be indicated in the course of the discussion.

Instances will be cited of early American voyages to Manila, which overlapped the age of the galleons, often in connection with the Canton trade, and resulted in the founding of two American merchant houses in the 1820s. In that decade, following the end of trade with Mexico, there was a Schumpeterian clustering of new western merchant firms. The locus of entrepreneurial decisions in each of the two American firms is examined, as are entrepreneurial motivations as these were expressed in the words of one of the leading protagonists. Aside from the influence of the Canton trade, evidence will be seen that Philippine trade eventually became an objective in itself.[1]

Early Foreign Interest

Of the non-Spanish western merchants who started coming to the Philippines late in the eighteenth century and early in the nineteenth, those most deserving of attention for their eventual importance are the British and the Americans, with the French in a secondary position. British and French interest in the Philippines evidently arose out of the East India trade. It has been pointed out in earlier chapters how they came to Manila under false colors even when Philippine ports were still legally closed to them. The British in addition formed some notion of the country's possibilities during their occupation of Manila in 1762–64. In the 1790s, there was some discussion of giving Spain a factory in India in exchange for one in Luzon; the object was to gain a foothold at China's doorstep for the China trade and a window on the Pacific for the Latin American trade.[2] Around 1801, the firm of Gordon & Murphy, which secretly transported funds for the Spanish treasury as well as dyes from Oaxaca, listed Manila as one of the places where it had representatives (this was its only office in Asia, the others being in Europe or Spanish America).[3]

American interest arose in part out of whaling and the China trade. Reference has earlier been made to Zamboanga as a port of call for American whalers. In the years following the American Revolution, Yankee ships and sailors became frequent visitors in distant parts of the world and gave their former rulers competition in the China trade. As is evident from a perusal of the accounts of that time and the records of such firms as Bryant & Sturgis of Boston, one of the more common procedures was for American ships to go down the east coast of South America and around Cape Horn, sail up the west coast of both Americas to the Oregon country, and from there go across the Pacific to Canton. Several objectives were accomplished by this. They sold general cargo in Latin America and picked up silver dollars in exchange. They acquired furs on the west coast of North America and sandalwood in Hawaii. The Philippines lay along their route to Canton, and it was often to their advantage to stop there and pick up a cargo of rice, since any vessel with such a cargo (three thousand *piculs* of it, according to one account) could sail upriver to Whampoa without having to pay a fee.[4] Apparently, this was a measure taken by the Imperial Chinese government to reduce the likelihood of famine and keep rice prices down. This was one way in which American sailors and merchants came to know the Philippines.

It was not the only way, however. The alternative route for American vessels was to cross the Atlantic, perhaps sell a cargo at Gibraltar to pick up Spanish silver, sail around the Cape of Good Hope and through the Indian Ocean, and proceed through the Sunda Straits to Canton. Again, the Philippines was on the sailing route, and if rice was not available in Java the ships could call for it at Manila. The Cape of Good Hope route was also used by vessels going to Mauritius, Reunion, and Bengal for sugar and indigo.

There were occasions when the Philippines was an object of commercial expeditions in its own right. Elias Haskett Derby, the famous Salem merchant, sent the *Astrea* with Nathaniel Bowditch as supercargo to Manila in 1796 with a cargo of Madeira wine for the purpose of acquiring sugar and indigo, as was seen earlier. These two products helped stimulate American commercial interest in the Philippines. On a subsequent voyage to Manila in 1799–1800, in the same ship and under the same captain (Henry Prince), Bowditch met a Scotsman named Murray,[5] whose connection with the later firm of Ker, Murray & Co. remains to be determined.

Well into the nineteenth century there was an element of probing and experimentation in the American voyages to Asian waters. The Salem ship *Aurora* was sent in 1819 to Cochin China to procure sugar for Trieste, but if unable to do so it was instructed to proceed to Manila for sugar and return to Salem. If that was not possible, it was to go to Canton, invest its funds in sugar, and fill up with freight for Boston or Salem. In Vietnam, four American and several French ships had preceded it, so, finding the official regulations restrictive, the *Aurora* proceeded to Manila, where it procured a cargo of first- and second-quality sugar at eight and five pesos per *picul*, respectively, as well as a small quantity of dyewood. The outbound cargo consisted of $40,050 in Spanish dollars, while the return cargo of sugar and dyewood was valued at a little over $38,000, including charges.[6]

For the most part in the early days, however, Manila was a way station in the American trade with Canton, and because of its nearness to the mainland it came to be regarded as an alternative loading point whenever teas and silks were not to be had in China. A representative voyage might be that of the Salem ship *Perseverance*, which sailed from Salem to Batavia late in 1796, proceeding from thence to Manila, where it arrived on June 12, 1797, then on to Canton on July 31, and back to Salem on November 30. Its captain was Richard Wheatland, and its keeper was Nathaniel Hathorne (without the *w* in the family name, which was added by his son, the novelist).[7]

At a later date, the same priorities were still in evidence. In 1843, R. G. Shaw & Co. wrote from Boston to Russell & Sturgis in Manila that it favored having its ship *Surat* go to China for a part or the whole of its cargo of tea. If this was not possible, "you can ship sufficient Hemp and perhaps 1000 bags of Sugar . . . by her before leaving Manila to enable her to come home with a full cargo."[8]

236

Another early voyage was that of the Providence ship *Resource* to Manila and Canton in 1802–3, which illustrated more clearly even than Nathaniel Bowditch's earlier visit the state of commerce in Manila at a period when western voyages overlapped with the operation of the galleon trade. The customs brokers in Manila were the Messrs. Kerr and White, the Kerr in this instance being the same John Stuart Kerr who had attended to Bowditch in 1796. There were a number of investors in the voyage, among them J. & T. H. Perkins (of whom more will be seen), who were sending clarified ginseng to Canton and verdigris to Manila, with instructions to take the proceeds in cash if possible or in blue and yellow nankins as an alternative.

At Manila, Captain Megee "found the place glutted with every kind of goods." Sixteen ships had preceded him: three Danish, three French, three American, three Portuguese, and five from Bengal, with a large quantity of goods that flooded the market as no galleon was sailing that year. The Danes [from their enclaves in India] and the Bengal ships were expected to "sink at least thirty p. cent on their capital . . ." Megee disposed of his cargo by selling at retail and any other means just "to get hold of the *plata*." One of these means was to barter for "Black Wood" (probably *kamagong*, or ebony), taken at nineteen reales ($2.375) per *picul* from a Chinese named Appa by two of the minor investors in the voyage, Henry and Stephen Higginson Jr. of Boston. The smaller investors accounted for about $7,000 in sales of green baize, lace, glassware, sperm candles, saddles, and bridles, but two-thirds of such sales were accounted for by the Higginsons, who also took some cochineal (a transshipped commodity from Spanish America) at $3.25 per pound and left part of the wood with Kerr and White to be sent to Canton by the first available ship. Also left with the brokers, but on consignment, were some lace and green baize, the proceeds to be remitted to Canton. (This practice of consignment was censured by Fr. Martínez de Zúñiga as a monopolistic price-raising tactic.)

Megee reported that he would "make a freight" from Manila to Canton of about four thousand dollars, and he carried in cash and cargo (including black wood and cochineal) about twenty-three thousand dollars' worth. In order to raise more cash, he had borrowed twenty-one thousand dollars from a galleon captain who had made his fortune and was being paid 8 percent interest plus passage to Canton (on his way to America). The loan was payable in bills on the United States at sixty days sight but not to be forwarded there until he had sailed from Canton.[9] American vessels could also, if they expected a long wait at Canton for cargoes of tea and silk, make several trips to Manila to pick up rice and thus earn a little money on the side.

Manila's proximity to Canton, therefore, imparted a greater measure of flexibility to the operations of Yankee merchantmen in Asian waters. This was especially convenient during the War of 1812, when American shippers feared that access to Canton might be denied them by British warships. American captains were instructed to put in at Manila if they could not negotiate the passage to Canton in safety. As was seen earlier, Bryant & Sturgis of Boston wrote Perkins and Co. of Canton on November 22, 1813, to either send a cargo to Manila to be picked up by their ship or furnish it with credit to load Philippine sugar, indigo, and saltpeter. But this was only an alternative; their primary interest lay in tea, as is shown in the letter forwarded two days later to Edward Carrington in Providence, also quoted previously.

J. and T. H. Perkins of Boston wrote Perkins and Co. of Canton on New Year's Day in 1814 that they were sending two fast schooners to Manila, where they could pick up tea sent down from Canton. The tenuous relations existing between the Philippines and world trade at this time are evidenced by the fact that information about conditions in Manila had to be ascertained through Spanish residents in Macao and Canton. The Perkinses of Boston, however, were already interested in indigo, sugar, and cotton (in that order of importance), a cargo of which costing seventy-five thousand dollars would, they calculated, bring in four hundred thousand.[10]

In subsequent years, contacts with the outside world increased, and the Philippines began to assume some importance in its own right. In 1817, for instance, Captain Ezekiel Hubbell of Bridgeport, Connecticut, broke a retirement of nine years' duration and went to Manila in the *Citizen* for the firm of Hoyt & Tom. There he invested one hundred thousand Spanish dollars in sugar and indigo, with which he loaded his own ship bound for New York and a French ship going to Hamburg. (The 1818 customs return shows a *Sitasen*, obviously a Spanish misspelling of the name of Hubbell's ship, as having brought in 80,400 pesos in specie and 12,626 pesos' worth of cargo.) Although the return on this venture was said to have been only moderate, Hubbell sent the *Citizen* to Manila in 1819 with his son, George William, as supercargo. George loaded it for Hamburg and from there sent it back again to Manila, while he returned to the United States, arriving in February 1821. George Hubbell took the time to get married in March of that year, and the following month he sailed with his father and his brother, Henry Wilson, on the *Ajax* for Manila on a trip that was to have important results, for it led to the founding of a business house that was to be very influential in Philippine commerce until late in the century and whose successor was active in Philippine business until recently.[11]

The *Ajax* carried ninety thousand Spanish dollars on this voyage, and in this connection it should be noted that the Americans at that time were importing heavy amounts of specie into the Philippines. Of total specie imports of 752,839 pesos in 1818, the American ships brought 328,260, or 43.57 percent of the total, exceeding even the return on the Mexican trade, which was 327,312 pesos or 43.48 percent.

Of the American specie imports, all came from the United States except for 45,000 pesos from Gibraltar. In 1825, of total specie imports on foreign vessels amounting to 337,686 pesos, 162,384 were listed as coming from the United States. In addition, 151,980 pesos were listed as coming from China, but since the Chinese, as has been pointed out, did not bring specie to the Philippines these can be presumed to have come on western ships, including probably many American vessels.[12]

While specie movements in these years cannot be taken as representing total capital movements because of the employment of negotiable instruments like bills of exchange, the use of such instruments was still very restricted. Thus, specie movement is instructive. It also confirms what has been seen in earlier chapters, namely, the American interest in the Philippine export trade, which in the absence of sizable imports must have required capital financing.

The Establishment of Business Houses

At about the time the Hubbells were making their voyages to Manila, other contacts were being established between Philippine commerce and world trade. The Barretto family's connections with Canton and India were mentioned in the previous chapter. There was another local firm called Calvo & Co., which acted as an agent for the Forbeses of Canton.[13]

This was also a time when foreign business firms were being founded, many of which were to play a crucial role in the shaping of the Philippine economy. In 1818, one John Christopher O'Farrell was described by Capt. Charles Stewart of the *Christopher* from Providence as the only agent that did American business. (John Stuart Kerr was apparently gone from the scene, although his descendants continued in the country until at least the 1980s). Stewart found out that, contrary to expectation, all business was based on regular commissions. Because of the "trouble and formality in doing the most trifling business," the assistance of someone of influence and responsibility was needed, for which a commission of 2.5 percent was paid.

At the time of Stewart's visit, there were other American vessels in port, all mentioned in the Manila customs report for 1818, including Hubbell's ship. O'Farrell handled their local contacts, steering some to Domingo Roxas, son-in-law of an old sugar merchant, Doña María Vita (called by Captain Stewart "the old lady Beete"), whose family is still in the sugar business. Others went to Agustín Scarella, described as a very substantial sugar merchant.

The garrulous O'Farrell, both in a circular and in personal correspondence, presented as his credentials his having been in business all his life and his membership in the Board of Trade since March 1811 by virtue of a royal appointment that cost him $2,500, "so you may say that i am now a Spaniard in place of an Irishman or a Citazen [sic] of the U.S. of America . . . belov'd and respected by this Government and populace . . ." Although a marine officer from Baltimore named Andrew Stuart was the American consul, the local authorities did not "acknowledge" him, perhaps because of his relatively low rank, even drafting him for duty as a second officer aboard a galleon in a privateer-chasing expedition. So O'Farrell tried to get Edward Carrington to have him appointed U.S. consul in Manila. O'Farrell charged Stuart with snatching business away from him while he was ill, but added that in the current year Stuart had not handled a single vessel. He noted with perhaps a touch of malice that Stuart was married to the daughter of an Armenian, Pedro Abraham, whom he described as being poor as a church mouse.

O'Farrell's account of the purchases made by the ships in port showed Ezekiel Hubbell's driving energy and willingness to take risks. He purchased much more sugar than anyone else, and at higher prices, going as high as $7.00 and $7.25 per *picul* for part of his cargo (as against the price paid by others of $6.375), drawing on London for an extra $10,000 at 5/6, and chartering a French vessel (jointly with Capt. Eben Clark of the *Ladoga* from New Bedford). O'Farrell doubted that they would make a profit, but Hubbell may have been following a high-volume, low-margin strategy; as previously mentioned, the Hubbells would keep coming back.

Aside from the normal commercial and climatological risks, there was at that time danger from pirates in the Gaspar Straits (between Bangka and Billiton Islands), impelling the trading ships to sail in pairs or in informal convoys for mutual protection until they made open sea. "The Pirates this season has been extreamly troublesome," wrote Capt. Charles Stewart, and "I shall sail in Company with a French ship till i get through the Straits of Sunday [sic] . . ."

Philippine exports then were few, the principal one being sugar, as there was not enough at Batavia, where the price was a nominal nine dollars per *picul*. Also mentioned in O'Farrell's circular was indigo but with the warning that it was of very bad quality because the manufacturers mixed all grades of the product and tried to pass it off as being of first quality. Andrew Stuart's notification of November 12, 1818, was more optimistic, stating that indigo was improving because the manufacturers were now aware of its bad reputation in Europe and America. Stuart also foresaw that owing to a recent government regulation (contents unspecified) up to fifty thousand *piculs* of coffee would be exported in three years.[14]

In 1819 and 1820, Perkins and Co. of Canton was corresponding with one Peter Dobell in Manila, although no further contact seems to have taken place after the middle of the latter year. In that year, however, a commission house bearing the Welsh name of J. & T. Apthorp was established in Manila. There is no indication of whether it was British or American, although about a decade and a half later an Apthorp from Boston was recorded as having visited Manila and it may therefore have been American. For about a year and a half—throughout 1821 and halfway through 1822—there seem to have been relatively frequent contacts between Apthorp and Perkins of Canton. The latter consigned some of its ships to the former; gave instructions for the buying of Philippine sugar, indigo, pearls, and tortoiseshell and the selling of European merchandise; and instructed its captains to secure Apthorp's assistance in the trading operations in Manila. It also requested information on the kinds of imports salable in Manila and their prices. This seemingly fruitful relationship was abruptly ended in 1822 due to the death of Thomas Apthorp about the middle of that year. A letter from Luis Barretto dated August 8 transmitted the sad news to Canton and announced that he had assumed control of Apthorp's interests. Perkins of Canton answered Barretto the following month and expressed its pleasure at his assumption of Apthorp's concerns and its satisfaction with the arrangements Barretto proposed to make regarding Perkins's property. During the next few years, the Barrettos seem to have been Perkins's correspondents in Manila.[15]

The house of Apthorp was the precursor of several others that were founded in Manila during the same decade. Kierulf & Co. was founded by a young Dane of twenty, William Kierulf, who arrived in 1820 at about the time of a mob massacre induced by hysteria over cholera but who got over his initial aversion to the country to the extent of marrying locally and leaving numerous descendants who still bear his family name (some having served in the Philippine Public Health Service and the armed forces).

In court cases in which he figured, he was known as Guillermo Kierulf.[16] By the late 1830s, Kierulf & Co. was said to be the oldest foreign merchant firm in Manila.

Others that can be dated are George W. Hubbell, 1822, later to become Peele, Hubbell & Co.; Wise & Co. (known for a time as Holliday, Wise & Co.), 1826, extant to this date; Ker, McMicking & Co. (known for a time as Ker, Murray & Co.), 1827, today known as Ker & Co.; and Russell & Sturgis, 1828, which was for a time to enjoy the reputation of being the greatest company in the country. There were undoubtedly other firms established around that time. For example, Paterson & Co. (which seems to have been a precursor of Martin Dyce & Co.) was founded at about the same time as Wise & Co. In 1827, John Wise reported the number of foreign firms as being nine (ten including a Spanish firm managed by an American). Of the four companies definitely dated, the two British firms, Wise & Co. and Ker & Co., seem to have been branches of partnerships with head offices in the United Kingdom and initially were mainly concerned with the importation of British goods, although the second one was later to build up a substantial export trade.[17] The two American houses, George W. Hubbell and Russell & Sturgis, on the other hand, seem to have taken an interest in exports from the early years of their existence.

The establishment of so many firms within the same decade, many of which were to play important roles in the economic growth of the Philippines, suggests a correspondence with one feature of Schumpeterian theory, namely, the clustering of entrepreneurial activity in discontinuous groups and swarms. The evidence suggests that such a cluster occurred in the Philippines in the 1820s. And, aside from all the particular circumstances of the case that might tend to explain the same thing, it is possible to surmise on theoretical grounds that the impact of these foreign firms on the Philippine economy was extraordinarily strong because of the clustering.

The importance of the two American houses founded in the 1820s and the availability of material concerning them make it convenient to look in more detail into the circumstances surrounding their establishment and their early operations.

The Founding of Peele, Hubbell & Co.

The Hubbells' trip to the Philippines on the *Ajax* in 1821 resulted in the founding of a firm under the name of George W. Hubbell. The first commercial circulars were issued on January 1, 1822. Henry W. Hubbell served as a clerk in his brother's establishment. By 1823, George Hubbell was exporting sugar to South America (together with a cargo of China silk), and in 1825 he personally delivered a shipment of the same product to Cádiz in Spain. In the meantime, there was increasing business with the United States, particularly New York and Salem.

Hubbell went to the United States after delivering the Cádiz cargo and remained there for two years (1825–27), promoting the business of his Manila firm. On his return trip to the Philippines, he took a shipment of imports, part of which was landed at Manila and part in China, where the ship loaded for New York. From this time on, several such voyages were made in which goods were consigned to Hubbell in Manila and the ship then proceeded to China to load tea.

George Hubbell died on May 3, 1831, at the age of thirty-five. His brother Henry was more interested in the trade with England and China than with the Philippines, so he entered into an arrangement with J. W. Peele of Salem through which the Manila house would continue with both of them as partners. Peele arrived in Manila in May 1832 on the *Sapphire*, and on August 1 circulars were issued announcing the new firm of Peele, Hubbell & Co. Two years later, Henry Hubbell retired from the partnership and was succeeded by Henry Lawrence of New York. However, he continued to promote the firm's interests in the United States, England, and China and also maintained personal relations with the new partners. Peele and Lawrence retired in 1843, selling out to O. E. Edwards, Nathaniel Cook, and William H. Osborn, the first from Connecticut (the son of a former governor) and the latter two from Salem. Edwards would remain with the firm until its demise in 1887.[18]

Just who the entrepreneur was who decided to found the firm in the 1820s is not certain, but there is reason to believe that Capt. Ezekiel Hubbell himself may have had much to do with it, judging from his actions during earlier trips. His continued voyages to Manila until 1828 suggest that he was active in helping run the firm during its first years of existence. However, one must also consider George Hubbell an entrepreneur. Once the firm was established, he was on his own in a distant part of the world, and he had to make decisions on the spot. It is possible that he was responsible for the methods the firm used in its local operations and for the export products in which he chose to deal. Suggestive material regarding this will be presented later.

In the light of Redlich's schema,[19] it may be said that the locus of entrepreneurial decision making was at least partly external to the firm of George W. Hubbell, although it was internal to the Hubbell family. The function of capitalization was also at least partly external in the early voyages (Hoyt & Tom and others), although it is reasonable to assume that the Hubbells put more and more of their own funds into the venture. The managerial function seems to have devolved mainly on George Hubbell.

The founding of the house of Hubbell derives added significance from the fact that the initial impulse does not seem to have come as a by-product of the China trade. The venture was apparently conceived in the United States, and the Manila trade seems to have been judged on its own merits and regarded as a worthwhile commercial object in itself.

The Founding of Russell & Sturgis

The establishment of what came to be known as the great house of Russell & Sturgis was intimately connected with the Canton trade and especially with the Boston merchants in that trade. A conjunction of able men in different parts of the world figured in the events that led to its founding—Thomas Handasyd Perkins of J. & T. H. Perkins of Boston; John Perkins Cushing of Perkins & Co. in Canton; Thomas T. Forbes, who was at one time or another active in both Canton and Manila; and finally the founders of the firm itself, George Robert Russell and Henry P. Sturgis.

The central figure seems to have been J. P. Cushing, who had already demonstrated his ability when, as a clerk at the age of sixteen, he had taken charge of Perkins & Co. in Canton upon the sudden demise of its head and had managed so skillfully that it became unnecessary for his uncles in Boston to send out anyone to replace the deceased manager.[20]

Around the mid-1820s, the Perkins interests seem to have felt the necessity of having a more confidential agency in Manila than could be provided by the Barrettos, their correspondents theretofore. On April 28, 1824, T. H. Perkins wrote J. P. Cushing that his only reservation about sending a ship to Manila was on account "of the necessity of putting ourselves entirely into the hands of an agent in Manila, in whom we do not like to confide so extensively as we must." And somewhat later he wrote the following: "We will thank you to be explicit in your next, in relation to your agent in Manila—how far he might be trusted to decide impartially if his interest was in favor of a vessel stopping at Manila in deciding between that plan and the River."

At this time, Cushing seems to have foreseen a rise in Philippine trade, and T. H. Perkins concurred in the opinion. In the same letter, but dated the sixth of May, the latter wrote: "Your observations in your letter 5 Dec. are in conformity with our ideas. We have no doubt that the trade of Luconia will increase rapidly, & constant information should be given of its wants."

One of the reasons why a rise was foreseen was the availability of specie. T. H. Perkins anticipated a decline in the American trade with Java because of the local shortage of specie. Foreign shippers taking goods there had to receive payment in coffee, which in periods of low coffee prices was bound to be a losing proposition. On the other hand, more flexibility was possible in the trade at Manila, where an importer might elect to receive payment in either goods or specie.

Perkins also anticipated (somewhat prematurely) that the Philippines would fight for its independence if the South American colonies succeeded in their struggle for freedom, and he was ready to supply powder and arms in such an eventuality (although it must be said that he was just as willing to supply the same goods to meet the normal needs of the Spanish garrison to show them that this would cost them less than if they had to supply themselves).

Finally, Perkins looked on Manila as a possible market for the output of textile mills in which the Perkinses had an interest. "In a national point of view," he wrote to Cushing on September 18, 1824, "it is proper to promote the introduction of those goods whenever we can, and it is interesting to us, inasmuch as our funds are intensively engaged in the factories, and our Senior is interested in works which are near erecting, where the Snuff Mills were in Newton."

Even before this, he had dispatched two vessels to Manila and suggested to Cushing in Canton that Thomas T. Forbes be sent there to attend to them.[21] Forbes appears to have arrived in Manila early the following year and to have stayed slightly over a year, which was somewhat longer than had been anticipated. He was very active in that period, working with the Barrettos, drawing up schemes with them to sell arms and ammunition to the Cavite arsenal, and exporting cargoes of sugar, abaca, cotton, rice, dyewoods, coffee, cigars, wax candles, mat bags, indigo, and cassia (the last probably an aftereffect of the Royal Philippine Company's ventures in cinnamon). He also seems to have had some contact with Kierulf & Co.[22] This stay must have been a profitable one, because T. H. Perkins wrote on April 8, 1826: "Mr. Forbes has certainly managed well at Manila as well as possible . . ."[23]

After Forbes returned to Canton, he wrote Francisco Barretto on March 25, 1826, asking the latter to sell his carriage and horses in Manila, collect some money from H. P. Sturgis, and let that gentleman have his boat (his Forbes sporting blood being evident even in his transitory commercial contacts). This is the earliest known reference to Henry P. Sturgis, who was less than twenty years old at the time.

T. T. Forbes went to Boston in 1826–27, and when he returned to Asia it was to take over Perkins & Co. in Canton from J. P. Cushing, who was retiring. His operations in Manila in 1825 may have encouraged the Perkins interests to strengthen their connections with the Philippines. His estimate of the situation agreed with the optimistic prospects for Philippine trade held by J. P. Cushing and T. H. Perkins, and he opined that there was room enough in which to expand, despite the competition from the many English houses, which he mentions as having been founded by that time, and from the Hubbells, who were that year expected to make a "demonstration" with their ship, the *Cadet*.[24] During his absence from Asia, events occurred that led speedily to the establishment of Russell & Sturgis.

The main event was the coming to East Asia of a young Providence-born lawyer, George Robert Russell, in search of a mercantile fortune. His importance in Philippine entrepreneurial history and the availability of material about him justify a somewhat detailed look at the circumstances surrounding his coming and his first years in business.

Born on May 5, 1800, Russell graduated from Brown University in 1821 and then studied law in Philadelphia.[25] Early in 1824, he wrote his uncle, Otis Ammidon, that he had concluded to practice law at his birthplace. Midway through the following year, however, he wrote his sisters a farewell letter from New York in which he consoled them by saying that his absence would be a necessary but temporary evil. There is a hint that domestic troubles—perhaps financial—had made him change his plans and seek his fortune in the commerce of foreign lands.

Armed with a letter from General Lafayette to Simón Bolívar, he stopped at Lima, Peru, toward the end of 1825 but missed seeing the South American liberator, who was away at the time. He did, however, get to witness the siege of Callao from the front lines of the Peruvian forces. Concluding that the prospects for commercial gain in Peru were not too rosy, he decided to join his uncle, Philip Ammidon, a partner in the famous house of Russell & Co. in Canton (founded by Samuel Russell of Middletown, Connecticut—apparently no relation). He sailed on an English brig early in 1826 from Lima to Manila, where he remained sixteen days, "& was much pleased with it," as he wrote his sisters. "The Island of Luconia is one of the richest in the world & its luxuriance afforded an agreeable contrast to the country I had left." Falling in with a Providence friend in Manila, he took passage on the friend's ship to Canton, arriving April 25. "I have no reason to regret leaving South America," he wrote his sisters in the same letter, dated May 21. "On the contrary—I am convinced that my prospect of success is much better in this part of the world."

Although he planned to leave Canton after Philip Ammidon's departure, he seems to have impressed Samuel Russell favorably, and on December 14 he wrote his uncle Otis that Mr. Russell had asked him to stay and, as soon as circumstances permitted, to become a partner in the house. "In the meantime," he wrote, "I am to assist (as I have done since my residence here) in the business & am to be furnished with means & every assistance in adventuring on my own account. I have the privilege of engaging in any enterprise which may take me from Canton & can resume my footing in the House on my return." On January 19 of the following year he wrote his sisters that Mr. Russell "is a very pleasant amiable man & we live together in a most comfortable manner—that is—as much so as one can so far from home & in so confined a place as Canton."

But Samuel Russell was not the only one with an eye for character in Canton. About a month later, on February 23, George Russell wrote his uncle Otis that he had been engaged by Perkins & Co. as supercargo of a brig whose cargo was to be disposed of in Manila and Batavia; he was also to settle the affairs of the Perkinses in Java. He told his uncle:

> You are aware that Mr. Cushing composes the firm of P. & Co. at this place. This gentleman has evinced much friendly regard for me & the very important business he has now confided to my management is the strongest evidence of the favourable place I hold in his good opinion. I feel much flattered by the confidence he has reposed in me & the warmest gratitude for the very friendly wishes he expresses in my behalf. I deem myself fortunate in entering his employment & have the most sanguine hopes that it is the commencement of very cheering prospects.[26]

It was, indeed, the commencement of big things for the Philippines, for a few months later, on July 19, a letter received at the Boston end of the Perkins interests announced: "We shall put the settlement of our affairs at Manila in the hands of Mr. Geo. R. Russell, a young man of excellent character, who will implicitly obey our instructions."[27]

Russell wrote to his sisters from Manila on October 2, 1827, that after his trip to Batavia, "I was immediately engaged by my excellent friend Mr. Cushing to return here for the purpose of taking charge of the business of the Messrs. Perkins' & have been here nearly three months. I shall probably remain here several months and perhaps longer." He proceeded to make himself comfortable, rented a house, brought furniture from Canton, and engaged a cook, a coachman, and two servants. "I keep a carriage, for legs are of no sort of use here, it being extremely ungenteel to walk. I have plenty of employment & find no idle hours." Evidently things looked promising in Manila, for he added: "You will be pleased to learn my Dear Sisters that my prospects are very good and I have sanguine hopes that I shall one day be able to offer you a home." At this time, he already felt prosperous enough to instruct them to call on him unhesitatingly should they find themselves in financial straits.

On Christmas Day, 1827, he wrote his sister Amelia (later to be a resident of Brook Farm) that he had been joined by Henry P. Sturgis, "who arrived lately from Canton & at the strong recommendation of our friends at Canton we have decided to establish a house at this place." This was the genesis of the firm of Russell & Sturgis, which opened its doors for business formally on July 1, 1828.[28] (What Henry Sturgis was doing in Manila at the time of T. T. Forbes's visit in 1826 is unknown). The reference in George Russell's letter to their Canton friends makes it a virtual certainty that J. P. Cushing had much to do with encouraging the two young men to establish their firm; indeed, he seems to have presided like a tutelary deity over Russell's early career in Asia.

Here again is a case in which an entrepreneurial decision, that to establish a new house, seems to have been arrived at by several persons, including perhaps outsiders, rather than by the principals alone. Cushing's relationship with Russell & Sturgis is of course ambiguous, since the partners shifted from being mere agents of the Perkinses to doing a general commission business. Formally, Cushing was in the same group of organizations in their former status but not in their latter. If his influence was not therefore completely external, neither was it wholly internal. What is certain is that he must be given credit for character judgment and his choice of personnel. His decisions were made in the face not only of risk but of uncertainty, in Knight's sense of the word. This is not to minimize the role played by George Robert Russell and Henry Sturgis. Obviously, they had something that recommended them to Cushing; once the firm had been founded, its progress depended on them more than on anyone else, and they appear to have run it quite skillfully indeed.

Both partners seem to have been men of more than ordinary ability, and they held each other in high regard. One proof of this is that they named their first-born sons after one another—George Robert Russell Sturgis and Henry Sturgis Russell. Writing to a sister on October 12, 1831, Russell characterized Sturgis as "amiable & worthy. . . . [H]e is an excellent young man very industrious, very capable, with an inexhaustible fund of good nature, a most enviable disposition & of first rate principles."

Russell himself seems to have won the regard of those who came in contact with him, and the number of times his name is mentioned by travelers who visited Manila or wrote about the country at that time is truly remarkable. Harriet Low, a young New England girl who stopped in Manila on her way to Canton in September 1829, wrote of having gone on a couple of evening rides with Russell, and the hospitality she met with was so enjoyable that she declared: "I have never left any place but my home with so much regret, and shall always remember my visit to Manila with pleasure."[29] Admiral Laplace, who was in Manila about a year later, speaks of him as "an American merchant distinguished in every respect" and of being accompanied by him on a visit to Gironiere's estate at Jala-jala.[30] The last-named gentleman in one of his works mentions him as "a very competent person," "a good and true friend, the recollection of whom, often present to my mind, will never be effaced."[31] A British surgeon visiting Manila in 1833 heard of "a gentleman named Russell" who was described as a crocodile killer.[32] The crocodile in question, an exceptionally large monster, was killed by Russell near Jala-jala while he was convalescing from "a bilious fever" at Gironiere's place. The event "caused a considerable sensation not only on the field of battle but at Manila, none of equal size having been before seen & it is rarely that any of small size are taken," he wrote on October 6, 1831, to his uncle Otis Ammidon. But he hastened to assure his relative: "You must not be alarmed thinking that I may repeat an experiment which has been so unusually successful. My Crocodile battles are over & I am content with the trophy I have already acquired viz the head which I shall preserve." (This skull is now in the Harvard University Museum.) Gironiere gives an extended account of the crocodile hunt but, exercising literary license, attributes the main role to himself and relegates Russell to an auxiliary part.[33]

The first few years of the firm seem to have been busy and prosperous ones. On November 14, 1828, Russell wrote to his uncle Otis: "I am much engaged at this time & have as much business on my hands as I can attend to." Sixteen days later he wrote to his father: "My business so far answers my expectations & have reason to believe it will continue." Canton merchant Isaac M. Bull, while visiting Manila in 1831, wrote, "Mess. Russell & Sturgis are now the only established Commission (American) House here. (Mr. Hubbell having died some months ago) they have done a good business worth 20,000$ each, but they work hard."[34]

To his sisters, Russell wrote of the social duties concomitant with his position in society. On December 1, 1828, he spoke of having received an invitation addressed to himself "and friends" to attend the one annual public ball at Manila. Since his house was always full of ship's captains, visitors, business correspondents, and so forth, it devolved upon him to lead the way to the festivities, which he found very pleasant, although quite exhausting after a hard day's work. On February 6, 1830, he wrote of having to play host to the officers of the *U.S.S. Vincennes*, "the first national vessel of ours that has been here for many years & the second that has ever been here. The duties of hospitality fall in a great degree on us & I shall endeavor to soak the gentlemen that they may remember the last day of their visit to Manila."

The early success of the firm seems to have aroused jealousy among its competitors. In a letter of April 11, 1831, to his uncle Otis, Russell indignantly relates:

> It has been industriously circulated by interested persons that we have been & are more the special agents of Perkins & Co than general commission merchants & that their interests are preferred by us to those of others. This is entirely false for in no instance has their business in the least interfered with that of others. Indeed, since the death of Mr. Forbes it has been very trifling & since the new arrangements in China it is dwindling down to nothing.[35]

That year also seems to have been a poor one for the firm, and Russell reported in the same letter that he was not doing much business. But he was not one to let grass grow under his feet. The following year he quickly made up his mind to return to the western world, as George Hubbell had done previously, to improve his firm's connections there. He arrived in New York on June 3, 1832, and four days later wrote of having had as fellow passenger on the voyage Mr. Robert Ker (of Ker & Co.), "a Scottish gentleman . . . a sterling good fellow of most excellent character & with first rate principles. He is an old resident of Manilla as agent for a very respectable English House & we have been on the most friendly terms." Ker was on his way to Scotland but managed to spend a month sightseeing in America with the help of Russell's relatives.

After completing his business in the United States and calming his family's fears about the spread of the cholera epidemic that was raging in New York that summer, Russell took passage late that year to England and France, where he made more business contacts, including a call on Mr. Bates of Baring Brothers & Co. He also found time to hobnob with Lafayette, the Bonapartes, Fenimore Cooper, and the poet Campbell. His curiosity led him to watch part of the siege of Antwerp and to observe the House of Commons in session in London ("as graceless & stupid a set of stammerers as ever figured in a college class meeting").

By the middle of the following year, he was back in Boston, and he must have returned to Manila in late 1833 or early 1834. The new connections he had made apparently proved profitable, and in June 1835 he retired from Asia for good (though he formally severed his connection with the firm only at the end of 1841).[36]

One qualification Russell possessed that few other merchants in Asia had, namely, his training at law, may have contributed to his business success in the often litigious environment of Manila. For example, on November 14, 1828, he wrote to Otis Ammidon:

> The most tedious business in which I am engaged is one which reminds me of the little office in 4th Street, viz, the management of three law suits. One is enough to make a man crazy even in a land of Law & Justice what must *three* then be before a *Spanish Tribunal*. These law suits are in consequence of the dishonorable & very ruinous failure of Messrs. Barretto & Co Merchants of this place who have done a large business for some years past. The Parsee Houses of Bombay are sufferers & we have received full powers from their regents in China to act as their attornies [sic] & to take general charge of their business at this place.

Barretto & Co. had declared bankruptcy on September 20, 1828, followed two days later by the allied firm of Yrastorza Brodett & Co. Both failures were termed extremely ruinous, causing much distress.[37]

Russell need not have been surprised at Barretto's failure because early that year T. T. Forbes, then in charge of Perkins & Co. at Canton, had transferred his Manila business from Barretto to Russell & Sturgis, and this must have been a rather heavy blow to Barretto. Little did Russell foresee the fate that was to overtake his own firm in less than half a century or the fact that his firm's creditors at that time would celebrate their meetings at the house of a Barretto.

The most suggestive fact, however, is that Russell's legal background helped him in business and may have partly accounted for his firm's preeminence in Philippine commerce. Nor did his departure deprive the firm of a partner with legal training, for by then Henry Sturgis's eldest brother Russell (later to be Russell Sturgis of London), who was also a lawyer, was in Asia, and he divided his time between Canton and Manila. Of the ten years he spent in Asia (1834–44), he passed four at the latter place and laid his second wife to rest there in 1837.[38] Thus, Russell & Sturgis in its first decade and a half of existence seems to have benefited, in the legalistic atmosphere of Manila, from the legal background possessed by one of its principals.

Even more interesting to students of entrepreneurial history are the motivations and philosophy of George Russell. On February 2, 1831, in reply to queries as to when he was coming home, he wrote his sister Amelia:

> My motions will be regulated by my success & my residence here will be no longer than is absolutely necessary to obtain an independence. I never expect to be able to nabobize but hope at some future day to live comfortably in my own country. Time will however be necessary. . . . [I]t makes me sad when I think that I am spending my best years in a strange land. I do not wish however to leave this country till I can live as I please in my own. The sacrifice I am making is very great but as it has commenced it should be completed. Whenever I do return I hope my business days will be over & that I may feel able to live in peace.

To the same sister, he again wrote on May 20 of that year, expounding his views further:

> I never expect to be able to *nabobize* & indeed my happiness would not be increased by doing so. All I wish is to be able to live like a gentleman quietly & peaceably with the power of commanding all the comforts of life. It seems to me folly for a man to spend the greater part of his life in a Foreign Country merely that he may return to his own with overgrown wealth, but his constitution ruined, his disposition soured, & his tastes for everything in this world entirely altered. A long absence from civilized society makes him unfit for it & he finds that money, the God he has so long worshipped, is not every thing in life. Is it not better to return with a comfortable independence while the constitution is unimpaired & the feelings unchanged, while old friends are living to welcome & the world yet offers enjoyment? I think you will answer yes. I believe I am about the same in all respects as when I left home. My health is excellent & the regular & temperate life I lead is calculated to maintain it.

While visiting Boston in 1832, he learned that his old uncle, Philip Ammidon, was thinking of returning to Canton to establish a house there. He expressed his amazement to Otis Ammidon in a letter dated August 10, 1832:

> It is strange that an infirm man who has laboured all his life should, instead of enjoying as well as he may, the remainder of his days, now wish to start on a new career where success cannot add to his comfort & ill fortune may make him a beggar.

His own immediate motives in going into business in a distant land were founded on a more general philosophy, which he expounded to a sister in a letter dated October 12, 1831:

> It is the true philosophy of life to laugh as much as possible in this world & make the most of it. I think that this world should be enjoyed as much as possible & that the person who makes him or herself as comfortable as possible, taking every opportunity that offers for rational amusement, lives a wise & religious life. I of course mean a strict adherence to morality for I really believe that nothing is more correct than the old maxim that "vice brings with it its own punishment" & that conscience is a better guide to our conduct in life than can be found in books even though expounded by men with long faces & black coats. If one attends strictly to the duties of life (& I consider the principal one to be attention to personal comfort & that of others whose happiness is dependent on our own) there is precious little use in attending to anything else & I would ensure the soul of a virtuous man at a very small premium even though he had never crossed a church door & did not know which comes first, Genesis or Revelations. However though I do not myself feel the necessity of being "born again" yet I have all due respect for those who do, provided they do not insist on my undergoing the same operation. I would interfere with no belief & ridicule no creed, which is followed with honest intentions . . .

If the initial impetus behind Russell's departure from his native land has been correctly interpreted as coming from domestic financial troubles, then his is a case of straitened gentility seeking to recoup a competence in order to enjoy again the blessings of a genteel life. He was most certainly not an exponent of business for business's sake or money for money's sake. Commercial activity and money were useful but only up to a certain point and as a means to an end, which in his case was the independent life of a gentleman. It is probable that he accomplished his objective; but when he married and settled down in Milton, Massachusetts, he did not divorce himself entirely from economic affairs; he evidently invested some money in industry and was also interested in railroads.

Russell & Sturgis was carried on for a while by the Sturgises. Before Russell left, Henry's younger brother, George, who will be seen in another role later, joined the firm as a clerk, and on January 1, 1848, he became a partner, together with Charles Griswold, while Henry P. Sturgis withdrew. Russell liked him very much, describing him as "very correct in his habits, attentive & industrious and always amiable." Russell Sturgis arrived in East Asia in 1834 and left the firm on the same day as G. R. Russell at the end of 1841. There was also the bookkeeper, Josiah Moore, who later became a partner but died on March 18, 1848, leading Henry P. Sturgis to resume his connection with the firm the following year. Henry Sturgis had married a Calcutta girl, Mary Georgiana Howard, around 1835, and their eight children were born in Manila. Their son, George Robert Russell Sturgis, was in Manila as late as 1864 and may have died there in 1866.[39] In the meantime, George Sturgis left the firm on July 1, 1850, and on February 1, 1851, Edward H. Green and Jonathan Russell became partners, the latter George Russell's half-brother who had sailed from the United States for Manila on May 21, 1846, and was fated to be the firm's last senior partner. Three other names should be mentioned, which would figure in the firm's eventual bankruptcy: Edward Jackson, who was granted signatory powers on April 14, 1866, and Henry Upham Jeffries and William Griswold Heron, who were given the same power on January 1, 1867.[40]

It is now time to take a closer look at firms such as those founded by Hubbell, Russell, and Sturgis and see what features made them important entrepreneurial institutions.

CHAPTER 9

Entrepreneurial Activity:
The Organization and
Operation of Merchant Houses

This chapter will examine the organization and operation of the Anglo-American merchant houses. Certain advantages, such as consanguinity, a correspondent network, cultural and institutional affinities, and access to London's banking facilities will be cited. The differences between American and English practice will be noted. The three main variables facing the merchant firms will be reviewed, namely, commodity prices, freight rates, and exchange rates.

The last item centered on the rate between the Mexican dollar (or peso) and sterling, the main currency for external payments, and reflected rates for bills of exchange drawn on London. The bill market grew apace after an initial period of specie transactions and of fungibility of certain export commodities. Bill rates on regional ports made for a multiple rate system, with the London rate as the variable central rate, supplemented with a cluster of geographically based subsidiary rates, until the early 1870s, when the disappearance of these subsidiary rates signaled the virtual unification of the exchange rate. At about this time the great currency depreciation stemming from the fall in silver prices began, although it appears not to have affected the bill market until the next decade.

The rise of bill financing induced the merchant firms to raise local currency by issuing notes, that is, by taking deposits from largely urban depositors drawn not only from the affluent strata of society but from people of quite modest backgrounds. The funds thus raised were given out as advances in the course of agricultural financing operations, diffusing liquid wealth to Filipinos in the rural areas. By means of these advances, the merchant firms were able to exercise considerable control over the supply of export commodities. By engaging in financial intermediation, these firms were doing de facto banking and could be called merchant-financiers. With economic initiative (in foreign hands) separated from political authority (in Spanish hands), the Philippines fell into a more East Asian (China and Japan) than Southeast Asian mold (Malaya and Indonesia).

The Anglo-American Firms: Advantages and Comparisons

The foreign firms that established themselves in Manila in the 1820s and 1830s had several advantages over their local counterparts, even abstracting from the Iturbide incident and the loss of the Mexican trade. They were, as we have seen, in close contact with the centers of economic progress, Western Europe (especially Great Britain) and the United States, which were also the regions of the world with rising real income and therefore good markets for tropical products. They had commercial relations with firms that were not only commodity traders but shipowners and thus had a flexible choice between trading on their own account or taking freight. These firms had to put their affairs in distant ports in the hands of agents, and they usually felt more at ease if these agents were countrymen whom they knew personally rather than a local firm that was only a name to them. The transfer of the Perkins agency in Manila from the Barrettos to Russell & Sturgis is illustrative of this.

In the case of the Boston merchants, there was an additional bond, that of kinship. The Perkinses, Forbeses, Russells, and Sturgises were all related to one another by ties of blood and marriage. Moreover, some of them, like the Sturgises, had the habit of naming their children after their brothers and sisters, so that anyone who reads their correspondence is liable to get lost without the aid of a genealogical table.

Family connections, however, while they meant opportunity, did not mean favoritism; Boston was too puritanical for that. To take a position with a relative meant an opening, a chance to get ahead in the world, but it also meant having to demonstrate a high level of competence. The career of Capt. Robert Bennett Forbes, for example, well illustrates this. In the Philippine case, when fourteen-year-old George Sturgis advised his brother Henry of his desire to begin a career in Manila, the latter frankly outlined the conditions of work and offered a good deal of general advice. In a letter dated November 20, 1831, he wrote to George:

> You will recollect that you will be subject to two masters, and you must make up your mind to make every exertion to please both, and to take the same interest in our affairs as if they were entirely your own.
>
> I can assure you of kind treatment so long as that is the case and can promise you that you shall have no cause to repent your exertions to forward the interests of your employers.[1]

In the 1850s, family connections enabled Russell & Sturgis to displace the British firm of Ker & Co. as the Plymouth Cordage Co.'s correspondent in Manila, but the cordage firm's dissatisfaction with Russell & Sturgis's conduct led it to return to the British firm, as will be seen.

What might be called the British pattern diverged in some respects from American practices. There was a more formal connection between the head offices in Britain (Liverpool, Glasgow, or London) and the Manila firms, and quite commonly partners leaving Asia did so not to retire from business but to continue in their head offices. The established pattern was residence in Manila for some years by young men who were considered best fitted to survive the vicissitudes of climate and health, followed by management of the firm in Britain.

British practice favored keeping overall control with the mother company and giving signing powers in the Philippines only to the resident partner there. Thus, Ker & Co. in 1878 had for partners Ker, Bolton & Co.; Joseph Cheney Bolton and John Ross of Glasgow; Gilbert McMicking of London; and Albert Coats of Manila. The latter was admitted into the partnership by Ker, Bolton & Co., the managing partners and overseers. Although Coats's contract ran for seven years, he apparently left after a short stint, and the following year a new resident partner in Manila and Iloilo was named in the person of Thomas Worthington. Another change was that Robert Jardine of London joined the firm as a partner that year.

On November 29, 1884, Jardine informed his correspondents of the retirement of the senior partners William Ker, Joseph Cheney Bolton, and Gilbert McMicking, as well as that of Thomas Worthington. He in London and John Ross in Glasgow would continue the business, to be joined shortly by Frederick Bolton, and Robert J. Paterson would take charge of Manila and Iloilo. Formal notices sent out on New Year's Day included not only Ker, Bolton & Co. of Glasgow and London and Ker & Co. of Manila and Iloilo, but also Syme & Co. of Singapore and Pitcairn, Syme & Co. of Batavia and Surabaya. Southeast Asia was well covered.

As in the American case, family ties played some part; successive junior partners were often related to the senior members of the firm. An example of such ties was the employment of T. McMicking in Iloilo in 1878 and 1879 while Gilbert McMicking was still a senior partner. But T. (Torrence) McMicking departed from the norm somewhat by marrying locally, then leaving his Iloilo family and remarrying in Scotland. (Tragically, most of the Philippine McMickings were massacred by the Japanese during the destruction of Manila in 1945.)

One can visualize concentric circles defining areas of common contact among the Anglo-American firms, with the smallest circle consisting of family groups and personal friends, a larger circle defined by nationality (British or American), and the largest circle comprehending the general Anglo-Saxon culture, with a common language, similar religious and ethical beliefs, almost identical legal systems, and shared traditions. But the various groupings were not watertight compartments. American buyers could and did shift their business from American to British houses depending on perceived advantages.

Some idea of the advantages of the Anglo-American firms can be had by comparing their references to merchants of other nationalities. When Russell & Sturgis opened for business on July 1, 1828, they gave as references the following: Baring Brothers & Co. and Thomas Dickason & Co. in London; Hope & Co. and Daniel Crommelin & Sons in Amsterdam; Perkins & Co. in Boston and Canton; Bryant & Sturgis in Boston; Russell & Co. in Canton; Joseph Peabody and Pickering Dodge in Salem; Brown & Ives and Edward Carrington & Co. in Providence; John Jacob Astor and Nathaniel L. & George Griswold in New York; Samuel Archer and Perit & Cabot in Philadelphia; and William Lorman & Sons and William Wilson & Sons in Baltimore. In 1834, the partners, together with John W. Perit and Russell Sturgis, formed a copartnership in Canton under the name Russell, Sturgis & Co. "in connexion with the House of Russell & Sturgis of Manila."[2]

By contrast, the French merchant Edmond Plauchut (who was later to write an article on the Cavite Mutiny of 1872) gave as references in 1854 N. Monteaux et Fils, bankers in Paris, London, and Brussels; Comptoir Commercial de la Gironde in Bordeaux; and Dulary, Bellamy & Co. (brandy merchants) and Premont et Plauchut (bankers) in Angoulême. In 1846, B. A. Barretto & Co., considered as late as 1875 to be a British firm (although Barretto himself was listed as a Spanish merchant, so the firm was actually domestic), gave as references Magniac, Jardine & Co. of London; Jardine, Matheson & Co. of Hong Kong; Jardine, Skinner & Co. of Calcutta; and Remington & Co. of Bombay. The Jardine connections were understandable, since it was Jardine who had set Barretto up in Manila. (Early in the nineteenth century, Beale & Co., private East Indian traders holding Danish papers, had employed B. Barretto as an agent in the Macao opium market; he was also for many years the Macao agent for Jardine, Matheson & Co.).[3] The superiority of the Anglo-American network is immediately apparent.

Finally, the foreign traders had the advantage of being in touch with London, banker to the world. And here they were in a position to introduce a business innovation into Philippine commerce, namely, the use of bills of exchange. Until they came upon the scene, and probably for some time after, the principal mode of payment in the Asian trade was by means of Mexican silver dollars or pesos. During his visit to Manila, T. T. Forbes wrote the Perkinses in Boston that he was remitting the proceeds from the sales of certain shipments in silver to Canton because bills were scarce and almost unknown there (this was in 1825–26).[4]

Walter Hubbell dates the first American confirmed credit on Baring Brothers & Co. in London to 1829. However, there were limitations to the use of bills. That same year Capt. C. B. Peirce reported that G. R. Russell "thinks bills could not be negotiated on London." Five years later, Russell & Sturgis were still reporting "Bills on England not . . . negotiable here." But there was a demand for bills because, according to Isaac M. Bull in 1831, "the agents of English Houses are directed to make their returns in Bills in preference to shipping produce." He reported having sold three thousand pounds in bills at four shillings to the dollar.[5] All during those years, there were quotations for bills, so there appeared to be a distinction between negotiability and salability, the latter perhaps involving only the final users. But before the end of the decade trading in bills of exchange was in full swing.

With the increasing use of bills of exchange, the greater flexibility of negotiable instruments favored the foreigners. A foreign house would send a ship to Manila with a letter of credit (usually on Baring's) for the local correspondent, which would buy local products and sell them to the captain for bills drawn on London at six months' sight. These the local merchant could negotiate by means of an endorsement and thus close the transaction as far as he was concerned. Meanwhile, the goods would arrive at a destination such as London in four or five months, and the bills would not fall due for nine or ten months, so the importer had ample time to sell the goods before then and could economize on capital. He could also authorize better prices for the goods and thus outbid his agent's local competitors, who were unversed in this procedure.[6]

In fact, the use of American bills on London with Baring's as the chief guarantor has been identified as an innovation in the whole Canton trade that the British merchants initially treated with reserve. But a credit crisis in Calcutta in 1829–34, which caused all the great agency houses to fail, finally persuaded the Canton merchants to use such American bills extensively. In 1831 and 1833, which may have been exceptional years, American vessels imported into Canton 86 and 87 percent, respectively, of their means of payment in bills, with the residual in specie.[7] This occurred at a time when, for the first time in recorded history, China's trade balance had turned adverse. Silver output in Spanish America also had fallen—to a level in 1820–29 only 41 percent of what it had been in 1790–99.[8] It will be recalled that in Manila Ezekiel Hubbell's cargo of 1818 had consisted of 80 percent specie and 20 percent goods. Specie would now decrease in importance, and bills of exchange were the coming thing. In fact, rather than exporting specie the Philippines would become a net importer. In the twenty-year period 1837–56, silver specie imports were 10.8 million pesos while silver specie exports were only 2.8 million.[9]

Operation and Organization: Basic Functions

Of even greater importance was the entrepreneurial organization that developed over time to take care of the business that the firms conducted. Officially, the foreign firms were simply commission merchants, and they seem to have started modestly enough. As Henry Sturgis wrote his brother George in 1831: "Mr. Russell and myself make it a rule of our establishment to transact our business with as little assistance as possible in order to have no idlers, consequently we ourselves and those connected with us are generally constantly employed."[10] Nearly four years later, on January 13, 1835, George R. Russell wrote his sister that besides himself and four other Americans who resided with him he had four native assistants, who came during office hours but did not live in the house.[11] In Redlich's schema, not only would these merchants be partly capitalists, besides being entrepreneurs and managers, but they would also be employees. It was a relatively simple and uncomplicated form of entrepreneurial organization, which required little initial capital.

Three Variables

In their commodity trading, the merchant houses operated within limits set by their customers in the West. These limits pertained to the set price of the commodity at its destination and had to take into account three main variables—namely, the local cost of the commodity, freight rates, and the rate of exchange—in addition to duties at the importing end. The movements of the three major variables—commodity prices, exchange rates, and freight rates—are available in a single source for about three decades, from 1851 to 1882, and for earlier years in other sources (table 16).

There were asymmetrical relations between some of these variables; for example, low freight rates enabled the merchants to offer high prices for the commodity, but the reverse was not true because the level of freight rates was independently determined by the number of "seeking" vessels putting into port at a given time. In 1847, for example, Russell & Sturgis reported the "extraordinary number of *twenty* ships" in port or expected shortly, of which "but *two* have cargoes ready leaving eighteen more waiting." At other times, the situation was reversed either for particular places (e.g., in 1853 for Australia) or in general. In 1855, tonnage was scarce and "much wanted for all quarters, large quantities of produce having accu-

TABLE 16
Prices and Exports of Hemp and Sugar
Selected Years, 1818-1882

Year	Prices[1] Pesos per picul		Exchange Rate Shillings per Peso	Freight Rates to				Exports[2] (piculs, '000)	
	Hemp	Sugar		U.S. Pesos Per Ton[3]		Great Britain Pounds Per Ton[3]		Hemp	Sugar
				Hemp	Sugar	Hemp	Sugar		
1818	4.00	7.00	5/6	-	-	-	-	26	14.4
1819	-	6.50	-	-	-	-	-	-	-
1820	-	8.00	-	-	-	-	-	-	-
1822	-		-	-	-	-	-	1.9	-
1823	-	-	-	-	-	-	-	2.0	-
1824	5.25	3.88	-	-	-	-	-	2.6	-
1825	-	-	-	-	-	-	-	4.4	-
1826	5.50	4.63	-	-	-	-	-	5.2	-
1827	6.00	6.00	-	-	-	-	-	5.1	28.4
1828	-	-	-	-	-	-	-	10.0	116.5

Continued next page

Table 16 *Continued*

	Prices[1] Pesos per picul		Exchange Rate Shillings per Peso	Freight Rates to				Exports[2] (piculs, '000)	
				U.S. Pesos Per Ton[3]		Great Britain Pounds Per Ton[3]			
Year	Hemp	Sugar		Hemp	Sugar	Hemp	Sugar	Hemp	Sugar
1829	6.25	4.86	$4/0^{1/2}$	-	-	-	-	8.4	120.3
1830	5.00	6.94	-	-	-	-	-	17.3	138.4
1831	6.00	3.69	4/	-	-	-	-	27.9	-
1832	-	-	-	-	-	-	-	38.2	-
1833	6.13	3.88	4/3	-	-	-	-	46.6	-
1834	5.38	3.94	$4/10^{1/4}$	-	-	-	-	28.0	-
1835	4.81	4.25	4/8	-	-	-	-	42.1	-
1836	-	-	$4/7^{1/2}$	-	-	-	-	57.2	-
1837	-	-	$4/10^{1/2}$	-	-	-	-	59.4	-
1838	-	-	$4/6^{3/4}$	-	-	-	-	80.1	180.7
1839	4.22	3.56	4/8	-	-	4-7/6	4-10/	81.7	288.3
1840	3.88	3.75	4/6	-	-	5-1/3	4-7/6	83.8	251.0
1841	4.25	3.63	4/7	-	-	4-2/	4-5/	87.0	235.6
1842	4.13	2.75	4/6	-	-	3-5/	3-0/	104.3	-
1843	3.53	3.25	4/4	-	-	3-5/	2-16/3	86.1	230.6[4]
1844	4.16	3.75	$4/2^{1/2}$	-	-	3-16/6	3-15/	195.1	217.3[4]
1845	4.22	3.94	4/4	-	-	5-2/	4-2/6	102.5	326.5
1846	4.02	3.72	$4/4^{1/2}$	-	-	6-0/	4-12/6	109.2	323.0
1847	5.22	3.05	$4/4^{3/4}$	13.0	13.0	-	4-12/6	117.0	376.2
1848	7.88	3.00	4/3	-	-	5-10/	3-10/	143.6	248.7
1849	5.38	2.81	$4/1^{3/4}$	16.0	14.0	4-10/	3-10/	153.4	371.4
1850	5.91	2.88	$4/5^{1/2}$	16.0	14.0	4-0/	3-5/	123.4	433.8
1851	6.62	4.00	4/10	7.0	5.8	3-0/	2-1/	174.6	453.4
1852	7.12	3.44	4/8	10.0	9.0	3-15/	2-5/	249.3	430.6
1853	7.55	3.37	5/0	10.0	10.0	3-17/6	3-2/	222.7	566.4
1854	8.42	3.25	$4/9^{1/4}$	17.5	13.0	3-12/6	4-14/	322.7	715.7
1855	7.25	3.44	4/8	15.25	13.44	5-10/	4-10/6	239.0	775.4
1856	7.50	5.38	4/5	10.8	10.7	5-12/6	3-18/	355.3	817.6
1857	7.75	8.72	4/2	8.65	5.0	5-5/	3-5/	347.6	717.1
1858	5.37	5.87	4/0	8.0	9.0	4-0/	2-5/	412.5	557.1
1859	5.00	5.81	4/3	5.0	4.0	2-5/	1-5/	426.2	832.8
1860	4.56	5.34	$4/2^{1/2}$	7.0	7.0	3-10/	2-17/6	396.9	874.8
1861	3.75	5.25	4/1	8.25	7.75	4-5/	2-18/9	368.0	849.8
1862	4.88	3.94	$4/3^{1/2}$	13.0	11.0	4-12/6	4-7/6	472.1	1,292.3
1863	4.56	4.31	$4/5^{1/2}$	12.5	12.0	4-15/	3-5/	424.1	1,200.2
1864	5.56	5.19	4/9	13.5	16.0	5-5/	3-15/	493.9	1,020.6
1865	6.75	5.06	$4/2^{1/2}$	9.5	7.5	2-10/	1-17/6	397.8	882.8

Continued next page

Table 16 *Continued*

Year	Prices[1] Pesos per picul Hemp	Sugar	Exchange Rate Shillings per Peso	Freight Rates to U.S. Pesos Per Ton[3] Hemp	Sugar	Great Britain Pounds Per Ton[3] Hemp	Sugar	Exports[2] (piculs, '000) Hemp	Sugar
1866	8.25	4.78	4/2	9.5	11.5	3-2/6	2-16/3	406.7	887.5
1867	8.82	4.25	4/2$^{1/2}$	10.75	10.5	3-12/6	2-15/	435.8	1,033.0
1868	8.88	4.63	4/3$^{1/4}$					465.1	1,185.3
1869	10.06	5.22	4/5	110.0	13.0	3-16/	3-	426.3	1.101.1
1870	10.75	4.91	4/3	9.63	9.0	3-15/	2-18/9	488.6	1,251.4
1871	9.44	5.16	4/3$^{3/4}$	11.0	11.25	3-15/	3-	463.7	1,399.4
1872	9.25	4.88	4/4$^{1/4}$	14.25	12.25	4-7/6	3-11/3	625.2	1,528.4
1873	8.38	4.66	4/1$^{1/4}$	15.0	16.75	5-7/6	3-7/6	622.7	1,429.4
1874	7.13	4.31	4/1$^{1/16}$	13.0	15.75	4-10/	3-16/3	616.0	1,661.8
1875	6.50	4.00	4/1	8.0	14.5	3-17/6	4-18/9	525.8	2,019.2
1876	5.56	4.50	4/2$^{5/8}$	7.25	13.0	3-7/6	2-18/9	630.9	2,093.3
1877	5.75	5.06	4/3$^{5/16}$	8.5	10.5	3-13.6	2-10/	630.5	1,965.9
1878	5.31	4.44	4/1$^{1/4}$	6.0	6.0	2-7/6	1-10/	667.4	1,890.3
1879	6.63	4.63	3/11$^{3/4}$	8.0	7.75	3-2/6	2-	648.0	2,145.4
1880	6.94	4.94	4/0$^{1/2}$	7.5	10.0	3-11/3	4-14/6	800.9	2,904.3
1881	9.34	4.63	4/2	10.5	11.0	3-15/	3-15/	868.9	3,362.6
1882	10.28	4.94	4/2	8.5	10.5	3-2/6	2-6/3	707.3	2,452.0

Notes:

[1] Prices for 1851-78 are averages of figures taken from Peele, Hubbell & Co. memos. For other years, the prices are median values of the high and low quotations.

[2] Export quanitites are private trade figures that slightly differ from official figures. There are discrepancies between Peele, Hubbell & Co. and Russell & Sturgis figures. I have relied primarily former in the interests of statistical homogeneity.

[3] Units to which freight rates were applicable were not given in PHC's tables but were known to commercial users from quotations in circular letters. The most common unit for Great Britain was 20 cwt. or one ton. For hemp the unit occasionally given in the early years (1839-41) was "per 50 cu. ft." For the U.S. the unit used was most coomonly "per ton of 40 cu. ft." and later "per ton of 4 bales." The difference in cubic capacity of a ton over time may be traceable to the introduction of screwage machines, which baled the hemp more compactly, so that a ton took up less space.

[4] Europe and the U.S.

Sources: Yldefonso de Aragon, *Estado que manifiestan la importacion y exportacion 1818* (Manila 1820); Peele Family Papers, Peabody Essex Museum; Edward Carrington Papers, RIHS; *Price Current Manila*, 13 March 1824; *Manila Price Current*, various dates, 1826-27, 1829; Russell & Sturgis, "Prices Current of Exports at Manila," various dates, 1831, 1833-35, 1841, 1843; *Precios Corrientes de Manila*, various dates, 1839-41; *Manila Prices Current*, 1 September 1842; *New Weekly General Price Current*, Manila, various dates, 1843-46; Circular letters, various dates, Ker & Co., Peele Hubbell & Co., Russell & Sturgis; Peele Hubbell & Co., memos dated 1 January 1863, January 1880, 19 January 1883; Max Tornow, "A Sketch of the Economic Condition of the Philippines," Senate Document No. 62 (1899); Ramon González Fernández and Federico Moreno Jerez, *Manual del Viajero en Filipinas* (1875).

mulated and constantly arriving. . . . [V]essels are also wanted to take Rice to Whampoa and Sugar to Shanghai at good rates."

The Manila merchants of course preferred to see such limits set on a free-on-board (f.o.b.) basis. Ker, Bolton & Co. wrote from Liverpool to Stone, Silsbee & Pickman in Salem on August 9, 1866: "Our friends [Ker & Co., Manila] would much prefer having limits f.o.b. including freight in Manila, but if you desire to send limits laid down please give them a statement showing your mode of calculating the laid down cost . . ." Judging from subsequent transactions, the buyers had their way.[12]

The Manila merchants were to act not so much in reaction to prices actually realized as on price anticipations based on underlying factors such as inventories of goods in export markets and volume of shipments. "If you wait to hear of high prices at those places produced by these causes, you will be almost sure to find the demand supplied before your cargo can reach there," wrote Stone, Silsbee & Pickman to Capt. E. A. Emmerton, whom they sent as agent to Manila in 1856.

Acting on price anticipations was not confined to the international traders but also characterized the conduct of local businessmen like the operators of coasting vessels. In 1855, although shipments remained normal from the abaca-growing provinces of Albay and Leyte, some of the largest vessels in the coasting trade were diverted to carrying rice cargoes to China, effectively taking them out of the hemp trade for two or three months. "This does not *seem* to be owing to the high rates of freight offered for Rice," reported Russell & Sturgis, "so much as to the positive indications of a short supply of Hemp, caused in part no doubt by the material decline threatened from last season's prices."[13] Market information was paramount. And correct price anticipations of course shortened the response time when prices did eventually move.

The price fluctuations of the two major exports, abaca and sugar, differed somewhat in overall trends and amplitude (table 16). Abaca prices moved along a clear secular upward trend in well-marked cycles of large amplitude; in one particularly long upward movement in 1861–70, abaca rose from $3.75 to $10.75 per *picul* and then fell almost equally steeply to $5.31 in 1878. Sugar prices displayed no strong secular trend, although from the early part of the century a slight declining tendency seems discernible. During two periods, price movements were fairly limited. Between 1839 and 1854, most quotations fell in the $2.75 to $3.75 range; between 1862 and 1882, they were mostly in the $4.25 to $5.25 range. In between, there was a brief, atypical spurt in 1854–57 from $3.25 to $8.72. It can be argued that the lengthy periods of relative price stability probably extended the planning horizons of those in the sugar business and helped stimulate the great increase in output.

As commodity traders, the merchant houses could shift between the two principal Philippine exports, depending on price. But this was not a matter of "price buying," of getting the cheaper commodity, but of business expectations. "In view of the scarcity of Hemp, & the relative cheapness of sugar," wrote Ker & Co. in 1869, "Captain Allen is hesitating as to the advisability of taking a somewhat larger quantity of [the] former than the maximum mentioned in your instructions to him."[14] Low prices indicated slack demand or ample supplies, while high prices indicated brisk demand or reduced supplies and therefore better sales prospects.

As commodity importers, the overseas buyers had what might be called complementary cargo items, goods that might not be purchased for their final use alone but for the role they played in relation to the major commodity items, the voyage itself, or the funds allocated for the venture. Such, for example, would be *sapan* wood, which was the most common item for dunnage and at the end of the voyage was useful in the dye industry. In itself, it was not an item of major interest, and in later years it would even be supplanted as dunnage by bamboo or firewood.[15] Another case of cargo complementarity might be rice, whose carriage to Canton enabled vessels to get into Whampoa, with some savings in river charges, in order to load Chinese products. Finally, certain secondary items (such as indigo) could be included to use up the unspent portion of funds allocated to a voyage, even though such items in themselves might not merit primary attention.

Decisions regarding substitution and complementarity were part of the function of the merchant house. They were also to make sure the goods were up to quality and packed properly. When not supervised by them, another reputable house could be called in. On a hemp shipment in 1875, Ker, Bolton & Co. wrote that it was not packed under the supervision of Ker & Co. or their agents and "the guarantee of Messrs. Smith, Bell & Co. was given that any difference in value would be paid if it should not turn out good current quality . . ."[16]

The major items, abaca and sugar, were traded by the merchant houses themselves, but their individual partners or associates could also trade on their personal accounts. Apparently, there was enough mutual confidence among the protagonists to obviate any suggestion of conflict of interest. "I have invested $1500 on my own account & shipped the Goods on the Australia, leaving the freight to be fixed by you," wrote Captain Emmerton in his final letter to his principals in 1856.[17]

The demarcation line between company and private trading appeared to be that between major exports (abaca and sugar) and minor exports (all others). J. Willard Peele, during his stay in Manila in 1836–43, traded in indigo, tortoiseshell, grass cloth, and hats on his own account, although some invoices were shared half and half with Peele, Hubbell & Co.[18] Private trading could also take place at the importing end. George H. Allen of Stone, Silsbee & Pickman ordered fifty thousand cigars for his account in 1868, and in 1883 he asked for timber samples, provided by one Henry G. Brown of Laguimanoc, to be shipped as dunnage in order to save on freight costs.[19]

The demarcation line between major and minor items was not, however, hard and fast. George H. Peirce (of Peele, Hubbell & Co.) had a half interest (together with a local Albay merchant named José Crespo) in sales of "Lupiz" Hemp to one of his firm's competitors, Smith, Bell & Co., in 1862. For the rest, he traded in a wide range of both exports (cigars, coffee, cordage, rattan, and indigo) and imports (saddlery, carriage ware, glassware, refined beeswax, medicine, ham, champagne, wheat, paint, and wagons) as well as engaging in domestic sales of rice. Among his local customers were two Barrettos, J. Zóbel, and the Chinese Chuidian and Tiaoqui. But he was charged by the company for a large loss on an indigo shipment to New York purchased before the restoration of peace in the United States in 1865.

The tolerant stance toward private trading changed in later years, possibly as awareness rose of the risks inherent in conflict of interest. The last copartnership agreements of Peele, Hubbell & Co., from about 1874, provided that "no member of the firm shall trade or speculate for his individual account, either with his own funds, or with the funds of the house."

The dual role of overseas western buyers as shipowners and commodity importers gave them operational flexibility. When rates were high, they could elect to take freight; when rates were low, they could purchase commodities (principally abaca and sugar). Thus, services (freight) and commodities were substitutable. When shipping was tight, freight rates could rise to fifteen or sixteen dollars per ton; when shipping was ample, rates could fall to eight to ten dollars.

Shipowning also gave them a lock on cargo space. "Many ships are sent here to load Exclusively on ships account," wrote Ker & Co. to Bourne Spooner in 1852, "and even tho' in our hands we frequently cannot venture to put any other freight on board."[20]

Freight rates for hemp and sugar to both the United States and Great Britain described wide cyclical movements, with some divergence in the movement over time but with peaks and troughs generally coinciding. The influence of the American War between the States showed in the price and rate increases of the early 1860s as well as the brief fall that followed the restoration of peace. The opening of the Suez Canal in 1869, however, which would have been expected to lead to a decline in freight rates, was accompanied by a rise that peaked in the early to mid-1870s (the start of a world depression). Quantity exports of hemp and sugar also reflected the effects of the American war, with ups and downs in the 1860s before they began a sustained rise. Price and freight rate fluctuations were not generally synchronous except that they all coincided in the rather deep trough of 1878.

There is some evidence for a decline in freight rates, both in absolute terms and as a percentage of the commodity price. This is quite clear in the case of abaca, whose annual average freight rate to the United States edged down from $10.00 per ton to $9.79 between 1851–62 and 1871–82. With a rising secular price trend, the decline was more marked as a percentage of the average commodity price; this fell from 10 percent in 1851–62 to 7.54 percent in 1871–82.[21]

The case is not so clear for sugar, for which the twelve-year annual average freight rate went up from $8.97 to $11.52 per ton in the same time periods. The relative rate also went up from 11.6 to 15.4 percent of the commodity price. It has already been suggested, however, that the sugar price spurt of the late 1850s was extraordinary, and when the reference base is pushed back to the decade 1847–56 the picture changes. The absolute figure remains almost the same (an annual average of $11.44 per ton in 1847–56 compared with $11.52 in 1871–82), but with the absence of the atypical prices of the late 1850s the relative figure shows a decline from 20.7 percent in 1847–50 to 15.4 percent of the average commodity price in 1871–82.

For Great Britain, absolute figures comparing the decade 1839–48 with 1873–82 show an absolute fall in abaca freight from an annual average of £4.9.11 to £3.7.8 per ton and in sugar freight from £3.18.3 to £3.3.8 per ton (fractions of pennies excluded). As the trend was clear, no computations were necessary to obtain percentages of the commodity price.

The third major variable faced by the merchant houses, the exchange rate, was in practice determined by the rates for bills of exchange drawn on London. In 1818, Capt. Ezekiel Hubbell had drawn $10,000 on Thomas Wilson & Co. of London at an exchange rate of 5/6 (five and a half shillings) to the dollar. Charles Stewart at the same time had paid this rate on a ninety-day sight bill for $3,500.[22]

Those were early transactions, when bills were merely supplemental to specie. For bills to come into their own and for an exchange rate mechanism based on them to function smoothly, the market had to organize itself better. The difficulties in negotiability of the early 1830s were apparently overcome later in that decade, and by 1838 Isaac M. Bull could report specifically that bills on London on Baring Brothers & Co. and Morison Cryden & Co. "are now negotiating @ 4/7 a 4/7 1/2."

Indicative of bill market imperfections in the early days (the 1830s and early 1840s) was the fungibility of exports when their prices fell to low levels. In 1837, it was reported:

> *Indigo* has been a subject of attention to the English Houses who are looking for a saving mode of remittance for proceeds of goods, and . . . they can afford to pay more for an article that is deemed safe by those who purchase with a look for a profit from the transaction. They have therefore in a measure the market for indigo to themselves at present . . .

Five years later, the commodity involved was sugar, which had "reached a point at which shipments can be made to Europe, both for orders and as remittances." It was not thought likely that prices would go lower, so that the demand for commodities as a remittance medium put a floor to their prices. Naturally this affected the bill market; at that same time, it was reported: "*Bills on London* appear to be very little wanted at present, the low price of sugar . . . causing remittances to be made in this article."

But at times the impulse for using commodities as remittances came not from low but high commodity prices. In 1854, the hemp price in England rose greatly, stimulating competition in Manila. "The usual purchasers of Exchange [importers] are just now shipping produce largely and selling bills against it," reported Russell & Sturgis, "causing the amount to be much greater than can be got rid of, and the rates continue unfavorable to sellers."[23] Thus, the diversion of the demand for remittances from the bill to the commodity market weakened the former, leading to an appreciation of the local currency.

Another difficulty that had to be overcome was establishing the creditworthiness of the entities on which the bills were drawn. There was no question about what were termed Bank and Treasury bills, but private bills were something else again. Russell & Sturgis warned in 1839: "There are bills offered however on England . . . on houses well known *here* but which would not sell so readily in other places, where they were strangers." By midcentury, and perhaps earlier, two names stood out above others in the Manila bill market, namely, Baring Brothers & Co. and Brown,

Shipley & Co., and there was a premium on their paper of between a farthing and a penny per dollar (Mexican).[24]

The main instruments were Bank and Treasury 30-day sight (d/s) bills (sometimes carried as 3 and 30 d/s), and first-class private bills at six months sight (m/s); occasionally there were four m/s bills quoted.

The Bank and Treasury 30 d/s bills came in small denominations and were favored for remittances to Spain. On July 23, 1840, Ker, Murray & Co. advertised the sale of London Treasury 30 d/s bills, remitted in triplicate, in denominations of £100, £200, and £500 at 4/3.5 per peso (dollar Mex).

The instrument most widely used in commerce, however, was the 6 m/s bill, with Baring's as the favored drawee. On January 2, 1841, Russell & Sturgis advertised the sale of bills specifically drawn on Baring's. On December 22, 1852, they observed: "The 6 m/s paper finds a more ready sale, as the purchasers object to the difference of a penny in the rate." On that date, Bank 30 d/s paper sold at 4/7 to 4/7.5 per peso, while 6 m/s paper sold at 4/8. But it may not have been the price difference that attracted business as much as the longer maturity, which the price may have reflected at least in part. A more detailed breakdown in 1850 showed the following rate structure: bank bills 30 d/s, 4/3; private, Baring's and Brown's, 4/4.75; others 4/5 to 4/5.5.[25]

The exchange rates presented in table 16 are average rates reported by Peele, Hubbell & Co. for 1851–78 and median rates (factoring in both 30 d/s and 6 m/s bills) for the other years. It is possible to discern two periods of moderate movements: 1833–49, when, in the context of a falling trend, most quotations were found to be between 4/8 and 4/3 to the peso; and 1865–82, when, in the context of another falling trend, most quotations were found to be between 4/5 and 4/1 to the peso. In between, there was a period of rather steep movements in the 1850s and early 1860s, when the quotations spanned a whole shilling (or 20 to 25 percent), between 4/0 and 5/0 to the peso.

The market was subject to random arrivals of large amounts of bills, which had to be absorbed. In February 1854, the Russian admiral Putyatin, on a ten-day call with a squadron headed by the frigate *Pallada*, unloaded £12,000 in 30 d/s bills drawn on Baring's at 4/8.5, and 6 m/s bills on the same firm and on Brown, Shipley & Co. at 4/9.5. More than four years later, other lumpy transactions were effected by the French steamer *Dordogne* of the Indochina expedition, with sales in September 1858 of $20,000 in French 30 d/s naval bills, taken at 5.10 to 5.12 francs per dollar, and in November of about $40,000 in 30 d/s bills drawn on the Paris gov-

ernment at 5.34 francs per dollar. In between, the market experienced difficulties in absorbing the paper. "The amount of bills offering on London is
very heavy . . . with many left over unsold," reported Russell & Sturgis in
October 1858.

The market also had to absorb spikes in demand. In July 1854, it was
reported that bill rates on London had improved for sellers "in consequence of a large amount being required for remittance to Spain for government account and as returns for bills drawn on the Colony." Two
months later, Peele, Hubbell & Co. referred to "extraordinary demand for
bills on London for remittance to Spain."[26]

With rates subject to market fluctuations, time horizons were short
and exchange movements evoked rapid market responses, protagonists
calculating that movements could turn the other way at any moment. "Exchange has advanced to 4/6 p $ which appears to have somewhat weak-
ened the demand for the article [hemp], & we are now in hopes of being
able to secure the balance of the 'Mindoro' cargo on somewhat better
terms, while we also look for some re-action in Exchange shortly," wrote
Ker & Co. in 1869.[27]

Despite this flexible stance, a combination of high commodity prices
and high exchange rates, independently determined in separate markets,
could (as might be expected) cause some problems. In September 1853,
with exchange at 5/3 to 5/4 to the peso, abaca was at 7.5 to 7.625 pesos per
picul, which Russell & Sturgis judged too high compared with the exchange rate. But if there was any attempt to reduce buying prices the commodity would be held back in the provinces. "We trust, therefore to better
rates of Exchange to put prices at more reasonable figures rather than to a
fall in Hemp, but if we have to submit to anything like the rates in China,
the price must decline to meet it."[28] In fact, it was not the commodity
price that declined in this case but the exchange rate, as the abaca
price, then in a cyclical upward phase, would keep rising until it
peaked the following year.

One curious feature is that the exchange rate did not, up to 1882,
reflect the fall in the peso or Mexican dollar in terms of the gold dollar. The
Mexican dollar had fallen about 12.5 percent between 1874, when it was
almost at par with U.S. gold, and 1882.[29] But the exchange rate (as reflected
in the London bill rate) had actually moved from 4/1.0625 to 4/2. Why
this was so remains to be explained, but part of the answer may lie in the
bimetallic Philippine currency system of the time. It was only after 1882
that the fall in the price of silver began to have some impact on the exchange rate, as may be seen in table 17, which supplements table 16.

TABLE 17
Philippines: Exchange Rates, 1883-1898
(Median Rates, Sight Drafts on London)
(Shillings and Pence per Peso or Mexican Dollar)

1883	3/10	7/8	1889	3/4	5/8
1884	3/8 1/2	3/8	1890	3/6	3/8
1886	3/8	5/8	1892	3/1	7/8
1887	3/5	3/4	1897	1/10	3/8
1888	3/4	3/4	1898	1/11	1/8

Sources: John Foreman, The Philippine, 2nd ed., pp 292-293. In years where they overlap (not carried in this table) Foreman's figures are consistently lower than those of Peele, Hubble & Co., and this should be borne in mind in comparing Tables 16 & 17.

The London bill rate, while it was the principal foreign exchange rate, was not the only one. Two important features affected the foreign exchange system, namely, the presence of paper on other places with varying discounts and premiums and the fluctuation in the value of silver specie.

Some paper sold on other centers represented no modification in exchange rates. Australian bank bills had maturities of 30 d/s and were generally quoted at the same prices as London Bank and Treasury 30 d/s bills. There were also occasional quotations on Paris, and a French merchant with a Flemish name, A. van Polanen Petel, advertised the sale of bills on both Paris and London in 1846.[30]

More important were bills on regional trading ports—Singapore, Canton, Hong Kong, and Amoy. Paper on these ports traded at various premiums and discounts, giving rise to de facto multiple exchange rates. Paper on Singapore appeared largely before midcentury, usually at par or at small discounts. Paper on South China was generally drawn on Canton until 1856, when, with the outbreak of the Second Anglo-Chinese War (or the Second Opium War), western traders moved to Hong Kong. Quotations on Canton oscillated between discounts and premiums. Those on Hong Kong and on Amoy, which started appearing in the trade from about 1848, almost exclusively featured premiums.

Maturities were generally short, for thirty days or less, with even shorter maturities of fifteen, ten, seven, and five days coming into the market as time went on. There were rate differentials for different maturities. A report of November 23, 1861, said that 30 d/s bills on Hong Kong commanded a 14 percent premium, while sight bills had a 15 percent premium. In Amoy at that same time, there was a similar differential—a 15.5 percent premium for 30 d/s and 16.5 percent for sight. But longer maturities had no market. A. V. Barretto in 1863 wrote that Hong Kong 60 d/s bills were not negotiable in Manila (table 18).

Part of the discounts and premiums represented arbitrage difficulties. In April 1837, when bills on London fetched 4/8 to 4/9 to the peso in Manila, it was reported: "At Canton the rate is 5/ but the difficulty of getting bank proceeds prevents Bills being sent from that Market to this . . ."

Arbitrage costs should have resulted in fairly stable premiums or discounts, but the actual movements were quite variable on both the plus and minus sides, so arbitrage costs alone cannot explain them. The evidence is that the premiums and discounts were equilibrating rates in the trade and payments flows to the China coast. In April 1854, it was reported: "Rice shipments have caused rates on Canton to decline to 2% premium . . ." The premiums must also have reflected the influence of remittances of unknown magnitude made by the Chinese in the Philippines to their families and associates in their country of origin.

The rumblings of the Taiping Rebellion provided a background for some rate fluctuations. In July 1852, it was reported: "Advices from China have alarmed purchasers." In April of the following year, the news came that "the rebel army had advanced on Nanking, that all business had been suspended at Shanghae and that a large amount of paper had been forced on the Canton market, putting the rate at 5s, and they quote it of difficult sale even at that. Purchasers here demand the same, and the amount for sale being large, we have to submit to it." A year later, the situation had eased around Amoy, and it was reported that "late news from Amoy that Mexican dollars are now received there more freely is causing shipments of coin in that direction, and will tend to reduce the usual rates materially."[31]

The premiums and discounts, and the differences in level between various trading centers appeared to betoken a segmented system with obstacles hampering the triangular or multilateral movement of funds. The resulting premiums and discounts made for a multiple-rate system based on geographic criteria. If paper on ports in China was selling at a premium in Manila, it would be logical to surmise that paper on Manila in those ports, in a mirror image, would sell at a discount. In fact, bills on Manila were sold in Amoy in 1854 and 1855 at discounts of 8 to 10 percent, at a time when bills on Amoy commanded premiums of from 3 to 10 percent in Manila. But thereafter quotations for bills on Manila disappeared in Amoy, and only paper on Canton was quoted, changing (as noted earlier) to paper on Hong Kong after 1856. Possibly the financial transactions of the

TABLE 18

Philippines: Exchange Premia (+) or Discount (-), 1829-1874, (percent)

Year	Sinpore	Canton	Bills on Hong Kong	Amoy	U.S. Gold on Silver	Silver Dollars on Gold
1829	-	-2	-	-	-	-
1831	-	Par	-	-	-	-
1833	-	-2 $1/2$	-	-	-	-
1834	-	-3 to +1	-	-	-	-
1835	-	Par to +1	-	-	-	-
1837	-	+3	-	-	-	-4 to +6
1838	-	-	-	-	-	Par to +1
1839	Par	+4 to 5	-	-	-	-
1840	Par to +6	+2 to 6	-	-	-	-
1841	Par	+2 to 3	-	-	-	-
1842	Par	+3 $1/2$ to 4	-	-	-	-
1843	-3	+2 to 5	-	-	-	-
1844	-3 to Par	Par to 2 $1/2$	-	-	-	-
1845	-3 to +2	-2 to +2 $1/2$	-	-	-	-
1846	-3	Par	-	-	-	-
1847	-	Par to +1	-	-	-	-
1848	-	-1 to Par	-2 to Par	+2 to 3	-	-
1849	-	-2 $1/2$ to Par	-	+2 to 2 $1/2$	-	-
1850	-	Par to +2	-	+2 to 3	-	-
1851	-	Par to +8	+2 $1/2$	+3 to 8	-	-
1852	-	Par to +7	+3 to 5	+3 to 6	-	-
1853	-	Par to +6	-	+4 to 8	-	-
1854	Par	-4 to +4	-	+5 to 10	-	-
1855	-	-1 to +2	-	+3 to 6	-	+1 to 2
1856	-	+4 to 15	-	+8 to 18	-8 to -10	+5 to 13
1857	-	-	+15 to 28	+20 to 34	-10	+14 to 30
1858	-	-	+12 to 20	+12 to 30	-	+8 to 15
1859	-	-	+9 $1/2$ to 14 $1/2$	+13 to 17	-	+8 $1/2$ to 2$1/2$
1860	-	-	+11 to 15	+14 $1/2$ to 18	+10 $1/2$ to 15	
1861	-	-	+10 $1/2$ to 15	+12 to 16 $1/2$	-	+8 to 12 $1/2$
1862	-	-	+1 $1/2$ to 12	+3 $1/2$ to 15	-	Par to +9
1863	-	-	+1 to 10	+6 to 6 $1/2$	-	-
1864	-	-	Par to +6 $1/2$	-	-	+1 to 5
1865	-	-	+4 to 8	+6 to 9	-	+2 to 3
1866	-	-	+5 $1/2$ to 13	+15	-	-
1867	-	-	+3 to 12	+5 to 12	-	-
1868	-	-	+2 to 9	+7 to 8	-	-
1869	-	-	+1 to 6	+4	-	-
1870	-	-	-1 to +8	+3 to 12	-	-
1871	-	-	+4	-	-	-
1872	-	-	+2 $1/2$ to 7	-	-	-
1873	-	-	+1 to 7	-	-	-
1874	-	-	+1 to 7	-	-	-

Sources: ECP-RIHS; Russell & Sturgis, "Prices Current of Exports at Manila," 1833-43; 1839-41; Manila Prices Current and NWGPC, Manila, 1842-46; Shipping Intelligence, 1851-55; Circular letters, from: Fred Baker & Co.; Ker & Co.; PHC, Russell & Sturgis; and J.M. Tuason & Co.; AHC.

southern regions were consolidated first in Canton and then in Hong Kong, and the main financial complementarity in payments developed between Hong Kong and Shanghai, with paper on the former consistently selling for large discounts in the latter (about 26 to 30 percent).[32]

While the premiums and discounts on bills of exchange were unfolding, the other feature affecting the exchange system arose in the form of a silver crisis—an appreciation—that started late in 1855, peaked early and sharply in 1857, and lasted about a decade. Its origins involved the nominal anchor of the exchange system, namely, the price of doubloons, which the Spanish authorities were willing to purchase at sixteen dollars per doubloon. In April 1855, it was reported that "silver has been hoarded up for sometime under the impression that value of doubloons would be reduced soon." During his visit to Manila in 1856, Henry Sturgis Grew wrote that "at present silver is at 10 percent premium, so whenever I draw silver I have to pay for it." Heavy imports of doubloons and silver dollars were observed through 1857, and the premium on silver rose as high as 30 percent. Price quotations had to specify whether they were being made in silver or gold, and in their communications traders had to make the necessary adjustments constantly.

A stable source of specie was needed, and in November 1857 it was reported that large exports of doubloons to Singapore and Java and "advices from Spain that the Machinery for a Mint has been ordered in England and may be expected to arrive here early next year tend to alarm holders of Silver coin and to force it on the market, so that we look for a gradual decline in its value compared with the gold currency of the Country, until Mint goes into operation, and small gold coin becomes plentiful and causes silver to recede to par."

The silver premium also had an effect on bill premiums, and during the crisis years premiums on Hong Kong and Amoy bills rose to as high as 28 to 34 percent, respectively. As the silver premium declined, the trade in early 1858 expected specie exports to resume to China. Later that year, a new phenomenon was observed: Mexican dollars destined for the Philippines through Hong Kong were retained there, under orders from the Manila consignees, as bills drawn against them in Hong Kong "produce a better result than bringing the coin to this." (Does this partly explain the absence in Amoy of bills on Manila after the mid-1850s?)

The mint finally commenced operations on March 19, 1861, issuing gold and later subsidiary silver coins, and there was a decline in the premium on silver dollars. This went down in 1862 and disappeared in 1863, but it strangely reappeared, although at low levels, in 1864 and 1865. A. V.

Barretto early in 1864 explained this as being due to a "foolish Royal order lately received," under which the mint would not coin any gold on private account so that all importations of gold had to remain uncoined.[33] The premium on silver finally disappeared after 1865.

The premiums on bills took a little longer to work off, but those on Amoy disappeared after 1870, and on Hong Kong after 1874, probably attesting to a reduction of frictions and market imperfections in making external payments. But at that very time silver, under the impact of American silver discoveries and the international trend toward a gold standard, began its long price slide, which would lead to monetary disarray in the Philippines in the last years of the century.

In summary, the exchange-rate regime facing the Manila merchant houses throughout much of the nineteenth century might be termed a multiple-rate system with a cluster of subsidiary regional rates around a variable central rate. In dealing with the three major variables and their need to remain within their customers' limits, the merchant houses had to face both general world conditions and those particular to the region and the commodities and services in which they dealt.

The functions discharged by the commission houses were thus relatively straightforward. But as time went on they probably began to feel, as occurred in China, the need for modern banking and insurance facilities,[34] and since these did not exist in Manila at that time they decided to undertake them themselves. Thus, what began as simple commission houses were transformed into more complicated business organizations, which should be examined.

Merchant Financing

Until late in the century, the foreign merchant houses described themselves as general commission establishments. The last partnership agreement of Russell & Sturgis, dated April 11, 1872, for instance, declared "the business of the house as heretofore to be a general agency and commission business."[35] But most firms were much more than that. They also traded on their own account; were agents for marine, fire, and life insurance companies; were agents or consignees of shipping lines or were shipowners; owned shares in such enterprises as cordage works, banks, and slipways; owned real estate, including plantations; engaged in foreign exchange operations; and, most interesting of all, received funds at interest and made advances.

275

It is not difficult to find examples of all of these activities. In a book published in 1875, the merchant firms advertised their various agencies. Only a few will be mentioned here. Ker & Co. was agent for the British & Foreign Marine Insurance Co., the Union Marine Insurance Co., and the Sun Fire Office. Smith, Bell & Co. was agent for the Commercial Union Assurance Co., the Imperial Fire Insurance Co., the Netherlands-India Sea & Fire Insurance Co., and the China and Japan Marine Insurance Co. Russell & Sturgis was agent for the Colonial Maritime and Fire Insurance Co. of Batavia; the China Fire Insurance Co., Ltd.; the China Traders Insurance Co., Ltd., of Hong Kong; the North British and Mercantile Insurance Co.; the London Assurance Corp.; and the Batavia Sea and Fire Insurance Co. In addition, it was a correspondent of the American Lloyd Register, agent of the Messageries Maritimes, consignee of two ships in the China trade, and owner of a towing vessel. Peele, Hubbell & Co. was agent for the Board of Marine Underwriters of San Francisco, the Yangtsze Insurance Association of Shanghai, the Union Insurance Society of Canton, and the Queen Insurance Co. of Liverpool. In addition, it was agent for an English vessel in the China trade and a local interisland ship.[36]

Both American firms owned large blocks of shares in the Santa Mesa cordage works and also shares in the Banco Español-Filipino. Peele, Hubbell & Company had an interest in a slipway at the time of its collapse in 1887. Russell & Sturgis owned a cold storage plant and a coffee plantation in Majayjay at the time of its second bankruptcy in 1876, although the latter does not seem to have been anything remarkable, as it was listed as having cost only five thousand pesos.[37]

But from an overall economic point of view their banking operations have a major claim to attention. Russell & Sturgis was the Philippine (some say oriental) representative of Baring's, and Peele, Hubbell & Co. also had good connections in the financial centers of the world. Russell Sturgis's career after his ten-year stint in East Asia was to take him to a senior partnership in Baring's.[38]

Of perhaps equal importance from the standpoint of the internal Philippine economy were these houses' operations in domestic banking. According to De Mas's account, these were in full swing when he wrote in 1842.[39] In their barest essentials, they consisted of accepting funds on deposit at interest, and of making short-term advances to crop growers, also at interest. Clearly, they operated with intermediated funds, sourced from the general public and lent to a particular category of borrowers, namely, agricultural dealers or growers. Their entrance into deposit taking may have been related to the spreading use of bills of exchange. Until such bills became the principal means of effecting foreign payments, much of the incoming cargo consisted of specie, which was equally useful for domestic and foreign payments. Such specie imports served not only to pay for commodities but to make advances to growers. With the increased use of bills of exchange, their remaining sources of domestic currency were the sales of imported goods, which quite likely were not sufficient for their domestic operations. Taking deposits may have been a response to this challenge.

In their deposit operations, they provided an outlet for the savings of the community and a source of additional funds for mercantile ventures. Upon handing the money to the firm, the depositor got a receipt or a note called a *quedan*—from the first words of *Queda en nuestro poder la cantidad de. . .* (there remains in our possession the sum of . . .). The term has survived to this day in the warehouse receipts of the sugar business. The receipts were negotiable by endorsement and represented a further spread in the use of negotiable instruments as well as greater security in the safekeeping of funds, which was doubtless another reason for making the deposits. Depositors in the two great American firms included well-known Manila families, local firms, and several religious corporations. Well into the twentieth century, deposits were still being made at the provincial branches of British firms in the Philippines.

The Depositors of Russell & Sturgis

A glimpse into the deposit operations of Russell & Sturgis is given in the firm's bankruptcy papers, though in incomplete form. Total liabilities of the firm (including some intercompany accounts but consisting mostly of *quedanes,* or notes) amounted to 2,772,810 pesos. (Simply to get an idea of contemporary magnitudes, Philippine exports in 1875 amounted to 18,920,475 pesos.) Since depositors in amounts below 1,000 pesos were paid off at maturity, we have an idea of the identities of only those whose exposure was above that figure. Their number is not easy to extract from the various documents but seem to be around 230. A newspaper reported that the creditors were so numerous and fragmented that on at least one occasion there was not a sufficient quorum to take a decision.

As a group, the largest creditors were the four traditional religious corporations (the Dominicans, Augustinians, Franciscans, and Recollects), with total deposits of a little over 400,000 pesos. But this was only one-seventh of the total, and there were numerous other depositors, mostly in the four-digit class, or in some cases five digits, with one exception. This was J. M. Tuason & Co., also representing another party, with 111,880 pesos, which put it second only to the Dominicans, which had 122,081,51 pesos. If the deposits of the individual Tuason family members are factored in, however, the Tuason holdings (at about 130,000 pesos) easily surpass even those of the Dominicans. Reference has already been made to the Tuasons, and the question may be raised as to how they achieved financial parity with the long-standing religious corporations. A possible answer may be that the founding Tuason had established on February 25, 1794, the *mayorazgo* earlier referred to, covering a third and a fifth of his assets, thus keeping the family properties intact. Although the Civil Disentailing Law was promulgated in Spain on October 11, 1820, it was extended to the Philippines only on March 1, 1864, despite which the family maintained the estate until the 1922. (A Tuason descendant would marry a granddaughter of Jonathan Russell.)

The term of the *quedanes* evidencing the deposits was usually for one year, although some were for six months. The rate of interest in 1875 was usually 8 percent but could be lower by mutual agreement. Most *quedanes* were made to order, but there were some to bearer. Although most *quedanes* were payable in Manila, some were issued and payable in Cebu. There were depositors from various localities—the Elíos (Salvador and Joaquín) from Camiguin Island; Pablo Martínez of Cebu; Fray Marcos Hernández, parish priest of Bulacan; the governor of Laguna Province, Mateo Barrozo y Bonzón; Juan Nepomuceno, a development assistant in Bataan; and Evaristo Picazo, governor of Capiz. The list of depositors was replete with what might be called Manila's cosmopolitan element—with names like Ayala, Roxas, Zóbel, Barretto, Elizalde, Marcaida, Oppell, Witte, Burke, Summers, Gorricho, Zárate, Godínez, Rodoreda, Ynchausti, Genato, and Sáenz de Vizmanos. The Spanish historian José Montero y Vidal, whose three-volume history of the Philippines is still consulted a century after its publication despite its flaws, was in for 2,080 pesos. But there were also indigenous names like Bagay, Catipunan, Cuyugan, Macarandang, Magbanua, and Payumo. Were these examples of the rising Filipino middle class? Marcelo Adonay, the Filipino composer and conductor, who had begun as a poor provincial and in 1887 was to lead the first Philippine performance of Beethoven's *Missa Solemnis*, held an endorsed *quedan* for 1,087.20 pesos.

From the names of those who were active in business, it is possible to distinguish what stage in their progress some of them had reached. The

Barrettos were probably at or near their peak. So were the Tuasons. The Roxas-Ayala-Zóbel clan was on the rise. Joaquín Ma. Elizalde was probably not far behind. But the Ortigases, represented by infantry captain Ignacio Ortigas, with a *quedan* for 2,548.52 pesos, were in what might be called the precommercial stage. Captain Ortigas died in the course of the firm's liquidation, leaving three young sons in the care of a young widow, who also died not long after. It was the sons, who had to avail themselves of the free education granted to orphans and children of the military, who would propel the family to prominence in Philippine business.

A further reflection on the list of Russell & Sturgis's depositors would not seem out of place, and this is to note not only those included but those who are not. The political repression following the Cavite Mutiny of 1872 had brought imprisonment, exile, and, at a minimum, intercepted communications to the liberal elements of Philippine society. Might some of them have been among the depositors before then, say, the Basas, the Regidors, or the Pardo de Taveras? There were remnants of this progressive element on the list, for example, Manuel Genato, Jacobo Zóbel, and José Bonifacio Roxas, whose correspondence was ordered intercepted by the Spanish authorities or who were included in the charge sheets at the time, and there were echoes of others such as a Pardo and a Mauricio of the female line, whose menfolk had gone into exile.[40] The impression is that a pre-1872 depositors' list might well have included more representatives of the liberal element.

Advances to Agriculture

Of even greater significance were the banking operations of an obverse nature, namely, advancing funds to crop growers at interest. In effect, this meant estimating the value of a crop and buying it in advance. Some observers theorize that this procedure sprang up as a result of the Filipino farmers' need for working capital, which they found hard to secure except on ruinous terms because of the provision in the Laws of the Indies by which they could not be held liable for payment of debts exceeding twenty-five pesos. The limit was circumvented by land mortgages and usurious rates of interest. The foreign firms did not care to operate in this manner because no land of any value to them was securable, so they adopted the system of advances.[41] The argument is not completely satisfactory; it is useful to note that foreigners (with a few exceptions) could not in the early years of their coming settle outside Manila and therefore could not have any interest in land mortgages.

Whatever the merits of the above reasoning may be, it is possible to discern other reasons for the system of advances, namely, the control of supply and the forestalling of competition by the merchant firms. As early as 1825, T. T. Forbes mentioned making an advance of eighteen thousand pesos on sugar. On January 28 of the following year, he wrote the Perkinses of Boston that Barretto had made arrangements with the governor of the principal cotton province and "by making advances at the present time we shall no doubt succeed in getting the greater part of what is produced."[42]

The advances were probably governed by terms such as those set forth in a coffee contract between Peele, Hubbell & Co. and one Antonio Enríquez in 1873, which, because of the importance of the matter, is worth reproducing in translation.

Messrs. Peele, Hubbell and Co. and Mr. Antonio Enriquez have agreed on this date to the following:

1. The commercial house of the said Messrs. Peele, Hubbell & Co. shall make available to Enriquez the funds which he may ask from time to time for advances on coffee and these will bear interest at nine percent annually from the time they are given to their takers until the coffee is delivered in Manila. The funds will not be granted all at one time, but as Enriquez may ask for them, according to the needs of the business.

    2. Likewise, the house shall make funds available but without charging interest, to be used immediately in the provinces on coffee to be delivered in Manila at a specified price.

    3. The house has priority in taking the coffee acquired by means of advances at prices equal to those of other buyers. Funds advanced on coffee which it does not care to take shall be returned to it in cash.

    4. The house shall give Enriquez a bonus of two reals for each picul of coffee which he secures for it.

    5. With respect to risks arising from bad debts incurred in the business which is the subject of this contract, or from unavoidable chance accidents, Enriquez shall be liable for the full amount of the bonus referred to in the preceding article for the year or harvest in which the misfortune occurs.

    6. For any undue act or operation by which Enriquez might fail in the slightest to live up to the conditions of this contract, he

shall be liable to the extent of all his present and future assets to indemnify the house for any damage which it might suffer from such acts or operations.

7. The house may at any time it wishes make sure that its funds are not being diverted from exclusive use in the business to which they have been allocated.

8. The duration of this contract shall be until the next harvest, the matter at hand to be liquidated upon the conclusion of the same.

9. The maximum quantity which Enriquez may purchase is five thousand piculs of coffee by advances and another five thousand piculs by immediate purchase to be delivered in Manila at a fixed price; but if it should suit the house to extend these limits, it will so advise Enriquez in advance, and Enriquez shall try to attain them, using all his influence and his relations for the purpose, and he shall endeavor to make deliveries of coffee at an opportune time so that they may bring some advantage or economy to the house in its operations.

And so that it may thus be of record both of us sign the same agreement in Manila on the sixth of May of eighteen hundred and seventy-three.

(sgd.) Antonio Enriquez

(sgd.) Peele, Hubbell & Co.[43]

The provision of advances could vary from person to person. Ogden E. Edwards, a partner in Peele, Hubbell & Co. in the 1870s, for example, expressed dissatisfaction with his predecessor's (George Peirce's) lavishness in making advances and opined that the sugar growers had had enough money advanced them.

Dissatisfaction with the system of advances, despite the advantage of controlling supply and forestalling competition, stemmed from the system's ramifications, some of a cultural nature, not foreseen by those making the advances. From an economic point of view, if anything went wrong it meant a temporary embarrassment not for the recipient but for the grantor, who not only could not collect on the original loan but was often compelled to advance additional funds when faced with a choice between partial payment and a complete loss.

From the cultural point of view, the system was prevalent in almost all developing countries producing export goods by small landholders or free wage labor. It created a patron-client network emphasizing continuity, with debts never completely fulfilled. This was alien to the western concept of contracts as separate and complete individual transactions with well-defined quantitative and time limits. The cultural advantages to the recipient were security and recognized creditworthiness and to the grantor prestige and influence. As Owen points out, it was at bottom an indigenous system unintelligible to the participating Americans. Try as they might to get away from it, they never succeeded, despite decades of trying. But through it they were able to control one-half to two-thirds of the abaca trade in Albay (then including the modern provinces of Sorsogon and Catanduanes).

The advances were made through layers of intermediaries of diverse ethnicity. In the abaca trade, the merchant-financiers sent the funds to provincial agents, who advanced them to *personeros* (subagents), who in turn advanced them either to *personeritos* (sub-subagents) or directly to growers in return for future deliveries of the fiber at the provincial price (roughly a dollar below the Manila price). On delivery, the fiber would already be owned by the firm.

The provincial agents and *personeros* at and just after midcentury were mostly Peninsular Spaniards, but there were Spanish mestizos, Chinese mestizos, Tagalogs, Ilongos, and Bicolanos. Among the family names that have been passed down to the present are the Spanish Roco brothers (Juan Emeterio, Vicente, and Joaquin, the first of whom had financial and legal problems with Peele, Hubbell & Co.), Mariano Garchitorena, the Spanish mestizo Canuto Fuentebella, and the Chinese-Ilongo mestizo Joaquin Anson. There was also a Valentin de Vera (Spanish) and a Vicente de Vera (Bicolano). As time went on, however, another ethnic element acquired progressively greater importance, namely, the Chinese. Wickberg has described the great increase in Chinese immigration after 1850, partly as a result of more favorable official Spanish policies and partly because the Chinese population had risen from 5,700 in 1847 to 66,000 (officially) or even 90,000 (unofficially) by 1886.

The Chinese moved into the abaca industry both as growers and as merchants. In the latter role, unlike their competitors, they did not make cash advances but rather established stores, which operated as centers for bartering foodstuffs, textiles, and other goods for abaca. Money was rarely used, and the small producers preferred barter to cash transactions. By this means, a large portion of the country's exports was diverted into Chinese hands.

An imprecise but suggestive indicator of the direction of income flows in the late nineteenth century can be found in the number of luxury goods bazaars owned by the Chinese. There were fifty-three such in Albay, or more than 30 percent of all those in the country, and thirty-nine, or more than 20 percent, in Negros. Together the principal provinces producing the country's leading exports (abaca and sugar) had more than half the country's total of Chinese bazaar owners, clearly indicating where the purchasing power was.

The entrance of the Chinese merchants worked to the advantage of the British firms, which traded in both imports and exports, over the American, which concentrated on exports. This spreading of risk and profit centers over both imports and exports may have helped the British firms weather the crises that destroyed their American competitors.

The competition between the firms of two nationalities prompts a reflection on competition theory. The Americans in the abaca trade had tried to establish a monopsony, especially after the two major companies resumed joint-account trading in 1862, both to secure more favorable prices and to control the advances system. But they were thwarted by competition, particularly but not exclusively from the Spanish Muñoz brothers, backed at times by the British firm of Ker & Co. As will be seen later, in the mid-1860s just three firms accounted for more than 97 percent of the abaca trade, and two of these were operating jointly. It did not require a very great number of participants to achieve competitive prices that benefited domestic growers and dealers, but the absence of collusion was essential.

Aside from ethnicity, there was also a particular gender feature in the Bicol abaca trade, at least at the village market level of small cultivators. A French traveler in 1879 observed: "Buyers and sellers belong almost exclusively to the weaker sex, which is the stronger sex in the province of Albay; all the transactions, all the important decisions are dominated by the women; their husbands are reduced to the role of *prince consort*."[44]

Whether any domestic firms engaged in similar ventures is not certain, though we do have Azcárraga's remarks on the Aguirre, Fernández de Castro, and Tuason companies.[45] If such houses engaged in operations similar to those of the foreign firms, they were on a much smaller scale. It was probably easier for them to deposit their funds at interest with the American houses; J. M. Tuason & Company, as already seen, was one of the biggest depositors with Russell & Sturgis at the time of the firm's collapse.

283

Most of the local merchants acted as intermediaries for the foreign firms, as did many Chinese. The latter doubtless also made loans (as they still do to this day), but these were for the most part small and were different in nature from the advances made by foreign firms. There were also some Chinese who were directly engaged in the export and import trade, like a ubiquitous gentleman named Jose Castro Ong Chengco, who exported and imported a wide variety of articles in trading with his country.[46]

But all accounts agree that the most important trading firms were those run by the Americans and the British, and their preeminence was due in large part to their banking operations. In fact, they were not merely trading houses; they were merchant-financiers. This is the most important feature in the Philippine business landscape between 1820 and 1870 and perhaps later. At the center of economic change, growth, and progress in the nineteenth-century Philippines stands the figure of the merchant-financier. The consequences and results that have been seen in previous chapters and could not be imputed to plantations, government pressure on the peasantry, or official commercial policy can with little hesitation be largely attributed to him and his activities.

From the point of view of entrepreneurial theory, several things are worth noting. The function of private merchant financing as a whole was probably an innovation. Advances had been made long before then, notably by the Royal Philippine Company. But the combining of so many functions in one private firm on so large a scale was new, and it was introduced by the foreign firms. In particular, the two American firms seem to have been foremost in the banking business, partly because, being concerned much more extensively with the export trade than with imports, it naturally devolved upon them to undertake advances. By their use of credit, they not only forestalled competition and gained control over supply but also exercised a directing influence over the other factors of production, so that these were diverted from their former uses and combined in new ways to produce the goods wanted by the merchant-financiers. The similarity to the Schumpeterian schema is striking.

It is also worthy of note that accepting deposits at interest meant in effect that these firms were spreading the financial risk of their commercial operations, which is again a pattern of behavior associated with the entrepreneur in Schumpeterian theory. If they traded on their own account, they bore the risk in their role as capitalists. But when they traded with funds deposited with them they acted as entrepreneurs and the risk was borne by the depositors. In actual practice, of course, there was some admixture of the two roles, capitalist and entrepreneur, since the merchant-financiers also traded with their own funds, but it is noteworthy that the entrepreneurial endeavor to shift financial risk should show up so clearly in their deposit operations. When the two American firms suspended payment, the risk-bearing function of the depositors became painfully clear to them.

This is not to say that the merchant-financiers were mere promoters constantly scheming over how to get other people's money to finance their ventures. Their own fortunes, reputations, and hopes of eventual retirement were intimately bound up with the success or failure of their mercantile ventures. Furthermore, most of them seem to have been men of conscience. Ogden E. Edwards's distraught letters to Richard D. Tucker during the last days of Peele, Hubbell & Co. and after its bankruptcy are pitiful to read. He confesses to deep emotional disturbance and wonders what will happen to his children. He refuses to accept the full amount of the living allowance granted to him by the bankruptcy court but returns part of it to the assets of the liquidation. When the court finds him guiltless of any wrongdoing in the failure of the house and absolves him of any further obligation to the creditors beyond those that can be realized by the liquidation of the firm's assets, he makes it clear that although he is legally a free man he recognizes the moral obligation to make good his clients' losses. And he talks of having a few years ahead of him in which he can work.[47]

These are not the actions of a callous man. Nor is the spreading of financial risk the only noteworthy thing about accepting deposits, for by employing such funds in advances to growers the merchant-financiers were facilitating the circulation of wealth within the country. Since many of the depositors were city dwellers, being largely residents of Manila in the early days, merchant-financing operations meant that urban savings were being put at the disposal of rural producers. And since these operations were more sustained, more successful, and on a larger scale than those of the defunct Philippine Company, they had a greater effect in raising standards of living in rural areas and promoting the growth of a native middle class.

In some cases, the advances to rural growers only made available to the rural sector savings originating within it. Some deposits, notably those of religious corporations, can be presumed to represent income from land endowments, and there were identifiable deposits from outside Manila, so that their coming under the control of the merchant-financiers represented a means whereby the countryside could make use of some of the wealth originating within it. Agriculture was thus brought within the scope of commercial operations and participated in some of the gains from trade.

Merchant financing also had effects of a social nature. For many in the urban sector, it represented a new avenue of advancement and an increase in social mobility. "In Manila," writes Foreman, "many of the half-castes, pure natives, and some Spaniards, who at this day figure as men of position and standing, commenced their career as messengers, warehouse-keepers, scriveners, etc. of the foreign houses established." Long before his day, the spread of wealth was becoming visible in other forms. George R. Russell had equated carriage riding with gentility, and the sunset drive in Manila's Calzada was an occasion of social display. In 1856, Henry Sturgis Grew wrote: "All the foreigners, besides many Chinese and Indians, keep or hire by the month a carriage, and at night on the Calzada they make a very gay scene . . ." In the city, therefore, merchant financing seems to have had a leveling influence on the distribution of wealth and on social position.

In the rural sector, the evidence is not so clear, but there are suggestions that the opposite social effect may have resulted. The McHales have underlined the importance of the emergence of land as a productive factor in the output of export crops, leading to the development of the private hacienda system and the associated emergence of a Chinese mestizo landholding class, quite conspicuously in the Visayan sugar industry (this point will be taken up later on). [48] It was not haciendas that gave rise to exports, but exports that made possible the growth of haciendas. Both their owners and those of the more common small parcels benefited from having ready cash put into their hands, enabling them to raise their social and educational levels and their standards of living. But the rise of larger ownership units in itself represented a trend toward greater inequality.

This trend was not only social but geographic. The rise in total exports meant an aggregate increase in income, but this was unevenly distributed. The most obvious beneficiaries were the regions specializing in the rising export crops. For abaca, these would have been southern Bicol and the eastern Visayas; for sugar, the western Visayas and parts of central and southern Luzon; and for coffee, southern Luzon. As against these, there were areas with declining exports such as indigo and cotton in Ilocos and parts of southern Luzon. The disappearance of commercial quotations in the 1850s for "grass cloth" (most likely a coarse lining material locally called *medriñaque* or *guinaras* made from abaca) hit Samar and parts of Cebu especially hard (see table 10 for the steep drop in native textile exports between the 1840s and the 1850s).

Sectorally it could be argued that the rate of growth of the export sector outstripped that of the subsistence sector (mainly rice), giving rise to widening differences in income levels both geographically and occupationally. The turnaround of rice from an export to an import after 1870 not only augured a relative fall in income for the former rice-exporting regions (again, Ilocos) but the reduction or disappearance of grain surpluses and a reconfiguration of patterns of grain trading that led to more precarious local food supplies and even some regional manifestations of hunger.

Even within the progressing areas, the social effects could vary depending on the landownership pattern (e.g., small to medium parcels in Bicol, haciendas in Negros) and labor compensation systems (tenancy in Luzon, wage labor in Negros). The decline of the native textile industry had particular effects on the women workers who predominated in it, forcing them to seek other occupations (such as retailing, or field work in competition with men), thus upsetting the gender balance in village production systems. This may not have been disadvantageous where regional cultures gave women a significant decision-making role, as observed by the French traveler in Bicol in 1879, but this was not true of all regions.

The change from subsistence to commercial agriculture was bound to lead to greater social inequality. Although living standards may have been lower under subsistence agriculture, there was food enough for all grown by the people themselves, and social differences (except at the highest levels of officialdom) seem not to have been reflected as much in material conditions even in the seigniorial ambience of Spanish society. But with the rise in cash cropping, with greater opportunities but also greater risks, the balance in rural society was upset and the disparity between rich and poor widened.

The making of advances also facilitated the establishment of sugar plantations after the middle of the century, since, although there was plenty of vacant land, there was little capital with which to work it. A British consular report quoted by Sir John Bowring in 1859 gives the following hint of the Americans' role in opening new areas of the country to trade and cultivation:

The American houses (generally the first in enterprises of this kind) have already, through Spanish intermedia, established agencies at Negros, Leyte and Cebu, for the purchase of hemp and sugar, and it is stated from Manila, on apparently good authority, that one of them has lately advanced a sum of 170,000 dollars for this purpose, the distribution of which should have a stimulating effect on production, and thus give a collateral aid to the future exports from Iloilo.[49]

One observer attributes the existence of tenancy in the Philippines, despite the sparse population and the abundance of land, to the farmers' need for cash, which they could secure in the form of advances from larger land-owners[50] or from Chinese or mestizo middlemen who by means of this process were themselves able to become landlords.

The plantations established on the underpopulated island of Negros, however, which were opened with the help of funds advanced by the merchant-financiers, seemed to be something else again. Instead of using tenants, they employed wage laborers hired from neighboring is-lands, and their management seems to have been more modern and cen-tralized than that of estates in other parts of the country. The suggestion is that nothing corresponding to an enclosure movement took place in the regions of older settlement and that the introduction of more modern management in agriculture was associated with the opening of new lands rather than the integration of old parcels, although recent research has discerned an integration of new parcels. In itself an innovation, this was made possible by the merchant-financiers, with their advances, although the actual decisions regarding estate management were made by settlers on the land.

In occupying such an important position in the Philippine economy in the nineteenth century, the merchant-financing house was more akin to its counterparts in East (China and Japan) than Southeast Asia (Indonesia and Malaya). One reason for this is the obvious one that it was in part an offshoot of the Canton trade. Another is that in Southeast Asia westerners were supported by their own metropolitan authorities in the colonial terri-tories, who could rewrite laws and remold institutions in their interest, and this enabled them to engage not only in commerce but in production. In East Asia, on the other hand, such a profound penetration into the pro-ductive structure was resisted by independent governments, as it was also resisted by the government of the Philippines, which, although colonial, was of a different nationality.

In another respect, the Philippines fell between the two models. In East Asia, western enterprise was private, while in Southeast Asia it en-compassed both public and private entities.[51] In the Philippines, the pic-ture was mixed. The government did go into some utilities (steam navigation, telegraphy) while international trading by the westerners

288

came to be shared with a prospering Chinese community and a rising domestic merchant class. As will be seen, western enterprise also entered, in some cases through joint ventures with domestic capital, into processing (rice and sugar mills), industry (textiles), and shipping and utilities (railroads, electricity), where domestic enterprise also made its mark (tramways), as well as pioneering completely new endeavors (brewing). But the crucial dichotomy between economic initiative and political authority stamped the Philippine case as being more in the East Asian than the Southeast Asian mold.

CHAPTER 10

Innovations and Domestic Enterprise; Endings and New Beginnings

Enough has been said about the pervasive effect on the Philippine economy and on Philippine society of the operations of the merchant-financiers. It is well at this point to take a brief look at other instances of entrepreneurial activity in the Philippine economy at that time.

Examples will be given of the conquest of new markets, the development of new products, and the introduction of new production methods. Examples of domestic enterprise will also be cited. This is followed by an account of the collapse of the two great American merchant houses and an examination of the obsolescence of the merchant-financing firm. The rise of joint business ventures is next looked at, both those that included the foreign western merchants and those that did not. There is evidence of increasing assertiveness by domestic Philippine business, as distinct from Spanish-based enterprises, and a quickening of economic activity. The last case looked at is the founding of the first brewery in East Asia, which was temporarily embargoed by the Spanish authorities at the outbreak of the Philippine Revolution, whose early history highlighted the distinction between entrepreneurship and management. An epilogue surveys economic crosscurrents in the quarter century or so prior to the Revolution.

The Conquest of New Markets: Textiles

In the import trade, the principal development was the early capture by foreign importers, especially the British, of the Philippine market for textiles, as has been demonstrated by the overwhelming importance of textiles among Philippine imports. In 1822, Luis Barretto wrote Perkins & Co. of Canton that the Portuguese and British had imported a large quantity of British goods into Manila.[1]

In the early years, the Americans were just as interested in selling textiles in the Philippines. T. H. Perkins wrote J. P. Cushing in Canton in 1824 that since American cottons were better than English he expected the Chinese to prefer them eventually. He also expressed a desire to introduce them in Batavia and Manila; at the latter place, Barretto was to be urged to use his influence to bring them into use.[2]

J. P. Cushing, after his retirement from Canton, was even more interested in the Philippine textile trade. He asked Russell & Sturgis in 1830 to send him patterns of *cambayas* and handkerchiefs then in demand in Manila, and when these were lost in transit he selected some patterns for handkerchiefs in France on his own initiative. While he was in Canton a few weeks later winding up the affairs of Perkins & Co. following T. T. Forbes's death, he wrote William Sturgis in Boston proposing the sending of more New England textiles to the Asian market and even suggesting the construction of a factory to manufacture the amount needed annually in East Asia; in view of the improvements in machinery for cotton manufacture, he thought this would be a better plan, and he was willing to subscribe a quarter of the capital if the Boston merchants would follow his suggestions. Evidently, he included the Philippines in his calculations, for he wrote Russell & Sturgis from Canton on November 23 of that year that, although the Manila market appeared too limited to hold out any prospect of extensive operations, he was so convinced that American goods would eventually be preferred that "I shall be inclined when I go home to get up an establishment for the express purpose of manufacturing goods for this country & Luconia."[3]

Despite the existence of such initiative, the Americans played only a minor part in the Philippine textile trade. For this, various reasons may be assigned. The first and probably principal one was a combination of consumer preference and lower prices from competitors. In 1829, Russell & Sturgis reported: "American Domestics are not so well liked as English Longcloths and they generally come too high. They are not yet well known here, but the success of those which have been imported is not very encouraging."[4] The second reason is that at about this time, with the triumph of protectionist sentiment and the opportunity offered by the vast possibilities of the American West, the United States turned its economic face toward the development of its internal resources and markets. William Sturgis and the free traders of that time did not carry the day politically. The third reason is that the Americans were shipowners as well as merchants, and if they could make more money on freight or by purchasing European goods for resale in Asia they did not hesitate to do so. The fourth is that the British merchants in Manila were from the beginning primarily interested in imports, whereas the Americans divided their attention between imports and exports and eventually concentrated on the latter. By the middle of the century, Mac Micking could write:

> The trade of my countrymen consists principally in selling cotton manufactured goods, and in purchasing the produce of the islands for export; while the business of the Americans, who sell few goods, consists almost entirely in purchasing produce for the markets of the United States, and elsewhere.[5]

The extension of commercial credit was another factor that, in a capital-short country, helped in the success of the western foreign traders. But credit extension had problems of its own. Early in 1841, the following news item appeared:

> Cotton goods. The foreign houses having agreed not to give more than three months credit in sales to Chinamen and natives and to make them sign a bill or promissory note for the amount, and many of them objecting to this, there have been but few transactions since the holidays.

But the trade was too lucrative for all parties involved for any prolonged halt, and some way to continue must have been found, perhaps a recourse to litigation in the manner of domestic firms (of which more will be seen).[6]

The British merchants seem to have won the major role in the Philippine textile market not only by means of their low prices but by their alertness to local demand and their readiness to imitate designs and patterns that were popular in the country. In some cases, they sinned due to their eagerness to capitalize on local circumstances. The story is told that after Gironiere's first book was published an enterprising Manchester manufacturer sent to Manila some "Gironiere" pocket handkerchiefs illustrated with many of that worthy man's alleged exploits. The scheme was a failure, for "those who knew him thought them funny, and those who knew him not, could not see the fun of them, and neither party bought any."[7] Although unsuccessful, the venture illustrates some of the qualities that enabled the British to win and hold the Philippine textile trade until the last decade of the nineteenth century.

With respect to the imitation of native patterns and alertness to local demand, Vice Consul Shelmerdine in Iloilo had the following to say in 1887:

> The merchants here appear quite alive as to the taste and requirements of the natives, the real difficulty to contend with being that house manufactures often do not follow sufficiently minutely the instructions of merchants on the spot, and frequently are not strict enough in keeping up the standard of their original shipments.[8]

No further comment need be made about the initiative displayed by the British importers of that time.

The Development of New Products: Abaca

The case of abaca was not only an instance of innovation but also showed aspects of product substitution and differentiation and the workings of monopoly in both the trading and processing sectors. Until 1818, according to one source, the only buyer of abaca was the government, which received it in tribute at a maximum price of four escudos per *quintal* and used about six thousand *quintales* for cordage on galleons and other royal vessels. That year 261 *piculs* were exported worth $1,044, or a price of $4 per *picul*, as well as $625 worth of abaca rope.[9] Even after the foreign western merchants came, its importance does not seem to have been fully appreciated except by one group. Admiral Laplace in 1830 had grave doubts concerning its usefulness on vessels. He much preferred European hemp for his rigging after an experiment with it but conceded that it would make good rope. His attitude toward it was not one of enthusiasm. Spain, despite long acquaintance with it, never adopted it for its domestic navy nor imported much of it and even made a vain and tardy protectionist effort around midcentury to compel government-built ships even in the Philippines to use rigging made from European hemp in its Cartagena factory.[10]

But the Americans had other ideas. They seem to have been the only ones at the time who saw in the fiber a new and important addition to world trade. It seems to have come to their attention first for use in their vessels in Asian waters. Very soon they saw its commercial possibilities, and in 1820 the first commercial quantities were landed at Salem. Its exportation from Manila began to show progress in 1823,[11] the year after George W. Hubbell founded his firm, which probably was not a coincidence. The following year Luis Barretto recommended that a ship with available lading space be filled with "Manila Grass, an article that has been taken by the American ships to the United States for the last three or four years past . . ."[12] This certainly referred to abaca, as may be discerned from the fact that abaca textiles, called hemp cloth by J. M. Tuason & Co., were called grass cloth by the western traders.

On Christmas Day of 1828, J. P. Cushing in Boston wrote a memorandum to T. T. Forbes about articles in the Asian trade. Of abaca, he had the following to say:

> Manila Hemp is getting into more general use, & will hereafter become a more important article than is generally supposed. It makes the best cordage for use on the great rivers in the Western Country where the demand will annually increase. It would be well to give Russell & Sturgis orders to purchase all that can be got, & even go half, or a dollar higher than the old prices to obtain it, & when freight can be had low to ship it on our account, or resell it when freight cannot be had at low rates.[13]

"Purchase all that can be got"—it was a sweeping order, and the American firms acted on it so well that they not only purchased the available output but took steps to increase the production of the fiber. Competitors though they might be in other respects, the two firms decided it would be to their advantage to unite in the hemp trade, the better to face its uncertainties. The following year Russell & Sturgis reported: "This article is not produced in sufficient quantities to meet the demand & there is no certainty as to the time of its being in the market." By the end of the following decade, they had a clearer picture of the requirements of the trade. "Hemp can be produced to almost any extent required," they wrote on New Year's Day, 1841, "but experience leads us to conclude that the quantity brought to market would be much reduced, whenever the price offered for it falls as low as Ds 3 4/8." In fact, from table 16 it can be seen that exports in the intervening period had gone up about tenfold, while prices were down nearly 40 percent from the peak in the 1820s, in some years of the 1840s nearly down to the identified minimum export price of $3.50 per *picul*.

This could have resulted from cyclical forces, but the circumstances of the case point more strongly to the monopsonistic position of the trading firms. By 1842, Captain Wilkes could write that "the whole crop is now monopolized by the two American houses . . . of Manila, who buy all of good quality that comes to the market." It may be indicative of the importance of the abaca trade in the fortunes of the American traders of those times that Russell Sturgis's crest, a modification of the Sturgis family coat of arms, contains a knot of rope.[14]

Abaca was a natural monopoly of the Philippines, but this could carry it only so far in world markets, as its price was circumscribed by the availability of substitutes in the form of Russian and American hemp. Morison's price quotations for cordage of different fibers for 1843–48 make this clear. The finest grades, commanding the highest prices, went for whaling lines (formerly made from ordinary hemp), which were not always available.[15]

Abaca had to make its way in western markets against already established fibers like Russian and American hemp. In the case of the amply documented operations of the Plymouth Cordage Co., which began buying abaca in 1830, Bourne Spooner, the company treasurer and manager for forty-six years, was chiefly interested at first in "Russian hemp yarn" and was not overly impatient for abaca. Although the first steam-powered spinning machines in 1838 were for abaca, an automatic system introduced in 1842 was designed for Russian hemp, and there was some delay in fitting the old machines to handle abaca.

The new fiber, however, soon won greater acceptance for its superior characteristics. Hemp had to be tarred in order to resist deterioration in salt water, and at first this was also done with abaca. But it was found to be naturally resistant to such deterioration, and without tar it was clean, durable, and flexible, thus gaining popularity particularly for use as running rigging. Spooner calculated that abaca rope cost 15 to 18 percent more than tarred rope but lasted 75 percent longer and was therefore cheaper. If there was substitutability between hemp and abaca, there was also product differentiation based on actual physical characteristics rather than imputed consumer preferences. Both elements were susceptible to cost calculations. Abaca was also far superior to another fiber, sisal, that came on the market at the same time and was used as an adulterant in Manila rope, particularly by New York manufacturers. By 1855, Spooner was so proud of his Manila boltrope that he was urging it on his customers, claiming he was selling two or three times as much of it as he had ever sold of Russian hemp, which he expected would be superseded to a great extent by abaca.

Aside from its physical characteristics, the abaca trade was helped by world events. With some cyclical interruptions, the high points were the Mexican-American War of 1846, at which time there was an "immense" number of vessels under construction; the California Gold Rush, which stimulated business in the early 1850s; and the Australian gold strike, which took place just as the California trade was settling down. These three events increased demand; the next two would reduce supplies of competing fibers. During the Russo-Turkish War and the ensuing Crimean War of 1853–56, Russian hemp disappeared completely from the market. Following a cyclical downturn in 1857 came the American War between the States, adversely affecting the output of American hemp (cultivation of which was centered in Kentucky and Missouri), which never recovered afterward.[16]

In the meantime, the competition attracted by the lucrative gains from the trade was bound to erode whatever monopoly trading position the American merchant firms had built up in the Philippines. "We fear an advance in the price of Hemp," wrote Russell & Sturgis in 1844, "the Ship Levant having arrived addressed to an English house and put a bidder against us." The following year the firm reported: "At the time we recieved [sic] their [Russell & Co.'s Canton] order, opposition in the market by English houses had caused high prices . . ."[17]

In 1848, the monopoly broke down. Russell & Sturgis circularized its correspondents:

> It is, we believe, generally known to our friends in the United States that for many years past the market for this article has been almost entirely controlled by two or three houses who were the largest purchasers and bought in company. The great rise in price in Europe and the United States has caused large orders to be sent to almost every house here, and the above-named arrangement having been thereby rendered nearly null, it was discontinued on the 1st Jan. each house now buying separately, and necessarily causing more competition. The effect of this, combined with excessively high quotations elsewhere, will henceforth keep prices far beyond the range of former years; a fact of which we recommend our friends to take note in sending future orders. It yet remains to be seen whether the high prices which have ruled of late will tend to increase the production.[18]

The same year B. A. Barretto & Co. optimistically announced it was ready to fill orders for hemp, having just acquired two screw presses. But its customers set a limit of $5.00 per *picul* at a time when local prices were $5.88 per *picul* unscrewed and $6.50 screwed plus commissions and shipping charges on board. The firm was reduced to watching, perhaps somewhat wistfully, the battle of the giants.

> We look forward to a further [price] rise, as the competition between the two American Houses established here is great, orders to some extent from the United States, having been received by the March mail. It is reported that one order alone, received by Mess. Peele Hubbell & Co., without limits as to price, is for 16,000 pls. We much doubt their being able to purchase the entire quantity within this year, as our advices . . . state the article to be scarce . . .[19]

Despite its favored position on the supply side, abaca was not immune from changes in demand. After the end of the American War between the States, with the U.S. merchant marine reeling from the inroads of Confederate raiders and later from vigorous competition and the spread of steam navigation, which used less cordage, it was clear that uses outside maritime markets would have to be sought. These were found in power transmission, in oil drilling, and above all in binder twine, which had previously been made of soft iron wire. Thirty years after its introduction in 1881, binder twine accounted for 40 percent of Plymouth's output.[20]

The American houses repeatedly complained of outside, especially British, competition, which kept prices up. "Hemp has been run up by offers from parties purchasing for Europe," reported Russell & Sturgis in 1851, "the heaviest purchasers (those for U/ States) requiring all they can control for the vessels in port and . . . though from their large purchases they have the preference for what comes to market, they are obliged to pay whatever price others offer." The following year they wrote: "Heretofore the orders have usually come into two or three hands, but this year there are many buyers, and, with the large amount of tonnage to be filled during the next two months, we cannot hope for a decline, but fear the contrary."

Early in 1856, they reported that "our Hemp market has been somewhat excited by purchases for the English market. These purchases, . . . unless they are . . . supplied through the hands of the houses who purchase constantly, are sure to cause excitement and an advance in price." Later in the year, they wrote somewhat breathlessly that "news from London of an advance and a better feeling in hemp . . . will no doubt effect [sic] our prices as orders will be sent to English houses from their funds at home which causes competition which is always followed by an advance here in prices of the article." The gathering of American vessels in Manila had the same price-raising effect. "We . . . fear the number of American vessels now in port supposed to be waiting for cargoes will have the effect to make dealers more firm in their demands."

British demand not only raised abaca prices in the aggregate but also served to support them during any weakening in the American market, the phasing of activity being implicitly nonsynchronous, at least in this line. Russell & Sturgis wrote late in 1858 that "the demand is active for shipment to Great Britain, the favorable advices thence having counteracted the tendency to decline caused by those of a contrary nature from the United States . . . some parties holding for shipment to the United States having sold freely to those wanting for Europe." All of this of course redounded to the benefit of the growers.

Russell & Sturgis's query in 1848 about the effects of high prices on production was soon answered. In November 1851, it reported that quotations from the United States and Europe were high and arrivals from the province were as a result much larger than usual. "The production this year will prove, we think, to be fully 25 percent in excess of any previous one." At the end of the following year, their circular read: "HEMP—Our table of Exports will show a very large increase in the quantity over that of last year, and yet the demand is so active that all the parcels which arrive are readily taken at $8 1/8 a 8 3/16 per *picul*, the highest price ever known."[21]

The British houses sold not only in their own country but also gained American customers. Around the mid-1860s, Stone, Silsbee & Pickman of Salem appear to have shifted their business from Peele, Hubbell & Co. to the British firm of Ker & Co. This firm claimed to control one-third of the production of Albay Province, which itself accounted for two-thirds of the country's abaca output, as well as having a "fair share" of the shipments from other provinces. If the ratio of inventories held by each trading firm to the total is taken as indicating its relative importance, the three firms accounting for practically the entire abaca trade in 1865 had the following shares: Peele, Hubbell & Co., 42.6 percent; Ker & Co., 30.9 percent; and Russell & Sturgis, 23.9 percent.[22]

Another American account won by the British was that of the Plymouth Cordage Co. Originally it had made its fiber purchases from merchants like Perkins and Bryant & Sturgis. But in order to eliminate the profits of middlemen and handlers it began in 1853 to import directly from Manila, choosing Ker & Co. as its agents. These were sent a letter of credit on Baring Brothers by their Boston representative, Samuel Ward, for four thousand pounds, with instructions to buy for the company about five hundred bales monthly, not to exceed a thousand bales in any one shipment, to reduce the risk of loss, on any vessel or vessels bound for Boston or New York, giving preference to the former. Much of the abaca was transported in the holds of the swift clipper ships of that era.

Two years later, Bourne Spooner reluctantly (having been favorably impressed by Ker & Co.) made a shift in agents, owing to "a change in the proprietors of this establishment having relationship with the firm of Russell & Sturgis . . ." It was sent a letter of credit on Baring's for six thousand pounds for a thousand bales of Manila hemp with instructions to procure a larger proportion of the whitest kinds of hemp and ship it in parcels of about six hundred bales a month or six weeks apart. Two years later, however, Spooner sent a caustic letter to Russell & Sturgis:

> Although the investing of our funds is subjected to your discretion, allusion is made to my extreme limit of "12 cs. laid down here" as if you might properly buy at any where below. . . . Why, Gentlemen, my meaning of instructions was that under no possible circumstances should a higher price be paid—all below was to be discretionary— and if shipments to the U. States had been "unprecedentedly large" and the price was "forced up", an opportunity had occurred requiring the exercise of your discretion, which exercise I will still hope has been duly accorded to us.

After a gap in the documentation, we find Plymouth in the late 1860s once again doing business with Ker & Co.[23]

During the price rise of the late 1860s, one of Ker & Co.'s provincial dealers wrote that "'if some steps be not taken by the Authorities, the native plantations will be quite destroyed'—the last remark refers to the reckless way in which the young trees are being cut down, leaving no reserve for future supplies." After prices peaked and fell there was a contrary trend; hemp became scarce "in the interior, the scarcity being the result of a partial suspension of production caused by the great fall in prices which recently took place and the greater care now exercised by buyers in the selection of Hemp." Moreover, price declines in abaca often led to a reflux of labor to rice culture.[24]

The price responsiveness of production signified that the effects of prices translated into income changes for the final growers. In 1894, Joseph Earle Stevens, an American businessman representing Henry W. Peabody & Co. of Boston and New York, met on the small southern island of

Camiguin "a rich Indian, who although the possessor of four hundred thousand dollars, lived in a common little *nipa* house."[25] The gains from foreign trade had reached deep into the countryside. Owen calculates that the abaca growers of Bicol received one-half to three-quarters of the Manila export price, while the laborers stripping the fiber would receive half of the provincial price as their wages. Competition kept the margin between Manila and provincial prices narrow. "We want to see lower prices but while there is so much competition you can hardly look for a greater difference between Albay & Manila than 5 rls.," wrote O. E. Edwards early in 1859 at a time when abaca fetched between $5.00 and $5.25 per *picul*, implying a trading margin of about 12 percent.[26]

And, although abaca growing was concentrated in southern Bicol and the eastern Visayas, some gains filtered to other regions; there were occasional commercial quotations for inferior quality abaca from Misamis in Mindanao and Capiz in Panay at 20 to 50 percent below ordinary trade prices.[27]

At the time of the final collapse of Russell & Sturgis in 1876, the two American companies were again trading abaca on a joint account, perhaps as a response to British competition. At that time, their half share of the trade included more than 269,000 pesos in advances. Peele, Hubbell & Co.'s participation in this joint trade got it into difficulties, and it would have had to suspend payment had its depositors not agreed to grant it a moratorium on withdrawals for three years. In fact, its share in the abaca trade declined after that, which may have contributed to its collapse in the succeeding decade.[28]

Before the century was over, abaca would have another brush with monopoly practices. These started mildly enough with the pool agreement of 1861, which was overtaken by the War between the States; the accompanying prosperity, lasting until 1873, removed all temptation to cut prices. The price declines thereafter led to a new agreement and various pooling arrangements that lasted unsatisfactorily until 1887. In that year, the Cordage Trust, officially known as the National Cordage Co., was formed. It started out controlling 30 percent of the industry's output; worked its way up by means of a campaign of "bluster and intimidation" to 90 percent, making it the biggest industrial colossus of the time; and tried to corner the abaca market. But the trust overreached itself, financing huge inventories with short-term paper and preferred stock, and it collapsed in a bear raid, touching off the panic of 1893. Plymouth Cordage had maintained its independence and came out stronger after the struggle.

If the consequences of monopoly for abaca in the earlier episode at the trading end had been low prices, the effects of monopoly at the processing end were wildly fluctuating prices, from 9 cents a pound in the summer of 1887 down to 6.6 cents in the summer of 1888, and up to 13 cents in the spring of 1889. Monthly price variations ranged from 3 to 4 cents in 1889–90, which on the basis of the prices just mentioned would mean between 20 and 60 percent. Competition restored prices to the normal workings of the market in both instances, but while the effect of ending the trading monopoly in the late 1840s was higher prices the return to normalcy in 1890s was a return to a marked cyclical pattern along a rising secular curve. It was this trend that pulled export volumes up, with some cyclical dips, to the end of the century.[29]

Who took the step of first promoting the development of this product is not known. It could have been any of a number of persons—George W. Hubbell, J. P. Cushing, or the partners in Russell & Sturgis. What is clear is that it was an American project from the beginning and it was the Americans who transformed abaca from an exotic curiosity into an article of commercial importance in world trade.

New Production Methods

There were doubtless many improvements in production methods made during the nineteenth century. Four instances in which the personal element is known will be briefly cited here.

Gironiere

One of the more remarkable personages in nineteenth-century Philippine economic history is the Breton doctor-planter Paul Proust de la Gironiere, who has already been referred to several times. His lurid narration of his adventures during his stay in the Philippines is not such as to inspire confidence in his intellectual sobriety, and yet the objective evidence points to him as a man of courage, intelligence, constancy, and enterprise. The learned Dr. T. H. Pardo de Tavera wrote: "He has exaggerated and fantasized regarding his own person, but no more than in that, because the facts to which he refers about the Philippines and Manila particularly, which he lived through and witnessed, are of the strictest truth."

Born of a father who had lost his commission in the Auvergne regiment because of the French Revolution, Gironiere studied medicine as a young man and then went on several voyages to the East Indies in search of fortune and adventure. He seems to have been similar to his friend George Russell in that he was of gentle birth and sought his fortune abroad, but his temperament was much more mercurial. Arriving in the Philippines in 1820 in time to witness a massacre of foreigners motivated by a cholera panic, he practiced medicine in Manila; married a rich and noble widow, the Marchioness Ana de las Salinas, who shortly afterward lost her fortune in the Iturbide incident; served with a Spanish regiment for a while, which involved him in the suppression of the abortive Novales mutiny for independence; and finally, having quit government service in a huff, decided to found his estate, Jala-jala, on the northeastern shores of Laguna de Bay.

Gabriel Lafond de Lurcy reported that the property purchased by Gironiere measured 880 *quiñones* (about 2,400 hectares). The village had 1,200 inhabitants, and 1,500 others from surrounding villages worked on the estate, which was about ten leagues in circumference. It was located at the extremity of a peninsula whose two coastlines stretched from seven to eight miles, and its boundary line probably measured six to seven miles, taking into account the height of Mount Sembrano, through which it passed. On it were found high mountains, rivers (including the Naglabas, where the crocodile fight took place), ancient forests, and magnificent quarries of granite and tuff. For a while, this was the economic showplace of the Philippines, both during Gironiere's tenure and after. Many visitors to Manila between 1825 and 1860 found occasion to go there and record their impressions, usually favorable, of what they saw.

Gironiere's achievements as an entrepreneur are noteworthy, and what is known about them largely comes from sources other than himself. His estate seems to have been the first modern plantation in the Philippines. Such, at least, is the suggestion of his countrymen, Dumont D'Urville and Admiral Laplace, which seems confirmed by its being an economic showplace for so long. The latter credits him with possessing perseverance, spiritual strength, learning, and a knowledge of agriculture and speaks of his establishment, "whose astonishing progress and happy influence on its surroundings have made the Spaniards recognize the value of these neglected lands, and has thus opened a new source of prosperity for the colony."

That Gironiere was no charlatan is amply demonstrated by his having won a prize of a thousand pesos from the Economic Society on June 27, 1837, for being the first to present a coffee plantation of more than sixty thousand trees in its second harvest. (It is not out of place to suggest here that such a prize should form part of the entrepreneurial return on the venture). He also claimed to have introduced improvements in the processing of indigo, substituting masonry basins dug into ground level for fermentation vats and directing a continuous flow of water through split bamboo to receiving vats at a slightly lower level, the new process representing a savings of two-thirds of the workmen formerly required. Finally, Meyen reported in 1831 that Gironiere had introduced improvements in the processing of sugar. At that time, his output was two thousand *piculs* yearly, but boilers were in the process of installation by which Gironiere hoped to double the output, shorten the length of the process of production, and reduce the floor space required for the operation.

The loss of his wife and son caused Gironiere to leave Manila in 1839. At the time he relinquished Jala-jala, he had 90,000 coffee bushes; 7 *quiñones* (nearly 20 hectares) planted to sugarcane; 40,000 abaca plants; 30 *quiñones* (about 84 hectares) planted to rice, with each *quiñón* yielding 400 measures of 75 pounds each; 3,000 bulls, cows, and calves; 600 carabaos; 600 horses; 100 sheep; and 150 goats. The estate also had around 2,000 *talaksanes* (around 3,500 cubic meters) of firewood, 200 loads of timber of 25 *talaksanes* each, and 200 loads (*casco* loads, perhaps?) of quarried tuff. Lafond added that it was to Gironiere that the Philippines owed the introduction of the production methods used on Reunion Island, with batteries of five boilers using bagasse for fuel instead of the firewood employed in less advanced mills even on the large friar estates. He had sent to Reunion for an experienced French agriculturist, Adolphe Delaunay.

Twenty years later, having suffered the tragedy of losing another family in France, he was back in the Philippines, and Jagor reports that he had established "a large sugar manufactory" in Calauan, Laguna, assisted by a Scot and a Frenchman, and had adopted Filipino dress and habits. The enterprise was reported to be a failure, but by then Gironiere had made his mark on Philippine agriculture.[30]

There is a curious footnote to Jala-jala. Correspondence exists datelined from there from an American named W. W. Wood in 1835–37. He mentions a flourishing "little coffee plantation" and the setting up of "an English sugar-mill and boilers." He also writes of the scarcity of labor in the locality and of having to import workers at high wages from Manila to install the machines. It is not known whether he worked for Gironiere, who is not mentioned in the correspondence, and he speaks as if he owned the place. He states that European machinery was being introduced and leading to great changes and laments Spanish neglect of the Philippines as compared to Cuba, calling Manila "little more than a genteel kind of

Botany Bay for offenders in the better classes, and is now the refuge of swarms of friars who have been expelled [from] the mother country." A Guillermo (i.e., William) Wood is listed among the creditors of Russell & Sturgis four decades later, and so are his unmarried daughters, Maria, Ysidra, Ysabel, and Julia.[31]

The Santa Mesa Cordage Factory

One of the most striking examples of American enterprise in the nineteenth-century Philippines was the steam-powered cordage factory that was established at Santa Mesa, then a suburb of Manila and now included within the city proper, about the mid-1840s. It was definitely in operation by 1845, according to a Quaker lady who visited there at the end of that year, and for a long time it was the only one of its kind in the country.

The enterprise seems to have been initiated by two men, Charles Mugford and an old shipmaster named Keating. Mac Micking said that the machine-made rope was known as "Keating's patent cordage" and that it was much superior to the handspun kind because of the steadiness of the pull of the steam engine in comparison with the unequal twisting of the handspun variety, which gave the machine-made kind greater tensile strength. Interestingly, a description of the factory exists in what is probably the first American novel set in the Philippines. Although fictional, the account bears all the earmarks of eyewitness authenticity, right down to flag waving, doubtless based on the author's stay in the country.

> On the left bank of the Rio Pasig, about five miles from Manila, surrounded by... luxuriant vegetation ... stands a number of whitewashed buildings; and during the long summer afternoons ... the buzz of a thousand spindles, and the panting of a steam engine as it regularly performs its work, can be heard ...
>
> The engine and the spindles are engaged in the manufacture of rope of all sizes, from the mighty hawser to the finest lead line, and is the only cordage factory of any magnitude in the Eastern world, or was, at the time I write.... The enterprise was formed by American energy, carried through by American intelligence, and was then, and is now, for all I know to the contrary, entirely under American control, and owned entirely by American capitalists.
>
> The machinery was purchased in Massachusetts; the long rope-walk was built, and then taken apart and put on board a vessel that sailed from Boston; and lastly, Massachusetts mechanics were

employed to go to Santa Mesa, put the whole in complete order, and remain in the country and superintend the works, with the condition of owning a certain number of shares in case the enterprise was successful . . .[32]

At an early stage in its existence, it encountered difficulties arising from adulterated imitations, and Keating was forced to publish the following notice:

A spurious article having appeared in this Market, under the name of Patent cordage and having experienced some difficulty from its sale under this name, I give notice, that no cordage faced or made of different materials inwardly, has been made at the factory at Sta. Mesa, and purchasers are requested to examine on delivery and satisfy themselves that the stock and yarns are the same throughout.

Manila 29th Augt. 1846   OLIVER KEATING[33]

A few years after it was established, George Sturgis acquired an interest in it, and it is well here to glance briefly at his previous career before this point.

George Sturgis came to Manila in 1831 at the age of fourteen and joined his brother Henry in the house of Russell & Sturgis as a clerk. Letters exchanged with his family in the early years tell of his satisfaction with his post, although he did confess to being lonely for their company, as they were an extremely close-knit family. In 1842, when his brothers, Henry and Russell, were away, he seems to have been in charge of affairs in Manila. At that time, he was "speculating pretty largely, and should I be successful may be able to establish at home 'ere long, and go to meeting again which is my principal privation here." He was also thinking of getting married, but "never . . . to a Spanish girl or one of this country—no, no, no, a yankey [sic] or an English girl for this child!" Fate was to decree otherwise.

He became a partner in Russell & Sturgis in 1848 but left the firm in mid-1850. Halfway through that period, on April 22, 1849, he married a Spanish girl, Josefina Borrás (whose father had come to the country on the promise of a provincial governorship, which did not materialize, and who was later to be George Santayana's mother by her second marriage). He appears to have gone into the cordage business after he left the firm. In a letter to his brother, Robert Shaw Sturgis, in Canton, he wrote:

The cordage factory, I am convinced, will be a good and agreeable business, but will not allow me to lay up much money. Well, I think Joe [his son] will be more virtuous if he had to work for his living. Keating is now ill and ere long will, I presume, have to go home for his health; at present he don't [sic] seem inclined to change places with me, and be a "gentleman at large" which is all well for a short period but I'm quite tired of it. I hope when I next write to you to be in his shoes.

What Sturgis's motives were in going into a business that would not allow him "to lay up much money" are vague. Evidently it suited his temperament, and perhaps, since he had married a Spanish girl, he foresaw an extended stay in the country and wanted to establish himself in an "agreeable business" for the long pull. Sturgis seems to have taken a creative pride in the factory. Early in 1856, he wrote his brother Robert: "I got $10,500 last year from our Cordage Factory—Mr. Mugford $9000—Mr. Allen the overseer $3000 = $22,500 profit from a little Cordage Factory isn't bad, Bob hey?"

Those first years were quite prosperous ones for the factory. In 1853, he reported that he was doing very well with rope, selling all his output at auction due to the high demand in Australia. The following year he was offering to send rope to Hong Kong for the California market. Late in 1855, he announced that since he had sold 50 percent more rope in that year than in the previous one at profitable rates, he planned to take his family home to Boston for a visit.

At that time, George and Josefina were in close touch with the orphaned Kierulf children. One, Carmen, lived with them and helped Josefina care for the children. Josefina later fell ill from her night and day watch at the deathbed of Adelaida Kierulf (Mrs. Belza), whom she had met on her six-month voyage from Cádiz to Manila in 1845 (Santayana misspells her name as Adelaida Keroll).

The entrepreneurial function in the factory at the time, like its capital, seems to have been divided between Sturgis and Mugford. The former, however, occupied himself more with the commercial end of the business and seemed to be in that respect the more important of the two, while the latter undertook the more technical end, together with Allen, who seems to have performed predominantly managerial and supervisory functions. Before leaving for Boston early in 1856, Sturgis wrote: "Mr. Mugford will be here very soon, and if he thinks well of increasing our factory, will send me the orders to Boston per mail."

Sturgis, however, seems to have been the principal risk bearer. On Holy Wednesday in 1851, while Mugford was at lunch, a spinner in the factory lit a cigar and carelessly set fire to the whole establishment, "excepting the long American rope walk with its enclosed machinery." Sturgis lamented: "It will be $10,000 out of my pocket I presume!! . . . Unless insurance is effected, I shall not, being unable, invest more money than is absolutely indispensable to prevent more loss."

Sturgis's visit to Boston was not a happy one. He arrived there just in time to be present at his father's deathbed. He also seems to have incurred heavy expenses in anticipation of continued prosperity in the rope business. When he returned to Manila in the spring of 1857, he found that his affairs there "have not flourished so well as I expected they would, therefore my expenditure at home has been too much." At that time, his philanthropic brother Robert made a gift of $10,000 to his wife and children and in addition lent him $2,500 at 6 percent interest.

There was at that time a monetary crisis in Manila, with silver dollars (pesos) commanding as high as a 26 percent premium on gold. He procured two thousand silver dollars from his friend Governor Toribio Escalera of La Union Province, who refused to accept any premium for them, much to Sturgis's amazement:

We must have [silver] dollars for house expenses and when they were at 26% premium, Escalera insisted upon receiving no premium on $2000 which he furnished me, thus losing $520 for which he could have sold them! Obliged to pay my factory people every Saturday in dollars at high premium, materially reduces out profits. The premium is falling, and I hope before long there will be none.

Escalera may have been doing his friend a favor, but even so the difference in attitude toward business matters such as the premium on exchange is indicative of the cultural differences between the two men. For one, brought up in a mercantile environment, the market was supreme and it was right to follow it; for the other, if the market diverged from notions of what was right or what was a long-term price, it was something that could be overridden by a conscious decision.

On July 1, 1857, ownership of the cordage factory changed hands. Mugford sold his half interest for $20,000 and Sturgis one-third of his half, so that the new owners were Governor Escalera and Sturgis, each with one-third, and Edward H. Green and Jonathan Russell, each with one-sixth. Sturgis remarked of Mugford at this time: "I'm sorry to lose from here so good a friend and excellent man of business."

A capital gain, probably attributable in Schumpeterian theory to entrepreneurship, showed up at this time. Sturgis reported that his half share had cost him $12,500 in November 1850 and was worth $20,000 in mid-1857, "with the many improvements made." A one-third interest was therefore worth $13,333.33 at this time.

The factory may have flourished again with the heavy rope exports of the 1860s, but by the time of Russell & Sturgis's final bankruptcy in 1876, its one-third share was worth $15,000, only slightly higher than the 1857 figure. By 1887, Peele, Hubbell & Co.'s one-third was worth only $12,000, indicating a decline in the fortunes of the establishment.

Of Robert S. Sturgis's loan to him of $2,500, George Sturgis said that "should my health be preserved I hope before a great while to return it, as I try my best to make our rope factory profitable." On July 3, 1857, he wrote: "Circumstances beyond my control (last year's gale and high sugar prices) cause 1856 & 7 to be rather poor years for the factory, but I hope for better results in future years." Four days later he was dead.

The factory continued operating after his death and in September 1874 was reported as being "fully employed, & the product remains in demand & firm at $13.50 p. pcl . . ." At that time, it was the only steam-powered cordage factory in the country. Its markets were in the Pacific and Asia. In 1851, cordage was in demand for "California, N.S. Wales and Ports in this neighbourhood." The following year it was listed as one of the articles (along with cigars, hides, and *sapan* wood) large quantities of which were exported to China, India, and Java. Two years later, it was calculated that "the demand for Cordage for East Indies and Australia causes about 2000 *piculs* of Hemp to be consumed monthly in its manufacture." Three decades later, most cordage exports were listed as going to British possessions in Asia, but by then the factory's activity seemed to be slowing down.[34] There is today in the riverside locale of Bacood in Santa Mesa, Manila, a street named Lubiran, and the one at right angles to it was formerly named Cordeleria, both meaning rope factory in Tagalog and Spanish, respectively. This marks the site where the cordage works stood.

Nicholas Loney

The opening up of the island of Negros, today the country's leading sugar area, has been attributed in great part to Nicholas Loney. Unlike so many other British merchants, who were Scots, Loney was a Devon man with naval antecedents. Like most of them, he was quite young (twenty-four) when he arrived in Manila in 1852. In letters to his family, he proved himself an urbane and witty correspondent, given to quoting poetry and writing extensive passages in French. By 1854, he had been authorized, together with Robert Jardine, to sign by procuration for Ker & Co. With the opening of the port of Iloilo, the British consul in Manila, W. Farren, recommended that he be appointed vice consul there.

He landed in Iloilo on July 31, 1856, and met the most important people, including three Kierulf sisters, one of whom was married to the governor. Aside from his consular duties, he initially engaged in the piece goods business, but he immediately recognized the export potential of the place. "At the island of Negros," he wrote Consul Farren in April 1857, "the soil . . . is eminently fertile and . . . possesses immense tracts particularly adapted for the growth of sugar . . ." The sugar was of low quality, however, and what was needed was a larger population and work force and a better system of crushing and boiling. At that time, there was not a single iron mill on the island. But the wide price difference between prices in Iloilo ($4.21 per *picul*) and Manila ($5.68 per *picul*) presented a great commercial opportunity. Earlier he had persuaded Russell & Sturgis to commit twelve to fifteen thousand dollars to build a stone storehouse and go into production. He felt it was wasteful to ship sugar by coasting vessels for export at Manila, at a freight rate of fifty cents a *picul* plus brokerage costs, and promoted direct trade between Iloilo and foreign countries, starting with Australia.

By 1861, there were in Iloilo three iron cattle mills, with seven more on the way to various plantations, as well as one driven by steam put up by a Spanish firm. On Negros, progress was even more noticeable; there were thirteen iron cattle mills in operation. It was anticipated that by the end of that year there would be thirty iron mills in both provinces compared to only one in 1857. Loney also recorded the arrival of a steam crushing mill for use in Negros, and he expected three other large steam mills to be set up in the next three years. European agricultural implements such as carts and improved plows were ordered. Loney observed in a consular letter in 1861 that

> very few of these distributions of machinery in Panay and Negros could have taken place in the absence of foreign agency for obtaining them at Yloilo, inasmuch as it is opposed to the practice of foreign importers at Manila to sell on other terms than cash particularly to planters in distant provinces, with the extent of whose means

they are but imperfectly acquainted. . . . The intermediate agency at Yloilo . . . has been enabled to supply the most reliable of them with machinery in terms of credit varying from 4 months to one year . . .

Increased output, despite a tendency toward falling prices abroad, was reflected in rises in the value of land and in both urban and rural wages.

Loney's concern in Iloilo went by the name of Loney & Ker. He added something new to the operations of foreign entrepreneurs, offering machinery to sugar planters payable out of the increased profits possible from the use of modern equipment. In this way, he was able to overcome the natural conservatism of rural folk, and when the first machines proved profitable there was a rush to acquire them. One source reports that in one year alone Ker & Co. imported 159 centrifugal iron mills (Derosne et Cail system) for Iloilo, together with 8 steam mills and another mill using other sources of power for Negros. Sugar exports from that region of the country soared within a few years, and prosperity began to be visible in the western Visayas.

Upon his untimely death in 1869 at the age of forty-one, "all Yloilo followed him to his grave and . . . over 100 carriages besides lots of buffalo carts filled with people were there," wrote a nephew to his relatives in England. "He was buried under some palm trees by the sea shore in the prettiest site that could be found and they are going to erect a monument there." The inscription on the monument was in four languages—Spanish, French, English, and Visayan. The high esteem in which he was held was reflected in part of the Spanish inscription: "This monument is dedicated to his memory by numerous friends: Spaniards, foreigners, and natives of the country, as a testimony of the regard and affection in which they held him." Further honors came to him when in 1904 the Municipal Council of Iloilo voted to name the waterfront the Muelle Loney (Loney Docks).

Unfortunately, his monument was bulldozed after World War II, and a new look at Loney's activities has led to some reappraisal. McCoy argues with some persuasiveness that the Negros sugar industry was built on the ruins of the weaving industry on Panay and that Loney's promotion of cheap British cottons made him the architect of the industry's demise. *Architect* may be too strong a word, as it connotes design and deliberation, and Loney rode a perceived change in factor flows rather than starting them himself. The Chinese mestizos of the Iloilo area had shifted from their investments in the piece goods trade, undercut by direct importation from Manila by increasing numbers of Chinese shopkeepers, to large tracts of fertile land on Negros. Despite disapproval of the Chinese intrusion by both the authorities and the local inhabitants, Loney saw little force in their arguments, considering as beneficial "their displacing native capital less beneficially employed and transferring it to other, and, for the colony at large, much more productive channels." In fairness to Loney, even Spanish writers who were neither his countrymen nor his coreligionists called him the "protector of the arts and industries in that province that flourished by his initiative."[35]

Ice and Bureaucracy

The cold storage project first proposed by Charles D. Mugford (cofounder of the Santa Mesa cordage factory) does not easily fit under the rubric of new production methods, but it was acknowledged categorically as an innovation by the Spanish authorities and illustrates the bureaucratic caprices encountered by such innovations. Signing as Carlos D. Mugford, the proponent petitioned the superintendent general of finance on May 25, 1846, for permission to import free of customs duties a cargo of ice from the United States together with the materials necessary to build an ice house, representing that it would be to the country's benefit and of great profit to public health.

This was not an unusual request, as exemptions from payment of duty were made from time to time on grounds of public benefit. Ker & Co. in 1862 successfully sought import duty exemption for the entry of Wetzel sugar-refining machinery, and Aguirre & Co. in that same year asked for a rebate of export duties paid on a shipment of refined sugar to Australia, although this only led to a lengthy and inconclusive two-year bureaucratic process.

Mugford met similar bureaucratic difficulties. The first official to pass on his petition, a certain González, professed not to know whether the use of ice was harmful to health and abstained from making a decision, endorsing the request to the Tariff Board (Junta de Aranceles) on June 8 for resolution on grounds of public benefit. This was duly transmitted two days later by the intendant general, Gervasio Gironella, knight pensioner of the Royal and Distinguished Order of Carlos III, but there it languished.

On April 20 of the following year, Russell & Sturgis entered the picture, advising that a cargo of 250 tons of ice had been consigned to it on the American frigate *Hizaide* and asking for duty-free entry on the grounds that this was a completely unknown article in the local market and was thus a trial shipment. Considerable expenses had been incurred, they said, and half the amount shipped from the United States had melted on the voyage.

The company evidently had much more clout than Mugford. Gironella acted with dispatch this time. On April 21, he wrote a note on the company's request, asking the administrator of customs for an urgent report. The report was written that same day, favoring duty-free entry of the ice because it was completely new in the market and even more because by its very nature it was neither possible to estimate the amount that would ultimately be salable nor to say whether the result would be a profit or a loss. From the outcome of the venture, it added, it should be possible to establish precedents for determining what should be done in the future; if the outcome should result in profits exceeding 10 percent, the company could pay the excess as a duty, provided this was not more than what other articles paid according to provenance and flag of vessel. This would observe the spirit of the existing tariff schedule without prejudice to the public treasury or to the interested parties, and it would favor an effort that might be productive if in the regular course of events it was not contrary to health.

The following day, Gironella decreed the duty-free entry of the ice on the basis of the customs administrator's report, adding only the conditions that it be one time only and would not serve as a precedent, so that when the results were known the appropriate measures could be determined. The following day, the administrator of customs and the Accounting Office acknowledged receipt of the order. The whole process had taken only three days.

On June 8, Gironella sent the decree to the Tariff Board so it could be taken into consideration in its deliberations on an existing case on the same subject (Mugford's). The board, stating for the record that it had been advised by His Lordship (the intendant general) that the supreme government had been informed of the concession, made haste to concur and further agreed to make no changes in what had been decreed until a resolution came from the court. This was hardly surprising, since the board was chaired by the intendant general himself and had for members the senior accountant, the accountant general of the army and finance, the administrator of customs, and a private merchant, with another merchant, Jose de Azcárraga, serving as secretary. It is not clear whether Russell & Sturgis's project was the same as Mugford's or distinct from it. In 1875, the ice plant's address was close to the company's on the same street (Barraca). All the bureaucratic complications became unnecessary after 1848, when a royal order of October 7 declared the importation of ice into the Philippines to be free of duty.[36]

312

Domestic Enterprise

While non-Spanish westerners in the Philippines were bringing about growth in trade directly and transformations in the economy indirectly, domestic enterprise was not idle, despite being hobbled by the Iturbide incident in the crucial 1820s and by the lack of connections with the western industrial world. However, its share in foreign trade transactions even at the end of Spanish rule was, judging from customs figures already cited, still minor, ranging from 12 to 27 percent.

Domestic enterprise is used here in its broadest denotation, as earlier suggested, comprehending all elements in a polyethnic and polycultural Philippine society from the indigenous to the various principal immigrant currents: Chinese, Luso-Iberian, and other western. This is in the spirit of the 1899 Malolos Constitution, the Philippine constitutional document closest in time to the period under study, which provided that foreigners who had established uninterrupted residence for two years on Philippine territory were Filipinos. Some entities considered Spanish at the time fall into this category, the test being whether the enterprises were domestically sourced and their protagonists domestic residents. There is some post facto validation for this, as descendants of such persons have served in the armed forces, in the diplomatic corps, at various levels of government, and even in the cabinet of the Philippine Republic. At least one walked as a Philippine army officer in the Bataan death march, and another was executed by the Japanese for resistance during World War II. Some families evolved over time; for example, the Kierulfs went from Danish through Spanish to Filipino nationality.

From time to time, the ethno-social group of various entrepreneurs may be indicated as a way of tracking their fortunes in business. Entrepreneurial interest and tradition were suggestively stronger among the non-Spanish westerners and the Chinese and less so among the Spaniards. There was an old commercial tradition among the indigenous Filipinos dating back to pre-Magellanic times, but all the traders, to recall what W. H. Scott has recently underlined, had been Muslims,[37] and this cultural bonding was broken by the Spanish struggles with the southern Muslim principalities and by external trading restrictions, shunting indigenous commercial energies to the coasting trade.

It is not easy to present a coherent narrative of nineteenth-century domestic entrepreneurship due to the lack of specialized studies and the paucity of private business records compared to those found in the western world. Much archival research obviously needs to be done. What little can be told must be culled from fragmentary reports and notices.

For the late 1840s and early 1850s, commercial circulars and shipping intelligence specify the consignees of the various vessels in port. The most frequently mentioned local names are J. M. Tuason, B. A. Barretto & Co., and Narciso Padilla. The differences among them are that Padilla's voyages were all to Amoy, Macao, and Hong Kong, while Tuason's were much more international in scope. The Barretto concern falls in between.

Also figuring in the list with some frequency are Lorenzo Calvo, F. V. de Orbeta, and Juan Bautista de Marcaida, almost certainly all Creole merchants. The last assisted J. W. Peele in 1841 in getting some furniture through customs. Another Marcaida, Antonio M., was a ship's captain. One A. Marcaida worked for the British house of Smith, Bell & Co. in 1862, taking charge of liaison with customs, finance, and other government authorities. There are still Marcaidas in Manila to this day. Also on the list was one Lucas Lucsin (probably Locsin in a modern rendering), evidently a Chinese mestizo.

One of the more interesting of the lot was Narciso Padilla. Family tradition holds that he was of indigenous origin. He seems to have been highly regarded. He was listed as a registered lawyer from the first visitor's handbook in 1834 until the last one in 1865, with the notation that he had been registered since December 8, 1822, and in another issue of the handbook he was listed as a Spanish merchant. As a lawyer, he was on the same register as Agustín Santayana, George Santayana's father, and served with him and the protonationalist cleric, Fr. Pedro Peláez, on the board of a pious foundation, the Misericordia. He was the grandfather of the prize-winning Filipino painter, Felix Resurrección Hidalgo.

His trading ventures were made on two brigs, both of Spanish registry, the 300-ton *Tiempo* and the 159-ton *Narciso*, the latter obviously named for him. In 1851, Captain Juan López of this vessel brought to Manila a six-year old Amoy girl purchased by George and Josefina Sturgis to learn to take care of their son Joey, nicknamed Pepín, who, however, died early. Josefina liberated and educated the girl, had her baptized Juana, and took her to Boston with her family after she was widowed. An Amoy report of 1854 specifically mentions the *Narciso* as having sold its cargo of Manila rice at $1.50 per *picul*.

Another glimpse at the movement of the various groups in Philippine trade is the list of local ship's captains, who merit mention here since captains of that time did not confine themselves to navigation but also performed commercial functions. Amid the multiplicity of Basque names like Aguirre, Basagoiti, Larrinaga, and Inchausti (the last having sailed for Padilla) is found an obviously indigenous name, Silverio Tayag (from the sound of it a Pampango), who not only commanded Padilla's *Narciso* on a voyage to Amoy but captained the 145-ton Spanish brig *Rodrigo* on a trip to Liverpool for one Vicente Valles. In the early 1840s, there was a frigate of Spanish registry, the *Esperanza*, which put in from Cádiz, captained by a certain Bocalan, who may have been of indigenous origin.

J. M. Tuason & Co.

The Tuasons merit more extended treatment. Reference has already been made to a *mayorazgo* created in 1794 by Antonio Tuason. On August 31, 1822, his grandson, Mariano Tuason, a lieutenant colonel of the Battalion of the Militia of the Prince Royal (composed of *mestizos sangleyes* or Chinese mestizos), mortgaged the Santa Mesa estate and its extensions in Diliman and elsewhere for the sum of 30,000 pesos at 5 percent per annum for eight years with the Cajas de Comunidad (the fund for local public works), despite an express prohibition in the document establishing the *mayorazgo* against any sale, alienation, encumbrance, or mortgage of any or all of the properties included therein, although certain laws were cited as covering the action taken. The property was said to have originally been purchased for 33,000 pesos and improved, so that now it was worth double that amount. It is not clear from a series of notations extending to 1871 when the mortgage was actually lifted. It was executed for Mariano's minor son, José María Tuason, who was in Spain and would give his initials to a company that would be active during the latter part of the century.

Before the company's apogee, Tuason in 1851 would be one of the first pair of comanagers of the Banco Español-Filipino de Isabel II (the other one being another merchant, Fernando Aguirre).

J. M. Tuason & Co. performed practically all the functions associated with the western merchants, and it added a few others besides. In its international trading, it was active in both exports and imports, more perhaps in the latter than in the former, and even issued to its customers in the late 1850s market reports in English similar to those of the western merchant houses.

In its export trading, it joined ten other firms in 1867 in agreeing on a standard sample for "Manila current" sugar; eight of the firms were western foreigners, and J. M. Tuason was the only firm of nonwestern origin, the other two being Aguirre and Barretto. In 1875, the firm was exporting lumber to China. Two years later, it represented, as did the British firm of Holliday, Wise & Co., that the duty on jute sacks, used for bagging coffee and rice exports, was excessive, representing 55.5 percent of the prime cost of the material, and secured a reduction.

In its import operations, it brought in textiles and a variety of other goods like playing cards, quill pens, buttons, and earrings. These it disposed of through Chinese merchants, who signed three-month promissory notes. If they defaulted, they were taken to court, as several cases attest, such as those against So Chico and Lim Tionchay. It then became necessary to foreclose on their stock in trade, which would be appraised and auctioned off to satisfy judgments by professional appraisers like Federico Calero and Manuel Genato.

It undertook customs brokerage, handling the packages shipped in 1865 through Heard & Co. in Hong Kong for the Spanish minister plenipotentiary in China, Sinibaldo de Mas, the author of two works on the Philippines. It also acted as the local representative of numerous Spanish pensioners who had retired to Spain but still had pending claims on the Manila treasury. In its purely domestic operations, it was deep into property management, which involved it in several ejectment cases.

The firm also opened a banking house, and a notice in 1860 said that it received deposits and current accounts at interest, drew bills on London and Madrid payable in all Spanish provinces, and discounted commercial bills and promissory notes. As late as November 19, 1895, it advertised in the *Diario de Manila* that it sold bills on Spain, London, and Paris.

Calling themselves "businessmen and bankers," the officials of the firm in 1860 proposed to the government that in order to economize on the expense and difficulty of moving specie its checks should be accepted for official payments up to a certain amount, say, 100,000 pesos, with the firm depositing a like amount in cash as a guarantee. This was rejected by the government on the grounds that its checks did not have the same standing as those of the Banco Español-Filipino, which the government considered its own bank, established, encouraged, and supervised by it. It pointed to the "immoderate latitude" granted to private banks in the United States, which encouraged them to overexpand and more than once had endangered commercial soundness and credit in that country. Somewhat grumpily, the public treasury charged that making this concession to one private company would force it in all fairness to extend it to other private firms and would convert the government into a cashier for private interests; besides, there was the danger of forgery.

Two years later, the firm tried again, representing that in view of the treasury's circumstances it was willing to advance to the government 70,000 pesos in gold and 50,000 in silver without interest, to be repaid by accepting its bills for payments at customs for manufactured tobacco, remittances to the provinces, and any extraordinary sales of tobacco for export. The answer was still no, but the proposal was received in better humor. Upon checking with the mint, it was found that it had a little over 167,000 pesos in gold, which, by working with some speed, could be reminted immediately for the treasury. The firm's proposal was therefore turned down, with many expressions of esteem and appreciation for its "disinterested and patriotic conduct."

One puzzling set of documents relates to the company's proposed dissolution in 1864. At that time, the partners were Mariano Tuason (not the previously mentioned Mariano), Josefa Patiño de Tuason, and José Severo Tuason. Mariano would liquidate the banking business and José Severo the commercial side. The notice, dated April 30, was filed officially on May 7. Yet the company continued operating until the end of Spanish rule and into the beginning of the American administration. One possible explanation is that the Spanish Disentailing Law of 1820 became operative in the Philippines on March 1, 1864, and that this was an initial reaction to what was believed would affect the *mayorazgo*, then held by José Severo Tuason. But they may have discovered that the measure was unnecessary, hence the continuation of the company's operations.[38]

Industry and Mining

Outside the commercial field, one example of local entrepreneurship was a spinnery powered by water in Calauan, Laguna, introduced by Domingo Rojas. At the time of De Mas's visit in 1842, there were plans for expanding the establishment to include more machinery, but little is known about it after that time. About 1860, the Rojases had a distillery for making rum, quite likely an offshoot of their sugar business.

A domestic innovation that impinged on a major export was the setting up of a steam-powered sugar refinery on Tanduay Street by Aguirre & Co. in the late 1850s. So little is known about it that even detailed historical studies on Philippine sugar do not mention it. Russell & Sturgis reported on June 28, 1858, that the sugar processed by the centrifugal machine was labeled superior grade, while refined sugar was sold for domestic consumption and future shipment to Spain. Contracts for the superior grade were reported to be reserved for export to California, Australia, and Spain. In 1875, Aguirre & Co. was reported to be in liquidation, but a sugar refinery was cryptically listed at a location in Binondo District.

Much local enterprise and capital also seem to have gone in the nineteenth century into mining ventures. Part of the capital for these ventures may have been raised in Spain, but much of it was domestic. There had been great interest in minerals and some activity dating to the eighteenth century, especially in the iron mines near Manila, as has been seen in the cases of F. X. Salgado and Isabel Careaga.

Gold mining naturally attracted attention. During the nineteenth century, a company called La Exploradora was formed to work gold deposits in Nueva Ecija and lead in Camarines Norte, and another one called El Ancla de Oro was established to work the deposits at Mambulao, Camarines Norte.

The most persistent local name was that of Rojas. The same Domingo Rojas of the water-powered spinnery as early as 1835 was interested in iron. In 1838, he sent two copper kettles made by Igorots to the Economic Society as samples of what could be made from local copper. The firm of Rojas Sons invested 200,000 pesos in coal mines in Cebu without result, and the Cántabro-Filipina Co., in which the Rojases had an interest, spent more than 300,000 pesos between 1860 and 1870 on the copper mines at Mancayan, which for a while produced some results but later had to be let out to a contractor.

There were many other projects and many other names. None of the mining ventures was successful, although between 1810 and the 1870s more than two million pesos were calculated to have been invested in them. What is ironic is that many of the sites given up were later worked successfully and profitably. The causes of failure were various. In some projects, it was a shortage in the initial capitalization. In others, it was the difficulty of securing a stable labor supply, since many of the laborers worked only long enough to meet their basic needs and then quit for as long as their funds lasted. Bad communications were another reason for failure. The loss of invested capital was lamentable, but some of the information gathered during those early ventures became useful later.[39]

Balbino Mauricio: A Lost Generation?

The merchant Balbino Mauricio was involved in July 1862 in a minor difficulty with Manila customs. He had imported vegetable wax from

Hong Kong, but the consular manifest erroneously listed 348 boxes instead of the 248 actually shipped, which involved duties of 163.80 pesos. Armed with a certification of the error from the Spanish Consulate in Hong Kong, Mauricio petitioned for a refund. This was opposed by the customs administration on the grounds that neither the captain nor the consignee had brought the error up at entry and it had only been discovered subsequently by the warehouse keeper and the control officer; a grace period could have been granted, but it was now too late, as the money had been deposited in the general treasury. He was overruled at a higher level, however, and Mauricio was granted his refund.

The incident was trivial in itself; what was significant was its very occurrence, which showed a growing Filipino presence in international trade. Born in Kawit, Cavite, into a Chinese mestizo family, Mauricio was listed as a Spanish merchant in various issues of the *Guía de forasteros*. He was one of the 154 unjustly implicated in the Cavite Mutiny of 1872 (aside from the three Filipino martyr-priests Burgos, Gomes, and Zamora) and suffered confiscation of his property, imprisonment, and exile. Three others are mentioned specifically as merchants—Crisanto de los Reyes, Máximo Inocencio, and Vicente Zabala. There were certainly more, to judge by the inclusion among the accused of Máximo Paterno, who, like Mauricio, had been listed as a Spanish merchant in the *Guía de forasteros* and who had taken part in the liberal demonstration in 1869 honoring the reputedly progressive Governor de la Torre. Mauricio, along with Paterno and several others, was exiled to Guam but escaped in May 1874 on an American vessel with Antonio Ma. Regidor, landing in Hong Kong, never to return to his country. De los Reyes was exiled to Cartagena in Spain but gained his freedom during an uprising, spending several years in North Africa and France before returning home. Paterno, with several others, took his case to Madrid and was granted amnesty in November 1874, although he was initially forbidden to go home. Máximo Inocencio, who had risen from apprentice carpenter to contractor for the Cavite arsenal and boat builder, was the living bridge between the events of 1872 and the Revolution of 1896 . Like De Los Reyes, he was exiled to Spain but escaped to France, returning home to resume his business after obtaining a pardon. After the Revolution broke out, he was arrested and, implicated by the testimony of an associate, executed. Did these men and others like them represent a generation of Filipino businessmen whose rise was slowed by the repression of 1872?[40]

The Collapse of the American Houses

The two great American firms, Russell & Sturgis and Peele, Hubbell & Co., went down in successive decades, the 1870s and the 1880s, and certain circumstances connected with their failures suggest that merchant financing had become an obsolescent form of entrepreneurial organization. The first suspension of payment by Russell & Sturgis, which occurred on November 6, 1875, seems to have been precipitated by the death of its managing partner, Jonathan Russell, on September 26 of that year in San Francisco, leaving the business in the hands of the more inexperienced junior partners. It was also admitted in court at the time that the company's affairs had not been going well for several years.

This unexpected event was a blow to Philippine commercial life, and there was a general lack of confidence in the business community. It has already been noted that Peele, Hubbell & Co. almost had to follow suit because it was so deeply involved. Jonathan Russell had bought Edward H. Green's half share in the firm in 1872 for $250,000, so the capital value of the partnership must have been around half a million pesos at this time, when it had the reputation of being the largest and most influential firm in the country. For all its prestige and greatness, the firm does not seem to have been very popular. There are references in the Peele, Hubbell & Co. correspondence to the fact that certain members of Russell & Sturgis acted as if they owned the country.

The month following the company's first suspension of payment, an agreement was arrived at with its creditors by which it was rehabilitated for business, with the condition that no creditor would be paid more than 50 percent whose credit exceeded 1,000 pesos and furthermore that 8 percent interest would continue to be paid on funds deposited with it. The agreement was based on the hope of securing more capital to the amount of 300,000 pesos in order to continue operations.

This, however, failed to materialize. Business conditions were bad the world over, and no money could be raised in London, especially after the death of the firm's senior partner. Panic in Manila deterred depositors from entrusting it with their funds. Its commission business was diverted to other houses. When it tried to sell its assets, no one was found with enough money to buy them all. On November 6, 1876, it suspended payment for the second and final time. For that year, it had more than 300,000 pesos tied up in sugar advances in Iloilo and Negros, more than 269,000 in abaca in Albay and Leyte, and more than 154,000 in shipping, besides sundry other items, on a balance sheet that totaled 2,749,489 pesos. Although it had in excess of 300,000 pesos in cash, more than enough to pay the 8 percent interest to its depositors, it decided to liquidate before things got worse.

There were ample economic reasons for the firm's difficulties, since hemp prices had fallen steeply since 1870, not to touch bottom until 1878, and sugar had experienced a shallower fall from 1869 to 1875. But these were conditions facing all the other firms, none of which went under. Particular reasons for this were offered by some observers.

One source says that the reason for the firm's failure was that the newly established branches and agencies of the English banks had begun to make loans at lower rates of interest and to accept land mortgages to secure loans, thus drawing business away from it. Another source blames the bad faith of the Visayan sugar planters, who, it was said, had failed to deliver the crops on which advances had been made because the funds they received had been spent on items of consumption and personal luxury such as pianos and jewelry, building fine houses, and sending their sons to college. According to Foreman, they "in a hundred ways satisfied their pride and love of outward show in a manner never known before, at the expense of the American capitalists. . . . Trade, was for the moment, completely paralysed. The great firm, which had for years been the mainspring of all Philippine mercantile enterprise, had failed!"

But the creditors probably retrieved their capital in the course of the liquidation. Depositors with less than a thousand pesos were paid at the maturity of their *quedanes*; those with more were paid 50 percent and the balance as the firm's assets were liquidated. The liquidators brought suit against Jonathan Russell's personal estate in Massachusetts and in 1882 were awarded $34,190.96, of which $5,913.91 went for the fees and expenses of their Salem lawyer, Arthur Lord Huntington. Edward H. Green got $72,500 of his $112,500 claim against the estate, representing the last two installments due from Russell when he bought out Green in 1872. (Green would be better known in history as the husband of Hetty Robinson Green, "The Witch of Wall Street.") Moreover, one L. S. Dabney, acting as guardian ad litem for Russell's three children in Manila under appointment of the Supreme Court, succeeded in obtaining a decree of $5,000 in favor of each of them. Holders of *quedanes* had them rubber stamped as dividends were paid. Those belonging to Richard Burke show rubber stamps for six dividends of 5 percent each and one of 10 percent, as well as one of 60 percent.

The bankruptcy of Peele, Hubbell & Co. in 1887 is a somewhat clearer case. It overtraded in sugar at a time of prolonged depression in

321

world sugar prices, and modern banking procedures caught up with it. At the time of the sudden suspension of payment in 1875 by Russell & Sturgis, with which it had traded jointly in abaca in Albay and Leyte since 1862, the ensuing general panic threatened to drag it down, too. But it secured an extension of three years, with interest continuing to be paid, from all creditors for sums of one thousand pesos and above. Excluded from the agreement was the bank, whose rules did not permit it to enter into such an agreement and whose loans the company had sufficient means to cover. The bank's share was relatively small, and the business regained its footing. (Although not named in the minutes of the creditors' meeting, this was the Hongkong and Shanghai Banking Corporation.)

In 1887, however, although the circumstances were in some respects similar, the bank held a huge chunk of the firm's liabilities. Total liabilities were 1,196,289 pesos, of which the bank held 449,689 in an advance account and 83,861 in the general account. There were only 703,986 pesos' worth of assets, its cash position was extremely low, and 486,226 pesos' worth of assets representing sugar shipments, shares, and the firm's office building were mortgaged to the bank. According to the *Diario de Manila* for March 24, 1887, although the other creditors were unanimously willing to grant it an extension, the bank was not, which earned it murmurs of public disapproval, for the firm was a well-liked and popular one. Peele, Hubbell & Co. had to file for bankruptcy. The news item in the paper ended by expressing warm good wishes and the hope for speedy rehabilitation.

The company's problems with the bank stemmed in part from unsatisfactory relations with one Hamlen, their import broker in the United States, who wired the company to draw on him for a hemp shipment and when told that the bank required credits simply repeated his original offer. "The Bank now is much more particular about Bills and dont want to take any but Credits," wrote H. N. Palmer to R. D. Tucker on January 14, 1887, "& the good old days when we used to turn into Barnes any kind of a Bill have passed . . ." Ogden E. Edwards also complained about Hamlen in a letter to Tucker dated the previous day: "You see how we are behind on the fibre thanks to Hamlen who has been nowhere in Hemp sales last year." On February 5, he wrote: "Hamlen is not in the swim of selling produce particularly Hemp and we suffer in consequence." (It is not clear why they stayed with Hamlen instead of changing to another broker, but stay they did, and as late as September 5 Palmer was writing that "we want to keep on with Hamlen, but we dont want to do any big business just for the sake of doing it . . .")

The firm had banking problems not only as regards foreign exchange payments but also with its domestic operations. "The Bank object to give any money unless on actual produce [this sounded like an objection to advances], and we cannot go on in that way, and I incline to think they will agree to our demands, as a panic here would hurt them very much" wrote Palmer to Tucker in his January 14 letter. But this was baseless bravado, as the firm was falling behind the competition. In the same letter, Palmer said, "S[mith] B[ell] & Co. and Ker & Co. are doing all the Hemp business to the States and we must try to catch on again somehow."

One reason for the bank's tightening up may have been its own losses on foreign exchange trading. "The Hkong Bank have again made an awful mull of this business," wrote Palmer to Tucker,

> & when 4 mos ago they were full of money & had to buy bills to cover their London a/c at a very heavy loss, they are now just the contrary, & have no cash and lots of Bills bought to pay for, which they will have to draw for at another heavy loss & . . . neither Bank will make any rate at which they will buy Bills & nobody knows where we are in produce, & there is no price for either Hemp or Sugar. . . . The telegram this morning quotes Exchange 3/9 nominal & the rate may go to 3/10 or higher.

Although this was written on September 5, 1887, the conditions dated back a year. Palmer wrote that "they have made an awful mull of this Exchange business here the past 12 months. Hemp of course will & must accomodate [sic] itself to Exchange, but Sugar will not, certainly for some time, & likely but little or no business will be done for the present." (Sugar's postulated unresponsiveness to exchange rate movements may have stemmed from the unlikelihood of replenishing low inventories owing to a diminished crop that had been affected by locust damage.)

The incident that precipitated the firm's downfall had come in mid-February. Palmer wrote Tucker on 21 February 1887:

> Last week when a quedan of some $3000 of those Yparriguirre [sic] girls was presented & had to be paid, the Bank said they saw no use in going on as they did not want to run the risk of having to pay an indefinite amount of these quedanes, & with almost a certainty that we should have to stop sooner or later, we did not think it was right to our other creditors to go on paying what might be called for as due, and so we have decided to stop.

The Yparraguirre *quedan* was only the occasion for the failure; the real reason was operational. In the same letter, Palmer wrote that "the end we have so long been dreading and been fighting against, has at last come. . . . [T]he highly respectable & old house of P. H. & Co. has gone down . . . and sugar did it." Edwards wrote the same day that "I know I ought to have wound up the house a year ago when I arrived." Perhaps managerial sclerosis was part of the problem; Edwards had been with the firm since J. Willard Peele had sold out forty-four years earlier.

The overconcentration in sugar was evident from the statistics. In 1881, the firm had shipped 648,227 *piculs* of sugar and 301,596 of abaca; a comparable English firm, Smith, Bell & Co., had shipped 962,730 and 255,684 *piculs*, respectively. Five years later, both had reduced their sugar shipments, the American firm to 529,354 *piculs* and the English to 744,905. But, while the latter increased abaca shipments to 304,356 *piculs*, the former suffered a diminution to only 90,348—a sad state of affairs for a pioneer in the industry. Smith, Bell & Co. had gained on it in abaca and could at least distribute its operations between a product that was depressed, sugar, and one that was not, abaca, while Peele, Hubbell & Co. had experienced a relative concentration in the depressed product. Ker & Co., another British competitor, advanced in both abaca and sugar (table 19).

The sugar crisis also affected the dealers, most of them Chinese, with whom the firm did business. One Champoo owed $400,000, including $170,000 to the Chartered Bank. Palmer wrote to Tucker on December 1, 1887, that

> as yet he has not been found or turned up any where, & with none of his books or a/cs, and with every body on his paper & he on theirs, you can imagine what a mixed up mess it is and I think several other Chinamen will have to come down, among them, our old friends Tioqui [i.e., Tiaoqui] & Co. . . . Chuidian, Buenaventura & Co. have decided to give up their dry Sugar business, so if Tioqui has to stop, the number of dealers is pretty well reduced, and those remaining ought to be able to make money. . . . I think Champoo and Tioqui both owe them for money advanced on Sugar contracts, & this bad practice ought to be stopped, though SB & Co. have done it to Palanca, since the failure of Champoo—some day or another that scoundrel Palanca will come to grief, & it will serve SB & Co. right if they got let in by him.

324

This last did not come true, as both Smith, Bell & Co. and Palanca prospered in coming years and decades.

Even as the sugar crisis was building, one small detail cropped up that was possibly a harbinger of things to come: "Of the late shipments of sugar by Ker & Co., some 30/40-M-*piculs* is on a/c of the dealers . . ." (Palmer to Tucker, February 21, 1887). This may have been an early indication that the local Chinese dealers were beginning to feel strong enough to assume foreign as well as domestic risks, and it represented a forward step in their firms' evolution into full-fledged foreign trading companies.

One of the accounts pending when Peele, Hubbell & Co. ceased operations was an *Alabama* claim. The Confederate commercial raider *Alabama* had entered the South China Sea through the Sunda Straits in November of 1863, destroying some American ships (among them the Boston bark *Amanda,* which was carrying hemp and sugar for Ker & Co., and the New York clipper *Winged Racer* from Manila, with a cargo of sugar, hides, coffee, and tobacco) and scaring numerous others into seeking refuge in safe ports. Twenty-four years later, Edwards wearily wrote to Tucker on February 21, 1887: "I hope you will settle the Alabama claims satisfactorily. Better take what we can get and be happy."

Life was difficult for those involved in the bankruptcy. "Edwards . . . still lives at Sta. Mesa where he is supposed to be under arrest, with the 'fianza' [guarantee] of Pompilio Jorge. He dines at the Club & We all get our breakfast at the Tiffin rooms in San Gabriel over the Chartered Bank & he travels on the river in a Banca, having sold his carriage," wrote Palmer to Tucker on March 30, 1887.

Every effort was made to take the bankruptcy out of the courts in order to hasten a settlement. To do this, the creditors' committee admitted the government's claims for fines, and the bank agreed to accept one-half of the proceeds of the sale of the house and lot in full payment for claims of all kinds. Thereafter the creditors' committee unanimously approved Edwards's proposal to consider the assets of the firm as payment in full (letters of September 5 and 6 and November 30, 1887, Palmer and Edwards to Tucker). The depositors appear not to have been as fortunate as those of Russell & Sturgis. *Quedanes* held by Juan (John) Burke and his mother Victoria Butler de Burke show the first two dividends at 5 percent each, a third at 2.5 percent, and a fourth and fifth at 5.5 percent each, or a total of 23.5 percent.

Of the last partners in the firm, Palmer died suddenly in London in 1889 while Edwards, Tucker, and Rufus A. Lane were restored by a judicial

Table 19
Abaca and Sugar Shipments from the Philippines by Shipper
1881 and 1886
(Piculs)

Shipper	Abaca		Sugar	
	1881	1886	1881	1886
Peele, Hubbell & Co.	301,596	90,348	648,227	529,354
Smith, Bell & Co.	255,684	304,356	962,730	744,905
Ker & Co.	92,914	141,512	284,655	440,016
MacLeod & Co.	49,668	63,368	136,000	302,097
W.F. Stevenson & Co.	44,056	58,826	474,749	483,030
E.J. Longard, Jr.	24,786	-	74,472	-
Luchsinger & Co. (Ilo-ilo)	-	-	-	153,104
Baer, Senior & Co.	-	4,110	48,565	106,394
Geo. Mackenzie & Co.	86,792	26,704	-	28,209
Findlay Richardson & Co.	-	3,620	28,966	25,459
F.M. Heriot & Co.	-	13,546	-	8,000
J. Smith (Cebu)	-	3,000	-	8,000
W.H. Hindley & Co.	-	31,120	-	1,440
Martin Dyce & Co.	-	-	308,142	-
Others	13,408	2,854	396,166	142.781
Total	868,904	743,364	3,362,672	2,972,789

Note: Official figures given in the Census of 1903 are slightly lower than those given here.

Sources: R.D. Tucker Papers, Peabody Essex Museum.

decree of December 22, 1891, to the exercise of the mercantile profession, although there is no record that they again became active in Manila's commercial life.

From the shambles of the company was formed the Anglo-American firm of Warner, Blodgett & Co., later to become the British firm of Warner, Barnes & Co., active until recently under different ownership. The new firm's cofounder, E. H. Warner, wrote to Richard Tucker on April 9, 1887, that on the advice of a friend he and his partner Blodgett had "picked up the crumbs from the wreck & they have proved far better than I ever expected we got all the agencies & on admitting Barnes eeked [sic] enough capital together to get the Samar business."[41] It is not certain, however, that the new firm came to occupy the same place in Philippine business that its predecessor had, for its experience with regular commercial banking procedures seems to indicate that the palmy days of the merchant-financiers were over.

The Obsolescence of the Merchant-Financier

The merchant-financing firm flourished at a time when communication with the Atlantic world was slow and it was necessary for the importers there to deal with persons on whose judgment and discretion they could rely implicitly. Those importers also operated with considerable flexibility in their dual role as commodity traders and shipowners.

From about the middle of the nineteenth century, forces based on technical improvements came into play. These would undercut the usefulness of the merchant-financing firm, drive to the wall those who could not adapt to the new conditions, and induce the survivors to look to new lines for their viability. The main factors were steam navigation, cable communications, and modern banking. The first one affected the business in two ways. It made it progressively harder for the importing firms in the West to continue in their dual role of traders and shipowners. Increasingly, they had to specialize and, in the face of increasing capital requirements for high-seas navigation, decide which role they would adopt. This did not happen overnight, as sailing vessels were in use through the end of the nineteenth century, but the trend was inexorable.

The second effect was felt at the other end of the business. Early in 1854, it was officially announced that a government steamer would be dispatched regularly from Manila to Hong Kong in the latter part of each month in order to connect with the latter's overland mail (through Suez). This was the first reduction in communications time with the West, which had until then taken five to six months (except for the fast American clipper ships, which could sail from Manila to Boston in ninety days).

An even more drastic reduction in communications time came with the extension of telegraphic service from Britain to Hong Kong and Singapore. Messages that had taken months to deliver now took at most a few weeks, depending on sailing schedules, as may be seen in the correspondence between Stone, Silsbee & Pickman and Ker & Co. from about the mid-1860s. The final step was the opening of cable communications between the Philippines and Hong Kong in May 1880. From then on, communications could be sent instantly and in code.

The last factor was the establishment of full-service, internationally oriented banks with the coming of the British Chartered Bank and the Hong Kong and Shanghai Banking Corporation in the 1870s. These banks made superfluous, at least in Manila, the deposit-taking functions of the merchant houses and at the same time provided a source of loan funds, which made it unnecessary for the merchant firms to resort to numerous *quedan* holders. They also supplanted the merchant houses as foreign exchange dealers. By the late nineteenth century, the merchant firms in their trading operations were simply following the orders of their correspondents in the West, taking the cargoes sent to them and sending back return cargoes as ordered.

The wreck of the 1,100-ton Salem ship *Panay* perhaps illustrates the changes in conditions. Sailing ships, before the introduction of tankers, were used in the interest of safety to transport oil in cases, which is what the *Panay* was doing in 1890, and then take advantage of the lading space to carry return cargoes of hemp or sugar. Having discharged its oil cargo in Manila, the *Panay*, which wanted to make all possible speed to Iloilo to load sugar, arranged to be towed by a steamer. It ran aground on July 14 on Simara Island, and on August 13 Ker & Co. telegraphed Silsbee and Pickman that the wreck had been sold for $2,500 by public auction.[42]

Diversification and Joint Ventures

If they were not to degenerate into mere agencies, the merchant firms had to engage in new activities, and this they did by diversifying and delving more deeply into the country's productive structure. Warner, Barnes & Co. in the last decade of the nineteenth century began building a railway in Mindanao from Iligan to Lake Lanao. (The railroad had already come to Luzon with the building of the Manila-Dagupan line in 1887–92 by British investors.) But construction was halted with the outbreak of the Spanish-American War, and the incoming American administration disapproved the project. The locomotives, rails, and other materials were sold to the Philippine Railway Co. for an Iloilo-Capiz line.

Smith, Bell & Co. established the Luzon Sugar Co. between 1880 and 1885 in Malabon, near Manila, claiming (erroneously) that it was the first sugar refinery in the country. (Its competitors at Peele, Hubbell & Co. cast a skeptical eye on its capital structure; "I calculate that of the $700,000 capital $400,000 is water . . . say, $250,000 over value of Patent right and $150,000 false price for the real estate," wrote O. E. Edwards to R. D. Tucker on January 23, 1882.) It arranged and supervised the construction in 1891 of the all-steel San Sebastian Church, prefabricated in Belgium and assembled in Manila piece by piece. (There is a suggestion that Gustave Eiffel designed its metal structure.) It secured a franchise in 1890 to run a railroad east of Manila to Antipolo, but this was annulled in 1892 and awarded to one Albert Coates, formerly the Manila manager for Ker & Co. in the late 1870s.

Perhaps more significant from the point of view of capital structure was its founding of Luzon Rice Mills Ltd. to establish the first mechanical rice mills in the country in collaboration with Filipino capital. This started in Bayambang, Pangasinan, and later spread to Bautista, Dagupan, Gerona, and Calumpit. During the Revolution and the Philippine-American War, the Smith Bell rice mills in Pangasinan and Tarlac donated hundreds of sacks of rice to the Filipino revolutionary forces.[43]

The participation of domestic capital was symptomatic of the growth and increasing economic role of the rising domestic business class. In one of the earlier joint ventures, George Peirce was a partner in the *S.S. Visayas* in 1872–72, managed by Macleod, Pickford & Co. together with such persons as Julio Arnáez, Teodoro Benedicto, Juan Climaco, Lucas Lacson, Anastasio Ledesma, A. de Marcaida, three Velosos, E. Villanueva, Toribio Reyes, Yap Juan & Co., Sy Chuangco & Co., Dy Jong, Sy Giap, and others. The list shows that westerners, Chinese, Creoles, and a strong Chinese-mestizo Visayan sugar planter element participated together in the venture. Another joint venture, the *S.S. Panay*, had more Manila names: A. V. Barretto, A. Inchausti & Co., Francisco Cembrano, Andrés O. de Zarate, and José Rocha.[44]

Other joint ventures did not include the merchant firms. One involved a change in headquarters. On April 22, 1881, Jacobo Zóbel was given a tramway concession by the governor-general of the Philippines, and the following year he formed a company for that purpose with a Madrid banker named Adolfo Bayo (a correspondent of Russell & Sturgis). On December 9, 1883, the first tramcars went out over five lines from the central station on Plaza San Gabriel (today Plaza Cervantes). Ambitious studies were made for tramways in the provinces of central and southern Luzon, Bicol, Panay, and Cebu.

But first the horse-drawn Manila trolley system had to be upgraded, and on October 20, 1888, the steam tramway to Malabon was opened. Joseph Earle Stevens described the service as "slow, but pretty generally good." A single pony pulled the tramcar, "and it is no uncommon sight on a slight rise or sharp turn for all hands to get off and help the vehicle over the difficulty." In his testimony before the Philippine Commission in 1899, Horace Higgins, manager of the British-owned Manila Railroad Co., agreed with his interrogator, the crusty Professor Dean C. Worcester, that the line was "a disgrace to civilization." But they offered no alternatives, and by then Zóbel had passed away.

From the point of view of joint ventures, the company's meeting in Madrid of June 17, 1890, is of special interest. Three points merit mention.

First, Jacobo Zóbel was not the largest stockholder. With 196 shares, he was surpassed by Pedro Roxas (a variant spelling for Rojas) and other Roxases (his relatives by marriage) with 260 shares and Gonzalo Tuason and other Tuasons with 240 shares. Second, in addition to Manila Creoles like Manuel Genato and Angel Marcaida, we find Chinese mestizos (besides the Tuasons) like Máximo Paterno (20 shares) and shipowner "Capitan Luis" Yangco (15 shares), as well as the Chinese Carlos Palanca (10 shares). Third, the meeting's first order of business was a decision to transfer the company's seat to Manila, now that the new Code of Commerce permitted it, where most of the shareholders resided. The Manila board of five members included Gonzalo Tuason, Pedro Roxas, and Jacobo Zóbel. Pedro Roxas, as the representative of the Philippine shareholders, argued vigorously and successfully that the Manila board should have the same powers as the outgoing Madrid board and not have its powers reduced. This was yet another manifestation of the growing assertiveness of Filipino domestic interests as distinct from Spanish interests.[45]

Another type of joint venture involved the practice of capital goods valuation. On September 16, 1892, the La Electricista company took over the electric lighting concession won at public auction earlier that year by Messrs. Millat, Marti, and Mitjans. The new company was formed by these gentlemen, José Moreno Lacalle, and the Tabacalera company. It was capitalized at 500,000 pesos, of which 50,000 represented the value of the concession, contracts, and preparatory work contributed by the three original franchise holders and 100,000 represented the value of the machinery and electrical equipment contributed by Thomson-Houston International Electric Co. of Boston. The rest of the capital would be contributed in cash by the other stockholders. The first board of directors, aside from Marti and Moreno Lacalle, included Armando Villemer, P. E. Heermann, and Gonzalo Tuason. Joseph Earle Stevens described the scene when electric lights were first turned on at the opening of the Royal Exposition in Manila on January 23, 1895:

> All of the elite of Manila were present at the ceremonies, from the Archbishop and Governor-General down to my coachman's wife . . . Governor Blanco opened the fair with a well-worded speech. . . . And just as the speaker had finished and the closing hours of the day arrived, the new electric lights were turned on for the first time. Then all Manila, hitherto illuminated by the dull and dangerous petroleum lamps, shone forth under the radiance of several hundred arclights and a couple of thousand incandescent ones.[46]

San Miguel Brewery: Enterprise, Revolution, and Embargo

The last of the wealthy Barrettos, Enrique Ma. Barretto y de Ycaza, launched what was an innovation not only in the Philippines but in East Asia with the inauguration on October 4, 1890, of the San Miguel Brewery (now San Miguel Corp.), antedating the first breweries in Japan by several years. Referred to as El Príncipe Negro for his dark complexion and his lavish style of entertaining, Barretto's innovativeness encompassed the taking out of a patent making possible the brewing of beer in a warm climate where usual methods are not feasible. This had been granted five months earlier on March 4, 1890, by the director general for agriculture, industry, and commerce. On his property in San Miguel District (from whence the brewery derived its name), he put up, adjacent to his residence, on a riverside lot of just over four thousand square meters, an industrial complex consisting of an ice plant and a brewery (including facilities for bottling and for caulking barrels).

Barretto contracted debts with the Banco Español-Filipino on August 14, 1891, and June 9, 1892, totaling 33,000 pesos secured by a mortgage on the property, and the following year he found it advisable to bring in fresh capital under a new organizational arrangement with other associates. The leader of the new group was Pedro P. Roxas y Castro, who purchased the business for 180,000 pesos by paying Barretto 147,000 and assuming the debt of 33,000. Thereafter, an organization was formed, called by the notary joint accounts (*cuentas en participación*) but later claimed by legal counsel to be an actual company (*sociedad*). In this company, Barretto held 102,500 pesos, Roxas 33,700, Gonzalo Tuason y Patiño 20,000, Vicente P. Fernández y Castro 9,900, and three others 13,900 in all. Roxas was put in charge of management and administration, and his compensation was set at 5 percent of the gross sales. The agreement, although it was signed on June 6, 1893, was effective from April 1. On July 25, 1896, Barretto sold 42,500 pesos of his portion to Roxas, leaving him with 60,000 and raising Roxas's share to 76,200.

Trouble arose with the outbreak of the Philippine Revolution in August 1896. An embargo was placed on all assets belonging to those who directly or indirectly cooperated or would have cooperated with the revolutionary movement. One of those targeted was Roxas, referred to in a Spanish article as "the opulent *indio*, blamed for many years by public opinion for being the first Filipino separatist (*filibustero*)," who took himself out of harm's way by jumping ship in Singapore on his way to Spain in September 1896. (He tried to induce his friend and fellow passenger on the *Isla de Panay*, the national hero José Rizal, to do the same, but Rizal, having given his pledge, declined; he kept his word and lost his life.)

San Miguel Brewery was embargoed, and the remaining owners, led by Barretto and Tuason, approached the governor-general on December 22, 1896, in an effort to have the embargo lifted on their portions of the business. This was denied on February 23, 1897, by the Board of Inspection of Embargoed Properties, on the ground that this would be equivalent to a total lifting since the co-owners held the factory pro indiviso and it was not possible to identify physically which parts belonged to Roxas and which to the rest. What was at issue was an embargo on the personal property of Roxas, to whom, the board disdainfully added, the petitioners had had the misfortune of delivering their funds owing to a lack of insight, ignorance of his personal qualities, or whatever reason. Lengthy proceedings ensued. The Board of Inspectors did put Barretto in charge of the factory, but, just to complicate matters, this was opposed by Roxas's administrator, Enrique Brías de Coya, who claimed the position for himself. On August 26, 1897, Albino Goyenechea, a minor co-owner, sold his share of 6,500 pesos to Luis Kiene, possibly because he feared trouble. On September 7, 1897, the judge advocate general expressed surprise at Barretto's appointment as administrator and ordered his removal.

Barretto's lawyer, Eugenio Purón, had the proceedings transferred from a military jurisdiction (where decisions were deemed final) to the civil courts by invoking an exception in favor of third-party suits (*tercerías*). He argued that the organization was not merely a contract for joint accounts, whose holders only had a right to share in profits or losses but not in property rights, but was actually a company since Roxas had sold to his colleagues part of his share in the business, the patent of invention, and the mortgage on his property. He added that 23,000 pesos of the 33,000-peso debt to the bank had been paid out of company profits, not from Roxas's personal funds. He managed the company not in his own right nor in his own name but by the free decision of his associates, who also had a right to dissolve the company. The associates had the right, in case anyone wished to sell his share, to purchase such share by matching the best outside offer (*derecho de tanteo*). The entity was a juridical person rather than a natural person with, among other things, a right to sell one's share to others, a right exercised in part by Barretto and in whole by Goyenechea. The state's embargo could be protected by being inscribed in the Register of Properties against Roxas's share, lifting it at the same time from the portions of the other associates.

Purón on November 17, 1897, petitioned the judge for permission to summon Roxas, whose whereabouts were unknown, by publication. On January 7, 1898, Purón notified the court that the summons had been published in the official gazette on November 24, 1897, giving Roxas twenty days to answer beginning on the following day. The civil proceedings were overtaken by a decision of a military judge, dismissing the charges against Roxas for lack of evidence, and because the witnesses against him had retracted their testimony. The decree of dismissal was signed on March 14, 1898, by Governor Primo de Rivera. The liberal statesman Francisco Pi y Margall reflected that Roxas was saved by being out of the country at the height of the political hysteria; otherwise he would have suffered the fate of his kinsman Francisco L. Roxas and his friend José Rizal. Six weeks later, with Dewey's victory in Manila Bay and the transfer of sovereignty to the United States, all of this became academic. The following year, Barretto sold out completely to Roxas—another example of an entrepreneur relinquishing his creation to other hands that might have better managerial skills.

A Manila commercial directory for 1901 carried Roxas's advertisement for the San Miguel Brewery as well as an advertisement for the San Miguel Oil Factory, listing him as manager and Vicente Fernandez and Enrique Brías as assistants. The oil factory was located at a nearby plant site but with the same office as the brewery. At that time, a case of six dozen quart bottles of double bock sold for seventeen pesos (or about half that figure in U.S. currency).[47]

Economic Crosscurrents
to the Time of Revolution and Beyond

The transformation of the Philippine economy into an agricultural export economy, completed by the 1870s, set a pattern that would endure for nearly a century. The details might vary, but basically its broad outlines featured the export of primary products and the import of finished goods and food grains. This was not necessarily bad in itself; the market for Philippine products had expanded greatly since the 1820s, and in line with Adam Smith's teaching that the extent of the market determines the division of labor, a reconfiguration of economic factors resulted in growing occupational and regional specialization. The full benefit of the division of labor would have accrued if the momentum of foreign trade growth had continued and the economic forces at work in the economy had developed into the secondary industries that would logically have been expected to follow, particularly with the protectionist policy of 1891.

But several factors conspired to blur the picture and confuse the trends, some connected with the foreign trade process and others exogenous to it. The annual growth of trade volume to midcentury was characterized as "explosive" at about 10 percent (understandably, since it started from a very low base). Thereafter, this annual rate slowed, and from the mid-1880s it was reduced to about 3 percent, although terms of trade had improved since about 1840.[1] As luck would have it, the Philippines achieved its economic transformation at precisely the time when its two leading markets were hit with economic crises, the "climacterics" of the 1870s and 1890s for Great Britain and the panics and depressions of the United States in 1873 and 1893.[2] Formulating the argument in terms of long-term rates of growth blurs, even as it absorbs, the effects of cycles. Earlier (chapter 4) it was seen that Philippine trade underwent marked cyclical episodes in the 1870s and the 1880s. Also blurred are the effects of high and low price years, for example, for sugar, high in 1857 and low in 1887. The latter phenomenon was a specific effect of the European and American promotion of beet sugar culture.

This case illustrates the hazards of the world market. English purchases of Philippine sugar declined permanently after 1881, and only sales to Asian markets maintained overall export levels, but for lower grades, which did not fully compensate for the higher grades consumed in the West.[3] There were no such offsetting factors for other commodities in decline—for example, indigo and *sapan* wood, displaced by aniline dyes, and such items as grass (hemp) cloth, which were subject to falling demand. The fourth-ranking export, coffee, was hit not by weakness in demand but by a blight that wiped out the plants and the industry. Against this, a new and vigorous export line began to appear in respectable quantities at about the time coffee was collapsing, namely, copra and coconut products. But this was late in the nineteenth century, and copra's peak periods, when it would outperform both sugar and abaca, were still in the future.

These divergent market trends showed the unevenness of the benefits that accrued from the economy's involvement in the world market. Rising exports contrasted with declining ones, and there were probably differential growth rates among the former—and also between them and products for domestic consumption. This unevenness led to greater income disparity between regions and occupations even as overall income levels rose. The decline of the domestic textile industry in the face of manufactured imports, it has been seen, had a particularly adverse impact on rural women, who almost exclusively formed the labor force in the industry.

There were also outside forces making for hardship amid prosperity. The 1880s have been called the "decade of death" because of the high mortality rates of the time. Aside from imported epidemics, the increased susceptibility of lower income groups to disease is attributed to the shift in the relative balance between commercial and subsistence agriculture and associated changes in land tenure,[4] with rice having to be imported instead of being available from domestic sources.

Another outside force was the depreciation of the Mexican silver peso, which had been used in the Philippines and Asian trade for centuries, starting in the 1870s. As has been seen, this did not affect exchange rates (based on bills of exchange) until the early 1880s. It was singularly ineffectual in accomplishing what depreciations should, namely, stimulating exports and restraining imports, although it may have helped sugar weather the depressed mid-1880s. In fact, export growth after 1885 was the lowest of the century, and the effect on imports was minor. Several fairly obvious reasons for this can be given. The depreciation affected not only the Mexican dollar but all other silver currencies; these would include those of some of the Philippines' competitors. It has also been seen how major Philippine exports were in the grip of cyclical forces and structural changes in demand at the time, beside which exchange rate effects were puny. On the import side, the depression in industrial countries led to price declines of about 30 percent.[5] Other factors cushioning the effect on import prices have were discussed in chapter 4.

Internally, the effects of silver depreciation were ambiguous, with leading foreign merchants testifying later before the Philippine Commission that the common people in effect operated under a money illusion and that a move to gold would be inadvisable. A Spanish military official writing in 1896 on the eve of the Revolution observed that export traders grew rich from buying domestically in depreciated silver currency while selling on a gold basis on the world market. One particular class was hard hit, namely, Spanish government officials. Already subject to uncertain tenure with the frequent changes in personnel starting with the liberal revolution of the late 1860s, their salaries were paid at face value in silver, but their lifestyles and personal prestige involved heavy consumption of imported clothing and food and their remittances to families in Spain were reduced by more than half of their nominal value. This was not conducive to honesty in public administration.[6]

Against these negative influences there was economic expansion and progress in the aggregate. Certain policies helped. The abolition of the tobacco monopoly, effective in 1882, opened up one of the leading exports to the full play of private enterprise and market forces. Eyewitnesses living at the time testified to the public rejoicing in Manila, with the celebration of *Te Deums* and religious processions despite extremely foul weather. It also gave rise to one of the few examples of private, peninsula-based, Spanish capital investment in the Philippines with the founding in 1881 of the Tabacalera (Compañía General de Tabacos de Filipinas), which, however, would attain its greatest profitability under the subsequent American administration in lines other than tobacco. (Previously, little peninsular Spanish capital had entered, in part because Spain itself was regarded as an economic colony of France.)[7]

Abolition of the tobacco monopoly had not only commercial and entrepreneurial implications but, more importantly, fiscal ones because it had since the late eighteenth century been both the biggest revenue source and the largest expenditure category. In anticipation of the abolition, an urban property tax and an industrial tax were imposed in the late 1870s. With the abolition, the government endeavored to replace the lost revenue by changing the tribute into the *cédula personal* (or poll tax) on a graduated basis, now including Spaniards in its scope (in contrast to the old tribute). At the same time, the *polo,* or statute labor, was reduced from forty days to fifteen. *Gobernadorcillos* and *cabezas de barangay* and their wives were free from tribute and the *cédula personal*. With the higher tariffs of 1891, customs duties and the *cédula* became the main sources of government revenue. The *cédula* may have aroused resentment, as the first overt act of the Philippine Revolution in August 1896 was the tearing up of *cédulas*, but this may have had greater significance as a political act of repudiation of sovereignty than as an economic act of protest. On the expenditure side, the overtly exploitative item for remittances to Spain, amounting at times to nearly 10 percent of expenditures, had disappeared by the 1890s, but some of these remittances continued under the category of "General Obligations."[8]

There was an accumulation of improvements in communications, finance, and infrastructure, some of which have already been mentioned but may be recapitulated here. Steam navigation was introduced in 1848, enabling the Spanish government to put a definitive end to Moro slave-raiding forays and stimulating economic activity in the Visayas. In 1851, the Banco Español-Filipino was established, partly with funds from the *obras pías*, and it continues to this day as the Bank of the Philippine Islands. In 1854, monthly mail delivery between Manila and Hong Kong was established.

The pace accelerated beginning in the 1870s. The extension of the cable to Hong Kong in 1871 brought up-to-date information from western markets just a short steamer trip away. The first telegraph line, between Manila and Cavite, was established in 1872 and later was extended north to Ilocos and south to Bicol. Regular direct steamship service between Manila and Spain, passing through the newly opened Suez Canal, was initiated in 1873. The previous year, the Chartered Bank of India, Australia, and China sent an officer to open a Manila agency, followed three years later by the Hong Kong and Shanghai Banking Corp.[9] In 1880, cable service was opened between Hong Kong and Manila, allowing instant communication with world markets. This revealed a regional demand for the services of the Jesuit-run Manila Observatory, previously supported largely by private merchants and mariners, and the government conferred official status on it in 1884. In 1882, another financial institution, the Monte de Piedad, opened its doors, using more funds from the *obras pías* and functioning as both a savings bank and a pawnshop.

That same year Manila obtained a municipal water system with the inauguration of the Carriedo waterworks, built with *obras pías* funds whose principal had been lost during the British occupation of 1762–64 but whose profit from the cargo on the galleon *Filipino*, which escaped the British blockade, was saved and reinvested until it was deemed sufficient to start construction.

The following year horse-drawn tramways began operating, and in 1888 a steam tramway to Malabon was inaugurated. Two years later came the installation of a telephone system in Manila, the same year that San Miguel Brewery opened. The following year the first traffic went over the partially finished, British-financed Manila Railroad, and in 1892 the Manila-Dagupan railway was completed. (Unfortunately, the latter did not prove profitable, according to testimony later given before the Philippine Commission, although it passed through rice-producing provinces whose output, now easily transportable to markets, greatly increased, raising the possibility for a brief period that the country might return to self-sufficiency in rice. There was a declining trend in rice imports in the early 1890s, and import unit values, after a sharp spike in 1889, fell to levels below those of the 1880s for most of the early 1890s.) In 1894, it was Iloilo's turn to install a telephone system, and the following year both it and Manila got electric lighting.[10]

While these material improvements were taking place, the expansion of the middle class and its growing assertiveness, as noted by Pardo de Tavera, continued apace. One other element must be factored in: unlike the case in many other colonies at the time, it was possible to get an education in such subjects as law, medicine, pharmacy, pedagogy, theology, and fine arts at local institutions of learning, and the members of this class took full advantage of these educational opportunities. By means of scholarships, even youths of poor peasant background like Apolinario Mabini (later to be called the brains of the Revolution) were able to become lawyers. Several were appointed to judicial posts. For example, in Batangas in mid-1888 Felipe Agoncillo and Sotero Laurel figured in the same list of appointments as justices of the peace.[11] Ten years later, Laurel was a delegate to the Malolos Congress and Agoncillo was campaigning for diplomatic recognition of the Aguinaldo government. Tiburcio Hilario of Pampanga, a lawyer and the son of a lawyer, was appointed an interim judge of the Court of First Instance in Pangasinan. Later, after undergoing much hardship and after Aguinaldo declared independence on June 12, 1898, he was elected revolutionary governor of Pampanga.[12]

The first Filipino entrepreneur immolated on the altar of the Revolution was Sancho Valenzuela. John Foreman described him as "a hemp-rope maker in a fairly good way of business" employing more than a hundred men. He had been a gold medalist at the 1895 Regional Exposition for exhibiting seven coils of abaca rope of different diameters. Together with Andres Bonifacio, he was a leader in the first major action of the Revolution at San Juan del Monte (Pinaglabanan) on August 30, 1896, but when the revolutionary forces were repelled by government troops he had to retreat to his starting point in Bacood, Santa Mesa, probably the site of George Sturgis's old rope walk. A photograph of his arrest shows a tall man in a white suit flanked by a few followers and surrounded by Filipino Civil Guards in Spanish uniforms. He was executed on September 4, 1896.[13]

In the meantime, foreign (mostly British) investors seemed undeterred by the turn of events. Although they were neutral, they probably sympathized with the Filipinos' democratic aspirations and the latter held them in high regard. It has already been mentioned that the country's railroadization would have been extended by the railroad begun by Warner Barnes from Iligan to Lake Lanao in Mindanao. Mention has also been made of a British textile factory set up in 1897 as a probable response to the protectionist tariff of 1891, which was a logical next step in the country's economic development. As the nineteenth century waned, all indications were suggestive, and Victor Clark wrote:

> A period of industrial development and expansion immediately preceded the insurrection that marked the beginning of the end of Spanish rule in the Philippines. . . . With political stability and a tolerable administration an era of great prosperity seemed promised during the last decade of the century. These happy anticipations, however, ended in disappointment on account of domestic revolt and foreign war.[14]

With the temporary frustration of the Filipino struggle for independence, sovereignty passed to the United States and conditions changed. Many material and institutional improvements were made—in public health, public works, public education, public administration, and mon-

339

etary management, to say nothing of the greater individual freedoms protected by law. Innovations such as the internal combustion engine would revolutionize transportation and affect settlement patterns. Preferential access to the huge American market would stimulate great increases in exports and promote levels of living undreamed of before the twentieth century. But this very export growth would lead to something the country had never known before. Under Spain, the Philippine economy had never been complementary to that of the metropole. This would now change. The price of twentieth-century progress would be economic dependence.

Political authority and economic initiative would now be joined under U.S. rule, and the Philippines would move from the East Asian to the Southeast Asian mold. An earlier generation of nonpolitical, economically motivated Americans had contributed materially to the rise of a Filipino middle class. The members of this class would now lead the people in dealing with the new suzerains, at times in cooperation, at other times in confrontation, as the Filipino struggle for independence moved from the fields of battle to the halls of legislation.

NOTES

Notes to Chapter 1

1.   Robert B. Fox, "Looking at the Prehispanic Community: The Structure of Prehis-
toric Filipino Communities," in *Filipino Heritage: The Making of a Nation,* edited by Alfredo R.
Roces, 2:352–59 (Manila: Lahing Pilipino, 1977); Robert B. Fox, "The Archeological Record of
Chinese Influences in the Philippines," *Philippine Studies* 15, no. 1 (January 1967): 41–62; F.
Landa Jocano, *Philippine Prehistory* (Quezon City: Philippine Center for Advanced Studies,
University of the Philippines System, 1975), 136–45, 161–76; F. Landa Jocano, *The Philippines
at the Spanish Contact* (Manila: MCS Enterprises, 1975), 2–26; William Henry Scott, "Class
Structure in the Unhispanized Philippines," *Philippine Studies,* 27 (2d qtr., 1979): 137–59. The
epigraph is from Marcelo H. del Pilar, *Filipinas en las Cortes* (Madrid: Imp. de Enrique
Jaramillo y Compañía, 1890), 11, 9.

2.   Miguel A. Bernad, S.J., *The Christianization of the Philippines: Problems and Perspectives* (Manila: Filipiniana Book Guild, 1972); Miguel A. Bernad, S.J., "The Ancient Slave Market," in Roces, *Filipino Heritage,* 2:330–36; Miguel A. Bernad, S.J., "A Booming Inter-island
Trade," in Roces, *Filipino Heritage,* 3:645–50; H. Otley Beyer, "Early History of Philippine Re-
lations with Foreign Countries, Especially China," historical introduction to E. Arsenio
Manuel, *Chinese Elements in the Tagalog Language,* vii–xxv (Manila: Filipiniana Publications,
1948); Horacio de la Costa, S.J., "The Legal Basis of Spanish Imperial Sovereignty," *Philippine
Studies* 1, no. 2 (September 1953): 155–62; S. V. Epistola, "The Day the Chinese Came to
Trade," in Roces, *Filipino Heritage,* 3:581–88; Friedrich Hirth and W. W. Rockhill, trans., *Chao
Ju Kua: His Work on the Chinese and Arab Trade in the Twelfth and Thirteenth Centuries, Entitled
Chu-fan-chi* (St. Petersburg: Printing Office of the Imperial Academy of Sciences, 1911; rpt.
Taipei: Literature House, 1964), 159–62; William Henry Scott, *Barangay: Sixteenth Century Phil-
ippine Culture and Society* (Quezon City: Ateneo de Manila University Press, 1994), 74–76;
Jocano, *Spanish Contact,* 55, 78; Cesar Adib Majul, "Celestial Traders in Sulu," in Roces,
Filipino Heritage, 3:589–92; E. P. Patanñe, "Overseas Trade before Magellan," in Roces,
Filipino Heritage, 767–69; E. P. Patanñe, *The Philippines in the World of Southeast Asia: A
Cultural History* (Quezon City: Enterprise Publications, 1972), 263–96, 321–55; "*Tome
Pires,*" in *Travel Accounts of the Islands (1513–1787),* 1–3 (Manila: Filipiniana Book Guild,
1971); Wu Ching-hong, "A Study of References to the Philippines in Chinese Sources
from Earliest Times to the Ming Dynasty," *Philippine Social Sciences and Humanities Review* 24, nos. 1–2 (January-June 1959): v–xii, 1–181, esp. 88–111. For a collection of material, some of it somewhat earlier, see Mauro Garcia, ed., *Readings in Philippine Prehistory*
(Manila: Filipiniana Book Guild, 1979).

3.   Rafael Bernal, *Prologue to Philippine History* (Manila: Solidaridad, 1967), 3–9.

4.   For a one-stop source of documentary material on all the expeditions, see Emma
Helen Blair and James Alexander Robertson, *The Philippine Islands,* 55 vols. (Cleveland:
Arthur Clark, 1903–9) (hereafter BR), esp. vols. 1–3 and 23–24 (documents and accounts,
some in summary form, mostly in English translation). For the first three expeditions, see
Martín Fernández de Navarrete, *Colección de los viajes y descubrimientos que hicieron por mar los
españoles desde fines del siglo XV,* vols. 4 and 5 (Buenos Aires: Editorial Guaranía, 1946). For the
Villalobos and Legazpi expeditions, see *Colección de documentos inéditos de ultramar* (Madrid:
Sucesores de Rivadeneyra), vol. 2 (1886) and vol. 3 (1887) (hereafter DIU). For the Legazpi

expedition, Spanish documents with English translations are found in Rafael López, O.S.A., and Alfonso Felix Jr., trans., *The Christianization of the Philippines* (Manila: Historical Conservation Society, 1965). For documents in English translation, see Mauro Garcia, Carlos Quirino, and Luis Ma. Araneta, eds., *The Colonization and Conquest of the Philippines by Spain* (Manila: Filipiniana Book Guild, 1965); and Virginia Benitez Licuanan and Jose Llavador Mira, *The Philippines under Spain, Book II (1564–1573)* (Manila: National Trust for Historical and Cultural Preservation of the Philippines, 1991). For secondary works on Magellan, see any standard biography, for example, Arthur Sturges Hildebrand, *Magellan* (New York: Harcourt, Brace, 1924); E. F. Benson, *Ferdinand Magellan* (New York: Harper, 1930); Charles McKew Parr, *Ferdinand Magellan, Circumnavigator* (New York: Crowell, 1964), first published under the title *So Noble a Captain* in 1953; Stefan Zweig, *Conqueror of the Seas: The Story of Magellan*, translated by Eden Paul and Cedar Paul (New York: Literary Guild of America, 1938); and George Sanderlin, *First around the World: A Journal of Magellan's Voyage* (New York: Harper and Row, 1964). For biographies of Elcano, see Mairin Mitchell, *Elcano: The First Circumnavigator* (London: Herder, 1958); and Eustaquio Fernández de Navarrete, *Historia de Juan Sebastian del Cano* (Vitoria: Hijos de Manteli, 1872). For an overview of the five expeditions, See J. V. Braganza, S.V.D., *The Encounter: The Epic Story of the Christianization of the Philippines* (Manila: Catholic Trade School, 1965); Alfonso Trueba, *La conquista de Filipinas* (Mexico: Editorial Jus, 1959); and Pablo Pastells, S.J., "Historia general de las Islas Filipinas," in Pedro Torres Lanzas, *Catálogo de los documentos relativos a las Islas Filipinas*, vol. 1: *1493–1572* (Barcelona: Compañía General de Tabacos de Filipinas, 1925), XLVIII–CCCIV. For secondary works on Legazpi, see José Arteche, *Legazpi. Historia de la conquista de Filipinas* (Zarauz: Editorial Icharopena, 1947); Bernad, *Christianization*; Edward J. McCarthy, O.S.A., *Spanish Beginnings in the Philippines, 1564–1572* (Washington, D.C.: Catholic University of America Press, 1943); Pompeyo de Mesa, O.P., and Isaias Villaflores, O.P., *Intramuros and Beyond* (Manila: Letran College, 1975), esp. the articles by E. P. Patanñe and Eric Casiño; José Sanz y Díaz, *López de Legazpi* (Madrid: Editorial "Gran Capitan," 1950); Andrew Sharp, *Adventurous Armada* (Christchurch, N.Z.: Whitcombe and Tombs, 1961); and William Henry Scott, *Looking for the Prehispanic Filipino* (Quezon City: New Day, 1992), 40–63. For a biography of Urdaneta, see Mariano Cuevas, S.J., *Monje y marino. La vida y los tiempos de Fray Andres de Urdaneta* (Mexico: Galatea, 1943). For secondary articles, see Jose Arcilla, S.J., "Raíces de la historia filipina," *Crónica de Manila*, September 26, 1993, 41; Ferdinand Blumentritt, "Los conquistadores militares y civiles de Filipinas. Apuntes para una crítica de la historia de la conquista. II," *La Solidaridad, Quincenario Democratico* (Madrid) 6, no. 132 (July 31, 1894): 154–56; Lucio Gutiérrez, O.P., "The Christianization of the Philippines: Myth and Realities," *Philippiniana Sacra* 11, no. 32 (May-August 1976): 203–91; and Charles E. Nowell, "Arellano versus Urdaneta," *Pacific Historical Review* 31, no. 2 (May 1962): 111–20.

5. Garcia, Quirino, and Araneta, *Colonization*, 162.

6. DIU, 2:284–92, 409.

7. Quotes are from Garcia, Quirino, and Araneta, *Colonization*, 114, 150, respectively.

8. Fernández de Navarrete, *Colección*, 5:424; Sanz y Díaz, *López de Legazpi*, 187–88.

9. Jocano, *Philippines at Spanish Contact*, 55; Fernández de Navarrete, *Colección*, 5:401.

10. DIU, 2:314–18; 3:188, 218–21; Licuanan and Llavador Mira, *Philippines under Spain*, 123–24; Bernad, *Christianization*, 100–101; Garcia, Quirino, and Araneta, *Colonization*, 127–226.

11. Garcia, Quirino, and Araneta, *Colonization*, 141, 146, 255.

12. DIU, 2:312–16, 3:127–28; Garcia, Quirino, and Araneta, *Colonization*, 174.

13. Rafael Bernal, "The Chinese Colony in Manila, 1570–1770," in *The Chinese in the Philippines,* edited by Alfonso Felix, 1:46 (Manila: Solidaridad, 1966); C. R. Boxer, "*Plata es Sangre*: Sidelights on the Drain of Spanish American Silver to the Far East, 1550–1700," *Philippine Studies* 18, no. 3: 457–78; *Enciclopedia universal ilustrada,* vol. 45 (Barcelona: Hijos de J. Espasa, 1921), 482.

14. Lopez and Felix, *Christianization,* 126–17, 341.

15. Joaquín] Martínez de Zúñiga, *An Historical View of the Philippine Islands*, translated by John Maver (London: J. Asperne and Nonaville and Fell, 1814), 1:125.

Notes to Chapter 2

1. The basic references are William Lytle Schurz, *The Manila Galleon* (New York: Dutton, 1939; rpt. 1959); Pierre Chaunu, *Les Philippines et le Pacifique des Ibériques* (Paris: SEVPEN, 1960); and Manuel Azcárraga y Palmero, *La libertad de comercio en las Islas Filipinas* (Madrid: Noguera, 1871). Passages without footnotes are based largely on Schurz and Azcárraga. See also Vito Alessio Robles, *Acapulco en la historia y en la leyenda,* 2d ed. (Mexico City: Ediciones Botas, 1948); Manuel Carballo et al., "El arte en el comercio con Asia," *Artes de México* (Mexico City) 22, no. 190 (1977); Francisco Santiago Cruz, *La Nao de China* (México: Editorial Jus, 1962); Maria Lourdes Díaz-Trechuelo, "Dos nuevos derroteros del galeón de Manila (1730 y 1773)," *Anuario de estudios americanos,* tomo XIII (Seville, 1956); John Galvin, "Supplies from Manila for the California Missions, 1781–1783," *Philippine Studies* 12, no. 3 (July 1964): 494–510; Percy Hill, "The Old Manila Galleons," *University of Manila Journal of East Asiatic Studies* 7, no. 3 (July 1958): 280–84 (reprinted from *Philippine Magazine* 32, no. 3 [March 1935]: 132, 155–57; Francisco Mallari, S.J., "The Wreck of the Santo Cristo de Burgos and the Trial of Its Officers," *Philippine Studies* 38 (1st qtr., 1990): 65–83; David F. Marley, "The Great Galleon: The *Santísima Trinidad* (1750–65)," *Philippine Studies* 41 (2d qtr., 1993): 167–81; Gonzalo Obregón et al., "El Galeón de Manila," *Artes de México* 27, no. 143 (1971); Gilbert S. Perez, "Manila Galleons and Mexican Pieces of Eight," *Philippine Social Sciences and Humanities Review* 19, no. 2 (June 1954): 193–215; Serafin D. Quiason, *English "Country Trade" with the Philippines, 1644–1765* (Quezon City: University of the Philippines Press, 1966); Serafin D. Quiason, "The Sampan Trade, 1570–1770," in Felix, *Chinese,* 160–74; Eulogio B. Rodriguez, *The Philippines and Mexico* (Manila: National Library, 1941); Vera Valdés Lakowsky, *De las minas al mar. Historia de la plata mexicana en Asia, 1565–1834* (México: Fondo de Cultura Económica, 1987); and Javier Wimer, ed., *El Galeón del Pacífico. Acapulco-Manila, 1565–1815* (State of Guerrero, Mexico: Gobierno Constitucional del Estado de Guerrero, 1992).

2. J. C. Van Leur, *Indonesian Trade and Society: Essays in Asian Social and Economic History* (The Hague and Bandung: W. van Hoeve, 1955), 121–22, 193–94.

3. Daniel F. Doeppers, "The Development of Philippine Cities before 1900," *Journal of Asian Studies* 31, no. 4 (August 1972): 769–92, esp. 781–82, 791. For more on Southeast Asian primate cities, see T. G. McGee, *The Southeast Asian City: A Social Geography of the Primate Cities of Southeast Asia* (New York: Praeger, 1967), esp. 23–25, 52–57.

4. Chaunu, *Les Philippines,* 15–17, 242–43.

5. Consuelo Maquivar, "Derrotero histórico del galeón de Acapulco," in Carballo et al., "El Arte," 14. In this source, tamarind is included among plants transshipped to Mexico, but this is contradicted in Rodriguez, *The Philippines and Mexico,* 28, which says that tamarind was brought from Africa to the Philippines through Mexico.

6. Rogelio Ruiz Gomar, "Metales," in Carballo et al., "El Arte," 72; Obregón et al., "El galeón de Manila," 97, 110, 113; Virginia Armella de Aspe, "Artes asiáticas y novohispanas" in Wimer, *El galeón del Pacifico*, 230–31; Fernando Benítez, "Introducción," in Wimer, *El galeón del Pacifico*, 38–39. The sources disagree on whether the work was done by Chinese or Japanese artisans, and also on the Christian name of the Mexican designer, Rodríguez Juárez, of the grille.

7. Galvin, "Supplies," 494–95, 500.

8. Clyde Hubbard, "Monedas de plata en los galeones del Pacífico," in Wimer, *El galeón del Pacifico*, 155; Carmen Yuste, "El galeón en la economía colonial," in Wimer, *El galeón del Pacifico*, 104; Valdés Lakowsky, *De las minas al mar*, 206; Perez, "Manila Galleons," 204–6.

9. Rodriguez, *The Philippines and Mexico*, 28; Perez, "Manila Galleons," 202–3. What is probably the best-known Filipino children's folksong lists the various plants growing around a humble nipa hut. Many if not the majority of them are introduced rather than indigenous. Thus, the galleons did have a lasting impact on the diet of the common people.

10. Valdés Lakowsky, *De las minas al mar*, 127–28.

11. Obregón et al., "El galeón de Manila," 74–93.

12. Quiason, "Sampan Trade," 162–65; "Galeones" books of photocopied documents, port entries (*peso marchante*) dated June 12, 1792, May 6, 1794, November 25, 1794, and June 6, 1796, Philippine National Archives (hereafter PNA); O. D. Corpuz, *The Roots of the Filipino Nation* (Quezon City: Aklahi Foundation, 1989), 1:530.

13. C. R. Boxer, *Jan Compagnie in War and Peace, 1602–1799: A Short History of the Dutch East India Company* (Hong Kong, Singapore, and Kuala Lumpur: Heinemann Asia, 1979), 23.

14. Joaquín Martínez de Zuñiga, *Estadismo de las Islas Filipinas* (Madrid: Viuda de M. Minuesa de los Ríos, 1893), 1:267.

15. [Francisco Leandro de Viana], "Ynforme que hizo el Conde de Tepa del Consejo de Indias sobre el comercio de Filipinas," transcript in "Libro de varios papeles," Ticknor Collection, Boston Public Library, folios 217, 218, 218 verso, 228 verso, 229 (author's translation); "Reglamento que se observará en el repartimiento del buque de la nao de Acapulco," in "Acapulco," bk. 3, photocopies of documents, PNA.

16. Díaz–Trechuelo, "Dos nuevos derroteros," 8, 44–46.

17. Viana, "Ynforme," folio 215.

18. Martínez de Zúñiga, *Estadismo*, 269; Tomás de Comyn, *State of the Philippine Islands*, translated by William Walton (London: T. and J. Allman, 1821), 70–81; Luis Prudencio Álvarez y Tejero, *De las Islas Filipinas* (Valencia: Imprenta de Cabrerizo, 1842), 60–62; Rafael Díaz Arenas, *Memorias históricas y estadísticas de Filipinas* (Manila: Imprenta del Diario de Manila, 1850), vol. 2, bk. 13 (unpaginated); Schurz, *Manila Galleon*, 15, 167–72, 190, 256; Felix Riesenberg, *The Pacific Ocean* (New York: Whittlesey House, 1940), 79; Chaunu, *Les Philippines*, 268–69.

19. Perez, "Manila Galleons," 199; Santiago Cruz, *La Nao*, 125–27.

20. Marco A. Almazán, "El Galeón de Manila," in Obregón et al., "El galeón de Manila," 7–8, 23–24; Honorio E. Ybera, Jr., "La búsqueda incesante," *Crónica de Manila*, July 31, 1994, 38. Rafael Bernal estimates that in 250 years thirty to thirty-five thousand Mexicans migrated to the Philippines and the Marianas, which he considers a small number. See his *Mexico en Filipinas. Estudio de una transculturación* (Mexico City: Universidad Nacional Autónoma de México, 1965), 124–25.

21. Santiago Cruz, *La Nao*, 203; Schurz, *Manila Galleon*, 211.

22. Quiason, *English "Country Trade,"* 5–6, 28–30.

23. Ibid., 5–11, 26–28, 43–49, 62–76, 87–90, 139–40, 183–88, 196–201; Chaunu, *Les Philippines*, 148–98, 219; Schurz, *Manila Galleon*, 59.

24. Chaunu, *Les Philippines*, 244–64; Santiago Cruz, *La Nao*, 114–15; Galvin, "Supplies," 494.

25. Chaunu, *Les Philippines*, 219; Schurz, *Manila Galleon*, 189.

26. Maria Lourdes Díaz-Trechuelo, "El comercio de Filipinas durante la segunda mitad del siglo XVIII," *Revista de Indias*, nos. 93–94 (July-December 1963): 474–77.

27. Juan Vicente Güemez Pacheco de Padilla Horcasitas y Aguayo, Conde de Revilla Gigedo, *Instrucción reservada que el Conde de Revilla Gigedo dió a su sucesor en el mando. Marqués de Branciforte sobre el gobierno de este continente en el tiempo que fué su virey* (Mexico: Imprenta de la calle de las escalerillas, 1831), 104–5; Schurz, *Manila Galleon*, 60, 396–99; Alessio Robles, *Acapulco*, 145–51; Valdés Lakowsky, *De la minas al mar*, 275.

28. Valdés Lakowsky, *De la minas al mar*, 216–31, 235–36, 357–58.

29. Schurz, *Manila Galleon*, 38; Nick Joaquin, *Manila, My Manila: A History for the Young* (Manila: City of Manila, 1990), 36. Joaquin has been awarded the title of national artist. The epigraph to this chapter is taken from the same book, page 33.

Notes to Chapter 3

1. Richard Herr, *The Eighteenth-Century Revolution in Spain* (Princeton: Princeton University Press, 1958), 11; Earl J. Hamilton, "The Decline of Spain," in *Essays in Economic History*, edited by E. M. Carus-Wilson, 215–26, esp. 221 (London: Edward Arnold, 1954). The expulsion of the Moriscos in 1609–14, contrary to prevalent opinion, was not a major cause of the economic decline.

2. Herr, *Eighteenth-Century Revolution*, 47–48; Schurz, *Manila Galleon*, 53–54; Roland Dennis Hussey, *The Caracas Company, 1728–1784* (Cambridge: Harvard University Press, 1934), 36–37; Andres V. Castillo, *Spanish Mercantilism: Gerónimo de Uztáriz—Economist* (New York: 1930), 76–77, 180. Castillo, cited in a note in Schumpeter's monumental *History of Economic Analysis*, went on to become governor of the Central Bank of the Philippines from 1960 to 1967.

3. W. E. Cheong, "The Decline of Manila as the Spanish Entrepot in the Far East, 1785–1826: Its Impact on the Pattern of Southeast Asian Trade," *Journal of Southeast Asian Studies* 2 (September 1971): 142, 150.

4. Maria Lourdes Díaz-Trechuelo, "Philippine Economic Development Plans, 1746–1779," *Philippine Studies* 12, no. 2 (April 1964): 203–9, 212–31.

5. Maria Lourdes Díaz-Trechuelo, "El comercio de Filipinas," 464–70.

6. Maria Lourdes Díaz-Trechuelo, "The Economic Development of the Philippines in the Second Half of the Eighteenth Century," *Philippine Studies* 11, no. 2 (April 1963): 218; *Ordenanzas de la Compañía de Comercio, que se ha Formado en esta Ciudad de Manila Bajo el Patrocinio de Nuestra Señora del Rosario y la Protección de Su Magestad, y en su Real Nombre, de la de el Muy Illustre Señor D. Pedro Manuel de Arandía, y Santestevan, Cavallero Professo del Orden de Calatrava, Gentil-hombre de Cámara de entrada del Rey de las dos Sicilias, Mariscal de Campo de los Exércitos de su Magestad, Capitán del Regimiento de sus Reales Guardias Españolas de Infantería, de su Consejo, Governador, y Capitán General de estas Islas Philipinas, y Presidente de su Real Audiencia* (Manila: Collegio, y Universidad del Señor Santo Thomás, 1755), preamble, paras. 8–12, 15, 19, 21, 23, 34.

7. Díaz-Trechuelo, "Philippine Economic Development Plans," 209–12; Maria Lourdes Díaz-Trechuelo, "Eighteenth-Century Philippine Economy: Agriculture," *Philippine Studies* 14, no. 1 (January 1966): 67–70; "Commerce of the Philipinas Islands," in BR, 47:251–84; "Viana's Memorial of 1765," in BR, 48:283–84.

8. Díaz-Trechuelo, "Comercio de Filipinas," 466–67.

9. Azcárraga y Palmero, *La libertad*, 117–18; Schurz, *Manila Galleon*, 397, 399, 401, 411; Eduardo Malo de Luque [Duque de Almodóvar], *Historia política de los establecimientos ultramarinos de las naciones europeas* (Madrid: Antonio de Sancha, 1790), 5:318; *Exposición de la Compañía de Filipinas relativa a su establecimiento y a su importancia político-mercantil: a los medios que ha empleado para llenar los fines de su instituto; y a la justicia y necesidad de su conservación para utilidad general del estado, dirigida por su junta de gobierno a las Cortes generales y extraordinarias de la nación* (Cádiz: Imprenta de D. Manuel Ximénez Carreño, 1813), 4–5; Díaz-Trechuelo, "Comercio de Filipinas," 478–82; Maria Lourdes Díaz-Trechuelo, "Eighteenth-Century Philippine Economy: Commerce," *Philippine Studies* 14, no. 2 (April 1966): 272–73; Miguel Capella and Antonio Matilla Tascon, *Los cinco Gremios Mayores de Madrid* (Madrid, 1957), 301–4. For a brief background in English on the major guilds, see Herr, *Eighteenth-Century Revolution*, 124–28; and Hussey, *Caracas Company*, 224–26.

10. Adele Ogden, *The California Sea Otter Trade, 1784–1848* (Berkeley: University of California Press, 1941), 1. See also Edwin Corle, *The Royal Highway* (Indianapolis: Bobbs-Merrill, 1949), 44, 116–20, for a semipopular account.

11. Díaz-Techuelo, "Dos nuevos derroteros," 55–72.

12. Holden Furber, "An Abortive Attempt at Anglo-Spanish Commercial Cooperation in the Far East in 1793," *Hispanic American Historical Review* 15, no. 4 (November 1935): 450, n. 8; Ogden, *California Sea Otter Trade*, 15–30; Galvin, "Supplies," 494–95.

13. Furber, "Abortive Attempt," 450–52; Ogden, *California Sea Otter Trade*, 19, 31, 155; *Hispanic American Historical Review*, 3, no. 4 (November 1920): 500, n. 36; Franciso de las Barras de Aragón, *Cuatro documentos del Archivo de Indias referentes a la obra realizada por España en Filipinas, en el siglo XVIII* (Seville: Sobrinos de Izquierdo, 1918), 3; Dr. Vernon D. Tate, interview with the author, August 3, 1954. Dr. Tate, of the Massachusetts Institute of Technology, did a great deal of research on the San Blas–Manila connection.

14. Francisco de las Barras de Aragón, "Don Francisco Xavier Salgado y sus obras en Filipinas en el siglo XVIII," in *Asociación española para el progreso de las ciencias, Congreso de Sevilla*, vol. 8, sec. 6, 53–122 (Madrid: Imprenta Clásica Española, 1917); Maria Lourdes Díaz-Techuelo, "Eighteenth-Century Philippine Economy: Mining," *Philippine Studies* 13 no. 4 (October 1965): 770–74, 787–90; Maria Lourdes Díaz-Trechuelo, "Economic Development of the Philippines," 216--17, 220–21; Díaz-Trechuelo, "Eighteenth-Century Philippine Economy: Agriculture," 74–92, 95–111, 113–14; Díaz-Trechuelo, "Eighteenth-Century Philippine Economy: Commerce," 264.

15. José Montero y Vidal, *Historia general de Filipinas* (Madrid: Viuda e hijos de Tello, 1894), 2:284–96, 307–15; María Luisa Rodríguez Baena, *La Sociedad Económica de Amigos del País de Manila en el siglo XVIII* (Seville: Escuela de Estudios Hispano-Americanos, 1966), esp. 1–20, 24–39, 81–89; María Belén Bañas Llanos, "Don Juan de Cuéllar y sus Comisiones Científicas en Filipinas (1739?–1801)," Ph.D. diss., Universidad Complutense, Madrid, 1991, 81–82, 181–82, 370–72; Ramón González Fernández and Federico Moreno Jerez, *Manual del viajero en Filipinas* (Manila: Establecimiento tipógrafico de Santo Tomás, 1875), 172, 299; Carlos Recur, *Filipinas: Estudios administrativos y comerciales* (Madrid: Imprenta de Ramon Moreno y Ricardo Rojas, 1879), 48; T. H. Pardo de Tavera, "Results of the Economic Develop-

ment of the Philippines," lecture delivered before the Philippine Columbian Association, Manila, 1912; Conrado Benitez, *History of the Philippines* (Boston: Ginn, 1926), 314–15; Max Tornow, "A Sketch of the Economic Condition of the Philippines," U.S. Congress, Senate, 55th Cong., 3d sess., S. Doc. 62, pt. 2 (Washington, D.C.: Government Printing Office, 1899), 618; Schurz, *Manila Galleon*, 54–55; Malo de Luque, *Historica politica*, 5:324–27, app. 1; Díaz-Trechuelo, "Eighteenth-Century Philippine Economy: Mining," 780–87; Díaz-Trechuelo, "Economic Development in the Philippines," 227, 229–30; Díaz-Trechuelo, "Eighteenth-Century Philippine Economy: Agriculture," 70–74, 92–95, 107, 119–23; Díaz-Trechuelo, "Eighteenth-Century Philippine Economy: Commerce," 262; Díaz-Trechuelo, "La defensa de Filipinas en el último cuarto del siglo XVIII," in *Anuario de Estudios Americanos* (Seville, 1964), 11–12; Comyn, *State*, l04–13, 148–49, 160, 288–89; Reynaldo Y. Palma and Benjamin C. de la Fuente, "The Economic Reforms of Jose Basco y Vargas (1778–1787)," *Anuaryo/Annales* 8 (1991): 96–107; Horacio de la Costa, S.J., *Asia and the Philippines* (Manila: Solidaridad, 1967), 69–71, 132. For a full-length treatise on the tobacco monopoly, see Ed. C. de Jesus, *The Tobacco Monopoly in the Philippines: Bureaucratic Enterprise and Social Change, 1766–1880* (Quezon City: Ateneo de Manila University Press, 1980).

16. Azcárraga y Palmero, *La libertad*, 114–15; Pardo de Tavera, "Results"; Hussey, *Caracas Company,* 203–4; Schurz, *Manila Galleon*, 410–11.

17. Hussey, *Caracas Company,* 296; Schurz, *Manila Galleon*, 412; Azcárraga y Palmero, *La libertad*, 119; *Exposición dirigida a las Cortes por la junta de gobierno de la Compañía de Filipinas* (Madrid: Imprenta de Don Mateo Repullés, 1821), app. 1, ii–iv, n. The value of the real vellon, generally computed at twenty per peso, varied from time to time; there were periods when the equivalence was only fifteen to one.

18. Azcárraga y Palmero, *La libertad*; Schurz, *Manila Galleon*; Hussey, *Caracas Company*, 299; *Real cédula de erección de la Compañía de Filipinas de 10 de marzo de 1785* (Madrid: Joachin lbarra, [1785]), esp. 6–8.

19. Malo de Luque, *Historica politica*, app., 11–94; Azcárraga y Palmero, *La libertad*, 120–28; Schurz, *Manila Galleon*, 412–16; Hussey *Caracas Company*, 296–99; *Real cédula,* esp. 19–20, 26, 30–32; *Exposición de la Compañía*, 9–10.

20. *Exposición de la Compañía*, 16; Weng Eang Cheong, "Changing the Rules of the Game (the India-Manila Trade, 1785–1809)," *Journal of Southeast Asian Studies* 1, no. 2 (1970): 1, 10.

21. James Cloghessy, "The Philippines and the Royal Philippine Company," *Mid-America: An Historical Review* 42, no. 2 (April 1960), 90, 98–101; Maria Lourdes Díaz-Trechuelo, *La Real Compañía de Filipinas* (Seville: Escuela de Estudios Hispano-Americanos, 1965), 71, 76, 80, 86, 88, 184–96.

22. Malo de Luque, *Historica politica*, 363; Azcárraga y Palmero, *La libertad*, 137–39; Schurz, *Manila Galleon*, 416.

23. Díaz-Trechuelo, *Real Compañía*, 77.

24. Malo de Luque, *Historica politica*, 334, 347–48, 365; Azcárraga y Palmero, *La libertad*, 133–34; *Exposición de la Compañía*, 39.

25. Malo de Luque, *Historica politica*, 350; Azcárraga y Palmero, *La libertad*, 134–35; *Exposición de la Compañía*, 40–41.

26. Malo de Luque, *Historica politica*, 350–51, 367–68; *Exposición de la Compañía*, 47–53. The term *Indian* (*indio*) was used by the Spaniards to designate a Filipino of native Malay stock. Originally a neutral word, it acquired a pejorative connotation about the middle of the nineteenth century as tension mounted between Filipinos and Spaniards.

27. Malo de Luque, *Historica politica*, 33, 351–52, 358–61, 366–67; Azcárraga y Palmero, *La libertad*, 134–37; *Exposición de la Compañía*, 41–47; Bañas Llanos, "Don Juan de Cuéllar," 157, 162–69.

28. Malo de Luque, *Historica politica*, 333, 354–56; Azcárraga y Palmero, *La libertad*, 132–33, 135; *Exposición de la Compañía*, 53–54. See also Barras de Aragón, *Cuatro documentos*, for memoranda on cinnamon culture in the Philippines.

29. *Exposición de la Compañía*, 56.

30. Jean Mallat, *Les Philippines* (Paris: Arthus Bertrand, 1846), 2:320; Malo de Luque, *Historica politica*, app. 69; Tornow, "Sketch," 616–17; Azcárraga y Palmero, *La libertad*, 150; Thomas R. McHale and Mary C. McHale, *Early American-Philippine Trade: The Journal of Nathaniel Bowditch in Manila, 1796* (New Haven: Yale University, Southeast Asian Studies, 1962), 23, 26. A shorter account of the same visit is found in the East India Marine Society Journals, vol. 1, no. 3 (mss.), Peabody Essex Museum, Salem, Massachusetts (hereafter PEM), but the year given is 1797. For the *Abigail*, see "Quenta y razon del peso marchante q.ᵉ ha satisfho. D. Christoval Thornton Capitan de la Frag.ᵗᵃ Inglesa Americana nomb.ᵃ Abigael Proced.ᵗᵉ de Rodesilan Puerto de America q.ᵉ vino en este pres.ᵗᵉ año a este comercio," in "Galeones," photocopies of documents, PNA.

31. Malo de Luque, *Historica politica*, 377–78; Azcárraga y Palmero, *La libertad*, 141–42; Schurz, *Manila Galleon*, 58–59; Montero y Vidal, *Historia general*, 302–3; Díaz-Trechuelo, *Real Compañía*, 275–77; Cheong, "Decline of Manila," 150; Cheong, "Changing the Rules," 5–8.

32. Azcárraga y Palmero, *La libertad*, 143–44; Comyn, *State*, 90; Montero y Vidal, *Historia general*, 304; McHale and McHale, *Early American-Philippine Trade*, 19, 34, 45, 48, 50.

33. Cheong, "Changing the Rules," 9, 16–17.

34. Azcárraga y Palmero, *La libertad*, 143; Cheong, "Decline of Manila," 149; Alexander M'Konochie, *A Summary View of the Statistics and Existing Commerce of the Principal Shores of the Pacific* (London: J. H. Richardson, 1818), 145.

35. Díaz-Trechuelo, *Real Compañía*, 260–63, 277–78; Azcárraga y Palmero, *La libertad*, 147.

36. Díaz-Trechuelo, *Real Compañía*, 111.

37. See, inter alia, *Exposición de la Compañía. Nueva real cédula de la Compañía de Filipinas de 12 de julio de 1803* (Madrid: En la imprenta de la viuda de Ibarra [1803?]); *Exposición dirigida*; and Díaz-Trechuelo, *Real Compañía*.

38. Cheong, "Decline of Manila," 148; Comyn, *State*, 290–91.

39. This writer follows Professor Usher's view that a factory is characterized primarily not by its use of machinery but by its centralized control and massing of laborers in the workplace, away from their homes.

Notes to Chapter 4

1. Michael Greenberg, *British Trade and the Opening of China, 1800–1842* (Cambridge: Cambridge University Press, 1951), 3–7; Romesh Dutt, *The Economic History of India* (Delhi: Government of India, 1960), 1:183–89; Hallett Abend, *Treaty Ports* (New York: Doubleday, 1944), 19; Cheong, "Decline of Manila," 142–51; Bryant & Sturgis, Boston, to Edward Carrington, Providence, November 24, 1813, in Bryant & Sturgis Letterbooks, vol. 8, 330, Baker Library, Harvard Business School (hereafter BL-HBS).

2. Azcárraga y Palmero, *La libertad*, 150–51. *Foreign westerners* as used in this study refers to non-Spanish westerners.

3. Valdés Lakowsky, *De las minas al mar*, 231.

4. Comyn, *State*, 283–84. Among those who reproduce Comyn's figures without due acknowledgment are, in chronological order, De Mas, Mallat, Itier, Azcárraga, González and Moreno, and Schurz.

5. [Yldefonso de Aragón], *Yslas Filipinas. Manila Año de MDCCCXVIII. Estado que manifiestan la importación y exportacón de esta ciudad, en todo el presente año; en que se hacen ver la contribución, productos líquidos de rentas, y reales derechos; como igualmente los frutos y efectos del país exportados; y sus valores en plaza, y venta* (Manila: Ynprenta [*sic*] de D. Manuel Memije, 1820), folios 1–2. Certain totals and subtotals in this report were found to be erroneous and were recomputed by the writer on the basis of the individual cargo value figures given. The geographic distribution of trade also had to be computed using the individual figures.

6. Alessio Robles, *Acapulco*, 99; Paul P. de la Gironiere, *Twenty Years in the Philippines* (New York: Harper and Brothers, 1854), 45–46; [José Felipe del Pan], *Las Islas Filipinas. Progresos en 70 años* (Manila: Imprenta de La Oceanía Española, 1878), 244; Valdés Lakowsky, *De las minas al mar*, 289–92, 301.

7. "Estado que manifiesta el número de buques nacionales y estrangeros que han concurrido a este puerto en todo el presente año de 1825, con expresión de los valores de importación y de exportación de cada uno de ellos así en frutos y efectos como numerario sacado de los registros de esta real aduana" (Manila, 1825?), photostat, PEM. As in the case of the 1818 report, some recomputation of certain totals and subtotals was necessary here as well as the computation of the geographic distribution of trade from the individual figures.

8. Rafael Díaz Arenas, *Memoria sobre el comercio y navegación de las Islas Filipinas* (Cádiz: Imprenta de D. Domingo Feros, 1838), 1.

9. Azcárraga y Palmero, *La libertad*, 147.

10. Díaz Arenas, *Memoria sobre el comercio*, 2.

11. Quoted, respectively, from *Centenary of Wise and Company in the Philippines, 1826–1926* (n.p., n.d.), 109; and [Sinibaldo de Mas,] *Informe sobre el estado de las Islas Filipinas en 1842*, vol. 2: *Comercio esterior* (Madrid, 1843), 27.

12. Joseph Lannoy, *Iles Philippines* (Brussels: Imprimerie de Delevingne et Callewaert, 1849), 107. Readers of this extremely interesting book should beware of accepting the figures for 1818, reproduced on pages 85–86, as they contain inaccuracies.

13. Del Pan, *Las Islas Filipinas*, 245; Jaime Vicens Vives, *Manual de historia económica de España*, 7th ed. (Barcelona: Editorial Vicens Vives, 1967), 552.

14. Comyn, *State*; De Mas, *Informe sobre el estado*, 2–4. The figure of 500,000 is an upper limit set by De Mas. Comyn's original figures identify positively only a median value of 425,000 pesos as native exports, but in addition some are included within the median value of 530,000 pesos classified as going to Lima, consisting of India and China goods and native products. The proportion of the latter cannot have been very high; in chapter 2, mention was made of indications that in the Acapulco galleon it was around 10 percent. The proportion in the Lima voyages was probably about the same and would give a median value of 53,000 pesos, which added to other native exports gives a total of 478,000. The figure of 500,000 pesos therefore seems to be a reasonable estimate.

15. Aragón, *Yslas Filipinas*.

16. Ibid.; Comyn, *State*; "Estado, 1825."

17. *Exposición de la Compañía*, 75.

18. Comyn, *State*; John White, USN, *History of a Voyage to the China Sea* (Boston: Watts and Lilly, 1823), 131; Aragón, *Yslas Filipinas*; "Estado, 1825"; Franz Julius Ferdinand Meyen,

Reise um die Erde ausgeführt auf dem königlich preussischen Seehandlungs-Schiffe Prinzess Louise, commandirt von Capitain W. Wendt, in den Jahren 1830, 1831, und 1832 (Berlin: in der Sander'schen Buchhandlung, 1835), 2:275. A note in the 1825 report states that the level of exports was so low because, for customs purposes, native products were undervalued about one-third below market prices in order to encourage exports. It goes on to say that the real value of native exports should have totaled 1,134,586 pesos. Poor harvests are also given as a reason for the low level of exports. Although it is not surprising to find undervaluation in foreign trade figures, in this particular case it seems to serve as a screen for the bad times the country's trade was experiencing. The undervaluation of exports is also reported in a commercial survey in 1829, which says that 2.5 percent export duty was paid "in a valuation usually below the actual cost" (Russell & Sturgis to E. Carrington, October 14, 1829, Edward Carrington Papers, Rhode Island Historical Society [hereafter ECP-RIHS]).

19. Aragón, *Yslas Filipinas*; "Estado, 1825"; Azcárraga y Palmero, *La libertad*, 157.

20. Aragón, *Yslas Filipinas*, folio 4.

21. Ibid.; *Exposición de la Compañía*, 39, 41, 47; Tornow, "Sketch," 618; Azcárraga y Palmero, *La libertad*, 18.

22. Del Pan, *Las Islas Filipinas*, 222; "Estado, 1825"; Lannoy, *Iles Philippines*, app.; "Balanza general del comercio de las Yslas Filipinas en el año de 1847," Manila, 1848, manuscript in PNA; Islas Filipinas, *Cuadro general del comercio exterior de Filipinas con la metrópoli potencias extrangeras de Europa, América, Africa, Asia y colonias de la Oceanía en 1856* (Manila: Imprenta de Ramírez y Giraudier, 1859); Islas Filipinas, *Balanza mercantil de las Islas Filipinas correspondiente al año de 1864* (Manila: Imprenta de Santo Tomás, 1868); Islas Filipinas, *Estadística mercantil del comercio exterior de las Islas Filipinas correspondiente el año de 1867* (Manila: Imprenta de los "Amigos del País," 1874). The various publications entitled *Balanza mercantil, Estadística general*, etc., were the annual reports of the Philippine customs agency in the last half-century of the Spanish period.

23. Meyen, *Reise*, 276; Tornow, "Sketch," 619; Islas Filipinas, *Cuadro general, 1856*, viii.

24. Aragón, *Yslas Filipinas*; Del Pan, *Las Islas Filipinas*, 231–32; González and Moreno, *Manual*, 238.

25. Del Pan, *Las Islas Filipinas*, 245.

26. Azcárraga y Palmero, *La libertad*, 164–66, 171–72; Jagor, "Travels," 10; John Bowring, *A Visit to the Philippine Islands* (London: Smith, Elder and Co., 1859), 307–8; Filomeno V. Aguilar Jr., "Beyond Inevitability: The Opening of Philippine Provincial Ports in 1855," *Journal of Southeast Asian Studies* 25, no. 1 (March 1994): 70–90. The census of 1903 reports that Zamboanga was made a port of entry and a customs establishment by virtue of a royal decree of January 24, 1833, and that the Cebu customs house was established in April 1842. See *Census of the Philippine Islands under the Direction of the Philippine Commission in the Year 1903* (Washington, D.C.: Government Printing Office, 1905), 4:558.

27. John Foreman, *The Philippine Islands*, 2d. ed. (New York: Charles Scribner's Sons, 1899), 285. This particular work should be used sparingly except in connection with matters of which the author might have personal knowledge.

28. *Boletín de la Real Sociedad Económica de Amigos del País* 3, no. 4 (August 1, 1884): 76–77, n. 2; Recur, *Filipinas: Estudios*, 124.

29. *Census of 1903*, 4:563, n. 1. See also U.S. Department of Agriculture, Section of Foreign Markets (Frank H. Hitchcock, Chief), *Trade of the Philippine Islands*, Bulletin no. 14 (Washington, D.C.: Government Printing Office, 1898), 11, n. 2. The gold-silver

ratios given here are often slightly different from those carried in the *Census of 1903*, although both were supposedly derived from the same source, the Bureau of the Mint of the U.S. Treasury Department. The discrepancies, however, do not affect the argument, as the trends are similar in both. Bulletin no. 14 was one of the compilations hurriedly made during the Spanish-American War. The most charitable statement that can be made about it is that the data it contains have been superseded by those in later publications.

30. In the discussion that follows, the argument is largely based on the tables found in Islas Filipinas, *Cuadro general, 1856,* viii (quantity figures to 1855); and *Census of 1903*, 4:15, 25, 33, 77, 98, 104 (quantity and value figures, 1854–94, or in some cases 1895, corrected in accordance with note c, table 1). Discrepancies in trends for the years 1854 and 1855 between the *Census of 1903* and the *Cuadro general* are probably due to the fact that the former relied on the original annual customs reports of these years whereas the latter contains revised data on previous years.

31. Lannoy, *Iles Philippines,* app.; Islas Filipinas, *Estadística mercantil, 1867,* 67; *Census of 1903*, 4:15, 25, 33, 77.

32. Islas Filipinas, *Cuadro general, 1856,* viii; *Census of 1903*, 4:33; Agustín de la Cavada y Méndez de Vigo, *Historia geográfica, geológica y estadística de Filipinas* (Manila: Imp. de Ramírez y Giraudier, 1876), 1:409, 2:377.

33. Aragón, *Yslas Filipinas*; Tornow, "Sketch," 618; *Centenary of Wise and Company*, 101; "Balanza general, 1847"; *Census of 1903*, 4:15.

34. *Census of 1903*, 4:98; Islas Filipinas, *Cuadro general, 1856,* viii; Del Pan, *Las Islas Filipinas,* 223–24; Greenberg, *British Trade,* 166.

35. Islas Filipinas, *Cuadro general, 1856,* viii; *Census of 1903*, 4:104.

36. Recur, *Filipinas: Estudios,* 61–62; F[rancisco] A[hujas], *Reseña acerca del estado social y económico de las colonias de España en Asia y reformas que exigen para su desarrollo,* I (Madrid: Imprenta de J. Noguera, 1874), 35–36.

37. *Centenary of Wise and Company*, 101.

38. Díaz Arenas, *Memoria sobre el comercio,* 58.

39. De Mas, *Informe sobre el estado,* 11–15; Lannoy *Iles Philippines,* app.; "Balanza general, 1847," table 5; Azcárraga y Palmero, *La libertad,* 159–60; Jean Mallat (trans. P. S. Castrence), *The Philippines: History, Geography, Customs, Agriculture, Industry, and Commerce* (Manila: National Historical Institute, 1983), 491–95, 502–4; Jules Itier, *Journal d'un Voyage en Chine* (Paris: Chez Dauvin et Fontaine, 1848), tables between pp. 362 and 363.

40. *Census of 1903*, 4:33, 77; Islas Filipinas, *Balanza mercantil de la renta de aduanas, 1855* (n.p., n.d.); Islas Filipinas, *Cuadro general, 1856*; Islas Filipinas, *Balanza mercantil de las Islas Filipinas correspondiente al año de 1857* (Manila: Establecimiento tipográfico de los Amigos del País, 1860); *Balanza mercantil de las Islas Filipinas correspondiente al año de 1858* (Manila: Establecimiento tipográfico de los Amigos del País, 1861); *Balanza mercantil de las Islas Filipinas correspondiente al año de 1859* (Manila: Establecimiento tipográfico de los Amigos del País, 1861); *Balanza mercantil de las Islas Filipinas correspondiente al año de 1860* (Manila: Establecimiento tipográfico de los Amigos del País, 1862); *Balanza mercantil de las Islas Filipinas correspondiente al año de 1861* (Manila: Imprenta del Colegio de Sto. Tomás, 1863); *Balanza mercantil de las Islas Filipinas correspondiente al año de 1864* (Manila: Imprenta del Colegio de Sto. Tomás, 1868); *Balanza mercantil de las Islas Filipinas correspondiente al año de 1862* (Manila: Ymprenta de los Amigos del País, 1864); *Balanza*

mercantil de las Islas Filipinas correspondiente al año de 1865 (Manila: Ymprenta de los Amigos del País, 1869).

41.   Benoni Lockwood, Manila, to Edward Carrington, Providence, February 18, 1834, ECP-RIHS; John A. Larkin, *Sugar and the Origins of Modern Philippine Society* (Berkeley: University of California Press, 1993), 51–52; Aguilar, "Beyond Inevitability," 76; Russell & Sturgis, circular, August 16, 1851.

42.   *Census of 1903*, 4:15, 25, 33, 54, 77; Cavada, *Historia*, 1:409, 2:377.

43.   *Census of 1903*, 4:54; Islas Filipinas, *Cuadro general, 1856*; Islas Filipinas, *Balanza mercantil, 1857*; Islas Filipinas, *Balanza mercantil, 1860*; Mallat, *The Philippines*; Itier, *Journal*.

44.   Islas Filipinas, *Balanza mercantil*, 1858; Islas Filipinas, *Balanza mercantil*, 1861; *Estadística general del comercio exterior de las Islas Filipinas en 1890* (Manila: Estab. Tipolitográfico de Ramírez y Compa., 1892).

45.   U.S. War Department, Bureau of Insular Affairs, *Monthly Summary of the Commerce of the Philippine Islands*, series 1904–5, no. 6 (December 1904): 605–6.

46.   Robert Mac Micking, *Recollections of Manilla and the Philippines during 1848, 1849, and 1850* (London: Richard Bentley, 1851), 231–33; Augustine Heard Papers, I, letters from Jonathan Russell, Manila, 5 January and 17 June 1864, to A. Heard & Co., Hong Kong.

47.   Peele, Hubbell & Co., "Exports from Manila" for 1850, 1853–55, 1871–72; Russell & Sturgis, "Principal Articles of Export from Manila," 1861–62, Peirce Family Papers, Stanford University Libraries (hereafter PFP-SUL), Stanford, California; Russell & Sturgis, "Comparative Total Exports from Manila for 1856 and 1857," BL-HBS; Islas Filipinas, *Balanza general del comercio de las Islas Filipinas, Año de 1851* (Manila: Imprenta de los Amigos del País, 1852); Lannoy, *Iles Philippines*, app.; Laura Esquivel, *Como agua para chocolate* (New York: Doubleday, 1992), 24.

48.   The basic data on which the preceding figures were based are found in Lannoy, *Iles Philippines*, app.; "Balanza general, 1847"; Islas Filipinas, *Balanza mercantil, 1857*; González and Moreno, *Manual*, 209–14; *Estadística general del comercio exterior de las Islas Filipinas, 1892* (Manila: Tipografía "Amigos del País," 1893); Society of Jesus, Philippine Mission, *El archipiélago filipino* (Washington, D.C.: Government Printing Office, 1900), 1:313–14.

49.   Aragón, *Yslas Filipinas*; Tornow, "Sketch"; "Balanza general, 1847"; Islas Filipinas, *Cuadro general, 1856*; *Balanza mercantil, 1864*; González and Moreno, *Manual*, 211; Islas Filipinas, *Estadística general, 1892*.

50.   Albert O. Hirschman, *National Power and the Structure of Foreign Trade* (Berkeley: University of California Press, 1945), 99.

51.   Ibid., 100–101, 106–7.

52.   Ibid., 105.

Notes to Chapter 5

1.   Comyn, *State*, 57–58.

2.   Díaz Arenas, *Memoria sobre el comercio*, 3.

3.   Díaz Arenas, *Memorias históricas*, vol. 2, bk.2 (unpaginated).

4.   Lannoy, *Iles Philippines*, 80–81.

5.   Ibid., 82–83.

6.   Mac Micking, *Recollections*, 227.

7.   "Balanza general, 1847"; González and Moreno, *Manual*, 207.

8.   Great Britain, Foreign Office, "Report by Consul Ricketts on the Trade and Com-

merce of the Philippines Islands for the Year 1870," in *Sessional Papers*, 1871, vol. 66 (London: Harrison and Sons, 1871), 752.

9. Recur, *Filipinas: Estudios*, 107.

10. The basic data are found in Lannoy, *Iles Philippines*, app.; "Balanza general, 1847"; *Cuadro general, 1856*; Islas Filipinas, *Balanza mercantil, 1857*; Islas Filipinas, *Balanza mercantil, 1864*; Islas Filipinas, *Balanza mercantil, 1865*; Islas Filipinas, *Estadística mercantil, 1867*.

11. *Census of 1903*, 4:87.

12. Aragón, *Yslas Filipinas*, folio 2; Lannoy, *Iles Philippines*, app.; Islas Filipinas, *Cuadro general, 1856*; Islas Filipinas, *Balanza mercantil, 1864*; Islas Filipinas, *Estadística mercantil, 1867*; *Estadística general, 1890*; *Centenary of Wise and Company*, 80.

13. Great Britain, Foreign Office, 1887, Miscellaneous Series, no. 48, *Report on the Native Manufactures of the Philippine Islands* (London: Harrison and Sons, 1887), 1–3. For the passages referring to Recur, see his *Filipinas: Estudios*, 107–8. For a fuller treatment of the decline of the textile industry in Iloilo, termed "deindustrialization," see Alfred W. McCoy, "A Queen Dies Slowly: The Rise and Decline of Iloilo City," in *Philippine Social History: Global Trade and Local Transformations*, edited by Alfred W. McCoy and Ed. C. de Jesus, 301–7 (Quezon City: Ateneo de Manila University Press, 1982).

14. *Exposición regional Filipina, 1895* (n.p., n.d.), 366–99.

15. Victor S. Clark, "Labor Conditions in the Philippines," *Bulletin of the Bureau of Labor* (U.S. Department of Commerce and Labor) 58 (1905): 809–10.

16. Comyn, *State*, 26; Mac Micking, *Recollections*, 276.

17. *Census of 1903*, 4:86.

18. Del Pan, *Las Islas Filipinas*, 229.

19. Tornow, "Sketch," 608–9.

20. Nicholas Tarling, "Some Aspects of British Trade in the Philippines in the Nineteenth Century," *Journal of History* 11, nos. 3–4 (September-December 1963): 290; "Remarks at Manilla in May and June 1826," ECP-RIHS.

21. Martínez de Zúñiga, *Estadismo*, 273.

22. Islas Filipinas, *Cuadro general, 1856*, viii; Greenberg, *British Trade*, 81, 96; Tarling, "Aspects," 293–300.

23. Olyphant & Co., Canton, October 22, 1832; Benoni Lockwood, Manila, February 18, 1834; Olyphant & Co., Macao, June 1, 1883; Russell & Sturgis, Manila, June 27, 1835; Benoni Lockwood, Manila, December 10, 1835; Isaac M. Bull, "Account Sales Paddy" and "Account Sales Rice," Canton, January 3 and January 7, 1836; all to E. Carrington & Co., ECP-RIHS; "Prices Current from Russell & Sturgis, Nov. 4, 1834," Russell & Sturgis circular, December 23, 1848, BL-HBS.

24. Tarling, "Aspects"; Russell & Sturgis to E. Carrington & Co., October 14, 1829, ECP-RIHS; Russell & Sturgis to William Appleton & Co., Boston, October 26, 1844, Dexter-Appleton Papers (hereafter DAP), BL-HBS; Russell & Sturgis circular, September 8, 1855, BL-HBS.

25. *Centenary of Wise and Company*, 101; Lannoy, *Iles Philippines*; "Balanza general, 1847"; Islas Filipinas, *Cuadro general, 1856*; Islas Filipinas, *Balanza mercantil* (for 1857–61, 1864, 1865).

26. Islas Filipinas, *Balanza general, 1854*; Russell & Sturgis circulars dated February 20, April 21, August 16, September 13, and December 18, 1851; November 22, 1847; February 21, 1848; December 22, 1852; and March 12 and April 15, 1853, all in BL-HBS.

27. Azcárraga y Palmero, *La libertad*, 19; Bowring, *Visit*, 298; J. M. Tuason & Co. circular dated October 7, 1857, Russell & Sturgis circulars dated November 26, 1857, April 6, Sep-

tember 4, October 21, and November 22, 1858, BL-HBS; Peele, Hubbell & Co. (hereafter PHC) circulars, 8 November 1859, PFP-SUL; Manuel Buzeta and Felipe Bravo, *Diccionario geográfico, estadístico, histórico de las Islas Filipinas* (Madrid, 1850), 1:33.

28. Díaz Arenas, *Memoria sobre el comercio*, 17; Mallat, *Les Philippines*, 2:330; Mac Micking, *Recollections*, 278; Russell & Sturgis circular, May 15, 1854, BL-HBS; *Precios corrientes de Manila* (hereafter PCM) 1, no. 20 (November 16, 1839), ECP-RIHS.

29. Mac Micking, *Recollections*, 271. A *cavan* of rice weighed differently for different grades; see PCM. See also Tornow, "Sketch," 619.

30. A. Heard & Co. to PHC, August 24, November 14, and November 25, 1860, in Letterbooks, vol. 516, 2, 40–41, 44–45, Augustine Heard Collection (hereafter AHC) II, BL-HBS.

31. A. Heard & Co. to A. V. Barretto, July 18, August 5, September 3, 1863, in Letterbooks, vol. 517, 232, 241–47; A. V. Barretto to A. Heard & Co., August 20, 1863, January 8, January 23, August 2, 1864; A. Heard & Co. to Arrechea & Co., January 28, 1864, all in AHC; *Tait & Co's. Market Report*, Amoy, June 19, 1869, BL-HBS.

32. Del Pan, *Las Islas Filipinas*, 229.

33. Russell & Sturgis circulars, March 4, 1856, October 16, 1874, BL-HBS; PHC circular, January 7, 1863, PFP-SUL.

34. Tornow, "Sketch," 609.

35. Corpuz, *Roots*, 1:545, 568–69; Daniel Doeppers, personal communication, July 30, 1996.

36. *Census of 1903*, 4:86.

37. González and Moreno, *Anuario Filipino para 1877* (Manila: Establecimiento tipográfico de Plana y Ca., 1877), 48.

38. Bowring, *Visit*, 388–89.

39. Jagor, "Travels," 305.

40. Clark, "Labor Conditions," 766. Elsewhere (768) he adds: "The collective wealth of the working people does not increase. If they produce more to sell abroad, they produce less to consume at home; if they raise more fiber they raise less food." This is persuasive, but on closer scrutiny it is not very convincing, for if the growing of fibers and food were equally indifferent to the cultivator there would be no reason to change from one to the other, as in fact occurred. One would have to factor in the directing role of capital and enterprise.

41. Cavada, *Historia*, 2:420; *Census of 1903*, 4:322, 325–28.

42. Bowring, *Visit*, 298, 389.

43. Azcárraga y Palmero, *La libertad*, 19–20.

44. Russell & Sturgis, "Yloilo Market Report, 31st December 1867," BL-HBS.

45. J. Montano, *Rapport a M. le Ministre de L'Instruction Publique sur une mission aux Iles Philippines et en Malaisie (1879–1881)* (Paris: Imprimerie Nationale, 1885), 195.

46. W. Gifford Palgrave, *Ulysses, or Scenes and Studies in Many Lands* (London: Macmillan, 1887), 160–61. His estimate of the country's population is much too high, being from 6 to 6.5 million (including animistic tribes) at the time his book was published.

47. Clark, "Labor Conditions," 767.

48. *Census of 1903*, 4:218.

49. Ibid., 86.

50. Palgrave, *Ulysses*, 161.

51. McCoy, *Queen*, 307, 311, 317.

52. Felix Renouard de Sainte-Croix, *Voyage commercial et politique aux Indes Orientales,*

aux Iles Philippines, a la Chine, avec des notions sur le Cochinchine et le Tonquin, pendant les années 1803, 1804, 1805, 1806, et 1807 (Paris: Imprimerie de Crapchet, 1810), 3:29–30.

53. Lannoy, *Iles Philippines,* 135.

54. Buzeta and Bravo, *Diccionario,* 2:89, 98–99.

55. Ibid., 2:91–92; Del Pan, *Las Islas Filipinas,* 367; Cavada, *Historia,* 1:94, 99, 101, 106–7.

56. Del Pan, *Las Islas Filipinas,* 367–68; Cavada, *Historia,* 1:411.

57. Ahujas, *Reseña,* 11–14; *Census of 1903,* 4:120; De Jesus,*Tobacco Monopoly,* 180, 189.

58. Cavada, *Historia,* 1:100, 108, 411.

59. Peter C. Smith, "Crisis Mortality in the Nineteenth Century Philippines: Data from Parish Records," *Journal of Asian Studies* 38, no. 1 (November 1978): 51–76. Ken De Bevoise's book *Agents of Apocalypse* (Princeton: Princeton University Press, 1995), dealing with the high mortality and morbidity levels of the late-nineteenth-century Philippines, reached the writer after the text of the present volume was done. It is not possible here to engage the analytical and factual points he raises. In his view, there were two adverse effects of rice imports on the population. The first was the progressive dependence on a Chinese mercantile network at all stages of the trade, including the "relief process," which was guided more by profit considerations than human need. The second was beri-beri, arising from a thiamine deficiency in Saigon rice, the principal variety imported, with infantile beri-beri singled out as "the hidden tragedy of Philippine cash cropping" (125–26, 136).

60. Maximo M. Kalaw, *The Development of Philippine Politics (1872–1920)* (Manila: Oriental Co., 1926), 32.

Notes to Chapter 6

1. Karl J. Pelzer, "The Resource Pattern of Southeast Asia," *South Asia in the World Today,* edited by Phillips Talbot, 109 (Chicago: University of Chicago Press, 1959).

2. Recur, *Filipinas: Estudios,* 47–48.

3. González and Moreno, *Manual del Viajero,* 290.

4. Ahujas, *Reseña,* 6–7.

5. Clive Day, *The Policy and Administration of the Dutch in Java* (New York: Macmillan, 1904), 336–37.

6. Azcárraga y Palmero, *La libertad,* 26; H. Lawrence Noble, *Philippine Digest* (Rochester, N.Y., and Manila: Lawyers Co-operative Publishing, 1927), 6:266, 4:3356–84.

7. Some instances of discontent in the nineteenth century are the Basi Revolt of 1807 in Ilocos, which was precipitated by the wine monopoly (*basi* is sugarcane rum); the Sarrat Revolt of 1815 in Ilocos Norte, directed against the local upper class rather than Spanish rule; and various semireligious or millenarian movements or uprisings such as that of Apolinario de la Cruz ("Hermano Pule") in Tayabas in 1840–41, that of "Apo Laqui" in Pangasinan around 1886, that of the "Santa Iglesia" in Pampanga in the 1890s, and that of "Papa Isio" in Negros (the last three spilled over into the American period). While scholars have cautioned against making causal connections between some of these movements and the more overtly political outbreaks of the late nineteenth century, connections seem to be indicated "in the common features through time of a consciousness that constantly seeks to define the world in its own terms" (Reynaldo Clemeña Ileto, *Pasyon and Revolution: Popular Movements in the Philippines, 1840–1910* [Quezon City: Ateneo de Manila University Press, 1979], 31). See Carlos Quirino, *Filipinos at War* (Manila: Vera Reyes, 1981; rpt. 1987), 92–96; *Extracto de la memoria*

escrita por el P. Fr. José Nieto, Cura regular de Sarrat en Ilocos Norte sobre la insurrección acaecida en el mismo el año 1815, Ahora publicada por primera vez, año de 1889 (extracted from W. E. Retana's *Archivo del bibliófilo filipino,* vol. 4); Ileto, *Pasyon,* 31–33, 211–14; and Miguel A. Bernad, "Popular Uprisings in the Philippines," *Kinaadman* 1 (1970): 145–48 (review of David R. Sturtevant's *Popular Uprisings in the Philippines, 1840–1910* [Ithaca: Cornell University Press, 1976]).

    8. Mac Micking, *Recollections,* 152–55.

    9. Palgrave, *Ulysses,* 159–60.

    10. *Census of 1903,* 4:261, 264, 268, 269. There is some reason to believe that there was a rise in the concentration of private landed property during the American period, when the country became even more of an agricultural export economy than before, but this phenomenon lies outside the scope of the present study. See Erich H. Jacoby, *Agrarian Unrest in Southeast Asia* (New York: Columbia University Press, 1949), 178–81.

    11. Chester Lloyd Jones, "The Spanish Administration of Philippine Commerce," *American Political Science Association Proceedings* 3 (1907): 193.

    12. Bowring, *Visit,* 306, 307.

    13. Tarling, "Aspects," 296.

    14. Díaz Arenas, *Memorias históricas,* vol. 1, bk. 7, vol. 2, bk. 16 (unpaginated); Mac Micking, *Recollections,* 42–44; Tarling, "Aspects"; Montero y Vidal, *Historia general,* 3:71–72; *Almanaque filipino i guía de forasteros para el año de 1834* (Manila: Imprenta de D. José Maria Dayot, n.d.), 158–60; *Guía de forasteros en las Islas Filipinas para el año de 1845* (Manila: Imprenta de D. Miguel Sánchez, n.d.), 95, 237–38; Corpuz, *Roots,* 1:448–50; George Santayana, *Persons and Places: The Background of My Life* (New York: Scribners, 1994), 31–36.

    15. Ahujas, *Reseña,* 2:63, n. 1.

    16. Aduana de Manila Papers (hereafter AdM), PNA.

    17. González and Moreno, *Manual,* 172–78.

    18. Carl C. Plehn, "Taxation in the Philippines, pt. 2,"*Political Science Quarterly* 17, no. 1 (March, 1902): 125–26. See also *Census of 1903,* 4:559–63, for a digest of pertinent portions of this work.

    19. Plehn, "Taxation," 129.

    20. *Arancel general para el comercio exterior de las Islas Filipinas* ([Manila]: Imprenta de Sampaloc, 1831). See also Díaz Arenas, *Memoria sobre el comercio,* 38–39.

    21. Díaz Arenas, *Memoria sobre el comercio,* 59.

    22. *Arancel,* 1831, 43–44; *Centenary of Wise and Company,* 122–23.

    23. Plehn, "Taxation," 128, 130, 132.

    24. Ibid., 131; *Arancel general . . . rectificado* (Manila, 1855), 74–76; Azcárraga y Palmero, *La libertad,* 151–52; *Aranceles provisionals de aduanas de las Islas Filipinas reformadas en virtud de la Real Orden de 12 noviembre de 1860* (Manila: Establecimiento tipográfico de Amigos del País, 1862), 9, 10, 16, 17, 47, 65, 74–85, 87.

    25. Azcárraga y Palmero, *La libertad,* 154–55.

    26. Bowring, *Visit,* 296–97.

    27. Mac Micking, *Recollections,* 218–19.

    28. *Aranceles de aduanas de las Islas Filipinas y disposiciones para la reforma de los mismos, dictados por decreto del gobierno provisional No. 63, de 29 diciembre de 1868, órdenes del Ministerio de Ultramar, números 64 y 65, de igual fecha y decreto del gobierno superior civil de 27 abril de 1869* (Binondo [Manila]: Imprenta de Miguel Sánchez y Cia., 1869), 3:VII.

    29. Ibid., IX.

30. See, for example, ibid., VII; and Azcárraga y Palmero, *La libertad,* 186, 199–200, 207–9.

31. Ricardo Fragoso, *Aranceles e instrucción de aduanas de Filipinas con las disposiciones que los reforman o adicionan, comentadas y concordadas; y con la exposición de todos aquellos datos convenientes al comercio y a la administración, seguidos de parte de la legislación aduanera de la Península* (Manila: Establecimiento Tipográfico La Industrial, 1886), 12–13.

32. Javier de Tíscar, ed., *Aranceles de las aduanas de las Islas Filipinas aprobadas en decreto de S.A. el Regente del Reino de 16 de octubre de 1870 y reformados por decreto del Gobierno Superior Civil de 26 de junio de 1871, con la instrucción reglamentaria del ramo aprobada en real orden de 29 de setiembre de 1855 y otras disposiciones importantes dictadas con posteriodidad* (Manila: Imprenta Ciudad Condal de Plana y Cía., 1874), 9–23.

33. Azcárraga y Palmero, *La libertad,* 192.

34. Tíscar, *Aranceles,* 174.

35. Ibid., 34–35; Azcárraga y Palmero, *La libertad,* 150.

36. Tíscar, *Apéndice a los aranceles de aduanas de las Islas Filipinas* [Manila, 1874?], 200–213.

37. Fragoso, *Aranceles,* 330–41.

38. Martin Ocampo y Reyes, *Manual del aduanista o compilación de aclaraciones y reglas arancelarias desde 1872 a 1888* (Manila: Establecimiento tipográfico *La Opinión,* 1888), 111.

39. *Estadística general, 1890.*

40. W. Bowden, M. Karpovich, and A. P. Usher, *An Economic History of Europe since 1750* (New York: American Book Co., 1937), 356–61, 616–18.

41. Fragoso, *Aranceles,* 108–9; Ocampo, *Manual,* 105–7.

42. [Spain, Ministerio de Ultramar,] *Aranceles y ordenanzas de aduanas para las Islas Filipinas,* edición oficial (Madrid: Establecimiento tipográfico *Sucesores de Rivadeneyra,* 1891), 7–8.

43. Plehn, "Taxation," 132.

44. *Aranceles,* 1891, 12; T. H. Pardo de Tavera, *Biblioteca filipina* (Washington, D.C.: Government Printing Office, 1903), 32; *Estadística general, 1894.*

45. Julián del Pozo y Bresó, *Guía práctica para el despacho de mercancías en las aduanas de Filipinas con arreglo a los nuevos aranceles y ordenanzas* (Manila: Tipo-litografía de Chofré y Compa., 1891), 177–96.

46. Plehn, "Taxation," 136, 134; González and Moreno, *Manual,* 198–221.

47. *Census of 1903,* 4:541; Hodsoll, "Britain."

48. Bank of the Philippine Islands, *LXXV Anniversary: Souvenir of the First Bank Established in the Far East* (Manila, 1928), 3.

49. Banco Español-Filipino Records, PNA.

50. Bank of the Philippine Islands, *LXXV Anniversary,* 1, 11.

51. Ibid., 11–14.

52. Ibid., 21–25; Banco Español-Filipino Records, PNA.

53. Banco Español-Filipino de Isabel II, *Memoria leída en la junta general de accionistas celebrada el día 3 de mayo de 1853. Año 1º* (Manila: Imp. *El Retoño,* [1853?]), 12, 20.

54. Banco Español-Filipino de Isabel II, *Año 5º, Memoria leída en la junta general de accionistas celebrada el día 17 de mayo de 1857* (Manila: Imprenta de los Amigos del País, 1857), 8–10.

55. Bank of the Philippine Islands, *LXXV Anniversary,* 18, 22.

56. Bowring, *Visit,* 303–4; Banco Español-Filipino, *Memoria, 1853,* 19.

57. Tornow, "Sketch," 617.

58. Antonio Regidor and J. Warren T. Mason, *Commercial Progress in the Philippine Islands* (London: Dunn and Chidgey, 1905), 22–23. This is another reference that should be used with caution.

59. Bank of the Philippine Islands, *LXXV Anniversary*, 16.

60. See, for example, Ahujas, *Reseña*, 2:47; and Gabino Pérez Valdés, *Situación económica de Filipinas y medios de mejorarla* (Madrid: Imprenta de Andrés Orejas, 1871), 22–23, 29–31.

61. Lannoy, *Iles Philippines*, 105.

62. Regidor and Mason, *Commercial Progress*, 22.

63. BR, 52:113–14. Le Roy is curiously hesitant about dating the trends he describes, as if he were not sure of the facts; only the more forthright, and in this writer's opinion accurate, passages have been quoted in the extract.

64. Mac Micking, *Recollections*, 267.

65. Samuel W. Belford, "Material Problems in the Philippine Islands," *American Monthly Review of Reviews* 19, no. 4 (April 1899): 455. Belford was assistant adjutant general on the staff of General Otis at Manila.

66. Tornow, "Sketch," 623.

67. Clark, "Labor Conditions," 862, 858; Tornow, "Sketch," 617; Belford, "Material Problems"; For an authoritative discussion of this point , see Wickberg, *Chinese*, esp. 45–123.

68. Bowring, *Visit*, 409–10.

69. Pardo de Tavera, "Results," 19. The term *middle class* is used in the western sense, following Dr. Pardo de Tavera, who wrote: "We call *clase ilustrado* [*sic*] in the Philippines what in other countries is called middle class. . . . We have already shown [how] this middle class was formed, how it was redeemed, created and fortified by economic phenomena" (28). The term is used for convenience and does not imply that the nineteenth-century Philippines had the same class structure as the West. Glenn A. May has remarked that "historians have done virtually no primary research on the social structure of the late nineteenth century Philippines . . ." (*A Past Recovered* [Quezon City: New Day, 1987], 12). Illustrative of the ambivalence toward Philippine class structure is Cesar A. Majul, who in one passage mentions "the educated class and the small but rising middle class" as though they were separate. A few pages later, he refers to "the educated segment of the Philippines (in particular those from the lower middle class)," clearly lumping the two together (*The Political and Constitutional Ideas of the Philippine Revolution* [Quezon City: University of the Philippines, 1957], 181, 186).

70. Islas Filipinas, *Cuadro general, 1856*; Islas Filipinas, *Balanza mercantil* (for the years 1857–60); *Estadística general* (for the years 1891–94).

71. [Nick Joaquin,] "Toward a Coffee Renaissance," *Philippines Free Press*, February 21, 1953, 10.

72. Ibid.

73. Recur, *Filipinas: Estudios*, 129; Henry Sturgis Grew, *Letters from China and Manila by . . . to his Parents, 1855 to 1862* (Paris: H.M.C.-H.G.C. [privately printed], 1927), 47.

74. Pardo de Tavera, "Results," 21–23. "Brutes loaded with gold," according to this author, was the term of contempt applied by the Spaniards to wealthy Filipinos. *Filibusterismo* means "separatism."

75. Del Pan, *Las Isles Filipinas*, 419–21.

Notes to Chapter 7

1. Joseph A. Schumpeter, "The Creative Response in Economic History," *Journal of Economic History* 7, no. 2 (November 1947): 149.

2. Gustav Cassel, *The Theory of Social Economy*, translated by S. L. Barron, rev. ed. (London: Ernest Benn, 1932), 1:172.

3. Schumpeter, "Creative Response," 150.

4. Joseph A. Schumpeter, "Economic Theory and Entrepreneurial History," in *Essays*, edited by R. V. Clemence (Cambridge: Addison-Wesley, 1951), 266.

5. Joseph A. Schumpeter, "Theoretical Problems of Economic Growth," *Journal of Economic History* 7 (1947): S1–9.

6. John H. Dales, "Approaches to Entrepreneurial History," *Explorations in Entrepreneurial History* 1, no. 1 (January 1949): 11.

7. Ibid.

8. Fritz Redlich, "The Business Leader in Theory and Reality," *American Journal of Economics and Sociology* 8, no. 3 (April 1949): 223–37. Schloss views all three functions as subfunctions of the "older" concept of entrepreneurship; see Henry H. Schloss, "The Concept of Entrepreneurship in Economic Development," *Journal of Economic Issues* 2, no. 2 (June 1968): 228–32.

9. Schumpeter, "Creative Response," 151.

10. Joseph A. Schumpeter, *The Theory of Economic Development*, translated by Redvers Opie, 132–36 (Cambridge: Harvard University Press, 1934); Arthur H. Cole, "An Approach to the Study of Entrepreneurship," in *The Tasks of Economic History*, supplement to the *Journal of Economic History* 7 (1946): S6.

11. Fritz Redlich, *History of American Business Leaders* (Ann Arbor: Edwards Brothers, 1940), 15.

12. Schumpeter, "Creative Response," 152.

13. Ibid., 154–55; Schumpeter, "Economic Theory," 256.

14. Schumpeter, *Theory*, 137.

15. Redlich, *History*, 2–3; Joseph A. Schumpeter, *Capitalism, Socialism, and Democracy*, 3d ed. (New York: Harper and Brothers, 1950), 81–86.

16. Schumpeter, *Theory*, 93–94.

17. Ibid., 288.

18. Ragnar Nurkse, *Problems of Capital Formation in Underdeveloped Countries* (Oxford: Basil Blackwell, 1953), 12–16.

19. Bowring, *Visit*, 18–19.

20. Frederic H. Sawyer, *The Inhabitants of the Philippines* (London: Sampson Low, Marston, 1900), 125.

21. *Enciclopedia universal ilustrada europeo-americana* (Barcelona: Espasa, n.d.), 10:1177–78. Detailed Barretto family information is found in Antonio María Barretto y Rocha, "Familia Barretto," translated from the Spanish original by Federico Valdés Barretto Jr. in 1993. A typescript was provided through the kindness of Mrs. Nena Barretto Olivares.

22. Perkins Russell letterbooks, 19:69–70 (BL-HBS).

23. Thomas T. Forbes letterbooks, vols. 3, 4 (BL-HBS).

24. Jonathan Russell Papers (BL-HBS).

25. San Miguel Brewery, *Golden Jubilee* [Manila: Catholic Trade School, 1940].

26. Díaz Arenas, *Memorias históricas,* bk. 5; Tarling, "Aspects," 303; *Canton Commercial List,* October 18, 1849.

27. The writer is indebted for background material on the Roxases to the late Mr. Fernando Zóbel y Montojo, a relative of theirs. See also Buzeta and Bravo, *Diccionario,* 1:27; Gregorio F. Zaide, *The Philippine Revolution* (Manila: Modern Book Co., 1954), 95, 97, 119, 133; and Teodoro A. Agoncillo, *The Revolt of the Masses* (Quezon City: University of the Philippines, 1956), 142–43.

28. W. E. Retana, *Índice de personas nobles y otras de calidad que han estado en Filipinas desde 1521 hasta 1898* (Madrid: Victoriano Suárez, 1921), 75; *Second Grand Reunion of the Descendants of Teresa de la Paz* (Manila: privately printed, 1990); Azcárraga y Palmero, *La libertad,* 29; Quirino, *Filipinos at War,* 98, n. 99; Corpuz, *Roots,* 1:271–72; *Barretto v. Tuason,* 50 *Phil. Rep.* [Supreme Court of the Philippines, no. 23923, March 23, 1926, "Antonio Ma. Barretto et al., plaintiffs and appellants, v. Augusto H. Tuason et al., defendants and appellants," in *Philippine Reports,* 888–971]; *Teresa de la Paz and Her Two Husbands: A Gathering of Four Families* (n.p.: The Descendants of Teresa de la Paz, 1996), 5–7, 20–28.

29. Introduction to Shirley Jenkins, *American Economic Policy toward the Philippines* (Stanford: Stanford University Press, 1954), 24.

30. Foreman, *Philippine Islands,* 209.

31. Bowring, *Visit,* 333, 18.

Notes to Chapter 8

1. Due to the circumstances surrounding the conducting of this study, much of the material refers to American enterprise, in itself not an undesirable thing because of the important role played by American firms in Philippine economic life at that time.

2. Furber, "Abortive Attempt."

3. Valdés Lakowsky, *De las minas al mar,* 260.

4. Mallat, *Les Philippines,* 2:330.

5. Alexander Young, *A Discourse on the Life and Character of the Hon. Nathaniel Bowditch, LL.D., F.R.S., Delivered in the Church on Church Green, March 25, 1838* (Boston: Charles C. Little and James Brown, 1838), 25–30.

6. Willard Peele et al. to Capt. Robert W. Gould, Salem, February 27 1819; R. W. Gould to Willard Peele et al., Manila, September 8, 1819; "Invoice of specie shipped on board the Ship Aurora, Robert W. Gould master. . . ," Salem, February 27, 1819; "Invoice of merchandise shipped on board Ship Aurora by Robert W. Gould. . . ," Manila, February 29 1820, all in Peele Family Papers, PEM.

7. *Perseverance,* shipping logbook, voyage to Batavia, Manila, and Canton, December 1796–April 1798, PEM.

8. R. G. Shaw to Russell & Sturgis, November 8. 1843, case LV–17, folder 21, AHC 2, BL-HBS.

9. *Resource,* William F. Megee, Master, "Accounts of Adventures, Voyage to Manila & Canton, 1802 & 1803"; J. and T. H. Perkins to Capt. Wm. Megee, Boston, May 5, 1802; William F. Megee to John Corlis, November 8 and November 29, 1802, Nightingale and Jenckes Papers, Rhode Island Historical Society (hereafter RIHS). See also Martínez de Zúñiga, *Estadismo,* 1:265.

10. Thomas G. Cary, *Memoir of Thomas Handasyd Perkins* (Boston: Little, Brown, 1856), 295.

11. Walter Hubbell, *History of the Hubbell Family* (New York: J. H. Hubbell & Co., 1881), 105–7, 127.

12. Aragón, *Yslas Filipinas,* folio 1; "Estado, 1825."

13. Perkins-Russell Papers, 19:383, BL-HBS.

14. Charles Stewart to E. Carrington, Manila, July 11, September 5, October 2, November 17, and November 27, 1818; Andrew Stuart to E. Carrington, Manila, November 12, 1818; John Christopher O'Farrell, circular, Manila, October 1818; letter to E. Carrington, Manila, November 8, 1818, in ECP-RIHS. O'Farrell's figure for Ezekiel Hubbell's specie imports is identical to that in the 1818 customs report, but that for the commodity component tallies more closely with the figure in the Hubbell family history, possibly owing to a difference between market and official customs values.

15. Perkins-Russell Papers, 19:76–77, 134, 278–79, 306–7, 365–66, 374–78, 382–83, 390–91; 20:145–46, 206–9, 317–22, BL-HBS.

16. Kierulf family file, mimeo provided by a member of the family; Guillermo Kierulf *legajo,* 1828–31, PNA.

17. Hodsoll, "Britain," 105–8.

18. Hubbell, *History,* 127–35; PHC announcement, August 1, 1832, in ECP-RIHS. J. W. Peele, "Waste Book," Peele Family Papers, PEM. Cook's and Osborn's first names are given by Mrs. N. Kinsman (chap. 10, n. 34). She refers to Edwards as the senior partner in 1845 (275) but does not give his initials; these are the writer's surmise. However, Norman Owen's article on Peele, Hubbell & Co. describes Ogden Ellery Edwards as a junior partner ten years later, so these could be two different but probably related persons. See Norman Owen, "Americans in the Abaca Trade: Peele, Hubbell & Co., 1856–1875," in, *Reappraising an Empire: New Perspectives on Philippine-American History,* edited by Peter W. Stanley (Cambridge: Harvard University Press, 1984), 203.

19. Redlich, "Business Leader," 223–37.

20. [Allan Forbes], *Other Merchants and Sea Captains of Boston* (Boston: State Street Trust Company, 1919), 17–19.

21. J. and T. H. Perkins Papers, box 2, folder 1822–1825, Massachusetts Historical Society, Boston (hereafter MHS).

22. T. T. Forbes Letterbooks, vols. 3 and 4, BL-HBS.

23. J. and T. H. Perkins Papers, "Extracts from Letterbooks of J. and T. H. Perkins et al.," 315, MHS.

24. T. T. Forbes Letterbooks, BL-HBS.

25. John Russell Bartlett, *Genealogy of That Branch of the Russell Family Which Comprises the Descendants of John Russell of Woburn, Massachusetts, 1640–1878* (Providence: privately printed, 1879), 70.

26. George Robert Russell Letters, owned by Dr. Charles P. Lyman, Cambridge, Massachusetts. These letters are the major source of information on G. R. Russell, except as otherwise noted.

27. J. and T. H. Perkins Papers, "Extracts from Letterbooks," 311, MHS.

28. Announcement dated July 1, 1828, from Russell & Sturgis, in ECP-RIHS.

29. Katharine Hillard, ed., *My Mother's Journal* (Boston: George H. Ellis, 1900), 21–25.

30. Cyrille Pierre Theodore Laplace, *Voyage autour du monde par les mers de l'Inde et de Chine execute sur la corvette de L'Etat La Favorite pendant les années 1830, 1831, et 1832,* I (Paris: Imprimerie Royal, 1833), 425.

31. Gironiere, *Twenty Years,* 217, 220.

32. Alick Osborne, *Notes on the Present State of Society in New South Wales, with an Historical, Statistical, and Topographical Account of Manilla and Singapore* (London: J. Cross, 1833), 56.

33. Gironiere, *Twenty Years,* 214–22.

34. I. M. Bull to E. Carrington, September 1831, ECP-RIHS.

35. T. T. Forbes had drowned the year before between Canton and Macao.

36. Bryant Tilden Journal, transcribed typescript, 9:926–44, PEM; Russell & Sturgis announcement, December 31, 1841, ECP-RIHS.

37. Russell & Sturgis to Edward Carrington & Co., November 30, 1828, ECP-RIHS.

38. Julian Sturgis, *From Books and Papers of Russell Sturgis* (Oxford: Oxford University Press, for private circulation, n.d.), 91, 210–11, 237. Mary Greene Sturgis's gravestone was visible in Manila's North Cemetery within living memory.

39. Roger Faxton Sturgis, ed., *Edward Sturgis of Yarmouth, Massachusetts, 1613–1695, and his Descendants* (Boston: Stanhope Press, for private circulation, 1914), 50–51.

40. See AHC 2, BL-HBS, case 31, folder 20, for various circulars announcing changes in the senior officers of various firms.

Notes to Chapter 9

1. George Sturgis Papers, in the possession of the family of Mrs. David Little, Weston, Massachusetts.

2. Anon., *Under Four Flags: The Story of Smith Bell & Co. in the Philippines* (Bristol: J. W. Arrowsmith, n.d.), 9; "Escritura pública de protocolización de un contrato social de los Sres. Ker y Compañía," November 8, 1878, and "Escritura pública de protocolización de un contrato social de los Sres. Ker y Compañía," October 16, 1879, PNA; R. Jardine to Weld, November 29, 1884—Partnership Announcements, January 1, 1885—Sale Account and Indent, Iloilo, August 31, 1878, and December 12, 1879, Stone, Silsbee & Pickman Papers (hereafter SSPP-PEM); Russell & Sturgis Announcements, ECP-RIHS; Consuelo H. McHugh, personal communication, October 24, 1995.

3. Heard Papers II, case 3, folder 20, Baker Library, Harvard Business School; Greenberg, *British Trade,* n. 47, 114; González and Moreno, *Manual,* 193; *Guía de forasteros en Filipinas . . . 1860* (Manila: Imp. de los Amigos del Pais, 1859), 126.

4. J. & T. H. Perkins Papers, MHS.

5. Hubbell, *History,* 132–33. See also C. B. Peirce to E. Carrington, June 14, 1829; Russell & Sturgis to E. Carrington, May 15, 1834; Isaac M. Bull to E. Carrington, October 1, 1831, all in ECP-RIHS.

6. De Mas, *Informe sobre el estado,* 2:27.

7. Greenberg, *British Trade,* 161–65, 219.

8. Cheong, "Decline of Manila," 150, 154.

9. Luis Camara Dery, *From Ibalon to Sorsogon: A Historical Survey of Sorsogon Province to 1905* (Quezon City: New Day, 1991), 129–30.

10. George Sturgis Papers.

11. George Russell Papers.

12. Russell & Sturgis circulars, September 16, 1847, March 12, 1853, and March 7, 1855, BL-HBS; Ker, Bolton & Co., Liverpool, to Silsbee & Pickman, Salem, August 9, 1866, SSPP-PEM.

13. Stone, Silsbee & Pickman to Capt. E. E. Emmerton, Salem, December 14, 1855, SSPP-PEM; Russell & Sturgis to B. Spooner, May 5, 1855, Plymouth Cordage Company Papers (hereafter PCCP), BL-HBS.

14. Ker & Co., Manila, to Stone, Silsbee & Pickman, Salem, March 15, 1869, SSPP-PEM.

15. Ker & Co., Manila, to Stone, Silsbee & Pickman, Salem, 28 March 1870, SSPP-PEM.

16. Ker, Bolton & Co., London, to Stone, Silsbee & Pickman, November 3, 1875, SSPP-PEM.

17. Capt. E. A. Emmerton to Stone, Silsbee & Pickman, Manila, October 22, 1856, SSPP-PEM.

18. J. Willard Peele, Waste Book, 1836–44, Willard Peele Papers, PEM.

19. Ker & Co., Manila, to George H. Allen, Salem, February 4 and March 17, 1868, August 3, 1883; George H. Allen, Salem, to Ker & Co., Manila, June 7, 1883, all in SSPP–PEM.

20. George H. Peirce ledger books, 1860–68, PFP-SUL; Ker & Co. to B. Spooner, July 11, 1853, PCCP.

21. Per ton rates were converted to a per *picul* basis by dividing by sixteen since a *picul* is equivalent to 140 pounds and one ton is 2,240 pounds. Abaca was a "measured good" whose freight rates were quoted in capacity terms equivalent to a ton in weight (see notes to table 16).

22. J. C. O'Farrell, Manila, to E. Carrington, November 8, 1818; Charles Stewart to E. Carrington, November 7, 1818, both in ECP-RIHS.

23. I. M. Bull to E. Carrington, November 15, 1838; Russell & Sturgis to E. Carrington, April 1, 1837, June 14, 1842, and November 3, 1843, all in ECP-RIHS; Russell & Sturgis circular, June 15, 1854, BL-HBS.

24. Russell & Sturgis to E. Carrington, November 18, 1839, ECP-RIHS; Russell & Sturgis circulars, January 21, March 19, and June 12, 1850, BL-HBS.

25. PCM, August 22, 1840, and January 9, 1841, ECP-RIHS; Russell & Sturgis circulars, April 21, 1851, December 22, 1852, and March 19, 1850, BL-HBS.

26. Russell & Sturgis circulars, March 20 and July 28, 1854, and September 4, October 21, and November 22, 1858; PHC circular, September 14, 1854, BL-HBS; Ivan Goncharov, "Voyage of the Frigate 'Pallada,'" in *Travel Accounts of the Islands (1832–1858)* (Manila: Filipiniana Book Guild, 1974), 153–214.

27. Ker & Co. to Stone, Silsbee & Pickman, March 15, 1869, SSPP-PEM.

28. Russell & Sturgis circular, September 7, 1853, BL-HBS.

29. *Census of 1903*, 4:563.

30. Russell & Sturgis circulars, December 22, 1854, and January 10, January 25, and March 7, 1855; *New Weekly General Price Current* (hereafter NWGPC), Manila, October 17, 1846, BL-HBS.

31. PHC circular, November 23, 1861, PFP-SUL; Russell & Sturgis to E. Carrington, April 1, 1837, ECP-RIHS; Russell & Sturgis circulars, April 1, 1854, July 12, 1852, and April 15, 1853, BL-HBS; A. V. Barretto to A. Heard & Co., August 5, 1863, AHC, BL-HBS.

32. Syme Muir circulars, Amoy, various dates, 1854–56, BL-HBS; Bull Nye & Co., Isaac M. Bull & Co., and Olyphant & Co. circulars, Shanghai, various dates, 1849–61, ECP-RIHS.

33. Russell & Sturgis circulars, April 11, 1855, November 7, 1857, February 20, 1858, and June 15, 1858; PHC circular, March 23, 1861, BL-HBS; A. V. Barretto to A. Heard & Co., February 22, 1864, AHC, BL-HBS; Grew, *Letters*, 50.

34. See G. C. Allen and Audrey G. Donnithorne, *Western Enterprise in Far Eastern Economic Development: China and Japan* (London: Allen & Unwin, 1954), 34.
35. Jonathan Russell Papers, BL-HBS.
36. González and Moreno, *Manual.*
37. Jonathan Russell Papers, BL-HBS; Richard D. Tucker Papers, PEM.
38. Regidor and Mason, *Commercial Progress,* 21–22.
39. De Mas, *Informe sobre el estado,* 26.
40. Jonathan Russell Papers, BL-HBS; Supreme Court of the Philippines, no. 23923, March 23, 1926, "Antonio Ma. Barretto et al., plaintiffs and appellants, v. Augusto H. Tuason et al., defendants and appellants," in *Philippine Reports,* 888–971; Raymundo C. Bañas, *The Music and Theater of the Filipino People* (Manila: privately published, 1924), 61–67; Felisa R. Hernandez, *Our Outstanding Filipino Composers,* mimeo, Manila, 1952, 65–71; members of the Ortigas family, interviews with the author; Manuel Artigas y Cuerva, *Los sucesos de 1872* (Manila: Imp. de La Vanguardia, 1911), 63–64, 115–17, 266–72.
41. Regidor and Mason, *Commercial Progress,* 25.
42. T. T. Forbes Papers, vol. 4, BL-HBS.
43. Richard D. Tucker Papers, PEM.
44. Ibid.; Owen, *Prosperity,* 67–70, 102–3; Owen, "Americans," 209–10, 214–25, 229, 369–70; Wickberg, *Chinese,* 61, 96–98; J. Montano, *Voyage aux Philippines et en Malaisie* (Paris: Hachette, 1886), 89.
45. Azcárraga y Palmero, *La libertad,* 29–30.
46. AdM Papers, PNA.
47. R. D. Tucker Papers, PEM.
48. Foreman, *Philippine Islands,* 289; Grew, *Letters,* 49; McHale and McHale, *Early American-Philippine Trade,* 20–21.
49. Bowring, *Visit,* 407.
50. Charles de Montblanc, *Les Iles Philippines* (Paris: Guillaumin, 1864), 55.
51. G. C. Allen and Audrey G. Donnithorne, *Western Enterprise in Indonesia and Malaya* (New York: Macmillan, 1957), 49–51, 59–60, 65.

Notes to Chapter 10

1. Perkins-Russell Papers, vol. 20, 208, BL-HBS.
2. J. & T. H. Perkins Papers, MHS.
3. Bryant & Sturgis Papers, vol. 21, BL-HBS.
4. Russell & Sturgis to E. Carrington & Co., October 14, 1829, ECP-RIHS.
5. Mac Micking, *Recollections,* 267.
6. PCM 2, no. 2 (January 9, 1841), ECP-RIHS.
7. Henry T. Ellis, *Hong Kong to Manila and the Lakes of Luzon, in the Philippine Isles, in the Year 1856* (London: Smith, Elder, 1859), 94–95. This writer some years ago acquired a piece of cloth (since lost) about the size of a card table with illustrations from Gironiere's work printed against a blue background. While much too large to be a pocket handkerchief, it was quite likely the sort of Gironiere item referred to by Captain Ellis.
8. Great Britain, Foreign Office, *Report on Native Manufactures of the Philippine Islands,* Miscellaneous Series, no. 48 (London: Harrison and Sons, 1887), 3.
9. Ahujas, *Reseña,* 2:62; *Estado, 1818.*

10. Laplace, *Voyage,* 550–51; Owen, *Prosperity,* 47.

11. Perkins-Russell Papers, vol. 20, 10, BL-HBS; Bryant & Sturgis Papers, vol. 10, 201, BL-HBS; Samuel Eliot Morison, *The Ropemakers of Plymouth: A History of the Plymouth Cordage Company, 1824–1949* (Boston: Houghton Mifflin, 1950), 34, n. 3; Lannoy, *Iles Philippines,* 134.

12. L. Barretto to E. Carrington, June 14, 1824, ECP-RIHS.

13. Bryant & Sturgis Papers, vol. 12, BL-HBS.

14. Russell & Sturgis to E. Carrington, October 14, 1829, and circular dated January 1, 1841, ECP-RIHS; Charles Wilkes, *Narrative of the United States Exploring Expedition during the Years 1838, 1839, 1840, 1841, 1842* (New York: G. P. Putnam, 1856), 5:288; John Bernard Burke, *A Visitation of the Seats and Arms of the Noblemen and Gentlemen of Great Britain and Ireland,* 2d ser. (London: Hurst and Blackett, 1854), 10 ("Arms") and pl. 1.

15. Morison, *Ropemakers,* 48, n. 10; Russell & Sturgis circular, February 20, 1851, BL-HBS. The material for Morison's book contains price quotations for the years 1840–42, which are not used in the final text. See "Notes Made by Winston Lewis, May to September 1948—Competition and Expansion, 1837–1857," 40, PCCP, BL-HBS.

16. *Plymouth Cordage Company: One Hundred Years of Service* (Plymouth, Mass.: Plymouth Cordage Company, 1924), 37, 83; Morison, *Ropemakers,* 39–40; "Notes Made by Winston Lewis, May to September 1948—Competition and Expansion (43, 54–55), Machinery (28, 34), Materials (2–3), Some Notes on Products (2–3)," PCCP, BL-HBS.

17. Russell & Sturgis to William Appleton & Co., Boston, July 24, 1844, and July 8, 1845, DAP, BL-HBS.

18. Russell & Sturgis circular, January 19, 1848, BL-HBS.

19. B. A. Barretto & Co., Manila, to A. Heard & Co., Canton, May 26, June 12, and July 4, 1848, AHC II, BL-HBS.

20. Morison, *Ropemakers,* 63–65; *Plymouth Cordage Company,* 41.

21. Russell & Sturgis circulars, August 16 and November 14, 1851, November 22, 1852, January 7 and October 7, 1856, and November 22, 1858, BL-HBS.

22. Handwritten note at end of PHC circular of January 5, 1866, PFP-SUL.

23. Treasurer's Journal, 1824–1837, PCCP, BL-HBS; B. Spooner to Ker & Co., April 8, 1853, and January 18, 1855; B. Spooner to Russell & Sturgis, December 23, 1854, October 29, 1855, February 16, 1857 (in B. Spooner's Letterbooks, June 21, 1845, to February 9, 1854, and August 6, 1855, to November 7, 1857); Agreement between Plymouth Cordage Co. and New Bedford Cordage Co., January 1, 1867, all in PCCP, BL-HBS.

24. Ker & Co., Manila, to Stone, Silsbee & Pickman, November 12, 1868, March 2, 1869, November 10, 1868, June 1, 1871, SSPP-PEM; O. E. Edwards to G. H. Peirce, June 29, 1859, PFP-SUL; Russell & Sturgis circular, April 21, 1851, BL-HBS.

25. Joseph Earle Stevens, *Yesterdays in the Philippines* (New York: Charles Scribner's Sons, 1899), 158.

26. Owen, *Prosperity,* 107; O. E. Edwards to G. H. Peirce, February 2, 1859; PHC circular, February 9, 1859, PFP-SUL.

27. Russell & Sturgis circulars, December 18, 1851, and August 21 and November 22, 1854, BL-HBS.

28. Jonathan Russell Papers, BL-HBS; Richard D. Tucker Papers, PEM.

29. Morison, *Ropemakers,* 71–75, 77–85; "Notes Made by Winston Lewis, May to September 1948—Association, Pool and Trust," 1–31, PCCP, BL-HBS.

30. Gironiere, *Twenty Years,* 17–20, 296, 318, 330, 337–39, 355–56, 365; Laplace, *Voyage,* 432–33; Pardo de Tavera, *Biblioteca Filipina,* 185–86; González and Moreno, *Manual,* 173;

Meyen, *Reise,* 263; Jagor, "Travels," 67; Gabriel Lafond de Lurcy, *Voyages autour du Monde et Naufrages Celebres. Mers Du Sud, de la Chine et Archipels de l'Inde* (Paris: Pourrat Freres, Editeurs, 1844), 4:195, 223.

31. W. W. Wood (Jala-jala and Manila) to A. Heard, Boston, August 18, 1835, and January 9 and November 17, 1837, AHC I, BL-HBS; Jonathan Russell Papers, BL-HBS.

32. W. H. Thomes, *Life in the East Indies* (Boston: Lee and Shepard, 1872), 11–12.

33. NWGPC, Manila , October 17, 1846, BL-HBS.

34. Mrs. Frederick C. Munroe, "The Daily Life of Mrs. Nathaniel Kinsman on a Trip to Manila," *Essex Institute Historical Collections* 87, no. 3 (July 1951): 299–300; Mac Micking, *Recollections,* 223–24; Santayana, *Persons,* 32, 41–43; George Sturgis Papers; Jonathan Russell Papers, BL-HBS; Richard D. Tucker Papers, PEM; Russell & Sturgis circulars, February 20, 1851, August 18, 1852, July 28, 1854, September 1, 1875, BL-HBS; González and Moreno, *Manual,* 280; González and Moreno, *Anuario Filipino,* 247; *Estadística general, 1882; Estadística general, 1883.*

35. Nicholas Loney, *A Britisher in the Philippines* (Manila: National Library, 1964); Nicholas Loney, "Trade in Panay, 1857–67," in Mac Micking, *Recollections,* 207–87 (four letters from Loney published as an appendix to the 1967 edition); Regidor and Mason, *Commercial Progress,* 27–28; Foreman, *Philippine Islands,* 286; González and Moreno, *Manual,* 179; Carlos Recur, *Filipinas. El comercio nacional y el desestanco del tabaco* (Madrid: Imprenta de Fortanet, 1881), 16; PFP-SUL; McCoy, "Queen," 302–3, 314. Sir John Bowring's book contains extensive paraphrases of and excerpts from consular reports (*Visit,* 367–420).

36. "Los Sres Russell Sturgis de este Comercio solicitan se les permita introducir libre de derechos el Hielo q ha conducido la fragata Americana Hizaide. Va unida a otra instancia q.ᵉ sobre lo mismo promueve D.ⁿ Carlos D. Mugford," AdM, *legajo* 1861–64; "Yndice de los asuntos despachados que abajo se expresan," in a vellum-bound volume, "Año de 1848, Aduana"; "Yncidente promovido por los Sres Ker y Compañia pidiendo se declare como de utilidad pública una máquina para refinar azucar," Concepción Kerr *legajo*; "Demanda sobre esportación de azúcar de derechos satisfechos por la Cia Aguirre y Comp.ᵃ del comercio de esta plaza contra un decreto de la Yntend.ᵃ," AdM, *legajo* 1841–64, all in PNA; González and Moreno, *Manual,* 273, 279; *Guía de forasteros . . . 1845,* 104; *Guía de forasteros . . . 1850* (Manila: Imprenta de los Amigos del País, n.d.), 301–2, 308.

37. William Henry Scott, *Barangay,* 75.

38. On J. M. Tuason, see Quirino, *Filipinos at War.* See also Bank of the Philippine Islands, *LXXV Anniversary,* 2; *Barretto v. Tuason*; J. M. Tuason & Co. circulars, BL-HBS; *Diario de Manila,* Año XLVII, número extraordinario, 19 de noviembre de 1895; circular on sugar standards, June 1, 1867, PFP-SUL; "Año de 1822. Asignacion de 30,000 ps. a D. Mariano Tuason con la hipoteca delas haciendas de Diliman y Santa Mesa," Felipe Liao Collection, Quezon City, Philippines; "Disolucion dela Sociedad J. M. Tuason y C.ᵃ"—"La Ynspeccion de Montes . . . sobre abono de derechos de maderas exportadas a China"—"El aforo de los sacos a que se refiere la instancia de los Sres. Tuason y C.ᵃ"—"Expediente promovido por d.ⁿ Jose m.ᵃ Tuason y c.ᵃ pidiendo se admitan sus cheques en el tesoro publico como papel moneda oficial," all in *legajo* "Gonzalo Tuason Casos Civiles, 1860–1902," PNA; "Yncidente relativo al ofrecimiento espontaneo de 120 [mil] \$"—"Juzgado del Distrito de Tondo. Diligencias preparatorias de juicio ejecutivo promovidos por D. Jose Maria Tuazon [*sic*] y C.ᵃ contra el chino Lim Tionchay"—"Justiprecio y avaluo que el que Suscribe . . . ha practicado . . . en los bienes embargados al Chino So Chico . . ." (seven promissory notes of So Chico), all in *legajo* "Expedientes sobre J. M. Tuason y Compañía, 1853–1874," PNA.

39. On domestic enterprise in general, see De Mas, *Informe sobre el estado*, 3. See also Bowring, *Visit*, 278–79; Foreman, *Philippine Islands*, 378–88; Del Pan, *Las Islas Filipinas*, 234–36; Díaz Arenas, *Memorias históricas*, vol. 1, bks. 8 and 9; Russell & Sturgis circulars; A. Heard Papers; *Almanaque Filipino i guía de forasteros para el año de 1834*; *Guía de forasteros en las Islas Filipinas para el año de 1845*; *Guía de forasteros para el año de 1856* (Manila: Imp. de los Amigos del País, n.d.); *Guía de forasteros para el año de 1860*; *Guía de forasteros para el año de 1865* (Manila: Imp. de los Amigos del País, 1865); González and Moreno, *Manual*, 270–352; Anon., *Under Four Flags*, 12; Santayana, *Persons*, 52–53; Syme, Muir & Co., Amoy, circular, May 20, 1854; NWGPC, various dates, 1843–45. For some of the background on Narciso Padilla, I am indebted to the late Associate Justice (ret.) Teodoro Padilla of the Supreme Court of the Philippines. See also *Constitución política de la República Filipina promulgada el día 22 de Enero de 1899* (Barasoain: Z. Fajardo, 1899), Titulo IV, Articulo 6°, 9–10.

40. "Yncidente promovido por D.n Balbino Mauricio . . . sobre debolucion [*sic*] de derechos de importacion por cien cajas de cera vegetal . . ." AdM *legajo*, 1861–64, PNA; Artigas y Cuerva, *Los sucesos*, 63–64, 117, 222–23, 236–37, 261, 265; Celestina P. Boncan, *Remembering the Cavite Mutiny of 1872* (n.p.: Geronimo Berenguer de los Reyes Jr. Foundation, Inc., 1995), 10–13, i–ii, vii; Edmond Plauchut, *La algarada caviteña de 1872* (Manila: Imprenta "Manila Filatélica," 1916), 22; Clarita T. Nolasco, "The Creoles in Spanish Philippines," *Far Eastern University Journal* 15, nos. 1–2 (September–December 1970): 135, 140; Montero y Vidal, *Historia general*, 3:579, 584; Antonio M. Molina, *The Philippines through the Centuries* (Manila: UST Cooperative, 1960), 1:331, 335, 337; *Guía de forasteros en Filipinas para el año de 1860*, 127; *Guía de forasteros en Filipinas para el año de 1865*, 181; Zaide, *Philippine Revolution*, 121; E. Arsenio Manuel, *Dictionary of Philippine Biography* (Quezon City: Filipiniana Publications, 1955), 1:229–31. Father Gomes's name is often given as Gomez.

41. Jonathan Russell Papers, BL-HBS; Richard D. Tucker Papers, PEM; Burke-Miailhe Papers, Manila, Philippines; Foreman, *Philippine Islands*, 286–87; Regidor and Mason, *Commercial Progress*, 30; Boyden Sparkes and Samuel Taylor Moore, *The Witch of Wall Street, Hetty Green* (New York: Doubleday Doran, 1935), 82–84; Arthur H. Lewis, *The Day They Shook the Plum Tree* (New York: Bantam Harcourt Brace, 1969), 24–26; Raphael Semmes, *The Confederate Raider Alabama* (Greenwich, Conn.: Fawcett Publications, 1962), 309–13.

42. Russell & Sturgis circulars, SSPP-PEM; Society of Jesus, *El archipiélago filipino*, 1:331; C.H.P.C., "The Ship *Panay* of Salem," broadsheet, PEM.

43. Hodsoll, "Britain"; Anon., *Under Four Flags*, 22, 27; Ambeth R. Ocampo, "Eiffel's Church in Manila," *Philippine Daily Inquirer*, April 21, 1995.

44. PFP-SUL, box 9, folder 2.

45. *Tramways des Iles Philippines* (Liege: Demarteau, n.d.); Society of Jesus, *Archipiélago*, 1:325–26; Stevens, *Yesterdays*, 27–28; *Report of the Philippine Commission to the President* (Washington, D.C.: Government Printing Office, 1900), 2:321; Artigas y Cuerva, *Los sucesos*, 271–72; *Acta de las sesión celebrada por la junta general extraordinaria de la Compañía de Tranvías de Filipinas en Madrid a primeros de junio de 1890* (Madrid: Tipografía de los Huérfanos, 1890).

46. *Estatutos de La Electricista sociedad anónima domiciliada en Manila* (Manila: Ramirez y Compañía, 1892); Stevens, *Yesterdays*, 183.

47. Enrique Barretto Papers, photocopies in bound volume, PNA; Wenceslao E. Retana, *Vida y escritos del Dr. José Rizal* (Madrid: Victoriano Suárez, 1907), 350–52; *Commercial Directory of Manila, 1901* (n.p., n.d.), xix, xliii. Francisco Pi y Margall, *Historia de España en el siglo XIX* (Barcelona: Miguel Segui, 1902), VII (2), 1223–26.

Notes to the Epilogue

1. Richard Hooley, "A Century of Philippine Foreign Trade: A Quantitative Analysis," in *Choice, Growth, and Development, Emerging and Enduring Issues: Essays in Honor of José Encarnación,* edited by Emmanel S. de Dios and Raul V. Fabella (Quezon City: University of the Philippines Press, 1996), 258–62, 266, 281. In evaluating any computations based on Spanish trade data, readers should bear in mind the statistical reservations mentioned in the text.

2. Barry E. Supple, ed., *The Experience of Economic Growth: Case Studies in Economic History* (New York: Random House, 1963), 203–5, 266 (see especially articles by E. H. Phelps Brown and S. J. Handfield Jones, D. J. Coppock, and Alfred H. Conrad).

3. Larkin, *Sugar,* 51–52.

4. Smith, "Crisis Mortality," 68, 74–76.

5. Hooley, "Century," 288.

6. Francisco Borrero, *Cuestiones filipinas* (Madrid: Imprenta de la Viuda de M. Minuesa de los Rios, 1896), 18–21.

7. Florentino Rodao, "Spanish Interests in the Philippines after the Revolution," paper presented at the International Conference on the Centennial of the 1896 Philippine Revolution, Manila, August 21, 1996, 1–2, 6–7.

8. Benito Legarda y Fernandez, "The Philippine Economy under Spanish Rule," *Solidarity* 2, no. 10 (November-December 1967): 14–15.

9. Hodsoll, "Britain"; Compton Mackenzie, *Realms of Silver: One Hundred Years of Banking in the East* (London: Routledge and Kegan Paul, 1954), 133.

10. Legarda, "Philippine Economy," 16–17; *Census of 1903,* 4:81.

11. *Gaceta de Manila,* May 31 and June 1, 1888.

12. Rafaelita H. Soriano, "Tiburcio Hilario of Pampanga," *Historical Bulletin* 8, no. 4 (December 1964): 5–8, 11–12.

13. Zaide, *Philippine Revolution,* 115, 120–21; Foreman, *Philippine Islands,* 515–17; Umberto G. Lammoglia, "Valenzuela: Rope-Maker Who Made History," *Philippine Daily Inquirer,* August 30, 1996, 1, 20; *Exposición regional,* 349, 18 (of additional unnumbered pages).

14. Clark,"Labor Conditions," 731.

BIBLIOGRAPHY

Manuscripts, Archival Materials, and Unpublished Works

"Acapulco." Bound volumes of photocopies of documents about the galleon trade. Philippine National Archives, Manila.

Aduana de Manila. Collection of customs records. Philippine National Archives, Manila.

"Balanza general del comercio de las Yslas Filipinas en el año de 1847." Manila, 1848. Unpublished report of the Philippine customs, Philippine National Archives, Manila.

Bañas Llanos, Maria Belén. "Don Juan de Cuéllar y sus Comisiones Científicas en Filipinas (1739?–1801)." Ph.D. diss., Universidad Complutense, Madrid, 1991.

Banco Español-Filipino. Collection of manuscripts. Philippine National Archives, Manila.

Enrique Barretto Papers. Photocopies of documents in a bound volume. Philippine National Archives, Manila.

Barretto y Rocha, Antonio María. "Familia Barretto." April 1922. Translated from the original Spanish into English by Federico V. Barretto, Jr., July 24, 1993. Photocopy of typescript provided by Mrs. Nena Barretto Olivares, San Juan, Metro Manila.

Bowditch, Nathaniel. Account of a visit to Manila in 1796–97. East India Marine Society Journals, vol. 1, no. 3. Manuscript. Peabody Essex Museum, Salem, Massachusetts.

Bryant & Sturgis Papers. Letterbooks, vols. 8, 10, 11, 12. Baker Library, Harvard Business School.

Burke-Miailhe Papers. In the care of Mr. W. A. B. Miailhe, Manila.

Edward Carrington Papers. Rhode Island Historical Society, Providence, Rhode Island.

Dexter-Appleton Papers. Baker Library, Harvard Business School.

"Estado que manifiesta el número de buques nacionales y estrangeros que han concurrido a este puerto en todo el presente año de 1825, con expresión de los valores de importación y de exportación de cada uno de ellos así en frutos y efectos como en numerario sacado de los registros de esta real aduana." Manila, [1825?]. Photostat. Peabody Essex Museum, Salem, Massachusetts.

Thomas T. Forbes Letterbooks. Vols. 3, 4. Baker Library, Harvard Business School.

"Galeones." Bound volumes of photocopies of documents on the galleon trade, the sampan trade, and other vessels entering Manila. Philippine National Archives, Manila.

Augustine Heard & Company Papers. Baker Library, Harvard Business School.

María de la Concepción Kerr *legajo*. Philippine National Archives, Manila. This contains Ker & Co. material, although the Scottish company was unrelated to the lady in the title, a daughter of the American customs broker John Stuart Kerr.

Kierulf Family File. "General Account Regarding the Kierulf Family," with attachments. Mimeographed (privately circulated), Manila.

Guillermo Kierulf *legajo*, 1828–31. Philippine National Archives, Manila.

Nightingale and Jenckes Papers. Rhode Island Historical Society, Providence, Rhode Island.

Peele Family Papers. Peabody Essex Museum, Salem, Massachusetts.

Willard Peele Papers. Peabody Essex Museum, Salem, Massachusetts.

Peirce Family Papers. Stanford University Libraries, Stanford, California.

James Perkins and Thomas Handasyd Perkins Manuscripts. Originals and transcripts. Massachusetts Historical Society, Boston, Massachusetts.

Perkins-Russell Letterbooks. Vols. 19, 20. Baker Library, Harvard Business School.

Perseverance, Shipping Logbook, Voyage to Batavia, Manila, and Canton, December 1796–April 1798. Peabody Essex Museum, Salem, Massachusetts.

Plymouth Cordage Company Papers. Baker Library, Harvard Business School.

Prices Current, Baker Library, Harvard Business School (for Manila unless otherwise noted): Fred. Baker & Co., Ker & Co., Peele, Hubbell & Co., Russell & Sturgis, Syme Muir & Co., Amoy,Tait & Co. (Amoy), J. M. Tuason & Co.

Rodao, Florentino. "Spanish Interests in the Philippines after the Revolution." Paper read at the International Conference on the Centennial of the 1896 Philippine Revolution, Manila, August 21, 1996. Mimeographed.

George Robert Russell Letters. In the collection of Dr. Charles P. Lyman, Cambridge, Mass.

Jonathan Russell Manuscripts and Papers. Baker Library, Harvard Business School.

Stone, Silsbee & Pickman Papers. Peabody Essex Museum, Salem, Massachusetts.

George Sturgis Letters and Papers. In the collection of the family of Mrs. David Little, Weston, Massachusetts.

Tilden, Bryant. Journal. Transcribed typescript. Peabody Essex Museum, Salem, Mass.

[Tuason]. "Año de 1822. Asignación de 30,000 ps. a D. Mariano Tuason con la hipoteca delas [*sic*] haciendas de Dilimán y Santa Mesa." Felipe Liao Collection, Quezon City, Philippines.

[Tuason]. Expedientes sobre J. M. Tuason y Compañía, 1853–74. *Legajo* in Philippine National Archives, Manila.

Gonzalo Tuason Casos Civiles, 1860–1902. *Legajo* in Philippine National Archives, Manila.

Richard D. Tucker Letters and Papers. Peabody Essex Museum, Salem, Massachusetts.

[Francisco Leandro de Viana.] "Ynforme que hizo el Conde de Tepa del Consejo de Indias sobre el comercio de Filipinas." Dated March 9 but delivered May 9, 1780. Transcript in "Libro de various papeles," Ticknor Collection, Boston Public Library.

Printed Materials

Abend, Hallett. *Treaty Ports*. New York: Doubleday, 1944.

Acta de la sesión celebrada por la junta general extraordinaria de la Compañía de Tranvías de Filipinas en Madrid a primeros de junio de 1890. Madrid: Tipografía de los Huérfanos, 1890.

Agoncillo, Teodoro. *The Revolt of the Masses: The Story of Bonifacio and the Katipunan*. Quezon City: University of the Philippines, 1957.

Aguilar, Filomeno, Jr. "Beyond Inevitability: The Opening of Philippine Provincial Ports in 1855." *Journal of Southeast Asian Studies* 25, no. 1 (March 1994): 70–90.

A[hujas], F[rancisco]. *Reseña acerca del estado social y económico de las colonias de España en Asia y reformas que exigen para su desarrollo*. Vols. 1–2. Madrid: Imprenta de J. Noguera, 1874.

Alessio Robles, Vito. *Acapulco en la historia y en la leyenda*. 2d ed. Mexico: Ediciones Botas, 1948.

Allen, G. C., and Audrey G. Donnithorne. *Western Enterprise in Far Eastern Economic Development: China and Japan*. London: Allen and Unwin, 1954.

———. *Western Enterprise in Indonesia and Malaya*. New York: Macmillan, 1957.

Almazán, Marco A. "El Galeon de Manila." In Obregón et al., *El Galeón de Manila*, 4–30.

Álvarez y Tejero, Luis Prudencio. *De las Islas Filipinas*. Valencia: Imprenta de Cabrerizo, 1842.

Anon. *Under Four Flags: The Story of Smith Bell & Co. in the Philippines*. Bristol: J. W. Arrowsmith, n.d.

[Aragón, Yldefonso de.] *Yslas Filipinas. Manila Año de MDCCCXVIII. Estado que manifiestan la importación y exportación de esta ciudad, en todo el presente año; en que se hacen ver la contribución, productos líquidos de rentas, y reales derechos; como igualmente los frutos y efectos del país exportados; y sus valores en plaza y venta.* Manila: Ynprenta [*sic*] de D. Manuel Memije [1820].

Arancel general para el comercio esterior de Filipinas rectificado y añadido de orden del Escmo Sr. Capitan General de estas islas. Manila: Imprenta del Boletin Oficial, 1855.

Arancel general para el comercio exterior de las Islas Filipinas. [Manila:] Imprenta de Sampaloc, 1831.

Aranceles de aduanas de las Islas Filipinas y disposiciones para la reforma de los mismos, dictados por decreto del gobierno provisional no. 63, de 29 de diciembre de 1868, ordenes del Ministerio de Ultramar, numeros 64 y 65, de igual fecha y decreto del gobeirno superior civil de 27 de abril de 1869. Binondo [Manila]: Imprenta de Miguel Sánchez y Cía., 1889.

Aranceles provisionales de Aduanas de las Islas Filipinas reformadas en virtud de la Real Orden de 12 noviembre de 1860. Manila: Establecimiento tipográfico de Amigos del País, 1862.

Arcilla, Jose, S.J. "Raíces de la historia filipina." *Crónica de Manila*, September 26, 1993.

Armella de Aspe, Virginia. "Artes asiáticas y novohispanas." In Wimer, *El Galeón del Pacífico*, 203–39.

Arteche, José. *Legazpi. Historia de la conquista de Filipinas.* Zarauz: Editorial Icharopena, 1947.

Artigas y Cuerva, Manuel. *Los sucesos de 1872.* Manila: Imp. de La Vanguardia, 1911.

Azcárraga y Palmero, Manuel. *La libertad de comercio en las Islas Filipinas.* Madrid: Imprenta de José Noguera, 1871.

Baig Baños, Aurelio. "La Real Compañia de Filipinas, el Banco Nacional de San Carlos y el mayorazgo Don Valentín de Foronda." *Revista nacional de economía*, year 14, vol. 29, nos. 86–87 (July-August and September-October 1929): 75–92, 253–85.

Bañas, Raymundo C. *The Music and Theater of the Filipino People.* Manila: privately published, 1924.

Banco Español-Filipino de Isabel II. *Año 5°. Memoria leída en la junta general de accionistas celebrada el dia 17 de mayo de 1857.* Manila: Imprenta de los Amigos del País, 1857.

———. *Memoria leída en la junta general de accionistas celebrada el dia 3 de mayo de 1853. Año 1°.* Manila: Imp. *El Retoño* [1853?].

Bank of the Philippine Islands. *LXXV Anniversary: Souvenir of the First Bank Established in the Far East.* Manila, 1928.

Barras de Aragón, Francisco de las. *Cuatro documentos del Archivo de Indias referentes a la obra realizada por España en Filipinas, en el siglo XVIII.* Seville: Sobrinos de Izquierdo, 1918.

Barras de Aragón, Francisco de las. "Don Francisco Xavier Salgado, y sus obras en Filipinas en el siglo XVIII." Asociación española para el progreso de las ciencias, Congreso de Sevilla, vol. 8, sec. 6. Madrid: Imprenta Clásica Española, 1917.

Barretto v. Tuason, 50 *Phil. Rep.* 888. (Supreme Court of the Philippines, no. 23923, March 23, 1926, Antonio Ma. Barretto et al., plaintiffs and defendants, v. Augusto H. Tuason et al., defendants and appellants, *Philippine Reports*, 888–971.)

Bartlett, John Russell, *Genealogy of That Branch of the Russell Family Which Comprises the Descendants of John Russell, of Woburn, Massachusetts, 1640–1878.* Providence: privately printed, 1879.

Belford, Samuel W. "Material Problems in the Philippine Islands." *American Monthly Review of Reviews* 19, no. 4 (April 1899): 454–57.

Benitez, Conrado. *History of the Philippines.* Boston: Ginn, 1926.

Benítez, Fernando. "Introducción." In Wimer, *El Galeón del Pacífico*, 13–39.

Benson, E. F. *Ferdinand Magellan*. New York: Harper, 1930.

Bernad, Miguel A., S.J. "The Ancient Slave Market." In Roces, *Filipino Heritage*, 2:330–36.

_____. "A Booming Inter-island Trade." In Roces, *Filipino Heritage*, 3:645–50.

_____. *The Christianization of the Philippines: Problems and Perspectives*. Manila: Filipiniana Book Guild, 1972.

_____. "Popular Uprisings in the Philippines." *Kinaadman* 1 (1970): 145–48. Review of David R. Sturtevant's *Popular Uprisings in the Philippines, 1840–1940* (Ithaca: Cornell University Press, 1976).

Bernal, Rafael. "The Chinese Colony in Manila, 1570–1770." In Felix, *Chinese*, 1:40–66.

_____. *México en Filipinas. Estudio de una transculturación*. Mexico City: Universidad Autónoma de México, 1965.

_____. *Prologue to Philippine History*. Manila: Solidaridad, 1967.

Beyer, H. Otley. "Early History of Philippine Relations with Foreign Countries, Especially China," introduction to E. Arsenio Manuel, *Chinese Elements in the Tagalog Language*, vii–xxv. Manila: Filipiniana Publications, 1948.

Blair, Emma H., and James A. Robertson. *The Philippine Islands, 1493–1898*. 55 vols. Cleveland: Arthur H. Clark, 1903–9.

Blumentritt, Ferdinand. "Los conquistadores militares y civiles de Filipinas. Apuntes para una crítica de la historia de la conquista. II." *La Solidaridad Quincenario Democrático* 6, no. 132 (1894): 154–56.

Boletín de la Real Sociedad Económica de Amigos del País. Vol. 3.

Boncan, Celestina P. *Remembering the Cavite Mutiny of 1872*. N.p.: Geronimo Berenguer de los Reyes Jr. Foundation, 1995.

Borrero, Francisco, *Cuestiones filipinas*. Madrid: Imprenta de la Viuda de M. Minuesa de los Ríos, 1896.

Bourne, Edward Gaylord. *Discovery, Conquest, and Early History of the Philippine Islands*. Cleveland: Arthur H. Clark, 1907.

Bowden, Witt, Michael Karpovich, and Abbott Payson Usher. *An Economic History of Europe since 1750*. New York: American Book Co., 1937.

Bowring, John. *A Visit to the Philippine Islands*. London: Smith, Elder, 1859.

Boxer, C. R. *Jan Compagnie in War and Peace, 1602–1799: A Short History of the Dutch East India Company*. Hong Kong, Singapore, and Kuala Lumpur: Heinemann Asia, 1979.

_____. "*Plata es Sangre*: Sidelights on the Drain of Spanish American Silver to the Far East, 1550–1700." *Philippine Studies* 18, no. 3 (July 1970): 457–78.

Braganza, Jose Vicente, S.V.D. *The Encounter: The Epic Story of the Christianization of the Philippines*. Manila: Catholic Trade School, 1965.

Burke, John Bernard. *A Visitation of the Seats and Arms of the Noblemen and Gentlemen of Great Britain and Ireland*. 2d ser. London: Hurst and Blackett, 1854.

Buzeta, Manuel, and Felipe Bravo. *Diccionario geográfico. estadístico, histórico de las Islas Filipinas*. 2 vols. Madrid, 1850.

Canton Commercial List, October 18, 1849.

Capella, Miguel, and Antonio Matilla Tascon. *Los cinco Gremios Mayores de Madrid*. Madrid: n.p., 1957.

Carballo, Manuel, et al. "El arte en el comercio con Asia." *Artes de México*, year 22, no. 190 (1977).

Cary, Thomas G. *Memoir of Thomas Handasyd Perkins*. Boston: Little, Brown, 1856.

Cassel, Gustav. *The Theory of Social Economy*. Translated by S. L. Barron. Rev. ed. Vol. 1. London: Ernest Benn, 1932.

Cavada y Méndez de Vigo, Agustín de la. *Historia geográfica, geológica, y estadística de Filipinas*. 2 vols. Manila: Imp. de Ramírez y Giraudier, 1876.

Census of 1903. See U.S. Bureau of the Census.

Centenary of Wise and Company in the Philippines, 1826–1926. N.p., n.d.

Chaunu, Pierre. *Les Philippines et le Pacifique des Ibériques*. Paris: SEVPEN, 1960 (graphic appendix, 1966).

Cheong, Weng Eang. "Changing the Rules of the Game (the India-Manila Trade, 1785–1809)." *Journal of Southeast Asian Studies* 1, no. 2 (1970): 1–19.

———. "The Decline of Manila as the Spanish Entrepôt in the Far East, 1785–1826: Its Impact on the Pattern of Southeast Asian Trade." *Journal of Southeast Asian Studies* 2 (September 1971): 142–58.

C.H.P.C. "The Ship *Panay* of Salem." Broadsheet, n.d.

Clark, Victor S. "Labor Conditions in the Philippines." *Bulletin of the Bureau of Labor* (U.S. Department of Commerce and Labor) 58 (May 1905).

Cloghessy, James. "The Philippines and the Royal Philippine Company." *Mid-America: An Historical Review* 42, no. 2 (April 1960): 80–104.

Cole, Arthur H. "An Approach to the Study of Entrepreneurship." *Journal of Economic History* 6 (1946): S1–15.

Colección de documentos inéditos de ultramar. Vols. 2–3. Madrid: Sucesores de Rivadeneyra, 1886–87.

Commercial Directory of Manila, 1901. N.p., n.d.

Comyn, Tomas de. *State of the Philippine Islands*. Translated by William Walton. London: T. and J. Allman, 1821.

Constitución política de la República Filipina promulgada el dia 22 de Enero de 1899. Edición Oficial, Islas Filipinas. Barasoain (Bulacan): Imp. Bajo la Dirección del Sr. Z. Fajardo, 1899.

Corle, Edwin. *The Royal Highway*. Indianapolis: Bobbs-Merrill, 1949.

Corpuz, Onofre D. *The Roots of the Filipino Nation*. 2 vols. Quezon City: Aklahi Foundation, 1989.

Costa, Horacio de la, S.J. *Asia and the Philippines*. Manila: Solidaridad, 1967.

———. "The Legal Basis for Spanish Imperial Sovereignty." *Philippine Studies* 1, no. 2 (September 1953): 155–62.

Cuevas, Mariano, S.J. *Monje y Marino. La vida y los tiempos de Fray Andrés de Urdaneta*. Mexico: Galatea, 1943.

Dales, John H. "Approaches to Entrepreneurial History." *Explorations in Entrepreneurial History* 1, no. 1 (January 1949): 10–14.

Day, Clive. *The Policy and Administration of the Dutch in Java*. New York: Macmillan, 1904.

De Bevoise, Ken. *Agents of Apocalypse: Epidemic Disease in the Colonial Philippines*. Princeton: Princeton University Press, 1995.

Dery, Luis Camara. *From Ibalon to Sorsogon: A Historical Survey of Sorsogon Province to 1905*. Quezon City: New Day, 1991.

Diario de Manila. Año XLVII, número extraordinario, 19 de noviembre de 1895.

Díaz Arenas, Rafael. *Memoria sobre el comercio y navegación de las Islas Filipinas*. Cádiz: Imprenta de D. Domingo Féros, 1838.

_____. *Memorias históricas y estadísticas de Filipinas*. 2 vols. Manila: Imprenta del *Diario de Manila*, 1850.

Díaz-Trechuelo Spínola, María Lourdes. "El comercio de Filipinas durante la segunda mitad del siglo XVIII." *Revista de Indias* nos. 93–94 (July-December 1963): 463–85.

_____. "La defensa de Filipinas en el ultimo cuarto del siglo XVIII." In *Anuario de Estudios Americanos* 21 (1964): 145–209.

_____. "Dos nuevos derroteros del galeón de Manila." *Anuario de Estudios Americanos* 13 (1956): 1–83.

_____. "The Economic Development of the Philippines in the Second Half of the Eighteenth Century." *Philippine Studies* 11, no. 2 (April 1963): 195–231.

_____. "Eighteenth-Century Philippine Economy: Agriculture." *Philippine Studies* 14, no. 1 (January 1966): 65–126.

_____. "Eighteenth-Century Philippine Economy: Commerce." *Philippine Studies* 14, no. 2 (April 1966): 253–79.

_____. "Eighteenth-Century Philippine Economy: Mining." *Philippine Studies* 13, no. 4 (October 1965): 763–97.

_____. "Philippine Economic Development Plans, 1746–1779." *Philippine Studies* 12, no. 2 (April 1964): 203–31.

_____. *La Real Compañía de Filipinas*. Seville: Escuela de Estudios Hispano-Americanos, 1965.

Doeppers, Daniel F. "The Development of Philippine Cities before 1900." *Journal of Asian Studies* 31, no. 4 (August 1972): 769–92.

Dutt, Romesh. *The Economic History of India*. 2 vols. Delhi: Government of India, 1960.

Ellis, Henry T. *Hong Kong to Manilla and the Lakes of Luzon, in the Philippine Isles, in the Year 1856*. London: Smith, Elder, 1859.

Epistola, S. V. "The Day the Chinese Came to Trade." in Roces, *Filipino Heritage*, 3:581–88.

Estatutos de La Electricista sociedad anónima domiciliada en Manila. Manila: Ramírez y Compa., 1892.

Exposición de la Compañía de Filipinas relativa a su establecimiento y a su importancia político-mercantil: a los medios que ha empleado para llenar los fines de su instituto; y a la justicia y necesidad de su conservación para utilidad general del estado, dirigida por su junta de gobierno a las Cortes generales y extraordinarias de la nación. Cádiz: Imprenta de D. Manuel Ximénez Carreño, 1813.

Exposición dirigida a las Cortes por la junta de gobierno de la Compañía de Filipinas. Madrid: Imprenta de Don Mateo Repullés, 1821.

Exposición regional filipina, 1895. N.p., n.d.

Extracto de la memoria escrita por el P. José Nieto, Cura regular de Sarrat en Ilocos Norte sobre la insurrección acaecida en el mismo en el año 1815. Ahora publicada por primera vez, año de 1898. Extracted from W. E. Retana, *Archivo del bibliófilo filipino*, 4:171–80. Madrid: Viuda de M. Minuesa de los Ríos, 1898.

Felix, Alfonso, Jr., ed. *The Chinese in the Philippines, 1570–1770*. Vol. 1. Manila: Solidaridad, 1966.

Fernández de Navarrete, Eustaquio. *Historia de Juan Sebastián Del Cano*. Vitoria: Hijos de Manteli, 1872.

Fernández de Navarrete, Martín. *Colección de los viajes y descubrimientos que hicieron por mar los Españoles desde fines del siglo XV*, vols. 4–5. Buenos Aires: Editorial Guaranía, 1946.

[Forbes, Allan.] *Other Merchants and Sea Captains of Old Boston*. Boston: State Street Trust, 1919.

Foreman, John. *The Philippine Islands*. 2d ed., rev. New York: Charles Scribner's Sons, 1899.

Fox, Robert B. "The Archaeological Record of Chinese Influences in the Philippines." *Philippine Studies* 15, no. 1 (January 1967): 41–62.

———. "Looking at the Prehispanic Community: The Structure of Prehistoric Filipino Communities." In Roces, *Filipino Heritage*, 2:352–59.

Fragoso, Ricardo. *Aranceles e instrucción de aduanas de Filipinas con las disposiciones que los reforman o adicionan, comentadas y concordadas; y con la exposición de todos aquellos datos convenientes al comercio y a la administración, seguidos de parte de la legislación aduanera de la Peninsula.* Manila: Establecimiento tipográfico *La Industrial*, 1886.

Furber, Holden. "An Abortive Attempt at Anglo-Spanish Commercial Cooperation in the Far East in 1793." *Hispanic American Historical Review* 15, no. 4 (November 1935): 447–63.

Gaceta de Manila. Various issues.

Galvin, John. "Supplies from Manila for the California Missions, 1781–1783." *Philippine Studies* 12, no. 3 (July 1964): 494–510.

Garcia, Mauro, ed. *Readings in Philippine Prehistory*. Manila: Filipiniana Book Guild, 1979.

Garcia, Mauro, Carlos Quirino, and Luis Ma. Araneta, eds. *The Colonization and Conquest of the Philippines by Spain*. Manila: Filipiniana Book Guild, 1965.

Gironiere, Paul Proust de la. *Twenty Years in the Philippines*. New York: Harper and Brothers, 1854.

Goncharov, Ivan. "Voyage of the Frigate 'Pallada.'" In *Travel Accounts of the Islands (1832–1858)*, 153–214. Manila: Filipiniana Book Guild, 1974.

González Fernández, Ramón, and Federico Moreno Jerez. *Anuario filipino para 1877*. Manila: Establecimiento tipográfico de Plana y Ca., 1877.

———. *Manual del viajero en Filipinas*. Manila: Establecimiento tipográfico de Santo Tomás, 1875.

Great Britain, Foreign Office. "Report by Consul Ricketts on the Trade and Commerce of the Philippine Islands during the Year 1870." *Sessional Papers* 66 (1871): 749–56.

———. "Report by Mr. Consul Ricketts on the Trade and Commerce of the Philippine Islands during the Year 1868." *Sessional Papers* 64 (1870): 207–21.

———. "Report by Consul Ricketts on the Trade of the Philippine Archipelago for the Year 1871." *Sessional Papers* 58 (1872): 1320–27.

———. *Report on the Native Manufactures of the Philippine Islands, 1887*. Miscellaneous Series, no. 48. London: Harrison and Sons, 1887.

Greenberg, Michael. *British Trade and the Opening of China*. Cambridge: Cambridge University Press, 1951.

Grew, Henry Sturgis. *Letters from China and Manila by . . . to his Parents, 1855 to 1862*. Paris: privately printed, 1927.

Guía de forasteros. Information handbooks for visitors published between 1834 and 1865 (annually from 1842). The following were consulted: *Almanaque Filipino i guía de forasteros para el año de 1834* (Manila: Imprenta de D. José Maria Dayot, n.d.); *Guía de forasteros en las islas Filipinas para el año 1845* (Manila: Imprenta de D. Miguel Sánchez, n.d.); *Guía de forasteros en las islas Filipinas para el año de 1850* (Manila: Imprenta de los Amigos del País, n.d.); *Guía de forasteros en las islas Filipinas para el año de 1856* (Manila: Imprenta de los Amigos del País, n.d.); *Guía de forasteros en Filipinas para el año de 1860* (Manila: Imprenta de los Amigos del País, 1859); and *Guía de forasteros en Filipinas para el año 1865* (Manila: Establecimiento de los Amigos del País, 1865).

Gutiérrez, Lucio, O.P. "The Christianization of the Philippines: Myth and Realities." *Philippiniana Sacra* 11, no. 2 (May-August 1976): 203–91.

Hamilton, Earl J. "The Decline of Spain." In *Essays in Economic History*, edited by E. M. Carus-Wilson, 215–26. London: Edward Arnold, 1954.

Hernandez, Felisa R. *Our Outstanding Filipino Composers*. Manila, 1952. Mimeo.

Herr, Richard. *The Eighteenth-Century Revolution in Spain*. Princeton: Princeton University Press, 1958.

Hildebrand, Arthur Sturges. *Magellan*. New York: Harcourt, Brace, 1924.

Hill, Percy. "The Old Manila Galleons." *University of Manila Journal of East Asiatic Studies* 7, no. 3. (July 1958): 280–84. Reprinted from *Philippine Magazine* 32, no. 3 (March 1935): 132, 155–57.

Hillard, Katherine, ed. *My Mother's Journal*. Boston: George H. Ellis, 1900.

Hirschman, Albert O. *National Power and the Structure of Foreign Trade*. Berkeley: University of California Press, 1945.

Hirth, Friedrich, and W. W. Rockhill, trans. *Chao Ju Kua: His Work on the Chinese and Arab Trade in the Twelfth and Thirteenth Centuries Entitled Chu-fan-chi*. St. Petersburg: Printing Office of the Imperial Academy of Sciences, 1911; rpt., Taipei: Literature House, 1964.

Hodsoll, Frank. "Britain in the Philippines." Speech delivered to the American Association of Manila, published in the *Manila Chronicle*, December 3–8 and 10–19, 1954.

Hooley, Richard. "A Century of Philippine Foreign Trade: A Quantitative Analysis." In *Choice, Growth, and Development—Emerging and Enduring Issues: Essays in Honor of José Encarnación*, edited by Emmanuel S. De Dios and Raul V. Fabella, 255–303. Quezon City: University of the Philippines Press, 1996.

Hubbard, Clyde. "Monedas de plata en los galeones del Pacífico." In Wimer, *El Galeón del Pacífico*, 153–75.

Hubbell, Walter. *History of the Hubbell Family*. New York: J. H. Hubbell & Co., 1881.

Hussey, Roland Dennis. *The Caracas Company, 1728–1784*. Cambridge: Harvard University Press, 1934.

Ileto, Reynaldo Clemeña. *Payson and Revolution: Popular Movements in the Philippines, 1840–1910*. Quezon City: Ateneo de Manila University Press, 1979.

[Islas Filipinas, Intendencia General de Hacienda or Dirección General de Hacienda.] Annual reports were published by Philippine customs from 1851 to 1894 during the Spanish period. The years 1868 to 1872, however, were exceptions because a Central Statistical Board was created, which was supposed to take charge of publication at that time. But the board was dissolved before it could carry this out. The data sent to it by customs were thought to have passed to the Department of Civil Administration, and there the matter rested. (See "Real orden no. 400 de 18 de Marzo de 1876, recordando la formación [y] envío de las Balanzas Mercantiles correspondientes a los años 1868 a 1872," PNA.) The reports used in this study were the following:

- *Balanza general del comercio de las islas Filipinas. Año de 1851*. Manila: Imprenta de los Amigos del País, 1852.
- *Balanza general del comercio de las islas Filipinas. Año de 1853*. N.p., n.d.
- *Balanza general del comercio de las islas Filipinas. Año de 1854*. N.p., n.d.
- *Balanza mercantil de la renta de aduanas. Año de 1855*. N.p., n.d.
- *Cuadro general del comercio exterior de Filipinas con la metrópoli potencias extrangeras de Europa, America, Africa, Asia y colonias de la Oceanía en 1856*. Manila: Imprenta de Ramírez y Giraudier, 1859.
- *Balanza mercantil de las islas Filipinas correspondiente al año de 1857*. Manila: Establecimiento

tipográfico de los Amigos del País, 1860.

- *Balanza mercantil de las islas Filipinas correspondiente al año de 1858*. Manila: Establecimiento tipográfico de los Amigos del País, 1861.
- *Balanza mercantil de las islas Filipinas correspondiente al año de 1859*. Manila: Establecimiento tipográfico de los Amigos del País, 1861.
- *Balanza mercantil de las islas Filipinas correspondiente al año de 1860*. Manila: Establecimiento tipográfico de los Amigos del País, 1862.
- *Balanza mercantil de las islas Filipinas correspondiente al año de 1861*. Manila: Ymprenta del Colegio de Sto. Tomás, 1863.
- *Balanza mercantil de las islas Filipinas correspondiente al año de 1862*. Manila: Establecimiento tipográfico de los Amigos del País, 1864.
- *Balanza mercantil de las islas Filipinas correspondiente al año de 1863*. Manila: Imprenta de Miguel Sánchez y Ca., 1867.
- *Balanza mercantil de las islas Filipinas correspondiente al año de 1864*. Manila: Imprenta de Santo Tomás, 1868.
- *Balanza mercantil de las islas Filipinas correspondiente al año de 1865*. Manila: Imprenta de los Amigos del País, 1869.
- *Estadística mercantil del comercio exterior de las islas Filipinas correspondiente al año de 1867*. Manila: Imprenta de los "Amigos del País," 1874.
- *Estadística mercantil del comercio exterior de las islas Filipinas correspondiente al año de 1874*. N.p., n.d.
- *Estadística mercantil del comercio exterior de las islas Filipinas. Año de 1876*. Manila: Imprenta de los Amigos del País, 1877.
- *Estadística mercantil del comercio exterior de las islas Filipinas del año de 1878*. Manila: Imprenta de los Amigos del País, 1879.
- *Estadística mercantil del comercio exterior de las islas Filipinas del año de 1879*. Binondo (Manila): Imprenta de M. Pérez, hijo, 1880.
- *Estadística mercantil del comercio exterior de las islas Filipinas en el año de 1880*. Manila: Establecimiento tipográfico de Ramírez y Giraudier, 1881.
- *Estadística mercantil del comercio exterior de las islas Filipinas en el año de 1881*. Binondo (Manila): Establecimiento tipográfico de Manuel Pérez, hijo, 1882.
- *Estadística mercantil del comercio exterior de las islas Filipinas en el año de 1882*. Manila: Establecimiento tipo-litográfico de M. Pérez, hijo, 1884.
- *Estadística mercantil del comercio exterior de las islas Filipinas en el año de 1883*. Manila: Establecimiento tipográfico de Ramírez y Giraudier, 1884.
- *Estadística mercantil del comercio exterior de las islas Filipinas en el año de 1884*. Manila: Establecimiento tipo-litográfico de Manuel Pérez, hijo, 1886.
- *Estadística mercantil del comercio exterior de las islas Filipinas en el año de 1885*. Manila: Establecimiento tipográfico de Ramírez y Giraudier, 1886.
- *Estadística mercantil del comercio exterior de las islas Filipinas en el año de 1886*. Manila: Establecimiento tipo-litográfico de Manuel Pérez, hijo, 1887.
- *Estadística mercantil del comercio exterior de las islas Filipinas en el año de 1887*. Manila: Establecimiento tipo-litográfico de Manuel Pérez, hijo, 1888.
- *Estadística mercantil del comercio exterior de las islas Filipinas del año de 1888*. Manila: Establecimiento tipo-litográfico de Manuel Pérez, hijo, 1890.
- *Estadística mercantil del comercio exterior de las islas Filipinas en 1889*. Manila: Imprenta y litografía de Manuel Pérez (hijo), 1891.

- *Estadística mercantil del comercio exterior de las islas Filipinas en 1890*. Manila: Estab. tipo-litográfico de Ramírez y Compa., 1892.
- *Estadística mercantil del comercio exterior de las islas Filipinas en 1891*. Manila: Tipografía "Amigos del País," 1893.
- *Estadística mercantil del comercio exterior de las islas Filipinas en 1892*. Manila: Tipografía "Amigos del País," 1893.
- *Estadística mercantil del comercio exterior de las islas Filipinas en 1893*. Manila: Imprenta y litografía de J. Marty, 1894.
- *Estadística mercantil del comercio exterior de las islas Filipinas en 1894*. Manila: Imprenta David, 1896.

Itier, Jules, *Journal d'un Voyage en Chine*. Paris: Chez Dauvin et Fontaine, 1848.

Jagor, Feodor. "Travels in the Philippines." In *The Former Philippines through Foreign Eyes*, edited by Austin Craig, 1–356. Manila: Philippine Education Company, 1916.

Jenkins, Shirley. *American Economic Policy toward the Philippines*. Stanford: Stanford University Press, 1954.

De Jesus, Ed[ilberto] C. *The Tobacco Monopoly in the Philippines: Bureaucratic Enterprise and Social Change, 1766–1880*. Quezon City: Ateneo de Manila University Press, 1980.

Jimeno Agius, Jose. *El comercio exterior de Filipinas*. Madrid: Imprenta Nacional, 1878.

_____. *Memoria sobre el desestanco del tabaco en las Islas Filipinas dirigida el Excmo. Sr. Ministro de Ultramar*. Binondo (Manila): Imprenta de Bruno González Moras, 1871.

Joaquin, Nick. *Manila, My Manila: A History for the Young*. Manila: City of Manila, 1990.

_____. "Toward a Coffee Renaissance." *Philippines Free Press*, February 21, 1953, 10–11.

Jocano, F[elipe] Landa. *Philippine Prehistory*. Quezon City: Philippine Center for Advanced Studies, University of the Philippines System, 1975.

_____. *The Philippines at the Spanish Contact*. Manila: MCS Enterprises, 1975.

Jones, Chester Lloyd. "The Spanish Administration of Philippine Commerce." *American Political Science Association Proceedings* 3 (1907): 180–93.

Kalaw, Maximo M. *The Development of Philippine Politics (1872–1920)*. Manila: Oriental Commercial Co., 1926.

Lafond de Lurcy, Gabriel. *Voyage autour du Monde et Naufrages Célèbres. Mers du Sud, de la Chine et Archipels de l'Inde*, vol. 4. Paris: Pourrat Frères, Éditeurs, 1844.

Lammoglia, Umberto V. "Valenzuela: Rope-Maker Who Made History." *Philippine Daily Inquirer*, August 30, 1996.

Lannoy, Joseph. *Iles Philippines*. Brussels: Imprimerie de Delevingne et Callewaert, 1849.

Laplace, Cyrille Pierre Theodore. *Voyage autour du monde par les mers de l'Inde et de Chine execute sur la corvette de l'Etat La Favorite pendant les années 1830, 1831, et 1832*. Vol. 1. Paris: Imprimerie Royale, 1833.

Larkin, John A. *Sugar and the Origins of Modern Philippine Society*. Berkeley: University of California Press, 1993.

Laufer, Berthold. "The Relations of the Chinese to the Philippine Islands." *Smithsonian Institution Miscellaneous Collections* 50 (September 13, 1907): 248–84.

Legarda y Fernandez, Benito. "The Philippine Economy under Spanish Rule." *Solidarity* 2, no. 10 (November-December 1967): 1–21.

Lewis, Arthur H. *The Day They Shook the Plum Tree*. New York: Bantam Harcourt Brace, 1969.

Licuanan, Virginia Benitez, and José Llavador Mira. *The Philippines under Spain*. Book 2: *1564–1573*. Manila: National Trust for Historical and Cultural Preservation of the Philippines, 1991.

Loney, Nicholas. *A Britisher in the Philippines: The Letters of Nicholas Loney*. Manila: National Library, 1964.

_____. "Trade in Panay, 1857–67." In Robert Mac Micking, *Recollections of Manilla and the Philippines during 1848, 1849, and 1850* (Manila: Filipinana Book Guild, 1967), 207–87. This appendix to the 1967 edition of Mac Micking's memoir includes four letters by Loney.

Lopez, Rafael, O.S.A., and Alfonso Felix, Jr., trans. *The Christianization of the Philippines*. Manila: Historical Conservation Society, 1965.

M'Konochie, Alexander. *A Summary View of the Statistics and Existing Commerce of the Principal Shores of the Pacific Ocean*. London: J. M. Richardson, 1818.

Mac Micking, Robert. *Recollections of Manilla and the Philippines during 1848, 1849, and 1850*. London: Richard Bentley, 1851; rev. ed., Manila: Filipiniana Book Guild, 1967.

Mackenzie, Compton. *Realms of Silver: One Hundred Years of Banking in the East*. London: Routledge and Kegan Paul, 1954.

Majul, Cesar Adib. "Celestial Traders in Sulu." In Roces, *Filipino Heritage*, 3:589–92.

_____. *The Political and Constitutional Ideas of the Philippine Revolution*. Quezon City: University of the Philippines Press, 1957.

Mallari, Francisco, S.J. "The Wreck of the Santo Cristo de Burgos and the Trial of Its Officers." *Philippine Studies* 38 (1st qtr., 1990): 65–83.

Mallat, Jean. *Les Philippines*. Vol. 2. Paris: Arthus Bertrand, 1846.

_____. *The Philippines: History, Geography, Customs, Agriculture, Industry, and Commerce*, translated by P. S. Castrence. Manila: National Historical Institute, 1983.

Malo de Luque, Eduardo [Pedro Francisco Luxán y Suárez de Gongora, Duque de Almodóvar]. *Historia política de los establecimientos ultrmarinos de las naciones europeas*. Vol. 5. Madrid: Antonio de Sancha, 1790.

Manila Prices Current, September 1, 1842.

Manuel, E. Arsenio. *Dictionary of Philippine Biography*. Vol. 1. Quezon City: Filipiniana Publications, 1955.

Maquivar, Consuelo. "Derrotero histórico del galeón de Acapulco." In Carballo et al., "El arte," 5–15.

Marías, Julián. *La España posible en tiempo de Carlos III*. Madrid: Sociedad de Estudios y Publicaciones, 1963.

Marley, David F. "The Great Galleon: The *Santisima Trinidad* (1750–65)." *Philippine Studies* 41 (2d qtr., 1993): 167–81.

Martínez de Zúñiga, Joaquín, O.S.A. *Estadismo de las Islas Filipinas*: 2 vols. Madrid: Viuda de M. Minuesa de los Ríos, 1893.

_____. *An Historical View of the Philippine Islands*, translated by John Maver. 2 vols. London: J. Asperne and Nonaville and Fell, 1814.

[De Mas, Sinibaldo.] *Informe sobre el estado de las Islas Filipinas en 1842*. Vol. 2. Madrid, 1843.

May, Glenn Anthony. *A Past Recovered*. Quezon City: New Day, 1987.

McCarthy, Edward J., O.S.A. *Spanish Beginnings in the Philippines, 1564–1572*. Washington, D.C.: Catholic University of America Press, 1943.

McCoy, Alfred W. "A Queen Dies Slowly: The Rise and Decline of Iloilo City." In *Philippine Social History: Global Trade and Local Transformations*, edited by Alfred W. McCoy and Ed. C. de Jesus, 297–358. Quezon City: Ateneo de Manila University Press, 1982.

McHale, Thomas R., and Mary C. McHale. *Early American-Philippine Trade: The Journal of Nathaniel Bowditch in Manila, 1796*. New Haven: Yale University, Southeast Asian Studies, 1962.

Mesa, Pompeyo de, O.P., and Isaias Villaflores, O.P. *Intramuros and Beyond*. Manila: Letran College, 1975.

Meyen, Franz Julius Ferdinand. *Reise um die Erde ausgeführt auf dem königlich preussischen Seehandlungs-Schiffe Prinzess Louise, commandirt von Capitain W. Wendt, in den Jahren 1830, 1831, und 1832*. Vol. 2. Berlin: In der Sander'schen Buchhandlung, 1835.

Mitchell, Mairin. *Elcano: The First Circumnavigator*. London: Herder, 1958.

Molina, Antonio M. *The Philippines through the Centuries*. Manila: UST Cooperative, 1960.

Montano, J. *Rapport a M. le Ministre de L'Instruction Publique sur une mission aux Iles Philippines et en Malaisie (1879–1881)*. Paris: Imprimerie Nationale, 1885.

———. *Voyage aux Philippines et en Malaisie*. Paris: Librairie Hachette et Cie, 1886.

Montero y Vidal, José. *Historia general de Filipinas*. 3 vols. Madrid: Est. Tip. de la Viuda é Hijos de Tello, 1887–95.

Montblanc, Charles de. *Les Iles Philippines*. Paris: Guillaumin, 1864.

Morison, Samuel Eliot. *The Ropemakers of Plymouth: A History of the Plymouth Cordage Company, 1824–1949*. Boston: Houghton Mifflin, 1950.

Munroe, Mrs. Frederick C. "The Daily Life of Mrs. Nathaniel Kinsman on a Trip to Manila." *Essex Institute Historical Collections* 88, no. 3 (July 1951): 269–305.

New Weekly General Price Current, various dates, 1843–45.

Noble, H. Lawrence. *Philippine Digest*. Rochester, N.Y., and Manila: Lawyers Co-operative Publishing, 1927.

Nolasco, Clarita T. "The Creoles in Spanish Philippines." *Far Eastern University Journal* 15, nos. 1–2 (September-December 1970).

Nowell, Charles E. "Arellano versus Urdaneta." *Pacific Historical Review* 31, no. 2 (May 1962): 111–20.

Nueva real cédula de la Compañia de Filipinas de 12 de julio de 1803. Madrid: En la Imprenta de la Viuda de Ibarra, [1803?].

Nurkse, Ragnar. *Problems of Capital Formation in Underdeveloped Countries*. Oxford: Basil Blackwell, 1953.

Obregón, Gonzalo, et al. "El galeón de Manila." *Artes de México*, year 17, no. 143 (1971).

Ocampo, Ambeth R. "Eiffel's Church in Manila." *Philippine Daily Inquirer*, April 21, 1995.

Ocampo y Reyes, Martín. *Manual del aduanista o compilación de aclaraciones y reglas arancelarias desde 1872 a 1888*. Manila: Establecimiento Tipográfico *La Opinión*, 1888.

Ogden, Adele. *The California Sea Otter Trade, 1784–1848*. Berkeley: University of California Press, 1941.

Ordenanzas de la Compañía de Comercio, que se ha Formado en esta Ciudad de Manila Bajo el Patrocinio de Nuestra Señora del Rosario y la Protección de su Magestad, y en su Real Nombre, de la de el Muy Ilustre Señor D. Pedro Manuel de Arandía, y Santestevan, Cavallero Professo del Orden de Calatrava, Gentil-hombre de Cámara de entrada del Rey de las dos Sicilias, Mariscal de Campo de los Exércitos de su Magestad, Capitán del Regimiento de sus Reales Guardias Españolas de Infantería, de su Consejo, Governador, y Capitán General de estas Islas Philipinas, y Presidente de su Real Audiencia. Manila: Collegio, y Universidad del Señor Santo Thomás, 1755.

Osborne, Alick. *Notes on the Present State of Society in New South Wales, with an Historical, Statistical, and Topographical Account of Manilla and Singapore*. London: J. Cross, 1833.

Owen, Norman G. "Americans in the Abaca Trade: Peele, Hubbell & Co., 1856–1875." In *Reappraising an Empire: New Perspectives on Philippine-American History*, edited by Peter W. Stanley, 201–30. Cambridge: Harvard University Press, 1984.

_____. *Prosperity without Progress: Manila Hemp and Material Life in the Colonial Philippines.* Quezon City: Ateneo de Manila University Press, 1984.

Palgrave, W. Gifford. *Ulysses, or Scenes and Studies in Many Lands.* London: Macmillan, 1887.

Palma, Reynaldo Y., and Benjamin de la Fuente. "The Economic Reforms of Jose Basco y Vargas (1778–1787)." *Anuaryo/Annales* 8 (1991): 96–107.

[Del Pan, José Felipe.] *Las Islas Filipinas. Progresos en 70 años.* Manila: Imprenta de *La Oceanía Española,* 1878.

Pardo de Tavera, Trinidad H[ermenegildo]. *Biblioteca filipina.* Washington, D.C.: Government Printing Office, 1903.

_____. "Results of the Economic Development of the Philippines." *Revista Economica,* 1912. Lecture delivered by Dr. T. H. Pardo de Tavera before the Philippine Columbian Association, 1912.

Parr, Charles McKew. *Ferdinand Magellan, Circumnavigator.* New York: Crowell, 1964.

Patanñe, E. P. "Overseas Trade before Magellan." In Roces, *Filipino Heritage,* 3:767–69.

_____. *The Philippines in the World of Southeast Asia: A Cultural History.* Quezon City: Enterprise Publications, 1972.

Pastells, Pablo, S.J. "Historia general de las islas Filipinas." In *Catálogo de los documentos relativos a las islas Filipinas.* Vol. 1: *1493–1572,* edited by Pedro Torres Lanzas, XLVIII–CCCIV. Barcelona: Compañía General de Tabacos de Filipinas, 1925.

Pelzer, Karl J. "The Resource Pattern of Southeast Asia." In *South Asia in the World Today,* edited by Phillips Talbot, 108–18. Chicago: University of Chicago Press, 1950.

Perez, Gilbert S. "Manila Galleons and Mexican Pieces of Eight." *Philippine Social Sciences and Humanities Review* 19, no. 2 (June 1954): 193–215.

Pérez Valdés, Gabino. *Situación económica de Filipinas y medios de mejorarla.* Madrid: Imprenta de Andrés Orejas, 1871.

Philippine Commission. *Report of the Philippine Commission . . . to the President.* Vol. 2. Washington, D.C.: Government Printing Office, 1900.

Philippine Islands, Department of Commerce and Communications, Bureau of Commerce and Industry. *Statistical Bulletin No. 3 of the Philippine Islands, 1920.* Manila: Bureau of Printing, 1921.

Pi y Margall, Francisco, and Francisco Pi y Arsuaga. *Historia de España en el siglo XIX.* Vol. 7, pt. 2. Barcelona: Miguel Segui, 1902.

Pilar y Gatmaitán, Marcelo H. del. *Filipinas en las Cortes.* Madrid: Imp. de Enrique Jaramillo y Compañía, 1890.

Plauchut, Edmond. *La algarada caviteña de 1872.* Manila: Imprenta "Manila Filatélica," 1916.

Plehn, Carl C. "Taxation in the Philippines, Part II." *Political Science Quarterly* 17, no. 1 (March 1902): 125–48.

Plymouth Cordage Company: One Hundred Years of Service. Plymouth, Mass.: Plymouth Cordage Company, 1924.

Pozo y Bresó, Julián del. *Guía práctica para el despacho de mercancías en las aduanas de Filipinas con arreglo a los nuevos aranceles y ordenanzas.* Manila: Tipo-Litografía de Chofré y Compañia, 1891.

Precios Corrientes de Manila, various dates, 1839–41.

Quiason, Serafin D. *English "Country Trade" with the Philippines, 1644–1765.* Quezon City: University of the Philippines Press, 1966.

_____. "The Sampan Trade, 1570–1770." In Felix, *Chinese,* 1:160–74.

Quirino, Carlos. *Filipinos at War.* Manila: Vera Reyes, 1981; rpt. 1987.

Real cédula de erección de la Compañía de Filipinas de 10 de marzo de 1785. Madrid: Joachin Ibarra, [1785].

Recur, Carlos. *Filipinas. El comercio nacional y el desestanco del tabaco.* Madrid: Imprenta de Fortanet, 1881.

———. *Filipinas. Estudios administrativos y comerciales.* Madrid: Imprenta de Ramón Moreno y Ricardo Rojas, 1879.

Redlich, Fritz. "The Business Leader in Theory and Reality." *American Journal of Economics and Sociology* 8, no. 3 (April 1949): 223–37.

———. *History of American Business Leaders.* Ann Arbor: Edwards Brothers, 1940.

Regidor, Antonio, and J. Warren T. Mason. *Commercial Progress in the Philippine Islands.* London: Dunn and Chidgey, 1905.

Renouard de Sainte-Croix, Felix. *Voyage Commercial et Politique aux Indes Orientales, aux Iles Philippines, a la Chine, avec des notions sur le Cochinchine et le Tonquin, pendant les années 1803, 1804, 1805, 1806, et 1807.* Vols. 2–3. Paris: Imprimerie de Crapchet, 1810.

Retana, Wenceslao E. *Índice de personas nobles y otros de calidad que han estado en Filipinas desde 1521 hasta 1898.* Madrid: Victoriano Suárez, 1907.

———. *Vida y escritos del Dr. José Rizal.* Madrid: Victoriano Suárez, 1907.

Revilla Gigedo, Juan Vicente Güemez Pacheco de Padilla Horcasitas y Aguayo, Conde de. *Instrucción reservada que el Conde de Revilla Gigedo dió a su sucesor en el mando, Marqués de Branciforte sobre el gobierno de este continente en el tiempo que fué su virey.* Mexico: Imprenta de la Calle de las Escalerillas, 1831.

Riesenberg, Felix. *The Pacific Ocean.* New York: Whittlesey House, 1940.

Roces, Alfredo R[eyes], ed. *Filipino Heritage: The Making of a Nation.* Vols. 2–3. Manila: Lahing Pilipino Publishing, 1977.

Rodriguez, Eulogio B. *The Philippines and Mexico.* Manila: National Library, 1941.

Rodríguez Baena, María Luisa. *La Sociedad Económica de Amigos del País de Manila en el siglo XVIII.* Seville: Escuela de Estudios Hispano-Americanos, 1966.

Ruiz Gomar, Rogelio. "Metales." In Carballo et al., "El Arte," 72–77.

San Miguel Brewery. *Golden Jubilee.* [Manila: Catholic Trade School? 1940.]

Sanderlin, George. *First Around the World: A Journal of Magellan's Voyage.* New York: Harper and Row, 1964.

Santayana, George. *Persons and Places: The Background of My Life.* New York: Scribner's, 1944.

Santiago Cruz, Francisco. *La Nao de China.* Mexico: Editorial Jus, 1962.

Sanz y Díaz, José. *López de Legazpi.* Madrid: Editorial "Gran Capitán," 1950.

Sawyer, Frederic H. *The Inhabitants of the Philippines.* London: Sampson Low, Marston, 1900.

Schloss, Henry H. "The Concept of Entrepreneurship in Economic Development." *Journal of Economic Issues* 2, no. 2 (June 1968): 228–32.

Schumpeter, Joseph A. *Business Cycles.* Vol. 2. New York: McGraw-Hill, 1939.

———. *Capitalism, Socialism, and Democracy.* 3d ed. New York: Harper and Brothers, 1950.

———. "The Creative Response in Economic History." *Journal of Economic History* 7, no. 2 (November 1947): 149–59.

———. "Economic Theory and Entrepreneurial History." In *Essays,* edited by R. V. Clemence, 248–66. Cambridge: Addison-Wesley, 1951. Originally published in *Change and the Entrepreneur.*

———. "Theoretical Problems of Economic Growth." *Journal of Economic History* 7 (1947): S1–9.

———. *The Theory of Economic Development.* Translated by Redvers Opie. Cambridge: Harvard University Press, 1934.

382

Schurz, William L. *The Manila Galleon*. New York: Dutton, 1939.

Scott, William Henry. *Barangay: Sixteenth-Century Philippine Culture and Society*. Quezon City: Ateneo de Manila University Press, 1994.

_____. "Class Structure in the Unhispanized Philippines." *Philippine Studies* 27 (2d qtr., 1979): 137–59.

_____. *Looking for the Prehispanic Filipino*. Quezon City: New Day, 1992.

Second Grand Reunion of the Descendants of Teresa de la Paz. Manila: Privately printed, 1990.

Semmes, Raphael. *The Confederate Raider Alabama: Selections from Memoirs of Service Afloat during the War between the States*, edited by Philip Van Doren Stern. Greenwich, Conn.: Fawcett, 1962.

Sharp, Andrew. *Adventurous Armada*. Christchurch, N.Z.: Whitcombe and Tombs, 1961.

Smith, Peter C. "Crisis Mortality in the Nineteenth-Century Philippines: Data from Parish Records." *Journal of Asian Studies* 38, no. 1 (November 1978): 51–76.

Society of Jesus, Philippine Mission. *El Archipiélago Filipino*. Vol. 1. Washington, D.C.: Government Printing Office, 1900.

Soriano, Rafaelita Hilario. "Tiburcio Hilario of Pampanga." *Historical Bulletin* 8, no. 4 (December 1964): 1–22.

[Spain, Ministerio de Ultramar.] *Aranceles y ordenanzas de aduanas para las Islas Filipinas*. Edición official. Madrid: Establecimiento Tipográfico *Sucesores de Rivadeneyra*, 1891.

Sparkes, Boyden, and Samuel Taylor Moore. *The Witch of Wall Street, Hetty Green*. New York: Doubleday Doran, 1935.

Stevens, Joseph Earle. *Yesterdays in the Philippines*. New York: Charles Scribner's Sons, 1899.

Sturgis, Julian. *From Books and Papers of Russell Sturgis*. Oxford: Oxford University Press, n.d. For private circulation.

Sturgis, Roger Faxton, ed. *Edward Sturgis of Yarmouth, Massachusetts, 1613–1695, and His Descendants*. Boston: Stanhope Press, 1914. For private circulation.

Supple, Barry E. *The Experience of Economic Growth: Case Studies in Economic History*. New York: Random House, 1963.

Tarling, Nicholas. "Some Aspects of British Trade in the Philippines in the Nineteenth Century." *Journal of History* 11, nos. 3–4 (September-December 1963): 287–327.

Teresa de la Paz and Her Two Husbands: A Gathering of Four Families. N.p.: The Descendants of Teresa de la Paz, 1996.

Thomes, W[illiam] H. *Life in the East Indies*. Boston: Lee and Shepard, 1872.

[Tíscar, Javier de, ed.] *Apéndice a los aranceles de aduanas de las Islas Filipinas*. [Manila, 1874?]

_____. *Aranceles de las aduanas de las Islas Filipinas aprobadas en decreto de S.A. el Regente del Reino de 16 de octubre de 1870 y reformados por decreto del Gobierno Superior Civil de 26 de junio de 1871, con la instrucción reglamentaria del ramo aprobada en real orden de 29 de setiembre de 1855 y otras disposiciones importantes dictadas con posterioridad*. Manila: Imprenta Ciudad Condal de Plana y Cia., 1874.

"Tome Pires." In *Travel Accounts of the Islands (1513–1787)*, 1–3. Manila: Filipiniana Book Guild, 1971.

Tornow, Max L. "A Sketch of the Economic Condition of the Philippines." U.S. Congress. Senate. 55th Cong., 3d sess., S. Doc. 62, pt. 2. Washington, D.C.: Government Printing Office, 1899.

Tramways des Iles Philippines. Liege: Demarteau, n.d.

Trueba, Alfonso. *La Conquista de Filipinas*. Mexico City: Editorial Jus, 1959.

U.S. Bureau of the Census. *Census of the Philippine Islands Taken under the Direction of the Philippine Commission in the Year 1903*. Vols. 1–2, 4. Washington, D.C.: Government Printing Office, 1905.

U.S. Department of Agriculture, Section of Foreign Markets. *Trade of the Philippine Islands*. Bulletin no. 14. Washington, D.C.: Government Printing Office, 1898.

U.S. War Department, Bureau of Insular Affairs. *Monthly Summary of the Commerce of the Philippine Islands*. Series 1904–1905, no. 6, December 1904.

Valdés Lakowsky, Vera. *De las minas al mar. Historia de la plata mexicana en Asia, 1565–1834*. Mexico City: Fondo de Cultura Económica, 1987.

Van Leur, J. C. *Indonesian Trade and Society: Essays in Asian Social and Economic History*. The Hague and Bandung: W. van Hoeve, 1955.

Vicens Vives, Jaime. *Manual de Historia Económica de España*. Séptima edición. Barcelona: Editorial Vicens-Vives, 1967.

White, John. *History of a Voyage to the China Sea*. Boston: Watts and Lilly, 1823.

Wickberg, Edgar. *The Chinese in Philippine Life, 1850–1898*. New Haven and London: Yale University Press, 1965.

Wilkes, Charles. *Narrative of the United States Exploring Expedition during the Years 1838, 1839, 1840, 1841, 1842*. Vol. 5. New York: G. P. Putnam, 1856.

Wimer, Javier, ed. *El Galeón del Pacífico. Acapulco-Manila, 1565–1815*. State of Guerrero, Mexico: Gobierno Constitucional del Estado de Guerrero, 1992.

Wu Ching-hong. "A Study of References to the Philippines in Chinese Sources from Earliest Times to the Ming Dynasty." *Philippine Social Sciences and Humanities Review* 24, nos. 1–2 (January-June 1959): 1–181.

Ybera, Honorio E., Jr. "La búsqueda incesante." *Crónica de Manila*, July 31, 1994.

Young, Alexander. *A Discourse on the Life and Character of the Hon. Nathaniel Bowditch, LL.D., F.R.S., Delivered in the Church on Church Green, March 25, 1838*. Boston: Charles C. Little and James Brown, 1838.

Yuste, Carmen. "El galeón en la economía colonial." In Wimer, *El Galeón del Pacífico*, 91–111.

Zaide, Gregorio F. *The Philippine Revolution*. Manila: Modern Book Co., 1954.

Zweig, Stefan. *Conqueror of the Seas: The Story of Magellan*, translated by Eden Paul and Cedar Paul. New York: Literary Guild of America, 1938.

INDEX

A

Abaca (Manila hemp): advances for, 282; average export values of, 116–17; as cargo, 236, 245, 265, 270, 325, 328; Chinese in, 283; cloth, 60, 149, 153, 155, 335; competition for, 4, 94, 130, 142; cultivation of, 185, 190, 287, 303; export duties on, 195, 200; freight rates for, 266–67; on the galleons, 42; leading buyers of, 127; as a leading export, 1, 93, 115, 120, 122, 139, 167–68, 183; prices, 118, 264, 268, 321; profitability of, 173, 322–23; studies on, 192; transport of, 160; and women traders, 284; as a new product, 2, 104–5, 222, 288, 293–301;

Abigail, 84
Abraham, Pedro, 240
Acapulco, 31, 45, 53, 55, 72, 84, 86, 89, 96, 100, 147–48
Admiralty islands, 14
Adonay, Marcelo, 279
Ad valorem duties, 86
Advances to agriculture, 2, 81, 83, 87, 90, 255, 277, 280–82, 286, 288
Aetas, 66
Africa, 233, 319
Agoncillo, Felipe, 338
Aguilar, Gov. Rafael Ma. de, 82, 87
Aguinaldo, Emilio, 339
Aguirre, 315–16
Aguirre, & Co., 284, 311, 317
Aguirre, Fr. Andrés de, 20
Aguirre, Fernando, 315
Ahujas, Francisco, 176–77
A. Inchausti & Co., 329
Ajax, 238–39, 242
Alabama, C.S.S., 325
Alaska, 62
Albay, 42, 163, 169, 264, 266, 282–83, 298, 300, 320, 322
Alcaldes, 188–90
Allen (overseer), 306
Allen, Capt., 265

Allen, George H., 266
Almojarifazgo, 47
Alvarado, Pedro de, 14
Amanda, 325
Amboina, 15
America, Central, 34
America, South, 13, 101, 235, 243, 245–46
America, Spanish, 31, 48–49, 64, 78, 80, 88–89, 95–96, 98, 130, 183, 235, 237, 260
American Lloyd Register, 276
American merchants, mariners, 94, 116, 159, 210–12, 227, 234–35, 237–39, 258, 282–84, 288, 290–95, 297–98, 301, 321, 340
Ammidon, Otis, 246–47, 249, 250–51, 253
Ammidon, Philip, 246–47, 253
Amoy, 35, 56, 162, 164, 271–72, 274–75, 314–15
Amsterdam, 258
Anda, Gov. Simón de, 54, 58, 66–68, 71
Andalusia, 37–38
Angat, 75, 194
Anglo-American, 255, 258–59, 326
Angouleme, 258
Aniline dyes, 116, 335
Anson, Joaquin, 283
Antipolo, 328
Antique, 155, 163
Apacible, 214
Apóstol, Cecilio, 214
Appa, 237
Apthorp, 241
Apthorp, Thomas, 241
Arabs, 8
Aranceles, Junta de, 311
Arandía, Gov. Pedro Manuel de, 56, 59, 65, 71
Arbitrage costs, 272
Archer, Samuel, 258
Areca nut monopoly, 75–76
Areizaga, Fr., 13
Armenians, 47, 81, 240
Armenteros, José García, 56
Arnáez, Julio, 329
Arrechea & Co., 164
Asso y Otal, Juan de, 65

385

O

Oaxaca, 235

Obando, Gov. José Francisco de, 57, 64–66, 71

Obras pías, 36, 43–44, 50, 53, 57, 81, 208–9, 337–38

Octavio, Fr. Matías, 68–69, 75, 90

O'Farrell, John Christopher, 239–41, 361n. 14

Official customs values, 195

Olyphant & Co., 158–59

Ong Chengco, José Castro, 284

Oogong, San José de, 74

Opening of the port of Manila, 85

Opium, 95, 192, 259

Oppell, 279

Orbeta, F.V. de, 314

Oregon, 235

Orissa, 172

Ortega, Fr. Francisco de, 26

Ortigas, Capt. Ignacio, 279

Osborn, William H., 243

Otadui & Co., 158

Otaduy, Eulogio de, 191

Owen, Norman, 282, 361n. 18

P

Pacific, 11, 33, 44, 49, 95

Pactos de retro, 184

Padilla, Narciso, 314–15

Palanca, Carlos, 324–25, 330

Palapag, 66

Palgrave, W. Gifford, 172–73, 185, 354n. 46

Pallada, 269

Palmer, H. N., 322–25

Palm wine monopoly, 75–76

Pampanga, Pampangos, 66, 73, 76, 186

Pan, José Felipe del, 106, 157, 165–66, 168, 176, 315, 339

Panama, 5

Panama Canal, 146

Panay, 328

Panay Island, 22–26, 153, 155, 163, 169, 173, 175, 300, 310, 329

Panay, S. S., 329

Pancada, 29

Pancos, 169

Pangasinan, 42, 82, 162–63, 166, 170, 176, 190, 329, 339

Paoay, 175–76

Papal Bull of 1493, 11

Pardo de Taverra, 279; T. H., 213, 215, 301, 338, 358n. 69

Parián, 36

Paris, 258, 269, 271, 316

Parsee houses, 251

Pasacao, 163

Pasig River, 26, 304

Patadiong, 154

Patani, 27

Paterno, Máximo, 319, 330

Paterson & Co., 242

Paterson, Robert J., 257

Patriotic Society, 79

Payumo, 279

Peele, Hubbell & Co., 242–43, 266, 269–70, 276–77, 280–82, 285, 297–98, 300, 308, 320–26, 328

Peele, J. Willard, 243, 266, 314, 324

Peirce, Capt. C. B., 259

Peirce, George H., 266, 282, 329

Peláez, Fr. Pedro, 314

Pelzer, Karl, 181–82

Peninsulars, 228

Pepper, 73, 82

Perit & Cabot, 258

Perit, John W., 258

Perkins & Co., 238, 240, 244, 246–47, 250–51, 258, 291

Perkins, Thomas Handasyd, 244–46, 291

Perkinses, 229, 238, 245–47, 256, 259, 280, 298

Permiso, 40–41, 48–49

Perseverance, 236

Persia, Persians, 8, 11, 33

Personal account trading, 265–66

Personeros, personeritos, 282

Peru, 37, 55, 62, 86, 89, 246

Petate, 45

Philadelphia, 246, 258

Philip II, 14–15, 21, 51

Philippine-American War, 329

Philippine Commission, 329, 336, 338

Philippine National Archives, 213

Serrao, Francisco, 12
Seven Years War, 88
Seville, 33, 41, 60, 77
Shanghai, 113, 164, 212, 264
Shelmerdine, Vice Consul, 154, 293
Shillaber, John, 158
Shipping tonnage, 110
Siam, Siamese, 8, 27–28, 46, 55–56, 162
Sikatuna. *See* Katuna
Silk, 27, 31, 33, 35, 46–47, 53–55, 72, 81, 83,
    86, 148, 159, 192, 237, 243
Silkworm culture, 53, 74
Silver crisis, 274–75, 307
Silver-gold ratio, 30–31, 114, 350n. 29
Simara Island, 328
Sinamay, 153–54
Singapore, 100, 124, 126, 129–30, 137–38,
    144, 149, 161–62, 196–98, 258, 271, 274,
    327, 331
Sisal, 295
Situado, 41, 43, 53, 72, 183
Slaves, slavery, slave trade, 9, 10, 13, 19, 27,
    28, 33, 94, 121, 337
Smallholders, 147, 177, 184, 185–86, 286
Smith, Adam, 334
Smith, Bell & Co., 265–66, 276, 314, 323–25,
    328
So Chico, 316
Solano, Juan Francisco, 65
Soliman (Sulayman), Rajah, 24, 26
Sonsonate, 49
Son Tua, 230
Sorsogon, 42, 163, 282
Southeast Asia, 8, 27, 45, 182, 289, 340
Spain, Spanish Empire: 33, 51–52; analysis
    of Salgado's cinnamon, 71; coming
    and expansion of, 10–11; direct trade
    to, 61, 79, 86, 96; and increased import
    share, 143, 155–56; and Manila mer-
    chants, 99; as minor trading partner,
    94; and Philippine economy, 340; pro-
    tection of European hemp, 293; remit-
    tances to, 269–70, 337; share in
    Philippine trade, 127–30, 132–33, 137–
    38, tobacco exports to, 127, 142
Spaniards, Spanish (Castilians): 57; bureau-
    cracy, 311–12; capital investment in the

Philippines, 376–77; commercial
    policy, 186–87; employment of foreign-
    ers, 286; firms and merchants, 100, 103,
    212, 227, 258, 284, 288, 290, 319; in the
    Visayas, 19–23, 26; interaction with
    Filipinos, 228; Luzon expedition, 24–
    26; on Mindanao, 29; and Philippine
    Revolution, 216; and Philippine tex-
    tiles, 146–47; shipping subsidies, 113
Spanish-American War, 138, 328
Spanish mestizos, 282
Specie movement, 123, 137, 152, 239, 259,
    261, 275, 277
Spice Islands. *See* Moluccas
Spooner, Bourne, 266, 295, 299
Steam navigation, 113, 188, 195, 211, 289,
    327, 337
Steamer service to Hong Kong, 327
Stevens, Joseph Earle, 299, 329–30
Stewart, Capt. Charles, 239, 240, 267
Stone, Silsbee & Pickman, 264, 298, 327–28
Stuart, Andrew, 240–41
Sturgis, 256; George, 254, 256–57, 260, 305–
    8, 314, 339; George Robert Russell, 248,
    254; Henry P., 244–45, 248, 254, 256–57,
    260, 305; Josefina Borrás de, 305–6, 314;
    Mary Greene, 362n. 38; Pepin (Joe),
    306, 314; Robert S., 305–8; Russell, 251,
    254, 258, 277, 295, 305; William, 291–92
Sual, 110, 163–64, 170, 192, 201
Suez Canal, 111, 113–14, 146, 179, 198, 211,
    215, 267, 337
Sugar: 54–56, 58, 61, 72, 88, 95, 176, 181, 191,
    241, 245, 277; and Australian gold
    strike, 122; average export values of,
    116–17; Britain and U. S. exports of,
    127, 139, 142, 335; crisis, 323–25; culti-
    vation of, 167; domestic firms in, 315–
    16; early exports of, 60, 81–82, 94,
    104–5, 147, 236, 238, 240; freight rates
    for, 266–67; as payment for imports,
    268; prices, 118, 264; as principal ex-
    port, 1, 90, 93, 101, 115, 120, 168, 183,
    200, 265; processing and refining, 289,
    303, 317–18, 328; in Spain, 202; in the
    Visayas, 286–88, 308–10; and West In-
    dian emancipation, 120

Sulu, 3, 98
Sumatra, 12, 34
Summers, 279
Sunda Straits, 235, 240, 325
Sun Fire Office, 276
Supplemental non-agricultural household income, 178
Surabaya, 258
Surat, 236
Surigao, 22
Swidden farming, 10
Swiss, 212
Sy Chuangco & Co., 329
Sy Giap, 329
Syme & Co., 258

T

Taal, 9, 24, 148
Tabacalera (Compañía General de Tabacos de Filipinas), 115, 227, 330, 336
Tagalogs, 282, 308
Tahiti, 55
Taiping Rebellion, 272
Tambobong, 68, 148
Tanay, 65
Tanduay St., 317
Tariff: 112, 204–6; of 1832, 193–97; of 1860, 195; of 1869, 112, 198–99; of 1871, 199–202; of 1891, 155, 203, 337, 339; policy, 193–206, 211
Tarlac, 329
Tayabas, 67, 82–83, 175, 194
Tayag, Silverio, 315
Taydes, gold, 30
Tea, 95, 159, 192, 237–38, 243
Technology, transfer of, 50
Tehuantepec, 13
Telegraph, 289, 337
Telephone service, 338
Tenancy, 287–88
Terlingas, 83
Ternate, 56
Testoons, 24
Textiles, 1, 31, 56, 61, 84, 95, 114, 183, 193, 204, 245, 283, 316
Thomas Dickason & Co., 258
Thomas Wilson & Co., 267

Thompson, Philip, 62
Thomson Houston Electric Co., 330
Thornton, Capt. Christopher, 84
Tiaoqui, 266, 324
Tidore, 13–14, 56
Tiempo, 314
Tobacco, 34, 46, 54–55, 77, 93–94, 101, 115–17, 120, 127, 129, 132–33, 142, 176–77, 187, 194–95, 202, 325
Tobacco Monopoly, 76–77, 89, 90, 101, 115, 117, 129, 165, 179, 182–83, 188, 190, 197, 200, 202, 336–37
Tondo, 24–26, 83, 157, 190
Tordesillas, Treaty of, 11
Tornaviaje, 20, 29
Tornow, Max, 157, 166, 210, 212
Torre, Gov. Carlos de la, 319
Tortoiseshell, 10, 36, 54, 58, 60, 104, 195, 241, 266
Trade, concentration of, 115–16, 123–45, 178–79
Tramways, trolleys, 202, 289, 329, 338
Tranquebar, 86
Transshipments, 3, 10, 20, 88, 97–98, 125, 137–38, 148
Trieste, 236
Trinidad, 13
Tuason: 278–79; Antonio, 230, 315; Gonzalo, 330–31; José Ma., 210, 315; José Severo, 317; Josefa Patiño de, 317; Mariano, 210, 315, 317; Vicente Dolores, 230–31
Tuasiong, Capt. José, 35
Tuba Fresca, 45
Tucker, Richard D., 285, 322–23, 325–26, 328
Tupas, 19, 20, 23

U

Undervaluation of exports, 350n. 18
Union Insurance Society, 276
Union Marine Insurance Co., 276
United States, 139, 141, 191, 203, 213, 240, 250, 254, 292, 316, 322, 333
Urban property tax, 337
Urdaneta, Fr. Andrés de, 13–16, 19–21, 27–28
Ustáriz, San Ginés & Co., 61, 69
Uztáriz, Gerónimo de, 52

Center for Southeast Asian Studies
University of Wisconsin-Madison

MONOGRAPH SERIES

Voices from the Thai Countryside: "The Necklace" and Other Stories
by Samruam Singh, edited and translated by Katherine Bowie

Population and History: The Demographic Origins of the Modern Philippines
edited by Daniel F. Doeppers and Peter Xenos

Sitti Djoaoerah: A Novel of Colonial Indonesia
by M. J. Soetan Hasondoetan, translated by Susan Rodgers

Face of Empire: United States-Philippine Relations, 1898–1946
by Frank Hindman Golay

Inventing a Hero: The Posthumous Re-Creation of Andres Bonifacio
by Glenn May

The Mekong Delta: Ecology, Economy, and Revolution, 1860–1960
by Pierre Brocheux

Autonomous Histories, Particular Truths: Essays in Honor of John Smail
edited by Laurie J. Sears

An Anarchy of Families: State and Family in the Philippines
edited by Alfred W. McCoy

Salome: A Filipino Filmscript by Ricardo Lee
translated by Rofel Brion

Recalling the Revolution: Memoirs of a Filipino General
by Santiago Alvarez, translated by Paula Carolina S. Malay

Anthropology Goes to War: Professional Ethics and Counterinsurgency in Thailand
by Eric Wakin

Putu Wijaya in Performance: An Approach to Indonesian Theatre
edited by Ellen Rafferty

Gender, Power, and the Construction of the Moral Order
edited by Nancy Eberhardt

A Complete Account of the Peasant Uprising in the Central Region
by Phan Chu Trinh, translated by Peter Baugher and Vu Ngo Chieu